WORKER CENTERS

ERRATA SLIP

Figure 2.2 on page 38 should appear as follows:

2.2. Today at comparable levels of immigration

WORKER CENTERS

Organizing Communities at the Edge
of the Dream

JANICE FINE

ECONOMIC POLICY INSTITUTE

ILR PRESS
an imprint of
Cornell University Press
Ithaca and London

First published 2006 by Cornell University Press
First printing, Cornell Paperbacks, 2006
Printed in the United States of America

Library of Congress Cataloging-in-Publication Data

Fine, Janice (Janice Ruth)
    Worker centers : organizing communities at the edge of the
dream / by Janice Fine.
        p.   cm.
    Includes bibliographical references and index.
    ISBN-13: 978-0-8014-4423-4 (cloth : alk. paper)
    ISBN-10: 0-8014-4423-3 (cloth : alk. paper)
    ISBN-13: 978-0-8014-7257-2 (pbk. : alk. paper)
    ISBN-10: 0-8014-7257-1 (pbk. : alk. paper)
        1. Alien labor—Services for—United States.   2. Immigrants
—Services for—United States.   3. Employment agencies—
United States.   4. Community centers—United States.   5.
Community organization—United States.   6. Alien labor—
Labor unions—Organizing—United States.   I. Title.
    HD8081.A5F56   2005
    331.6'2'06073—dc22
2005025043

Cornell University Press strives to use environmentally responsible suppliers and materials to the fullest extent possible in the publishing of its books. Such materials include vegetable-based, low-VOC inks and acid-free papers that are recycled, totally chlorine-free, or partly composed of nonwood fibers. For further information, visit our website at www.cornellpress.cornell.edu.

Cloth printing   10 9 8 7 6 5 4 3 2 1
Paperback printing   10 9 8 7 6 5 4 3 2 1

This book is dedicated to low-wage workers and low-wage worker organizations. Their struggles at the point where America's promise and reality collide enrich us all.

CONTENTS

Acknowledgments ix

Introduction 1

1. Origins and Characteristics of Worker Centers 7

2. Putting Worker Centers in Context 27

3. Organizing at the Intersection of Ethnicity, Race, and Class 42

4. Delivering Services on the Front Lines 72

5. Economic Action Organizing 100

6. Relationships with Unions 120

7. Public Policy Enforcement and Reform 157

8. Immigrant Rights and Social Justice 180

9. The Internal Life of Worker Centers 201

10. Networking, Structures, and Practices 224

11. A Holistic Assessment of the Worker Center Phenomenon 244

Appendixes

A. Organizations Surveyed for National Immigrant Worker Center Study 269

B. Complete Contact List of Worker Centers as of January 31, 2005 271

Notes 283

Bibliography 297

Index 303

About EPI 315

About the Author 317

ACKNOWLEDGMENTS

Many people in numerous organizations helped me with this book. To promote a better understanding among funders, labor unions, public policy-makers, and worker centers, the Neighborhood Funders Group, in partnership with the Economic Policy Institute, commissioned the study that is the basis of this book. The wonderful and dedicated staff, leaders, and members of the worker centers I studied gave generously of their time in order to enrich my understanding of how the people involved in worker centers think about their work and carry it out. I want to especially thank the following: Bhairavi Desai, Kevin Fitzpatrick, Mohammed Fakhrul Islam, Tasleem Khan, and Rizwan Raja of the New York Taxi Workers Alliance; Lillian Araujo, Juan Calderon, Carlos Canales, Nadia Marin-Molina, Irma Solis, and Jaime Vargas of the Workplace Project; Jon Liss of the Tenants' and Workers' Support Committee (TWSC); Carol Bishop of the Carolina Alliance for Fair Employment (CAFÉ); John Arvisu, Tony Bernabe, and Angelica Salas of the Coalition for Humane Immigrant Rights of Los Angeles (CHIRLA). Also thanks goes to Raul Anorve, Jose Esquivel, Suzanne Foster, Porfiria Gaeona, Omar Leon, Nelson Motto, and Gloria Ronquillo of the Instituto de Educación Popular del Sur California (IDEPSCA); Cindy Cho, Ae Hwa Kim, Jessica Kim, An Le, Mrs. Jung Hee Lee, Paul Lee, Maximiliano Mariscal, Vy Nguyen, Danny Park, Mr. Park, and Derek Park of Korean Immigrant Worker Advocates (KIWA); Helen Chien, Alejandra Domenzain, Julia Figueria-McDonough, Lupe Hernandez, Kimi Lee, and Joann Lo of the Garment Worker Center; Jose Oliva, Kim Bobo, Connie Knutti, Tim Leahy, Daniel McMann, Francisco Orendain, Emily Rosenberg, and Moises Zavala of the Chicago Interfaith Workers Rights Center; and Marcella Cervantes, Alejandro Garcia, Julio

Gonzalez, Tom Holler, Sergio Sosa, and Rev. Damian Zuerlein of Omaha Together One Community (OTOC).

A hands-on advisory board of practitioners, intermediary organizations, funders, union leaders, academics, and others was put together to oversee the work that resulted in this book. Included on this board were Jeff Chapman, Economic Policy Institute; Victor Quintana, Unitarian Universalist Veatch Program at Shelter Rock; Ellen Widess, Rosenberg Foundation; Ann Bastian, New World/Phoenix Fund; Jennifer Gordon, Fordham Law School; Peter Cervantes-Gautschi, ENLACE; Nadia Marin-Molina, Workplace Project; Steven Pitts, University of California, Berkeley, Labor Center; Nikki Fortunato Bas, Sweatshop Watch; Eliseo Medina, Service Employees International Union; Marielena Hincapie, National Immigration Law Center; Sarah Fox, AFL-CIO; Kent Wong, UCLA, APALA; Pablo Alvarado, National Day Labor Organizing Network (NDLON); and Yanira Merino, Laborers International Union.

This board was instrumental in helping to define the universe of worker centers to be included on the map, select the nine case studies, raise funds, and identify and untangle various conceptual and practical issues that emerged over the course of the investigation.

The study was generously funded by the Arca Foundation, the Annie E. Casey Foundation, the Carnegie Corporation of New York, the Nathan Cummings Foundation, French American Charitable Trust, New World/Phoenix Fund for Workers, the Rockefeller Foundation, Rosenberg Foundation, Solidago Foundation, and the Unitarian Universalist Veatch Program at Shelter Rock. Special thanks to Ann Bastian whose knowledge and support of this field is amazing, Ellen Widess whose unflagging support of this project made a huge difference at a critical moment, and Victor Quintana who supported the study early and often, helped recruit others to do the same, and provided essential background information on worker centers always in a timely fashion. I am very grateful to Spence Limbocker and Debby Goldberg of the Neighborhood Funders Group who spent enormous amounts of time and energy on bringing this project to fruition. I also wish to thank Andrea Kydd whose support for this study early on made a critical difference, Shona Chakravartty of the Four Freedoms Fund who shared her knowledge of the field of worker centers with me on many occasions, and Katherine McFate of the Rockefeller Foundation whose critical thinking made this study sharper.

Jon Werberg, my amazing project research assistant, provided invaluable research, survey, data-analysis, and mapping skills. Jemila Martin plowed through interviews with total dedication, attention to detail, and good humor. Shannon Duncan transcribed hundreds of hours of interviews and provided fantastic technical support for too many PowerPoint presentations. The talented Tam

Doan enthusiastically met our final research and mapping requirements. Northeast Action, as always, gave me a room of my own, and Jean Moore agreed to take on odious administrative duties. Larry Mishel, president of the Economic Policy Institute, and my colleagues Jeff Chapman and Princess Goldthwaite strongly believed in this project and were of enormous assistance all the way through. Jeff shepherded the project through EPI at every stage with good advice, good humor, and strong interest in the subject, and I could not have asked for a more supportive and reliable companion in fund-raising than Princess. The Center for Community Change picked up this project when it went into extra innings and has shown me incredible generosity and support. Special thanks to Deepak Bhargava and Mary Ochs. Fran Benson, my editor at Cornell, kept hope alive about making this happen as an EPI/ILR book, and I am so grateful to her for doing so.

This study continued from where my dissertation left off. For this reason, I want to acknowledge the members of my committee at MIT: Joshua Cohen, Ira Katznelson, Richard Locke, and Michael Piore. The labor historians Dorothy Sue Cobble and Nelson Lichtenstein made many helpful suggestions at the beginning of this project. Howard Wial's ground-breaking work on enforcement issues and ideas about public policy change play a major role in this study, and Karen Pastorello, labor historian, generously shared her work on Bessie Abromowitz and Jane Addams with me. Abel Valenzuela graciously shared his ideas and research on day laborers with me, and Edna Bonacich spent an important afternoon going over the history of garment worker organizing in Los Angeles. Victor Narro, Peter Olney, and Steven Pitts of the University of California Institute for Labor and Employment Research provided advice, hands-on support, and forums for me to test my ideas. Peter and Steven helped me shape the project, and Steven read many drafts, listened to many stories and dilemmas, and always had helpful, important, and supportive things to say. Victor organized a fantastic forum with Los Angeles worker centers and shared his immense knowledge of the history of the Los Angeles worker center scene. I benefited greatly from all of the research and policy resources of the National Employment Law Project (NELP) as well as the helpful suggestions of Rebecca Smith. I also want to thank several people at the national AFL-CIO: Bruce Colburn of the Field Mobilization Department helped arrange a focus group that was helpful to my thinking; Ana Avendano Denier and Sarah Fox in the General Counsel's office offered great advice and strategic thinking. Ana's knowledge of labor and immigration law and her experience and knowledge of labor unions make her a unique asset to the labor movement and the broader struggle for immigrant rights. Sarah's knowledge of labor law and the labor movement and her clear thinking about ideas for structural change inside unions as well as labor law reform were extremely useful to me. Yanira Merino of the Laborers, who has been on the frontlines of union and worker center organizing, provided important stories and insights. John Martini, president of the Roofers Union, inspired me with his success stories of immigrant organizing in Arizona. Henry Huerta, senior deputy labor commissioner, and Lilia Garcia of the Maintenance Cooperation Trust Fund in Los Angeles both taught me a great deal about strategies for wage enforcement in low-wage industries.

Pablo Alvarado of the National Day Laborer Network (NDLON) devoted many hours to enriching my knowledge of the day labor scene in Los Angeles and nationally and went many rounds with me in good-natured debates and discussions. Paul Lee, formerly of KIWA, shared his original ideas about the origins, functions, and meaning of worker centers. For several years I have benefited from Peter Cervantes-Gautschi's information, insights, and ideas about low-wage worker organizing, as well as from his friendship. Jose Oliva, of Interfaith Worker Justice, hosted me in Chicago, introduced me to the national network of interfaith worker centers and helped pull together the first midwest worker center convergence.

Jennifer Gordon dried my tears, found my findings, read every word, and always knew exactly what would help. Marjorie Fine, my beloved sister, has been my number-one cheering squad for forty-four years. She is also a trenchant observer of the movement scene and a stentorian voice in the foundation world in support of organizing. David Donnelly, my amazing husband, absorbed my angst, put up with periods of constant travel, always looked for ways to ease the pressure, and never stopped encouraging me to keep at it despite the toll on him and our children.

Paul Saba, my editor, strongly believed in the importance of worker centers, read through early drafts of the study, and was always there with a helpful suggestion or citation from his immense knowledge of labor history. He helped me structure and restructure this manuscript and polished every single paragraph. Finally, without the incredible Sue Chinn, this study would never have happened.

WORKER CENTERS

INTRODUCTION

In the United States today, millions of workers, many of them new immigrants and people of color, are laboring on the very lowest rungs of metropolitan labor markets with weak prospects for improving the quality of their present positions or advancing to better jobs. It is unfortunate but true that ethnicity, race, and immigration status have enormous impact on the jobs they do, the compensation they receive, and the possibilities they have for redress when mistreated by employers.[1]

When my grandparents came to this country from Vienna at the turn of the last century, they were only a few lucky steps ahead of the Holocaust. Upon arrival at Ellis Island, they had already come through many hardships and knew that many obstacles awaited them here in the United States. But one obstacle they did not face was the legal right to work. From the moment they arrived here, European immigrants received legal authorization to work and started down the pathway to citizenship. In stark contrast to those immigrants of my grandparents' generation, labor migrants today often have an extremely difficult time obtaining legal status or employment authorization.[2]

The story of immigrant workers in America and the exploitation and prejudice they faced is obviously not a new one. Earlier waves of immigrants encountered serious discrimination, took up some of society's dirtiest and most dangerous jobs, looked to their families and coethnics to build economic stability over time, and fought to expand workers rights and establish labor unions. In the past, large numbers of American workers, including immigrants and African Americans, were able to join together through unions to wage a common struggle for dignity, better wages, and better working conditions, but now unfavorable labor law and employer opposition have made this much more difficult. In addition to unions, mutual aid, and fraternal organizations, political parties, settlement houses, and urban churches also offered immigrants and African-Americans a means of joining together to navigate their economic and political way through American society. But today, although there are some important and inspiring exceptions to the rule, many of these old institutions are no longer available to the vast majority of the nation's working poor. New forms of labor market institutions including new types of unions, community-based organizations, and social movement groups are struggling to fill the void.[3] This study examines one such promising emergent institution: worker centers.

Worker centers are community-based mediating institutions that provide support to low-wage workers. Difficult to categorize, worker centers have some features that are suggestive of the earlier U.S. civic institutions mentioned above. Other features, such as cooperatives and popular education classes, are suggestive of the civic traditions of the home countries from which many recent immigrants came. Centers pursue this mission through a combination of approaches:

- *Service delivery:* providing legal representation to recover unpaid wages; English classes; worker rights education; access to health clinics, bank accounts, and loans

- *Advocacy:* researching and releasing of exposés about conditions in low-wage industries, lobbying for new laws and changes in existing ones, working with government agencies to improve monitoring and grievance processes, and bringing suits against employers

- *Organizing:* building ongoing organizations and engaging in leadership development among workers to take action on their own for economic and political change

The combination of *organizing* with service and advocacy is what sets these centers apart from other worker centers and immigrant service organizations. The proportions of each of the three elements vary widely from center to center, as does the overall orientation the centers bring to their work.

MAPPING WORKER CENTERS

Given that they account for the majority, the focus of this study is immigrant worker centers in metropolitan areas, but these organizations exist as a subset of a larger body of worker centers—contemporary community-based worker organizing projects that have taken root in communities across the United States in recent years. As a starting point, before we focus on immigrant worker centers, it is useful to think about this larger set of organizations. Working with an advisory board created for this project, we hammered out the definition of "worker centers" given above and then attempted to identify all centers that fit the definition. As Lawrence Goodwyn observed in *The Populist Moment*,[4] a critical stage in the movement-building process is the "movement seeing itself." I plot all of these organizations on a map of the United States, a regularly updated version of which can be viewed on the Cornell University Press website (http://www.cornellpress.cornell.edu) on the page for this book. The full list of organizations included on the map are organized by state in Appendix B.

The study methodology was largely qualitative, although a survey of forty organizations was conducted and the data were analyzed and presented in quantitative terms. The worker centers included in the survey are listed in Appendix A.

As of May 2005, there were 137 worker centers. The majority of the organizations (122) are identified as *immigrant worker centers.* As will become apparent, a wide range of groups has been included—African-American organizations, groups that work with immigrants as well as nonimmigrants, organizations that focus on workfare participants, groups that call themselves unions, and even groups that do not call themselves worker centers. I have endeavored to capture the full breadth of new types of community-based worker organizing projects that are currently active among low-wage workers.

The final component of the study was to conduct nine in-depth case studies. For this first study of the field as a whole, our inclination was to choose established centers that were well thought of. We set out to identify the different worker center models, evaluate the effectiveness of the worker center strategy in improving the lives of low wage workers, and highlight key lessons, strengths, weaknesses, and future challenges. This study assesses immigrant worker centers from a number of different angles and through a variety of interpretive lenses.[5] Our questions going into it were urgent but straightforward ones. What are the institutional mechanisms for integrating low-wage immigrants into American civil society so that they, like those who came before them, are able to avail themselves of the benefits of ongoing organization, economic representation, and political action? Which organizations might become the fixed point in the changing world of work, able to provide the job training, skills development and placement, health insurance and pensions that many employees once accessed through firms? Given the racial polarization of the economy and the disproportionate representation of immigrants and people of color in low-wage employment, what role will race and ethnicity play as constitutive categories for analysis, education, strategy, and action?

Chapter 1 examines the origins and development of the worker center phenomenon. I describe and explain the distinguishing features of these centers and provide brief "snapshots" of some, which are discussed later in the book. I also provide a brief overview of the immigrant communities and subsets of those communities in which worker centers are active.

Chapter 2 begins with an examination of the changing immigration pattern in modern U.S. history to provide a context for looking at the contemporary immigrant scene. This is complemented by a review of recent changes in the U.S. economy that have had a decisive impact on the status and conditions of low-wage immigrant workers today. Finally, I survey the dramatic decline of immigrant support systems over the last century, arguing that this change has been critical to the rise of worker centers.

Chapter 3 looks at worker center methods of outreach and recruitment, and the important role that community institutions play in this regard. I highlight a central paradox for immigrant worker collective action in general. On the one hand, strong ethnic identities and vibrant social networks facilitate organizing; on the other, the fluid nature of immigration itself and the ability of workers to preserve strong ongoing home country connections can sometimes mitigate against civic participation in the United States. I also explore the challenges of working across ethnicity in industries in which more than one ethnic group is employed as well as the interplay between class, gender, and ethnicity in worker center organizing and advocacy.

Chapter 4 examines worker center service delivery models and explores some of the reasons why centers have decided to make direct service provision an important component of their activities. I offer a closer look at some of the most common services provided and the ways in which these organizations are trying to tie service provision more closely to their mission of organizing and advocacy.

Chapters 5 and 6 provide an overview of strategies pursued by worker centers for raising wages and improving working conditions in low-wage industries. In chapter 5 I look at organizing that targets single employers and entire industries. Also surveyed are efforts to organize day laborers and create independent economic enterprises. Chapter 6 offers case studies of a variety of worker center relationships with labor unions and the efforts of some centers to create independent unions.

Chapters 7 and 8 examine centers' public policy and advocacy activities. In chapter 7 I look at ways centers partner with governmental entities to foster enforcement of existing labor laws and regulations, and organize to push local, state, and federal government agencies for administrative and policy changes. I also review the ability of centers to promote policy and legislative reforms that raise wages and improve working conditions for low-wage workers. Chapter 8 looks at centers' public policy campaigns that fight for immigration reform and immigrant rights and for a broader social justice agenda. I end this chapter with an overall assessment of the strengths and weaknesses of worker centers' public policy campaigns.

Chapters 9 and 10 are devoted to the internal organizational structures and approaches of immigrant worker centers. In chapter 9 I examine how the centers handle leadership development and political education of members, and how they bring people of color and young people into leadership positions. In this chapter, I also look at decision-making, organizational budgets, formal membership, and dues collection structures. In chapter 10 I provide an overview of the variety of networks in which worker centers are involved and offers an evaluation of the strengths and weaknesses of worker center internal systems, structures, and practices.

Chapter 11 presents an overall assessment of the worker center phenomenon. I identify what I believe are the centers' greatest strengths and significant weaknesses and offer critical thoughts on their power and effectiveness. I also suggest changes to national labor, immigration, and social policies that could aid their efforts to improve the lives of low-wage workers.

Worker centers have emerged as central components of the immigrant community infrastructure and, in the combination of services, advocacy, and organizing they undertake, are playing a unique role in helping immigrants navigate the worlds of work and legal rights in the United States. They are gateway organizations that are meeting immigrant workers where they are and providing them with a wealth of information and training. Most centers provide a wide range of day-to-day work services: from one-on-one assistance to individuals who walk in the door with employment-related problems to mounting collective action campaigns to change employer, industry, or government policies and practices.

The world of worker centers is hopeful, compassionate, inventive, and dynamic. Confronting the "wild west" of America's largely unregulated low-wage labor markets, and the legal limbo in which many of their members live and work, worker centers have pioneered a host of innovative strategies that attempt to wrest order out of the chaos. The centers evince great skill at creative means of recruitment, leadership development, and democratic participation. They have effectively documented and exposed the exploitation of low-wage workers. They are altering the terms of debate, changing the way people understand the world around them, the problems they face, and the possibilities for social change. In all too many cases, these centers are the only "port in the storm" for low-wage immigrant workers seeking to understand U.S. labor and immigration laws, file back wage claims, and organize against recalcitrant employers.

Through their service provision, advocacy, and organizing work, worker centers are helping to set the political agenda and mobilize a growing constituency to make its voice heard on fundamental labor and immigration reform. This work, in and of itself instrumental to a brighter future for low-wage workers in the United States, is also indispensable to the revitalization of organized labor and progressive politics in America.

CHAPTER 1

ORIGINS AND CHARACTERISTICS OF WORKER CENTERS

Millions of workers, large numbers of whom are immigrants and people of color, are today the mainstay of America's service, manufacturing, and agricultural economy. They suffer under a double burden—as low wage workers and as immigrants and/or people of color. As discussed in the introduction, this study focuses on immigrant worker centers, but these organizations exist as a subset of a larger body of contemporary community-based, worker-organizing projects that have taken root across the United States in recent years. This chapter will be directed toward describing this larger set of worker centers. Most of the rest of the rest of the book will draw upon data derived from the nine organizations chosen for case studies, most of which work with an exclusively immigrant constituency base.

While worker centers exist in cities of all sizes, including many medium and some small cities, they are heavily concentrated in the largest ones. The largest cities without a known worker center are Detroit, Atlanta, and Dallas. The regional distribution of worker centers shown in figure 1.1 offers a telling snapshot of recent immigration trends and demonstrates that the highest number of worker centers is in the Northeast and the West, with a growing number in the South and Midwest. Most are still in urban areas, but more have cropped up in suburban areas as immigrant workers have become mainstays of the service economy and in rural places as immigrant workers—not just those who harvest the nation's agriculture but also those who slaughter, process, and package our beef and poultry—are organizing to improve conditions.

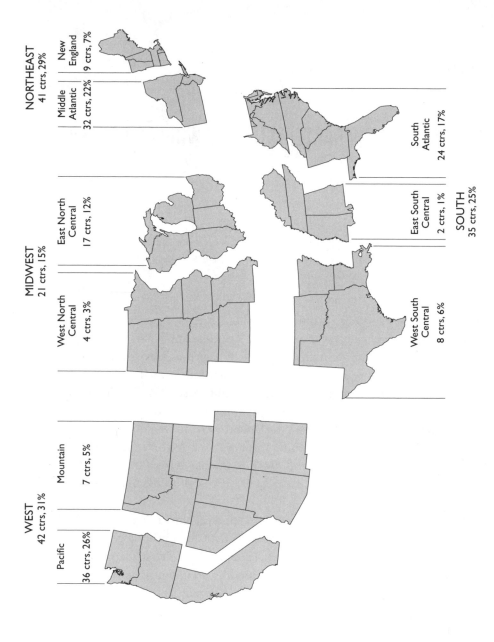

NORTHEAST
41 ctrs, 29%

Middle
Atlantic
32 ctrs, 22%

New
England
9 ctrs, 7%

MIDWEST
21 ctrs, 15%

East North
Central
17 ctrs, 12%

West North
Central
4 ctrs, 3%

WEST
42 ctrs, 31%

Mountain
7 ctrs, 5%

Pacific
36 ctrs, 26%

SOUTH
35 ctrs, 25%

South
Atlantic
24 ctrs, 17%

East South
Central
2 ctrs, 1%

West South
Central
8 ctrs, 6%

1.1. Regional breakdown of worker centers

THREE WAVES OF WORKER CENTER FORMATION

African American worker centers arose in the South in response to institutionalized racism in employment, the rise of manufacturing and "big box" retail, and the absence of labor unions as a vehicle for organizing. Immigrant worker centers have arisen in "generational waves" as certain immigrant groups have reached a threshold level of settlement and organization, and workers and their allies have grappled with ways to negotiate with the larger society about the terms and conditions of work and the larger set of integration issues (see figures 1.2 and 1.3). Often, the immigrant worker centers seem to have appeared after initial social service agencies and others have established themselves in these communities and begun grappling with employment-related problems.

The first contemporary worker centers were organized by black worker activists in North and South Carolina, immigrant activists in New York City's Chinatown, along the Texas-Mexican border in El Paso, and among Chinese immigrants in San Francisco. They arose during the late 1970s and early 1980s in response to changes in manufacturing that resulted in worsened conditions, factory closings, and the rise of lower paying service sector jobs. Disparities of pay and treatment between African American and white workers as well as exploitation within ethnic economic enclaves and in the broader economy (including the informal sector) were also major catalysts for the creation of the first wave of centers. Some of these first centers were founded by activists who had been active in peace, student, civil rights, and worker movements of the 1960s and 1970s. Although "pro-union," they were critical of the existing institutions of organized labor. For example, CAFÉ and Black Workers for Justice were founded by individuals and organizations with long connections to the labor and civil rights movements who were struggling to bring organization to workers in the South after the post–World War II failure of labor's southern offensive.[1] La Mujer Obrera (LMO) was founded by Central America solidarity and labor activists in El Paso in 1981 on the heels of a textile workers' strike by Mexican women workers at the Farah Clothing Factory. Over the next few years, thousands of women lost their jobs as major textile manufacturers shuttered their operations, giving way to small sub-contractors and substandard working conditions. During the first five years of NAFTA, 15,000 jobs left El Paso and LMO worked to join Mexican women workers to the global economic justice movement. A flagship worker center, the Chinese Staff and Workers Association in New York City was, was initially founded by Chinese activists eager to assist the Hotel Employees and Restaurant Employees Union (HERE) in helping Chinese restaurant workers unionize their workplaces.[2]

The second wave of centers emerged in the late 1980s and early to mid 1990s.

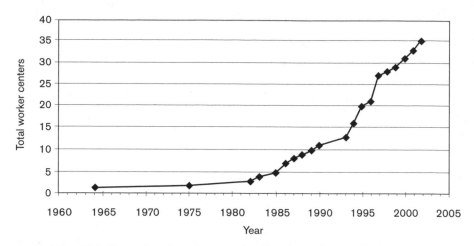

Note: While the number of worker centers has been increasing steadily since the late 1980s, new centers were opening most rapidly during the mid–1990s.

1.2. When did worker centers arise?

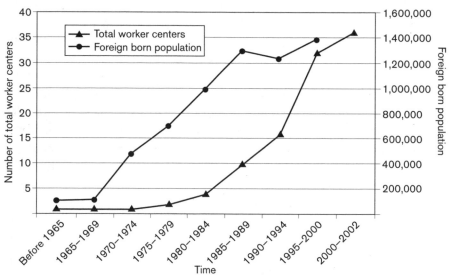

* Foreign born population includes Mexican, Central American, Chinese, and Korean immigrants in three major metropolitan areas (Chicago, L.A., N.Y.)

Source: U.S. Census 2000

1.3. Rise in worker centers and foreign-born population

They appeared as large new groups of Latino immigrants, some in flight from the Central American wars in El Salvador and Guatemala, came to live and work in urban metropolitan areas as well as the suburbs, and growing numbers of Southeast Asians immigrated to the United States seeking work. Drawing on the first-wave centers for their organizational models, these groups were founded by a diverse set of institutions and individuals, including churches and other faith-based organizations, social service and legal aid agencies, immigrant nongovernmental organizations (NGOs), and unions.

From 2000 to the present, a new wave of centers has emerged. Most of these continued to arise in the nation's cities. However, more of these centers are being organized in suburban and rural areas and in southern states in response to the large concentration of Mexican and Central American immigrants working in the service, poultry, meat-packing, and agricultural sectors. Also more centers are emerging among recent Filipino, Korean, African and South Asian immigrants, and more of them than in past waves are directly connected to faith-based organizations and unions.

DISTINGUISHING FEATURES OF WORKER CENTERS

Worker centers are community-based mediating institutions that provide support to and organize among communities of low-wage workers. As work is the primary focus of life for many newly arriving immigrants, it is also the locus of many of the problems they experience. This is why, although they actually pursue a broad agenda that includes many aspects of immigrant life in America, many of these organizations call themselves "worker centers."

Worker centers vary in terms of how they think about their mission and how they carry out their work. Nonetheless, in the combination of services, advocacy, and organizing they undertake, worker centers are playing a unique role in helping immigrants navigate life in the United States. They provide low-wage workers a range of opportunities for expressing their "collective voice" as well as for taking collective action.

Certain first-wave and early-second-wave centers have been the inspiration that others have modeled themselves on,[3] but there is not one specific organizational model, strategy, or structure that predominates across all or most centers. Some of them, such as the eleven that are affiliated with the National Interfaith Committee on Worker Justice, do share a common strategic approach that is characterized by working through the faith community, cooperating closely with government agencies, encouraging union organizing, and, whenever possible, matching workers with local unions for that purpose. Many others, while they might support and encourage union organizing, view their work less as feeding workers into unions and more as creating an independent power base of low-wage immigrant workers in their communities.

Regardless of which approach they take, most centers engage in many of the same types of activities. These include helping workers to claim unpaid wages, working with government agencies to improve enforcement, mounting direct action organizing campaigns against specific employers and sometimes across particular industries, and engaging in leadership development and popular education activities. Most of them also play an important role as general defender of immigrant rights in their communities.

One of the most interesting features of worker centers is their independence both from each other as well as from other national organizations or networks. As we will see, they have diverse origins and most did not start out as chapters of any national institution, or locals of a national union, or affiliates of a particular community-organizing network. Fifty-one of the 137 centers are now affiliated with one or more of the three national networks of worker centers: the National Day Laborer Organizing Network, Enlace, and Interfaith Worker Justice. (For more about the national networks, see chapter 10.)

While there is wide variation between centers in terms of program and emphasis, they have most of the following features in common:

Hybrid organization: All combine elements of different types of organizations, from social service agencies, fraternal organizations, settlement houses, community organizing groups, and unions to social movement organizations.

Service provision: Centers provide services, from legal assistance and ESL classes to check-cashing, but they also play an important matchmaking role in introducing their members to services available through other agencies such as health clinics. Many function as clearinghouses on employment law—writing and distributing "know your rights" handbooks and fact sheets and conducting ongoing workshops.

Advocacy: Centers conduct research and release exposés about conditions in low-wage industries, lobby for new labor and immigration laws and changes in existing ones, work with government agencies to improve monitoring and grievance processes, and bring suits against employers.

Organizing: Centers build ongoing organizations and engage in leadership development among workers to take action on their own behalf for economic and political change. This organizing may take different forms depending on the center, but all share a common commitment to providing a means through which workers can take action. Centers pursue these goals by seeking to impact the labor market through direct economic action on the one hand and public policy reform activity on the other.[4]

Place-based rather than work-site based: Most centers focus their work geographically, operating in a particular metropolitan area, city, or neighborhood. Often workers come into a center because they live or work in the center's geographic area of focus, not because they work in a specific industry or occupation. Within local labor markets they often target particular employers and industries for attention, but most worker centers are not work-site based. That is to say, their focus is not on organizing for majority representation in individual work sites or for contracts for individual groups of workers. Some day laborer centers do connect workers with employers and negotiate with them on wages and conditions of work.

Strong ethnic and racial identification: Sometimes ethnicity, rather than occupation or industry, is the primary identity through which workers come into a relationship with centers. In other cases, ethnicity marches hand in hand with occupation. Discrimination on the basis of race and ethnicity is a central analytic lens through which economic and social issues are viewed. In addition, a growing number of centers are working at the intersection between race, gender, and low-wage work.

Leadership development and internal democracy: Most centers place enormous emphasis on leadership development and democratic decision-making. They focus on putting processes in place to involve workers on an ongoing basis and work to develop the skills of worker leaders so that they are able to participate meaningfully in guiding the organizations.

Popular education: Centers identify strongly with the philosophy and teaching methods of "liberatory education" that Paulo Freire popularized and draw on models of popular education that originated in Latin American liberation movements and the American civil rights movement. They view education as integral to organizing. Workshops, courses, and training sessions are structured to emphasize the development of critical thinking skills and bringing these skills to bear on all information that is presented.

Thinking globally: Centers demonstrate a deep sense of solidarity with workers in other countries, have an ongoing programmatic focus on the global impact of labor and trade policies, and participate in campaigns that bring organizations together to take action transnationally. Some worker center founders and leaders had extensive experience with organizing in their countries of origin or were inspired by popular movements there and actively draw on those traditions in their current work. Many centers maintain ongoing ties with popular organizations in the countries from which workers have migrated, share strategies, publicize each other's work, and support each other as they are able.

A broad agenda: While centers place particular emphasis on work-related problems, they have a broad orientation and generally respond to the variety of issues faced by African Americans and recent immigrants to the United States, including education, housing, health care access, and criminal justice issues. They are also on the front lines regarding immigration-related issues such as defending access to drivers' licenses and helping workers deal with social security no-match letters.

Coalition building: Centers favor alliances with religious institutions and government agencies, and seek to work closely with other worker centers, non-profit agencies, community organizations, and student and activist groups by participating in many formal and informal coalitions.

Small and involved memberships: Most centers view membership as a privilege that is not automatic but must be earned. They require workers to take courses and/or become involved in the organization in order to qualify. At the same time, there is a lot of ambivalence about charging dues, and while about 40 percent of centers say they have a dues requirement, few have worked out systems that allow them to collect dues regularly.

ORIGINS OF WORKER CENTERS

Worker centers in general have emerged in response to the decline of institutions that historically provided workers with a vehicle for collection action. Immigrant worker centers have emerged as a consequence of the explosive growth of immigrant communities and the absence of infrastructure to support their needs. Concerned individuals and institutions have looked to the worker center model to address the increasing needs and demands of these newcomers. According to data collected from our survey, 23 percent of worker centers were founded by ethnic NGOs; 22 percent by churches, Catholic Charities, or other faith-based community organizing projects; and 27 percent by a combination of legal service organizations, social service agencies, and community-based organizations. Five percent were founded by Central America solidarity movement activists, as they realized that what had once been viewed as a temporary arrangement until refugees could return home had grown into permanent communities struggling to establish themselves economically and politically (see figure 1.4). Although 64 percent of worker centers are now stand-alone institutions, 36 percent continue to be connected to some larger institution.

While worker centers have grown out of a range of institutions, they have sprung from a common desire for a local organization that would provide services, conduct advocacy, and encourage organizing on the part of low-wage workers in the absence of anything else. Stories of their founding often share

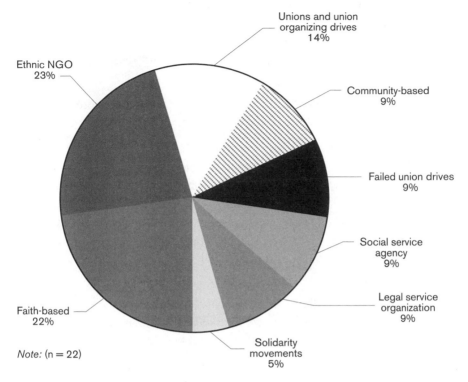

1.4. Worker center origins: Parent organizations

certain traits: a catalyzing event in which something happens to an individual or group of workers that leads them to seek support from an existing organization or visible leader. These workers and the allies they find to help them then try to figure out how to address the immediate situation but often discover that the particular issue they have confronted is emblematic of a much larger problem, and one that no existing organization is addressing. In this way, a host of ethnic NGOs, churches, legal aid centers, social service agencies, and university communities have almost literally "backed into" organizing and advocating for low-wage workers. They did so upon discovering that a service approach was simply not enough and that there was a void in terms of institutions for collective action among low-wage workers. As widely as these institutions differ from one another in form and function, most seem to have settled on the worker center model when their existing programs and strategies proved inadequate. Given below are some examples:

- The Workplace Project, one of the first of the second-wave worker centers, began as a project of CARECEN, a social service agency for Central American immigrants in Long Island, as more and more immigrants came to its offices seeking redress for unpaid wages and other employment-related problems.

- The Chinese Progressive Association established its worker center as a result of a campaign to fight for vocational training for dislocated garment workers in Boston's Chinatown.

- Casa Maryland, a social service agency for recent Central American immigrants, moved into organizing workers when a day laborer crisis developed in close proximity to their offices. This in turn catalyzed advocacy work at the state and federal level around the rights of day laborers to seek employment and led to voter participation efforts among the larger Latino communities in Silver Spring and Baltimore.

- The Filipino Worker Center of Los Angeles, founded by a group of young Filipino American UCLA graduates, provides support to the most recent waves of Filipino immigrants, many undocumented and working in the private sector home-health industry without benefits and access to organization.

- The Pomona Economic Opportunities Center, was founded after day laborers who had been gathering on the same corner and waiting for employers for fifteen years were banned from doing so by a new city ordinance. The day laborers, along with students from Pitzer College, city officials, and representatives from Home Depot, petitioned to get public money for a worker center and organized themselves to provide ESL and other classes to the workers.

Nine percent of worker centers were founded explicitly to fill the gap left by the decline of unionization in particular industries, and another 14 percent in connection to unions and union-organizing drives. These include:

- Black Workers for Justice (BWJ) grew out of a local campaign in 1981, in Rocky Mount, North Carolina, by three black women who were fired by the local K-Mart for raising questions with management about racially discriminatory practices. The vision of BWJ leadership has been to create an organization that straddled the civil rights movement, the labor movement, and community organizing. Over the years, in a state that has one of the lowest unionization rates in the nation, the organization has established worker centers, workers' schools, the first statewide public employees union and, with the Farm Labor Organizing Committee and others, a statewide African American Latino alliance.

- In response to the deaths of seventy workers and significant displacement of New York City restaurant workers following the September 11 attacks, Hotel and Restaurant Employees (HERE) Local 100 received special funding to assist the families of the workers at Windows on the World who were killed in the attack. At Here's request, two former Windows on the World workers and an organizer established the Restaurant Opportunities Center of New York (ROC-NY), an immigrant-led worker center seeking to bring organization to the overwhelmingly non-union restaurant industry workforce. Since its founding in 2002, through a combination of organizing, media, and litigation, ROC has won hundreds of thousands in back-wage and discrimination claims as well as specific commitments from some important industry leaders around wages, overtime, lunch breaks, paid vacations, promotions, and the right to organize.

- A coalition of legal aid and community organizations organized the Garment Worker Center (GWC) in Los Angeles a few years after the Union of Needletrades, Textiles and Industrial Employees (UNITE) was defeated in its efforts to organize in the garment industry there. The GWC provides legal, organizing, and advocacy support to the ninety thousand primarily Latina and Chinese immigrant women working for more than five thousand contractors, many under sweatshop conditions.

- The Laborers' Union decided to set up a worker center in collaboration with the National Interfaith Committee on Worker Justice after they won a hard-fought union organizing drive but were blocked from achieving a first contract by the employer, Case Farms, in the poultry industry of rural western North Carolina. Its goal: to support the thousands of Guatemalan immigrant workers living and working there, most of whom voted for the union.

- The new leadership of Service Employees International Union (SEIU) Local 615 opened a worker center at the union hall when they realized that they lacked effective means for communicating and building up participation among part-time Latino janitors, who had become the majority of their membership in Greater Boston. The center's goal, in addition to providing ESL, workforce development programs, and computer classes, is to build relationships between the union and its diffuse membership, to establish the union hall as a gathering place for immigrant members, and to build a vibrant core of new union leaders.

The vast majority of worker centers have grown up to serve predominantly or exclusively immigrant populations. However, as we have seen, there is a set of centers, especially in the south, that were founded by and focus on African Americans and some of these that bring immigrants together with African Americans. But they are exceptions to the rule.

In a 2004 study of jobs and activism in the African American community that was undertaken in close cooperation with this one, scholar Steven Pitts set out to understand why the worker center strategy has been largely concentrated among immigrants and not as widespread in black communities. First, he argues that the crisis around work in black communities is too often exclusively defined as a problem of high unemployment, and not also as one of a problem of bad jobs: "jobs that pay poorly; jobs with few benefits; jobs that offer no protection from employer harassment; jobs whose only future is a dead-end." Pitts found that responses to the crisis of bad jobs in the black community and the racially polarized nature of job markets often focused on individual skills development as opposed to putting forward a more systemic critique of the problem and strategies for transforming bad jobs on a larger scale. Those organizations that do take up the issues of jobs "do not attempt to improve the jobs held by black workers. Instead the emphasis is on the individualized provision of job readiness counseling, soft skills and hard skills." Pitts posits several other reasons for what he calls the "lack of transformative responses to the job crisis." These include a tendency for the African American freedom movement to focus on issues of ownership and control over assets rather than employer/employee relationships and the integration of African Americans into existing government agencies. Pitts also notes that McCarthy-era organizational attacks resulted in individuals who took a more systemic approach, "whose critique of segregation went beyond moral condemnation and contained an understanding of the social and economic structures that led to institutional racism" being purged from their organizations. In the too few cases where organizations were trying to transform the nature of the jobs themselves, strategies pursued were similar to immigrant worker centers: economic organizing to bring direct pressure to bear on employers and political organizing to enact public policy change.[5]

WHO WORKER CENTERS ORGANIZE

About half of all immigrants to the United States every year come from six countries: Mexico, Philippines, China, India, Dominican Republic, and Vietnam, and these same groups are also represented in large numbers among immigrant worker centers.[6] The majority of workers being organized through worker centers are from Mexico and Central and South America. As the 2000 census has shown Latinos to be the fastest rising minority group in the country, this makes sense. The largest number of immigrants, about 28 percent of all foreign-born persons, legal or undocumented, are Mexicans, and they are also the single largest presence in worker centers in the aggregate.[7]

Immigrants are more likely to live in cities, most likely in the twenty-seven largest urban regions of the United States, and these are also where the largest concentration of worker centers can be found. Cities with the largest percentage of the foreign-born are Los Angeles (30 percent); New York (20 percent); Miami (6 percent); San Francisco (6 percent); Chicago (4 percent); Houston (3 percent); and Boston, Dallas, San Diego, and Washington, D.C. (2 percent).[8]

The ethnic makeup of worker centers varies not only from region to region but also from industry to industry. For example, the taxi industry in New York City has become overwhelmingly South Asian, and this is reflected in the membership of the New York Taxi Workers' Alliance, while in northern Virginia there are large numbers of North African drivers. Restaurants in the Koreatown section of Los Angeles employ primarily Korean women and a smaller number of Mexican men. But grocery stores in Koreatown employ a large number of Mexican men and a small number of Korean women.

In their day-to-day work, worker centers are bringing together Latino immigrants who hail from a wide range of countries and have varied economic and political backgrounds. Over the course of conducting the research for this and earlier studies, it became quite clear that worker centers are one of the major local institutions where the forging of a pan-Latino identity and movement is taking place. However, very few workers identified with the term *Latino,* preferring instead to identify by their countries of origin.

Just as it would be a mistake to take a monochromatic view of workers who hail from the vastly different countries and cultures of Latin America, it would be a mistake to view worker centers as an exclusively Latino phenomenon. The Caribbean and East Asian regions each account for 15 percent of worker center participants, with West Africa and other African nations comprising 8 percent of the total (see Figure 1.5).

The majority of worker centers are either monolingual (Spanish only) or

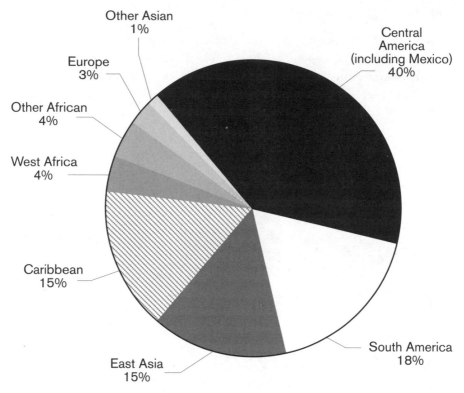

1.5. Region of origin of participating workers (immigrants only)

bilingual (Spanish/English). However in more than a third of the organizations, there are at least three languages spoken.

As we will explore in greater detail in chapters 5 through 9, worker centers take different approaches to organizing: 56 percent of those surveyed engage in industry-specific organizing, in which they build organizations of workers and engage in campaigns intended to improve wages and working conditions in a particular industry in a particular geographic area. Examples include:

- The Los Angeles Garment Worker Center, which focuses on women garment workers.

- The Tenants' and Workers' Support Committee (TWSC) in northern Virginia, which focuses on hotel housekeepers, taxi drivers, and childcare workers.

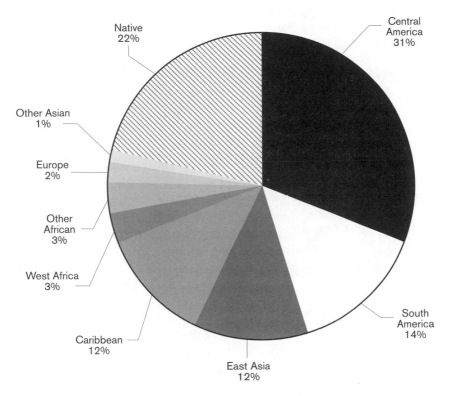

1.6. Who do worker centers organize? : Region of origin for worker center workers (including native-born Americans)

- Omaha Together One Community (OTOC) and the United Food and Commercial Workers, which has focused on meatpackers and related industries.

Forty-four percent of worker centers do not target specific industries for organizing, working instead to organize workers in a specific geographic area across a range of industries for action on non-industry specific issues. Examples include:

- Chicago Interfaith Workers Rights Center (CIWRC), which provides legal aid, helps workers in a wide variety of industries to act together for improvements, and matches groups of workers interested in organizing their workplaces with specific unions.

- Miami Workers Center (MWC), which organizes low-wage workers in Liberty City around job-related issues as well as housing, welfare, health care, and education.

- The Mississippi Workers Center for Human Rights, founded in 1996, which utilizes a human rights framework and works closely with the labor movement to educate and provide support to low-wage, non-union workers across a range of industries in the Delta.

As can be seen in Figure 1.7, although the day labor/construction and hospitality sectors are quite significant, worker centers organize within a wide variety of industries.

SNAPSHOTS OF THE NINE WORKER CENTERS

The Tenants' and Workers' Support Committee (TWSC) in Virginia began in 1986 as a community-organizing entity that focused on helping two thousand low-income residents of the Arlandria neighborhood of Alexandria fight eviction from their subsidized housing and convert a three-hundred-unit building into a limited equity co-op. Over the years the organization has grown into a local civil rights organization that is involved in a host of projects. It does community organizing in several other neighborhoods in Alexandria as well as Arlington and other northern Virginia communities. Broadening its scope, it has taken up a number of local issues, including public education and youth programming, health care, sustainable development and zoning, and living wages.

In addition, TWSC carries out worker organizing among immigrant and African American hospitality workers, childcare providers, and taxi drivers. Each of these groups of workers has an organization that is affiliated with the TWSC. Although the organization has sought union partners to work with, so far they have had limited success. For a time, they were also the northern Virginia affiliate of the Jobs with Justice national network. The organization does not provide services but places a strong focus on leadership development, with a stated emphasis on women of color and popular education. Once a year, it cosponsors with the City of Alexandria an ethnic festival that brings out more than ten thousand Latino families.

The Chicago Interfaith Worker Rights Center emerged out of the work of the Chicago Interfaith Committee on Workers Issues, a partnership of labor unions and area religious institutions. For more than eleven years, Chicago Interfaith organized hundreds of clergy to pray, fast, and rally in support of workers'

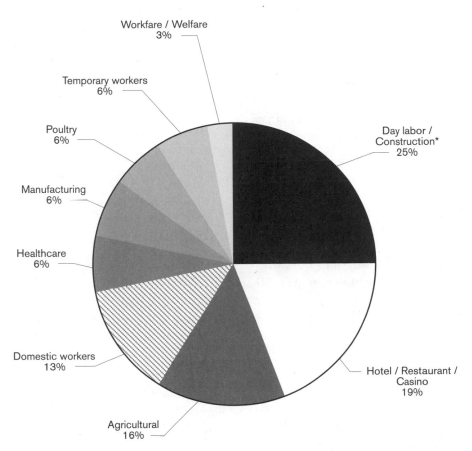

Note: While 44% of immigrant worker centers do not organize by industry, of the 56% that do, these are the most common industries.

* Centers that organize day laborers report that their workers work in construction, landscaping, warehouse, and other areas.

1.7. Worker centers: Most common industries

rights and union organizing campaigns on behalf of an estimated twenty-seven-thousand workers. Chicago Interfaith initiated a "Labor in the Pulpits" program organizing workers and union leaders to speak in religious congregations during Labor Day weekend, which is now carried nationally in more than one hundred cities and reaches more than 100,000 people. After years of work mobilizing clergy to support union organizing campaigns, the Interfaith Committee and a number of its churches became known as places immigrant workers could bring their employment-related problems.

In 1998, the Interfaith Committee published and distributed a workers' rights manual in English and Spanish that generated enormous response from area immigrant workers. Many who called had been unaware of their rights, and many were undocumented and afraid to seek help. Because of language barriers and limited office hours—it was only open from nine to five—the Department of Labor was largely inaccessible. Workers turned to their clergy and congregations for support, but these organizations didn't necessarily know how to help. Lacking an infrastructure to handle the growing numbers seeking help and organizing support, the Interfaith Committee opened two worker centers on Chicago's north and northwest sides. Both are located within the walls of religious institutions.

Six Day Labor hiring halls are operated by two community organizations in Los Angeles—the Coalition for Humane Immigrant Rights of Los Angeles (CHIRLA) and the Instituto de Educación Popular del Sur de California (IDEPSCA). The groups work with day laborers on an ongoing basis to set the rules that govern the centers. CHIRLA is the largest community-based immigrant rights organization in Los Angeles and began in 1986 in response to the impact of the changes in federal immigration law. While it initially functioned as an umbrella organization for a coterie of local groups, it added a focus on workers' rights and eventually direct organizing of immigrant workers as the day labor issues in Los Angeles grew increasingly serious in the late 1980s.

IDEPSCA is a nonprofit community-based organization that grew out of local community organizing efforts of a group of Chicano and Latino parents around issues of "racism, educational inequities, and the lack of affordable housing."[9] Dedicated to improving the educational opportunities and economic self-sufficiency of low-income Latino families through popular education and organizing, in addition to three hiring halls, it operates adult Spanish literacy and ESL programs, a computer literacy project, and youth and women's programs. Staff members for the two organizations work on-site helping to facilitate the day-to-day operation of the hiring halls. They offer a variety of services to day laborers, including help with unpaid wage claims and immigration issues, ESL classes, and tool lending. They engage in advocacy on a host of public policy issues that affect day laborers and make efforts to mobilize day laborers at rallies and hearings in support of these issues. So far they have not thought of their work as building worker power in the industry and have not built a worker association or union attached to the hiring hall project.

The Carolina Alliance for Fair Employment (CAFÉ) began as the Worker's Rights Project, a program of Southerners for Economic Justice (SEJ), in Greenville, South Carolina. In the 1970's the SEJ supported a national drive by the Amalgamated Clothing and Textile Workers Union (ACTWU) to organize textile workers at plants owned by JP Stevens. ACTWU reached a national settlement with JP Stevens in 1980. However, none of the Stevens plants in Greenville were unionized and calls from workers with job problems continued unabated. Sensing a clear need on the part of thousands of South Carolinians working in firms where union organization was highly unlikely, SEJ started the Worker's Rights Project (WRP) in Greenville in 1980.

By 1985, the WRP had been contacted by workers in more than fifty cities and towns across South Carolina. It developed "job rights workshops," which taught workers about employment laws and organizing, in ten cities around the state. In 1986, the organization won passage of a new state law that made it harder to fire injured workers. In 1987, WRP leaders voted to form a new statewide organization called the Carolina Alliance for Fair Employment. CAFÉ has continued to hold trainings on federal and state employment laws and to pursue public policy change on employment-related themes, including the regulation of the temporary employment industry. It has also broadened its agenda beyond employment issues to public education, criminal justice, and domestic violence. In recent years, the organization has also begun to organize chapters among the growing numbers of newly arrived Latino immigrant workers.

Founded in 1992, the Korean Immigrant Worker Advocates (KIWA) organizes restaurant and grocery store workers in the Koreatown neighborhood of Los Angeles. After a number of years of filing claims and lawsuits on behalf of individual restaurant workers, it launched the Restaurant Workers Justice Campaign in 1997. A major focus of the campaign was to increase compliance with minimum wage laws in the industry. By 2000, as a result of the campaign, KIWA estimated that the compliance rate of Koreatown restaurants had increased from about 2 percent to more than 50 percent.

In 2000–01, KIWA moved to create two independent organizations, one for restaurant workers, the other for workers in Koreatown's seven ethnic grocery stores. The Restaurant Workers Association of Koreatown (RWAK) is an independent organization based at KIWA, which operates as a quasi-union, offering a range of member benefits. It operates a free medical clinic and through KIWA helps members file claims for overtime and other wage claims as well as workers compensation. It has an ESL component that teaches workers English they need to know in the restaurant industry as well as a vocabulary for organizing.

The goal of KIWA's market workers' justice campaign, initiated in 2000, was to organize an independent union among the workers of Koreatown's seven grocery stores. The resulting Immigrant Workers Union faced fierce opposition from employers since its inception. In 2005, KIWA shifted strategies and kicked off a community and worker organizing campaign towards living wages and just treatment for workers employed at all seven Korean markets in Koreatown.

The New York Taxi Workers Alliance had its origins in 1992 in the Committee Against Anti-Asian Violence (CAAAV), a pan-Asian organization that was begun by young activists in New York City in the 1980s to create an organized voice for Asian immigrants around immigrant rights. CAAAV initially turned its attention to the taxi industry in response to violent attacks on immigrant drivers and had not intended to organize a separate cab drivers' organization, but over time, that is what happened.

Since 1997, when the organization became independent and renamed itself the New York Taxi Workers Alliance, it has built a membership base of close to five thousand drivers. It first demonstrated its ability to lead concerted economic action in 1998 when drivers struck in response to drastic policies promulgated by Mayor Giuliani to quadruple fines on drivers and make it much easier for them to have their licenses revoked. Over the next few years, the organization succeeded in consistently getting out the drivers' point of view in the media on issues like refusal of service. It established itself with the media and the relevant governmental bodies as the leading voice of Yellow Cab drivers in New York City.

In 2002 and 2003, the organization developed a successful multipronged strategy to campaign for a fare increase. It partnered with the Brennan Center of NYU Law School to produce research reports on wages and conditions in the industry, which provided the organization with a great deal of data to back up its claims to the media and government officials. By the fall of 2003, NYTWA had the attention of the major media and public officials. Over the next several months, it was the major voice of taxi drivers in the media and the major player on the drivers' side that negotiated a fare increase.

NYTWA is working to develop a strategy for fully consolidating a union model within the context of the current industry structure. As difficult as the wages and working conditions have become, many drivers identify as small businessmen and -women; in addition, independent contractor status gives the large number of undocumented workers in the industry an ability to work without facing as many risks regarding documentation.

CHAPTER 2

PUTTING WORKER CENTERS IN CONTEXT

In many parts of the United States today, the kind of work a person does, the compensation he or she receives for that work, and the possibilities that person has for redress when mistreated by an employer is enormously affected by that individual's immigration status, combined with his or her racial and ethnic origin. While businesses manifest an enormous hunger for immigrant workers—literally hiring them by the millions—the nation's immigration policies have exacerbated their vulnerability to exploitation. The silent compact between employers and employees is simple: in exchange for corporate indifference to their legal status, workers will not make a fuss about conditions or compensation. America's immigration policy has become one of its central, de facto labor market policies.

First-generation immigrants account for one out of eight workers in America today, but one in four low-wage workers.[1] Immigrants now comprise 20 percent of all low-income families.[2] Sixty-three percent of foreign-born workers are employed in service, manufacturing, and agriculture. Despite their economic importance,[3] immigrant workers are compensated at very low levels, routinely exploited on the job, and often lack access to health insurance.[4] In the five major immigrant cities, the percentage of immigrants living in poverty has risen steadily over the past three decades. For example, in New York before 1970, 10 percent of newly arriving immigrants were living in poverty; that number rose to 20 percent between 1980 and 1990 and then to 30 percent between 1990 and 2000. Los Angeles follows a very similar pattern: with a poverty rate of about 10 percent of immigrants arriving before 1970, between 1980 and 1990 it rose to 30 percent, and then to 40 percent between

1990 and 2000. Very similar patterns can be found in Chicago, San Francisco, and Miami.[5]

To understand the rise of immigrant worker centers and the role they are playing today, it is necessary to place them in a larger historical context. This context has two key elements: changes in U.S. immigration, and structural transformations in the U.S. economy. This chapter will examine each of these in turn, as well as their effect on national and state labor and welfare policies.

THE "SECOND GREAT MIGRATION"

During the so-called Golden Era of immigration to the United States—between 1880 and 1920—23 million immigrants arrived in a country that, in 1900, encompassed 76 million people.[6] By 1920, four out of ten inhabitants of the largest U.S. cities were foreign-born and an additional two in ten were children of immigrants. In contrast to earlier immigrants who hailed from northern and western Europe, the majority were Catholic, Jewish, or Greek Orthodox and hailed from eastern and southern Europe. These immigrants were joined by another Great Migration of southern blacks to the North, which began in the late 1890s but rose to its fullest height during and after the First World War.[7] As David T. Beito, one scholar of immigration puts it: "Never before had the United States experienced such an infusion of ethnic and cultural diversity in so short a time."[8]

On the other hand, America's immigration policy during the Golden Era was highly racially biased. Between 1851 and 1882, 300,000 Chinese immigrants arrived in the U.S., but Chinese immigration was brought to a halt with the passage of the Chinese Exclusion Act which effectively barred entry through the early 1940s. In 1907, a similar policy blocked the immigration of Japanese male laborers and by 1917 all Asians had been effectively banned. In 1924, Congress put in a system of national origins quotas which drastically reduced the number of new arrivals. Not until 1965 when the Hart Cellar Act opened up access to the United States once more, did immigration again become a dominant feature of American life.

Between 1990 and 2000, in terms of sheer numbers, more immigrants arrived in the United States than during any previous period in American history. The immigrant population in the United States increased from 19.8 million in 1990 to 31.1 million in 2000.[9] The two most striking differences between the Golden Era and today's immigrants are ethnicity and legal status. While 90 percent of immigrants to the United States during the Golden Era were white and European, only 15 percent of today's immigrants are from Europe, while half are from Latin America, with Mexicans comprising a full third of the total.[10]

The racial/ethnic character of this new Great Migration appears to be a deci-

WHY DO SO MANY IMMIGRANTS WANT TO COME TO WORK IN THE UNITED STATES?

- The principal magnet is U.S. wages relative to their countries of origin. Wages paid by U.S. employers are significantly higher than those available even for skilled and white-collar work in Mexico and other sending countries.

- Structural adjustment policies such as deep cuts in spending for government social or public works programs have pushed immigrants to leave their home countries. Also, new trade policies that have allowed cheap agricultural commodities such as corn to be imported from the United States have bankrupted thousands of small farmers and caused them to seek work in the United States.

- Labor immigration to the United States occurs because there is a strong and growing demand for it. In many places, urban and suburban employers and rural growers rely on this source of labor.

WHY DO SO MANY EMPLOYERS IN THE UNITED STATES SEEK OUT IMMIGRANT LABOR?

- Immigrant workers often cost employers far less than native-born workers—low wages, often less than full-time, and no or low-cost health insurance or other benefits.

- Employers are attracted to the low recruitment costs in hiring most immigrant laborers because they often come on their own.

WHY ARE SO MANY IMMIGRANTS UNDOCUMENTED?

- Family slots are either backed up for years, or people do not qualify for them.

- Employment is so narrowly defined, very few workers can enter the United States through the employment visa process.

The obstacles to legal immigration are much higher than they were for immigrants arriving in the United States at the turn of the twentieth century. Until 1921, there were no numerical limits or quotas for the number of immigrants allowed to enter the country. With the exception of those subject to the Chinese Exclusion Act, most immigrants who arrived at a port of entry and were not ill, insane, a convict, or likely to become a public charge were admitted into the United States as legal residents with permission to work.

Source: Jennifer Gordon, *Suburban Sweatshops: The Fight for Immigrant Rights* (Cambridge, MA: Harvard University Press, 2005).

sive factor in the unwelcome reception accorded to many newcomers. The vast majority of immigrants arriving during the Golden Era received immediate authorization to work and embarked on the pathway to citizenship. Approximately 28 percent of all immigrants (9 million) are living in the United States today without opportunities to legalize their status or obtain work authorization. About 5 million are part of the workforce; more than 50 percent of these are from Mexico, followed by El Salvador, Guatemala, Canada, and Haiti.[11]

TODAY

Legal status can only be acquired by those who fit within a restricted set of categories:

• Have a sibling, spouse, or parent who has green card or is a citizen;

• Can show that they will suffer persecution if returned to their home country;

• Have job skills that are in demand by employers and that U.S. citizens are not able to provide.

Most undocumented immigrants are labor migrants who do not qualify for any of these categories. Punishment for entering the country illegally also operates as a strong disincentive to apply for legal status, even for those who qualify. Even those who do qualify may face long waits before their admission is approved.

Caught in the tangled web of our nation's immigration laws, these newcomers risk being marginalized into a permanent new racial/ethnic underclass.

Like the European emigrants of the Golden Era, today's immigrants come to the United States in search of a better life and political freedom. Newcomers then and now find economic opportunity, but along with it, tremendous hardship, exploitation, and discrimination. An old story is told of an Italian immigrant in the late 1800s who learned three things upon his arrival in New York: "First, the streets aren't paved with gold. Second, they aren't paved at all. And third, you're expected to pave them."[12] In community after community, today's immigrant workers tell a similar story: "I realized that the American Dream wasn't what people thought it was. In America, it's more like you work and then you go to sleep. For a while after I arrived from Korea, whenever I saw a plane fly by, I would cry."

Immigrants are still glad to be in the United States but shocked by the hardships of daily life and their treatment by employers and the larger society. Then as now, the cultural, political, and social contexts of the home countries from which they hail affect their readiness to organize for social change. Jewish immigrants from Eastern Europe fled difficult circumstances at home to come to the United States. Some were from very small villages and had little experience of collective action. Others, who had been exposed to enlightenment ideas, socialist ideologies, and worker organization, arrived with a readiness for collective action. Similarly, some Mexican workers and Central American immigrants from El Salvador and Guatemala possess few repertoires of collective action while others were leaders or active participants in labor unions, student movements, agricultural cooperatives, or political parties in their homelands.

Scholars characterize the explosion of new immigration beginning in the

1980s as the "Second Great Migration," surpassing in size if not proportion of population that of the Golden Era. The nation as a whole, however, is only just beginning to appreciate this reality and come to grips with its full implications.

TRANSFORMATIONS IN THE U.S. ECONOMY

During the last half-century dramatic changes have occurred in the structure of industry, the organization of work, and patterns of employment in the United States. Between 1979 and 1996, 43 million jobs were lost—a large percentage in manufacturing. While millions more were created during that same period, many of these new jobs were of comparatively inferior quality.[13] The quickening pace of globalization, technological advance, and shifting markets has affected all aspects of the economy. Major industries have undergone massive restructuring, reengineering their processes and strategies. Economic restructuring has also stimulated a burgeoning service sector, which is highly decentralized; weighted toward low-wage, part-time jobs; and characterized by generally impermanent relationships between individual employers and employees. Bowing to pressure from financial markets, companies have become "leaner" and more "flexible," outsourcing or spinning off peripheral activities, employing fewer full-time workers, and relying more on contract and part-time employees. Individual firms are providing less training and fewer opportunities for job security and upward mobility for low-skill workers. Whereas in the fifties, sixties, and seventies, most U.S. workers, but especially blue-collar workers, were shielded from competitive unstructured labor markets, today a growing number of these workers are not.[14]

For the nation's 27.5 million working poor, the shift from goods-producing to service-producing industries has resulted in lower pay and fewer opportunities for upward advancement.[15] In many U.S. service and manufacturing industries, work that was once performed by employees of a single large firm is now being done by employees of many separate firms.[16] While the debate about the gains of "flexibility" to the U.S. economy continues, the story of structural economic change and its implications for workers at the bottom of the wage scale is by now well-established. Outsourcing and subcontracting has resulted in lower wages, little access to benefits, and fewer hours. The dramatic disaggregation of production has also greatly complicated minimum wage enforcement in low-wage labor markets as a shrinking number of inspectors strain to police a larger number of firms.[17]

Over the course of carrying out this study, the daily consequences of these structural changes on flesh-and-blood human beings in low-wage industries were made clear. What were once solid blue-collar jobs that made upward mobility possible for millions of immigrants now pay poverty-level wages and offer no hope of advancement. For example, today taxi drivers in New York City, who were once considered employees and accorded full-time salaries, benefits, and pensions, are commonly classified as "independent contractors." They have no access to employer-provided health insurance and are barely earning more than a hundred dollars after expenses for a ten- to twelve-hour day.

Home-based childcare providers in northern Virginia spoke of living in constant fear of becoming ill because they had no backup care for the children in their charge and no health insurance to go to the doctor. The stories of Omaha's newest generation of immigrant meatpackers, subject to kill-floor conditions that annually result in a 25 percent injury rate, are etched into their bodies in the multiple scars they point to with a mixture of sadness and pride.

The majority of American labor-market and social insurance policies at the federal and state levels are terribly mismatched to these current economic structures. They are premised on a 1930s understanding of employment relations that simply no longer exists for low-wage workers and has diminished for many white-collar workers. New Deal–era social-insurance programs (as well as labor laws) assumed long-term, stable employment at a single firm. Today, however, more and more workers are in nonstandard work arrangements and cannot access health benefits, unemployment insurance, pensions, and job training through their employers. As a result, the Fair Labor Standards Act—the cornerstone of government protections for low-wage workers—is failing millions of people. Federal and state departments of labor have four or five inspectors to cover hundreds of thousands of workplaces and penalties are minimal.

The National Labor Relations Act was premised on a similar set of assumptions that are now out of date. In the heyday of craft and industrial unionism, when workers' relationships to their occupations were more stable than their relationships with employers, millions were able to achieve decent wages, working conditions, and upward economic mobility through the organization of stable worker organizations.

Today, those ways of organizing and representing workers are largely gone. The right to organize in general has been extraordinarily weakened over the past several decades. Most employers wage aggressive, expensive, and successful campaigns to prevent unionization, and undocumented workers in particular have been held by the courts to have fewer rights and protections if fired for organizing activities. Many workers are understandably terrified of losing their jobs if they speak up. In a context in which 75 percent of employers hire consultants to help them fight unions that are organizing jobs, 25 percent illegally fire at least one worker for union activity, and 52 percent threaten to call immigration officials during organizing drives that include undocumented workers, this fear is more than understandable.[18]

Unions now represent 8 percent of workers in the private sector, where the vast majority of immigrant workers are employed.[19] In 2002, 4.5 percent of workers in the bottom tenth of the wage distribution (up to $6.70/hour) were represented by unions, for the bottom fifth it was 5.6 percent.[20] For many of these workers employed in the context of unstable firms, outmoded and ineffectual labor laws, and an institutional firm-based scaffolding around a social insurance system that makes less and less sense, it is not at all clear what alternative models make sense. In this context, as local actors grapple with the problems of low-wage workers and cast around for models, many are turning to the approach represented by worker centers.

IMMIGRANT AND LOW-WAGE WORKER SUPPORT SYSTEMS DURING THE GOLDEN ERA

A central thesis of this volume is that immigrant worker centers have arisen in part because of an absence of preexisting institutions to integrate low-wage immigrants into American civil society and provide them with pathways to economic stability through service, self-help, and self-organization. They are part of a cluster of organizations that comprise a newly emerging infrastructure for newcomers struggling for rights, respect, acceptance by society, and upward mobility through the labor market.

Today, as in the Golden Era, working-class immigrant life in America is frequently predicated on group identity and communal aid. Then as now, immigrants largely relied on their ethnic traditions and networks to help them make their way. Nonetheless, from the 1880s through the 1920s, a set of organizations played roles akin to today's worker centers in low-wage immigrant communities. The fought anti-immigrant abuse and discrimination, exposed exploitative conditions, lobbied for laws that protected workers, and assisted immigrant workers who wanted to form unions.[21]

A diverse group of fraternal organizations; settlement houses and women's civic organizations; labor radicals, socialists, and trade unionists were the earliest American reformers who fought to promote immigrant rights and establish a set of protections for the low-wage labor market. Many, such as the German and Jewish *Landsmanshaftn*, were based on homeland ties and culture, craft, or occupation, and offered mutual aid and services without a strong political bent.[22]

A minority of fraternal organizations, like the Workmen's Circle, or *Arbeiter Ring*, was explicitly political. Founded in 1892, the Workmen's Circle had a strong ethnic base among German and later eastern European Jewish workers, a deep ideological commitment to worker self-emancipation and economic equality, and a willingness to offer social benefits in addition to engaging in long-term organizing. The Workman's Circle was created to provide "(1) mutual aid in sickness and death; (2) furtherance of education; and (3) the establishment of cooperative enterprises." By 1920, it was furnishing life and burial insurance, and aid to influenza victims, the unemployed, and the "stricken" as well as summer camps and workers' schools. In 1925 it had eighty-four thousand members nationwide and engaged in a wide range of organizing and social services.[23]

Prolabor and socialist fraternal organizations that preceded the Workmen's Circle were pioneers in the struggle for workers' rights, including the fight for the eight-hour day. They were among the first to frame their demands as a struggle for a living wage, a rate of pay that would comfortably support a worker and his family, during the national railroad strike of 1877.[24] During the explosive growth of the labor movement in the 1880s, craft unionists in cities across the country took up this demand, creating central labor bodies that reached far beyond the skilled trades and embraced a broad social agenda.

For a period of time, the Knights of Labor brought together skilled and unskilled workers; small producers; women and men, blacks, whites, and immigrants; and by 1887 nearly one-tenth of the order's membership was female and a similar proportion was black.[25] The Knights believed that, to ensure the conditions of self-government in America, citizenship required the inclusion of a basic set of economic rights for wage earners, which included the right to reasonable hours of work, membership in unions, and the union pay scale. But beyond guaranteeing a just wage and the right to organize, the Knights called for industrial democracy.

The nation's first protective labor legislation emerged from these struggles, which also saw the emergence of a new institution—the settlement house. "In Chicago and other cities in the 1890s," writes Kathryn Kish Sklar, "social settlements stepped into the breach created by rapid urbanization on the one hand and traditions of limited government on the other." According to Sklar, settlements grew in number from six in 1891 to seventy-four in 1897, over one hundred in 1900 and four hundred by 1910.[26] During the progressive era, settlement house women worked to document the abhorrent conditions in the nation's sweatshops, and they were the leaders of a crusade to bring up conditions and wages not only for women and children but for all factory workers. In 1893, Hull House, the flagship settlement house founded in Chicago by Jane Addams, led the successful campaign to create an Illinois state law that provided for state inspection of factory working conditions. Hull House's Florence Kelley became the state's first chief factory inspector. Kelley and other middle-class women re-formers of the National Consumers' League worked with labor activists to ex-pand labor protections, strategically deciding to begin with the pursuit of regu-lations that would set rules in place about conditions of employment for women and children.

Kelley's work was instrumental to a 1908 decision by the U.S. Supreme Court, *Muller v. Oregon*, that established a new precedent in favor of protective legislation. In upholding the Oregon law that limited the hours that women could work in certain industries to ten hours a day, the decision reinforced the idea that employers' control over terms and conditions of employment was not absolute.

In 1912 alone, twenty-eight states set maximum working hours for women, and thirty-eight states enacted child labor laws. These laws paved the way for general reforms that covered all workers. By 1915, workers' compensation laws were on the books in thirty-five states, and twenty-five states passed laws that limited the hours of some male workers. By 1920, the majority of states passed compulsory education laws, banned the employment of children under four-teen, and established an eight-hour day for those under sixteen.[27]

However, when the courts struck down a number of Progressive-era re-forms, the American Federation of Labor became convinced that it had to wrest better wages and working conditions from capital directly and not via legislation. It took a decisive turn in the direction of "voluntarism," which stood in opposition to efforts to establish compulsory pensions and unem-ployment insurance. During this same period, the mainstream of the Ameri-can labor movement frowned on the idea of unions providing services, view-ing this as fostering dependency and undermining collective bargaining. The American Federation of Labor did not alter this stance and authorize service provision to its members until the Great Depression. Like the AFL, the Inter-national Workers of the World (IWW) eschewed traditional charities and ser-vices, but it did believe in providing alternative services to its members. Dur-ing the Paterson and Lawrence strikes, the Wobblies were able to create support committees that provided food, clothing, and emergency relief but were generally unsuccessful in establishing structured, consistent services be-yond emergency situations.[28]

Hull House, like the fraternal organizations, rejected this approach. It was always envisioned as a gathering place where immigrants could attend lectures, classes, concerts, and performances in addition to accessing needed social ser-vices. Hull House was also deeply engaged in the struggle to alter working con-ditions for immigrants plying the needle trades in Chicago. The organization's strategy always involved building cross-class partnerships, such as the Illinois

Woman's Alliance, a powerful coalition of middle- and working-class women's organizations that altered the terms of debate about industrial employment. Florence Kelley, as the leader of Hull House's efforts, carried out groundbreaking work documenting working conditions in the sweatshops and helped to strengthen "antisweating" campaigns in Chicago and elsewhere that worked toward legislative reform. While Kelley and Addams had their differences with the male-dominated Chicago Trade and Labor Assembly, they strongly supported union organizing efforts. They played a pivotal role, for example, in helping the Amalgamated Clothing Workers to organize and achieve a first contract.[29]

IMMIGRANT WORKER SUPPORT INFRASTRUCTURES—THEN AND NOW

It is important not to idealize the institutional infrastructure that existed for Golden Era immigrant workers or to exaggerate its importance (see figure 2.1). As historians have noted, during that period, self-help and informal financial giving dwarfed all other categories. This remains the case today as well. However, research for this project makes clear that the relatively robust constellation of institutions that existed to support new immigrants to the United States during the Golden Era no longer exists (see figure 2.2).

As figure 2.2 indicates, some important institutions that were critical supports for immigrant workers in the last century have essentially left the stage or now are playing a greatly reduced role. For example:

- Unions have been in decline for more than a generation and now represent fewer than one in twelve American workers.

- The old self-help organizations like fraternal organizations and mutual aid societies, which were once central to the provision of sickness, burial, and life insurance, for the most part no longer provide insurance and have declined dramatically in number and strength. The contemporary wave of Hometown Associations are primarily engaged in carrying out development projects back in their home communities and less focused on economic self-help activities between members here.[30]

- Political parties may be showing a resurgent interest in immigrants (at least in Latinos). But they have not, for this wave of immigrants, played the central role at the local level that they once did in certain American cities, in terms of integrating newcomers into political life and providing jobs and other services.

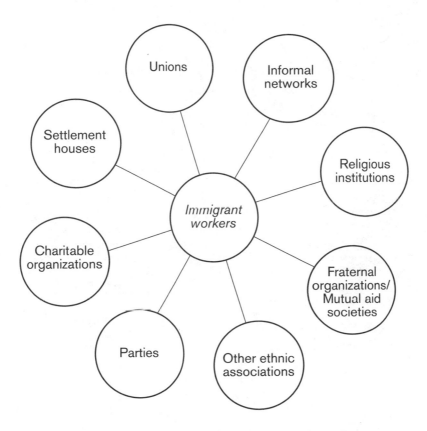

2.1. Golden era of immigration

- Settlement houses still exist but in diminished numbers, and while some are still involved in service provision and advocacy, in the main they seem to be less engaged in immigrant organizing activities than they were during the Golden Era.

- More recent additions to the immigrant social service infrastructure function with serious restrictions on their ability to provide support. The Legal Services Corporation created in 1974 to provide legal aid to the poor once played an important role for low-wage immigrant workers. But as of 1996, "all legal service agencies operating under funds provided by the Legal Services Corporation are prohibited from representing undocumented immigrants, as well as from filing class actions, challenges to welfare reform, rulemaking, lobbying, litigation on behalf of prisoners, and representation in drug-related public housing evictions."[31]

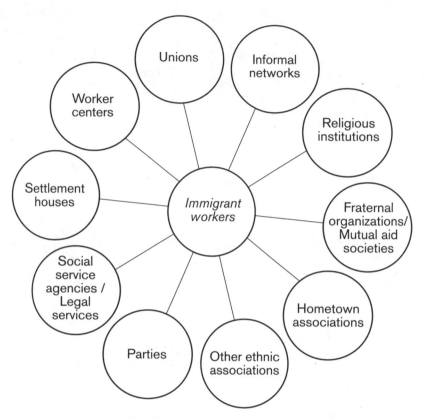

2.2. Today at comparable levels of immigration

Research makes clear that immigrant worker centers are part of a new wave of institutions that has arisen to fill the vacuum created by the disappearance or decline of these previous groups and institutions. As a result of attempting to respond to similar needs, immigrant worker centers share a number of features of these earlier institutions. One can readily distinguish parallels between the ideas and strategies of worker centers and organizations of the Golden Era— fraternal organizations such as the Workmen's Circle, settlement houses such as Hull House, and labor organizations such as the IWW, the Knights of Labor, and the Amalgamated Clothing Workers Union. Worker centers are not consciously emulating their historical antecedents, but the following similarities are worth noting.

The Workmen's Circle combined mutual aid and ethnic solidarity with a deep commitment to socialism and building the labor movement. It had a passionate commitment to the preservation of Jewish cultural traditions, but the celebration of *Yiddishkeit* was linked to the pursuit of social justice in America. Worker centers also combine a commitment to mutual aid via the services they provide and the celebration of workers' native cultural traditions; along with a strong commitment to organizing, cultural content is often woven into the events and activities they create. However, while the Workmen's Circle worked mainly through the Socialist party and the labor movement, worker centers now identify with and participate in larger "global democracy" and antiracist movements and engage in direct economic organizing activities on their own or in coalition with other immigrant and worker organizations.

Like the settlement houses that provided spaces for immigrants to come together and obtain services unavailable elsewhere, many worker centers today function as gathering places and matchmakers between service providers and today's low-wage immigrant workers. Many are actively engaged in education and youth activities as well as housing and health care issues. Also like settlement houses, they are playing a central role in documenting and publicizing workplace abuses of low-wage immigrant workers and fighting for necessary policy reforms.

While the settlement house movement built cross-class and cross-ethnic alliances between white middle-class women and low-wage immigrant women, not all worker centers take the same approach in their coalition-building activities. Some are more focused on building interethnic coalitions between people of color, and although they may be active in the broader global democracy movement, they are less interested in broad coalitions between whites and people of color. Others, including the day laborer centers who must work with neighborhood associations, local businesses, and law enforcement officials, as well as those who work within faith-based organizations, are building cross-class and cross-racial alliances.

Many of the strategies and tactics worker centers use today are the same as those first developed by organized labor in its efforts to improve wages and working conditions for low-wage workers. Then, as now, organizations engage in advocacy, compiling statistics and documentation on the problem of low-wage labor, struggle to create lasting organizations, and turn to the state to agitate and organize for the enactment of policy solutions.

Early U.S. guilds and craft unions struggled to "take wages out of competition." They fought to organize a majority of workers in order to establish a monopoly over the labor supply, which in turn enabled them to set higher wages and better working conditions. They pioneered the use of pickets, strikes, and boycotts. Craft unions required employers who were signatory to its contracts to contribute to "health and welfare funds" that provided health insurance and pensions. These same unions created union-run hiring halls to rationalize the hiring process.

Industrial unions helped workers combine across a specific sector to build enough power to bargain collectively with an association of firms in their industries at the national or regional level and set "patterns" for the industry as a whole. Some of the grassroots-led unions of the early 1930s and CIO local unions, as well as the United Farm Workers, AFSCME, and 1199 all twinned class with ethnic identity and the struggle for racial justice. In truth, the notion that "voluntarism" was American labor's guiding philosophy has been exaggerated. From the 1890s struggle for the eight-hour day, to minimum wage, workers' compensation, social security, occupational safety and health laws, full employment and national health care, the AFL-CIO has had a long tradition of pressing for public policy change as a major means of improving wages and working conditions.

In their local organizing efforts and public policy campaigns, worker centers deploy all of these tactics and strategies. Their day laborer worker centers are efforts to build leverage and establish terms and conditions of employment with transient employers. Their intensive picketing of employers and boycotts of specific companies are efforts to spin strong moral positioning into enough of a threat of potent economic pressure that companies make concessions. Their organizing efforts based in specific industries all share a long-run goal of winning industrywide improvements either through some form of collective bargaining with employers or enactment of public policy. In the new worker centers, ethnicity is the most stable identity, in many cases far more stable than craft or occupation, on which organizations are built, and the movement understands itself as much in racial or ethnic as economic justice terms.

Just as the individuals who founded and participated in Golden Era organizations were a mixture of "outsiders" and "insiders," so too are the founders and leaders of the immigrant worker centers. Some center founders were progressive individuals—antisweatshop activists, community organizers, public interest lawyers, ministers, and lay leaders all holding strong sympathies with the plight of immigrant workers but not arising out of the immigrant worker community itself. Other center founders were either immigrant workers themselves, with perhaps a few more years of navigating the American employment system under their belts, or second-generation immigrants keenly aware of what their parents went through in order to provide them with a shot at educational and economic opportunity. To succeed, these movement entrepreneurs have had to build relationships with immigrant workers, identify leaders among them, and develop narratives, structures, and strategies that resonated with them.

Worker center activists echo earlier social reformers in another sense—they have an expansive understanding of their role and mission as agents for social change. Many worker centers were created by activists whose political consciousness was decisively shaped by the social movements of the 1960s. Some drew additional inspiration from foreign examples such as the Cultural Revolution in China or popular guerrilla insurgencies in Central America and Mexico. Most are motivated by an ideology or worldview that seeks to tame or master the market for the benefit of all of society. Put another way, they are fighting not just for better wages for their own constituents, but for a societal "social wage."

As historian Nelson Lichtenstein reminds us, "This social wage includes monetary entitlements such as pensions, unemployment insurance and workman's compensation, but it also embodies a more far-ranging set of institutions: public education, city parks, mandated vacations, municipal services, health and safety regulations, minimum wage, child labor and women's protective laws."[32] Worker centers do not focus exclusively on labor and employment issues—or on immigration issues. They are about something much bigger and much more visionary—demonstrating, in the words of the World Social Forum, that "another world is possible."

CHAPTER 3

ORGANIZING AT THE INTERSECTION OF ETHNICITY, RACE, GENDER, AND CLASS

To understand immigrant worker centers and their role, it is necessary to understand the immigrant communities in which they work and from which their members and supporters are recruited. This chapter provides a contextual framework for looking at immigrant ethnic identities in the United States today, and how worker centers are rooting themselves in these complex and dynamic communities as they build organizations at the intersection of ethnicity, race, gender, and class. We will also explore worker centers' multi-cultural organizing and their efforts to unite immigrants and African Americans.

HOME COUNTRY CONNECTIONS AND ENDURING ETHNIC IDENTITIES

The gravitational force that grounds worker centers, especially those run by immigrants and the children of immigrants, is ethnic identity and solidarity. These ties bind workers from the same ethnic background to each other not only in the diasporan communities of the United States but also to their home countries. Given that immigration flows are so strongly conditioned by global economic policies, worker centers tend to view local and global issues holistically. For worker centers, "globalization" is not the abstract issue it sometimes appears to be in U.S. policy discussions; rather it is one of the reasons why immigrants come to the United States in the first place. Center staff and leaders stay in close touch with what is happening in the home countries of the immigrant groups with whom they work and strive to forge and maintain ongoing relationships with organizations engaged in similar work in those places.

Aquilina Soriano, executive director of the Filipino Worker Center in Los Angeles is an example of how these connections are developed. A third-generation Filipino American, she grew up in California and attended college at UCLA. She soon became active in immigrant rights and environmental justice issues as well as working with the dynamic and effective Hotel Employees and Restaurant Employees (HERE), Local #11, in Los Angeles. Through her college activism, Soriano began to explore her own heritage.

"I had always wanted to know what was going on in the Filipino community and I met someone who was an organizer in the Philippines; I left school and went to the Philippines for about a year." Soriano worked with student and peasant organizations and spent four months in the countryside where she did organizing in different barrios with farmer, worker, and youth organizations. On her return to the United States, she helped found the Filipino Worker Center to work with the newest waves of Filipino immigrants in California—a population that has higher numbers of undocumented and low-wage workers than in earlier waves.

"The situation in the Philippines has a lot to do with their situation here, too," says Soriano. "Partly it's the whole history of migration from the Philippines to the United States, the colonization of the country in the 1900s. Ten percent of the country's population is working abroad, which is a huge number. The economy is mostly surviving off the remittances of overseas workers—about eight billion dollars a year comes from the United States." Soriano says that what she learned in her year in the Philippines has shaped her approach to organizing in Los Angeles.

"The major influences on our work," she says, "are organizing in the Philippines and worker centers here." Soriano's understanding of the impact of globalization was shaped by her observations in the Philippines. "Working conditions there have caused this outpouring of people because there are no opportunities for jobs. Even the government supports sending people abroad because there are no more gold reserves and they are relying on the remittances." Just as globalization policies have affected the situation in the Philippines, Soriano believes they can also be seen in California in terms of "how they affect daily life, quality of jobs, and where budgets are spent."[1] In the belief that understanding globalization is critical to understanding the circumstances of immigrant workers, the Filipino Worker Center sponsors extensive political education that covers the history of immigration to the United States from the Philippines and U.S. immigration and globalization policies.

The Filipino Worker Center in Los Angeles is one of nine Filipino worker centers that have sprung up in the United States and Canada, including San Jose, Seattle, Vancouver, and New York City. The newest efforts are under way in

Washington, D.C., and Chicago. In the spring of 2004, they were in the process of trying to form a national network that would help the groups to support each other with fund-raising, organizational development, organizing, and research.

After immigration reform in 1965, Korean immigrants came to the United States in huge numbers. During the first decade of Korean immigration, immigrants tended to be highly urban, educated, and Christian, and came through occupational preferences in the immigration law. Beginning in the mid 1970s, and coinciding with changes in immigration law that demoted occupational preference in favor of family reunification, Korean immigration came to reflect a much larger cross-section of the Korean community. This period of immigration peaked at thirty-five thousand Koreans entering the United States each year in the mid 1980s and led to the growth and solidification of Koreatown in Los Angeles as an ethnic enclave. The more recent waves of Korean immigrants, especially those who came after the economic collapse in 1997, have been poorer and a much larger percentage has been undocumented.[2]

Like the Filipino Worker Center, the Korean Immigrant Worker Advocates (KIWA) emerged out of Korean student activism and cultural studies in San Francisco and Los Angeles around reunification and democracy issues in Korea as well as support for more recent Korean immigrant workers in the United States. It was founded in the aftermath of the Los Angeles riots in 1992 by two Korean organizers, Danny Park and Roy Hong. The organization's first campaign was to pressure the relief organization that had been created to rebuild Koreatown in the aftermath of the riots to provide financial help to individual workers, not just businesses.

Worker organizing was a natural focus for Korean-American activists who were strongly influenced by the democracy movement in South Korea and observed the strong role played by worker organizations there as well as the large number of low-wage Korean immigrants working in Los Angeles. Disturbed by the schisms between Koreans, Latinos, and African Americans exposed by the riots, KIWA started out with a strong commitment to interethnic organizing, especially between the Korean and Latino immigrants working for Korean businesses in Koreatown. From the beginning, the organization approached its work from an economic and racial justice framework.[3]

Observing the growing number of Korean companies setting up shop in free trade zones in Asia and Latin America that were notorious for labor rights violations, KIWA started the Asia–Latin America Solidarity Project. The project's main goal is to "to build a bridge between the struggles of workers in Asia and Latin America and to strengthen the workers' struggles against exploitative Asian transnational corporations,"[4] through monitoring Korean and other Asian plants in Latin American and supporting worker organizing. The director of the project, Ae Hwa Kim, a veteran of Korean worker centers and the labor movement, had long been interested in international solidarity work and came from Korea in order to direct the project.

Modernity has greatly facilitated closer ongoing connection and communication between immigrants to the United States and their home communities. For immigrants of the second great migration, the availability of long-distance phone cards, internet services, and check-wiring, and for those in the United States legally, the reduced price of travel, have shortened the distance between home and away. Some Mexican workers interviewed for this study made reference to annual trips home, although others noted greater difficulty in going back and forth since September 11, 2002. Meatpackers, among others, noted that their employers built in time for them to go home once a year to see family, renew visas, and tend to other issues.

Sending countries have very strong economic incentives for their citizens to work in the United States and to nurture ongoing connections between immigrants in the United States and their native countries. It is now well documented that low-wage immigrant workers send very significant amounts of money home, acting as important providers to family and social networks and playing a central role in the economies of their home countries. In 2003, at $38 billion dollars, immigrant remittances were the largest single source of foreign capital flowing to Latin America and the Caribbean.[5] According to sociologist Peggy Levitt, a growing number of countries are offering some form of dual citizenship "because they need the economic remittances and political influence that migrants offer."

In fact, in 1996, the Dominican House of Deputies passed legislation allowing dual citizenship, and in 1997 the Dominican Senate approved an electoral reform package that allows migrants to vote and run for office, including those who are naturalized American citizens of Dominican descent. Brazilians and Colombians in the United States are encouraged to vote by their consulates, which set up local polling places, and Colombians even have their own elected representatives in the legislature.

Although they are not yet permitted to vote or hold high office, Mexicans also have the right to hold Mexican nationality as well U.S. citizenship. In addition, Mexican consulates in a number of states play an ongoing role in providing support such as distributing identification cards to low-income nationals.[6] In South Carolina, CAFÉ has worked quite closely with the Mexican consulate helping to coordinate day-long events in Charleston, Greenville, and other cities where workers have come to meet with consular officials and receive immigration advice in addition to identification cards.

Writing about Dominican migrants in the Jamaica Plain neighborhood of

Boston, Levitt argues that migrants now have the ability to stay enmeshed in both societies. These "transnational villagers" have profound implications for longstanding ideas about immigrant incorporation and assimilation.

> Many Americans expect migrants . . . to sever their ties to their homeland as they become assimilated into the United States. They assume that migrants will eventually transfer their loyalty and community membership from the countries they leave behind to the ones that receive them. But increasing numbers of migrants continue to participate in the political and economic lives of their homelands, even as they are incorporating into their host societies. Instead of loosening their connections and trading one membership for another, some individuals are keeping their feet in both worlds. They use political, religious, and civic arenas to forge social relations, earn their livelihoods, and exercise their rights across borders.[7]

The "trans" in transnational villager can give a misleading impression—the truth is that accommodation of these workers is often one-way, with home countries but not the United States recognizing them and bestowing rights. Despite being increasingly able to maintain political and civic ties in their home countries, and having informal arrangements with U.S. employers who have an economic interest in a cheap workforce, many of these immigrants are unable to establish a political and civic voice in the United States. Levitt argues that migrants preserve strong home country ties and remain active in political and civic life there in part due to the blocked mobility, racism, and discrimination they experience in the United States and are "not allowed to become 'American' even if they want to."[8]

While many "transnational villagers" have their feet in two countries, only one gives them full political and economic rights. So how much should they "invest" in the other country, especially in terms of engaging in activities that could lose them their jobs or get them deported? These workers, especially those who are undocumented are constantly dealing with the tension between the desire to organize to improve wages and working conditions and the fear of being fired or deported. This tension poses great challenges to organizing.

From the turn of the century, Omaha has had many waves of immigrants come to work in the meatpacking industry, but the transnational nature of the Mexican workers who have come in the 1980s and 1990s seems different to close observers. "There's a transnational sense to this immigration pattern. People do come and there's permanence, but there are people from Mexico, they have families that go back and forth and they go back and forth," said Tom Holler, the Industrial Areas Foundation lead organizer in Omaha. "That was different when people came from Germany." This going back and forth presented difficulties for organizing in Omaha in the early days of the meatpacking drive because just when a solid leadership group had been organized, it had to be reorganized after key members left to return to Mexico. Marcella Cervantes, former Omaha Together One Community (OTOC) organizer, described the dilemma: "When we started organizing, one of the tactics Nebraska Beef used was to tell the workers, 'If the union gets in, you won't be able to leave and then get your job back.' It's really hard to control that because workers have their interests half in the United States and half in Mexico. All the companies have different ways of operating with the workers."[9]

Cervantes used the example of Nebraska Beef's informal arrangement with its workers to make her point. "The majority of them, 55 percent out of 750 workers, were undocumented. Those workers are men in their thirties and forties, and they left their families in their countries. They work for nine months and they visit their families. The company gives them a job back. That was difficult to organize those people. When I started that was the problem. We started finding people and in three months you go back looking for them and they're gone." But the terrorist attack of September 11 seems to have changed that. "I think since September eleventh they don't move as much. . . . People think if they left the country they would never get back in and if they went to a new company, they might get caught with bad papers," said Cervantes. "They started to stay in one place and this is a good chance for organizers to continue to reach people and establish more."

Workers from Central America, due to wars, distance, and lack of legal status, have been much less able to travel back and forth. Still, fear of deportation or detention can make them hesitant to organize. Some Salvadoran workers, for example, have received Temporary Protected Status (TPS). In Cervantes words, "they work for three years and they have to go back. They may not be able to renew their permit and instead start working as an illegal person." Other Salvadorans who never applied for TPS are stuck in a more or less permanent undocumented position. Many of these workers present false social security numbers to employers who look the other way: "They know because the majority of the companies here, their Human Resource people are Hispanics," said Cervantes. But when dealing with a troublemaker or threatened with an organizing drive, employers make clear that they could check workers' numbers with the Social Security Administration. "There is one company where a supervisor has a lot of family working here illegally. They know they are illegal, and that's why people get scared even if [they] know [they] work hard and [they] get low wages. What can [they] do? [They're] here to work and [the company] offered [them] a job."

As we will see in the case of the KIWA grocery workers in chapter 6, without a union, when workers receive no-match letters or are asked by their employers to resubmit their documentation, they have little power to resist. They know that if they do resubmit, they will expose themselves to arrest and deportation. If employers have taken this action in retaliation for organizing, workers can use the National Labor Relations Act, but few who are not engaged in a union organizing drive do so.[10] On the other hand, unionized workers are much more capable of defending themselves in these situations when their stewards and business agents understand immigration law. The presence of a union and a union contract means that employers are less capable of unilateral action and that union staff will fight any unilateral changes that are made in the terms and conditions of employment. Also, unions can negotiate clauses in their contracts to deal with these issues. For example, when Service Employees International Union (SEIU) settled a janitors' strike in Boston in 2002, one of the conditions of going back to work was that contractors would not "pull workers' papers" or ask them to resubmit their documentation. However, many union locals know very little about immigration law and are often unaware of the steps they can take to protect and defend the rights of their immigrant members.[11] To better inform unions about representing their immigrant members in 2004, the AFL-CIO has recently established a new national initiative based in the office of the general counsel.

It is in this environment of having a foot in two worlds and living in fear and legal limbo that worker centers endeavor to support immigrant workers and help them fight for their rights.

OUTREACH AND RECRUITMENT

All of the worker centers interviewed in the case studies and surveys viewed the building of a base of workers as a top priority and central focus of work. Worker centers recruit potential members and leaders through broad-gauge outreach, including getting features placed in the ethnic media, visiting neighborhoods, speaking in churches, and hand-billing workplaces. Here are some examples:

• Workplace Project leaders and staff make hundreds of community presentations every year. During the first seven years they have reached more than 10,000 workers directly through community presentations and 125,000 with information about their labor rights via stories in the Spanish language media. Since 1995, the organization has published and distributed *Voz Laboral,* a newsletter for immigrant workers in immigrant-heavy neighborhoods and commercial areas.

• Many workers are referred to the Chicago Interfaith Workers Rights Center by their churches. In addition, rather than setting up their own ESL classes, organizers and volunteers have created an interactive workshop on workplace rights and regularly offer it at the scores of ESL classes currently taking place in Chicago. This strategy brings them into contact with hundreds of immigrant workers every week. They also mass distribute a workers' rights handbook in English, Spanish, and Polish that has their contact information as well.

• Lupe Hernandez, who eventually became a part-time organizer for the Garment Worker Center in Los Angeles, first became involved with the organization when she heard an announcement on TV and decided to come down to the office to seek help with a problem she was having with an employer. "Sometimes we hand out flyers. When there were busses we'd put flyers on [these] or hand them out. I think . . . the best outreach is to pass the voice from one to another. A member will bring someone along. One time I saw someone who had gotten assistance from the center had stapled posters around downtown saying how we help workers and especially garment workers."[12]

• Working with federal and state agencies, CAFÉ sponsors and publicizes regular workshops across the state on employment-related issues for low-income workers. Workers come to learn their rights and are asked to join CAFÉ and become involved. With the Mexican consulate, the organization also cosponsors day-long informational events for Mexican workers that attract very large numbers. In Charleston on one day in 2003, twenty-two hundred people waited on line to speak with a consular official and apply for a Mexican passport or *matrícula consular,* the Mexican identification card.

For contacts that are not very personal, a surprisingly high number of workers seem to respond; perhaps this is because so many workers experience problems with employers and are hungry for information about what they can do. Several centers have had to limit the outreach they do because they cannot satisfy the demand for services, especially help with filing unpaid wage claims.

Kim Bobo, executive director of the Interfaith Worker Justice, talked about the Chicago centers' work: "We virtually don't promote or do much outreach because we don't have the capacity to handle it. Every time we get a hit on the radio or television, we get seventy-five phone calls that day. We can't handle that many. We don't have the volunteer structure set up to handle that quantity of calls. If we did regular PSAs [public service announcements], billboards, flyers, and workplace visits we could have a gazillion more—not only individual workers, but groups of workers. The potential in a city this size is overwhelming."[13]

Kimi Lee, executive director of Garment Worker Center (GWC) in Los Angeles spoke in similar terms about their initial experience with outreach: "The first six months was really just word of mouth and through the free media. After we got more workers involved, we did create flyers workers would pass out with our toll-free number on it. It wasn't twenty thousand flyers going out, it was like here's ten for you to take to your factory. It was very close-knit. We have workbooks and comic books that explain your rights as a worker and talks about the wage claim process, so workers would take handfuls to pass out. That's pretty much all we've done. From that we've gotten over seven hundred calls to the hotline and we've helped over two hundred and fifty workers. That's enough for us because there's still a small handful of us. We can't, we just don't have the capacity to advertise more. Every time we do a media event or a press release, we get more calls."[14]

Centers also recruit in a more targeted fashion, working through existing contacts to gain meetings with their friends and acquaintances in specific workplaces or industries and conducting one on one outreach to targeted groups of workers. Here are some examples:

- When the Tenants' and Workers' Support Committee (TWSC) was beginning to build a base around its home-based childcare work, it obtained a list of all home-based providers caring for children of parents in the welfare-to-work program, and organizers tried to visit all two-hundred-plus women on the list. In their outreach to the six hundred taxi drivers in Alexandria, TWSC organizers systematically charted and regularly visited all of the taxi stands in the City. On a day I spent out at the stands with the lead organizer, Kathleen Henry, in the spring of 2003, she knew almost every driver who pulled up, many drivers smiled and held up organizational fliers as they drove by.

- Workplace Project day labor organizer Carlos Canales regularly visits shape-up sites and street corners across Long Island, talking with workers and looking for potential leaders to try to interest in taking leadership at their particular site as well as in deeper involvement in the organization. The Workplace Project's UNITY co-op, a cooperative of house cleaners, recruits outside employment agencies and visits bus stations during hours when housekeepers are likely to be going to or from work, and Laundromats where they are likely to be doing laundry on days off.

- Omaha Together One Community worked through Spanish-speaking churches and soccer teams to attract an initial base of workers to participate in organizing. When the union organizing campaign began in earnest, OTOC and the United Food and Commercial Workers (UFCW) conducted home visits to workers employed at targeted companies and OTOC also organized small groups where workers could talk together about plant conditions, share information, and devise strategies for organizing.

- Making contact with the twenty-five thousand Yellow Cab drivers who ply the streets of New York is a daunting task. New York Taxi Workers Alliance organizer Bhairavi Desai, relies on a strong network of contacts embedded in ethnic-specific cab organizations, garages where drivers go to pick up their cars, and key neighborhoods and apartment-buildings. To get the word out on campaigns and events, she is also a regular visitor to the holding pens at La Guardia and Kennedy airports where hundreds of cab drivers wait each day in long queues to pick up passengers arriving at the terminals.

THE ROLE OF THE CHURCH

The first place immigrants often go on arrival to seek community and support, churches have been key points of connection and recruitment for worker centers as well as for garnering support for their issues in the larger community. The initial success of worker center outreach and recruitment often hinges on partnering or at least collaborating with religious institutions and the community networks of which they are a part.

Religious Denominations in General

Almost all of the centers surveyed, and most of those included in the case studies, cited churches as central to their efforts. Jose Oliva, of the Chicago Interfaith Workers Rights Center, described some of the reasons why: "If you're Mexican, you think about the government as sort of a corrupt monstrous thing that really isn't to be trusted and you think of the labor movement being in cahoots with the government. So you don't trust either of them, [and] when you come to the United States you go to your faith institution as sort of the first place you do trust."[15]

Central Americans, in Oliva's view, come to the same conclusion, but for different reasons: "The labor movement is seen sort of as opposition to the government, opposition to the state. The state is corrupt just like it is in Mexico, but if workers get involved with the labor movement, they can get killed by the state. So they want to stay away from that, not because unions are bad, but because it's too dangerous. And so, they see the church as the one institution that is safe to approach."

Because they are such central components of immigrant infrastructure, churches are major access points for worker centers in terms of the opportunities they present for membership recruitment as well as for general partnership on immigrant-related issues. Some churches are formally working in partnership with centers, others are informally referring members to centers and offering them opportunities to publicize events and conduct general outreach. Some worker centers receive in-kind support from churches and denominations, including free or reduced cost office and meeting space. In some cases, churches refer workers to worker centers and help support fledgling organizing efforts, and worker centers often refer workers to churches for services.

From the survey data, the churches that are most likely to become involved with worker centers are Catholic, followed by Presbyterians, Unitarians, Episcopalians, Lutherans, Methodists, and Quakers. Some Catholic, Protestant, and evangelical churches have large numbers of Latino parishioners and members of the clergy become involved in worker center efforts out of an interest in helping their own members improve their situations. Other churches, including nonimmigrant Catholic parishes as well as many different Protestant denominations, become involved out of empathy with problems new immigrants face, rather than direct experience.

The vast differences between religious denominations in terms of size, structure, and culture have important implications for involving them in support for worker organizing. Nationally, the Catholic church accounts for about 40 percent of religious institutions and is the church with whom millions of Latinos in the United States identify; its interests are also more directly tied in with those of immigrant Latino communities. "In terms of the faith-going community, they're the most significant numerically," says Kim Bobo, founder of the National Interfaith Committee on Worker Justice, "and, they have the most capacity because they have more structure than anyone else."

The Catholic church has a clear hierarchical structure that organizers can approach for support at the archdiocesan level, which can then pave the way for individual parish-based work. It has organization at the neighborhood, citywide, state, and federal levels. In addition to size and structure, strong social teachings locate worker organizing at the core of the church's mission and mean that they usually already have a social justice infrastructure in place at the parish level that has resources and access to church leaders, members, and financial resources. The Catholic Campaign for Human Development, a foundation that is funded through an annual collection throughout Catholic parishes nationally, is one of the largest and most consistent funders of economic justice community organizing in the country and heavily supports immigrant worker centers.

Of course, the evangelical movement is very powerful and popular among Latinos, but because it is much more decentralized than the Catholic church and also often espouses an "accept your fate" philosophy, most organizers believe it is less available as a resource. There is a big gap between the social and institutional resources the Catholic church offers and most Protestant denominations. The Baptists are the next largest denomination in terms of numbers but are very nonhierarchical structurally. Decisions are made and resources are concentrated at the individual congregational level, and they are much more difficult to engage on the regional, national, or even citywide level. Lutherans and Methodists are the third most significant numerically and both have more structure than the Baptists.

Bobo, who has extensive experience reaching out to religious denominations, believes that contrary to popular belief, evangelical and fundamentalist churches can also be important allies in supporting immigrant workers. "In local struggles it's just as easy to get the storefront Pentecostal church involved as the Episcopalian church because these are class issues," she argues.

Churches in Ethnic Communities

When OTOC began its organizing work in Omaha, the local Catholic church, Our Lady of Guadalupe, had been the locus of the Mexican community from the early twentieth century and was still the most important religious institution for the city's low-wage Latino workers. Father Damien Zuerlain, who was a young, non-Spanish-speaking priest when first assigned to the parish but went on to become a major leader in the meatpacking campaign, became involved out of an interest in bettering the lives of his parishioners. He explained, "My feelings about getting involved in social justice and those kind of things there just came out of responding to the needs of the people in my church. They were suffering so much and there was no way to fix anything. I could comfort them when they were hurting, but how could we stop the hurt from being there in the first place? It was organizing . . . OTOC happened to show up at the same time when we were struggling with some issues. All along there was this question about what were we going to do about the work situation in South Omaha."[16]

Zuerlain opened the church to OTOC and preached about organizing right from the pulpit, but he believes that the reason the meatpacking work took off was because the Latino community was ripe to hear the message and poised to make it happen. "I think in a sense it was easier to organize in the Latino community than in an Anglo community because of the networks and relationships within families. If you get the key leaders committed, they get to a lot of people." Zuerlain contrasted this with the "Anglo community," which has less of this kind of cultural orientation and community infrastructure.

> In the Anglo community, at least on a congregational level, we're all very independent, so you have to get to everyone one by one. There isn't a sense of "who can you bring with you?" That whole sense of bringing someone in the Anglo community isn't there. It is there in the Hispanic community. I said to Luis, "Bring your family," and we got a hundred people because he called all his brothers and sisters. In those early days of the meatpacking organizing, pastors would do turnouts for major events. People would say: "How many can you bring?" I'd say: "We'll bring 500."

This combination of church and vibrant neighborhood and family social networks was the basis of organization for the meatpacking drive. In describing OTOC's approach, former meatpacker and organizer Marcella Cervantes, said,

> Workers, especially immigrant workers, they congregate, for example, in churches. They have a lot of relatives that live in the same neighborhoods. The first place we looked in was the church. The second was in neighborhoods or relatives. We have ten meatpacking plants, but workers have relatives in the different plants. For example, there are workers in Nebraska Beef who have relatives at QPI. They're spread out, but they congregate. They talk about what's going on. The biggest place to get people is in the churches.

White Middle-Class Churches

When day laborers in Suffolk County were being attacked, a sympathetic religious institution of nonimmigrants responded, and the main elected official who rallied to their cause linked his actions to his religious beliefs. As we will discuss in greater detail in chapter 5, the town of Farmingville in Suffolk County, Long Island, in the past few years has been in the eye of the anti-immigrant storm. National anti-immigrant organizations targeted the area for aggressive organizing against day laborers. Local lay leaders in the largely white, middle-class Catholic parish, at one point fearing for the workers' safety, actually housed them at the church rectory for several weeks.

In the face of angry demonstrations at his home and place of work, Suffolk County legislator Paul Tona, a Republican, led the (ultimately unsuccessful) fight to fund a trailer and land on which to locate a day labor shape-up site. A former seminarian and active member of his church, Tona made repeated reference to his religious values and beliefs in explaining the position he took. In their leadership of a quest to establish a community center for Latino immigrants about twenty minutes away in Farmingdale, Peace and Justice Committee members of the local Catholic church talked about their work as a "calling." After being evicted from their first two locations, they have now moved to a third. It is completely staffed by volunteers from the church.

THE ROLE OF COMMUNITY INSTITUTIONS

No discussion of outreach and recruitment would be complete without covering the role that other community institutions play in sustaining the worker center movement. Two of the most important of these for many immigrant workers' centers are soccer leagues and hometown associations.

Soccer Leagues

In addition to churches, soccer leagues were an important recruitment network and organizing tool for the Omaha, Los Angeles, and South Carolina worker centers. A powerful match was made between sports and community organizing when South Carolina's key Latino soccer league organizer joined forces with CAFÉ. "When I came here I could count with my hands how many Hispanics were in the area," said Marcello Lopez, an organizer with CAFÉ.[17] "Then I started organizing the soccer league and I started seeing people coming from everywhere. For the first time we started with only seven against seven. In the next three months we had twelve teams," said Lopez. "South Carolina is not a big place," he continued, "but we get poor people from every city. We've got teams coming from seven different counties. We've got about four hundred to five hundred people every Sunday."

These soccer games, programs, and practices have evolved into a mixture of sports and workers rights. "I kind of take advantage, because even if I'm invited to the soccer meetings, I start talking a bit about my soccer stuff and then I start talking about CAFÉ and the rights they have," says Lopez. "About every single thing that I know about workers' rights [and] the law . . . I kind of translate to them. If I learn something in a workshop, then I come straight to them and say, 'Look today I learned about this and we cannot do this.' I update them with stuff I learn." Lopez has gotten hundreds of soccer players to join CAFÉ. "Not every single one in the soccer league is a member, but I've got most of them to be members."

As a way of building relationships with meatpacking workers in a prelude to union organizing in the tight-knit Omaha Latino community, OTOC organizer Sergio Sosa spent a lot of time on and off the soccer fields talking to players. Sosa, a former Catholic priest in Guatemala, has said that soccer players, their families, and networks, who were dispersed throughout the meatpacking companies, were the nucleus of the subsequent community and union organizing that took place in Omaha. "A lot of people like to play soccer and they have informal teams, so I started talking to them and saying to them we want to organize a Latino soccer league and apply for the fields and build an organization. They got excited and said yes."[18]

The Latino soccer league organized thirty-six teams with a total of about seven hundred players. "When we built that organization," Sosa said, "they became OTOC members." OTOC helped the soccer players to fight for access to the soccer fields. He estimates that about 70 percent of the players were working at meatpacking plants at that time. "So, I asked them if they were ready for organizing the plants. They said, 'We are ready.'" Through the Latino soccer league, OTOC was able to turn out more than five hundred workers to early actions and hearings with elected officials about the problems in the meatpacking industry.

Pablo Alvarado, the director of the National Day Labor Organizing Network (NDLON), was a literacy circle organizer in El Salvador and worked as a painter, factory worker, and gardener when he first arrived in Los Angeles. Hired by the Coalition for Humane Immigrants Rights of Los Angeles (CHIRLA) as the first day labor organizer, Alvarado believed that for organizing to be possible, it was important to build a community among the workers. In Pasadena, he organized the first day labor soccer team, which quickly grew into a league encompassing many shape-up sites in Los Angeles. Soccer trophies and team photographs adorned the walls of almost every hiring hall I visited in Los Angeles.

Home Country Connections

As growing numbers of immigrants from particular Latin American countries and communities have come to the United States, they have established hometown associations (HTA's) to provide economic support to their hometowns and regions, sending home money for the construction of schools, infrastructure improvement, and economic development. In Chicago, New York City, and Los Angeles, a highly developed network of these organizations has been quite vibrant and visible in Latino immigrant communities. However, my research did not uncover many formal organizational connections between worker centers and hometown associations. "They are pretty much in their own circles. We have not been able to tap into the networks," Raul Anorve, executive director and founder of Instituto de Educación Popular del Sur de California (IDEPSCA) said, "Like the Zacatecas Club [people from the Mexican state of Zacatecas], there are tons of clubs like that. They have wonderful fundraising events and raise lots of money. A couple have approached us and wanted to see if we could help them out. I always say yes, but they are too much into the cultural component, raising funds to send back home and not too much about organizing."[19]

Jon Liss, executive director of TWSC in northern Virginia, echoed Anorve's sentiments, saying, "We have a couple of committees here that are more focused on trying to build their own communities in El Salvador than trying to do something here. There are those kind of state-of-origin clubs but they don't do anything here, all they do is pretty much fund-raising to send back to their hometown and try to build their towns down there."[20]

While it appears that HTA's for the most part concentrate their activities on building up their home communities and are not formally involved with worker centers, recent scholarship in this area documents increasing involvement on the part of HTA's in labor unions and public policy issues, especially in California. In his research on one construction union local in California, David Fitzgerald writes "Mexican hometown networks dominate Local 123. About 500 of the Local's 3500 active members are from Guadalupe in the state of Michoacan. Guadalupanos have the largest and most influential hometown network. As one union captain put it, 'The strength of the union is in the town [Guadalupe].'" Running for election as business manager in 2000, the winning candidate visited Guadalupe to campaign among the families of union members. She estimated that 90 percent of her votes came from Guadalupanos. The union places its resources at the disposal of the Guadalupano and Zacatecan hometown associations, hosting fundraisers at the union hall, contributing funds and helping the organizations register as non-profit organizations.[21]

In terms of public policy, as Zabin and Rabadan observe, HTA's have so far been only episodically engaged. In Los Angeles, during the campaign to defeat the notorious anti-immigrant Proposition 187 in 1994, hometown federations and the majority of independent clubs came out forcefully against the proposition. They donated funds to the opposition effort, engaged in "get out the vote" efforts with members, turned members out for public protests, and worked through the ethnic media to advocate a no vote. However, club participation in the 187 fight proved to be the exception and not the rule during the 1990s.[22] In 2004 and 2005, many of the most influential hometown associations in Los Angeles became quite involved in the effort to preserve statewide legislation that would not have required social security numbers for drivers' licenses. Approved by Governor Gray Davis in 2003, it was repealed in 2005, at the behest of the newly elected governor, Arnold Schwarzenegger.

There are many examples in labor history and the contemporary period where "informal" networks among low-wage immigrant workers hailing from the same hometown or region have been crucial to worker organizing efforts. In recounting the history of the sweeping 1992 Southern California Drywall Strike, labor scholars Ruth Milkman and Kent Wong argue that "the fact that at least a few hundred men from the tiny Mexican village of El Maguey worked in the drywall trade and were bound together by close kin and friendship ties, was by all accounts an important source of the solidarity that emerged during the organizing campaign."[23] Historian Leon Fink tells a similar story in his book recounting the struggle waged by Guatemalan poultry workers of Mayan descent to form a union in North Carolina. He points to the central role played by Q'anjob'al speakers, Mayans from the province of Huehuetenango, who settled en masse in Morganton and were working the nightshift at Case Farms.[24] "We didn't organize anybody," a representative of the Laborers' International Union told him. "There was a union there before the union got there."[25]

For the New York Taxi Workers Alliance, networks of ethnic-specific taxi drivers have been critical to the organizing. While drivers are taking passengers all over the city they may not be able to make contact face to face, but they communicate with each other through cell phones and language-specific citizens' band radio channels. "In Manhattan if you're going from home, working, sometimes you can't see each other for a week. Only the points where you're on break can you see each other," said Muhammed Tasleem Khan.[26] "That's the only means of communication—CB channels—now in these days you have cell phones that you can talk on too. CBs and cell phones help the drivers get together and listen to each other. If a driver's having problems, you can go and help. Before if someone said something is going on or I'm getting robbed or somebody's beating me up, five to six drivers would come to help you."

While some worker center participants have used the skills they have developed through their participation at the centers to help establish hometown associations, until recently worker centers as institutions had not been directly involved in setting them up. An interesting model of a hometown association that is directly connected to a worker center was taking shape in 2003–2004 among Mexican immigrants from the Mexican state of Hidalgo, in Farmingville, Long Island. Whereas most worker centers and hometown associations have been developed separately, the Workplace Project as an organization had already worked with the workers and established a center in Farmingville before any hometown association had been set up in the area. This offered a rare opportunity for the organization to become involved from the outset and to bring its strategic and political orientation to bear in discussions of what a hometown association might do.

The project had developed a very close relationship with the Mexican immigrants because it had aided them in defending themselves against a highly organized local anti-immigrant campaign and in setting up and administering a local worker center. Its lead organizer in Farmingville, Irma Solis, had personally traveled to Hidalgo, carrying gifts and video letters from workers in Long Island to their family members back home. She also brought a video for government officials that had been made by the Farmingville workers to introduce themselves and their North American community.

As a result, Solis and one of the Farmingville workers were able to negotiate an agreement where, if the Farmingville workers needed anything like a birth certificate or a passport, they could get help from the Mexican consulate. Solis said, "Whenever a worker came here and wanted to get a passport, but didn't have a birth certificate, we'd contact them and they'd send it directly to us and then on to the Mexico consulate. That was one of the first testing grounds to see if that whole relationship would work, and it did. So far it has."[27]

In traveling back to the workers' hometowns, she was able to augment her knowledge of their lives in the United States with a clear picture of their lives back in Mexico and make connections and build relationships in both places. It made intuitive sense to her when the workers said "one of the purposes they saw for this space was to begin to talk amongst themselves as a community who had left their families behind in Mexico. It would be a way to be able to organize here to address some of the issues back home."

Solis had already been grappling with the challenge of frequent turnover among her leadership team in Farmingville. Building an organization that had a foot in each place provided the possibility of continuity. The leadership team in Farmingville had developed one way of dealing with the turnover: they established six-month terms of office for board members in their bylaws and timed the leadership changeover to parallel the migration pattern. Board members understood that part of their role was to tell the story of the organization to newly arriving immigrants and be on the lookout for leaders to take over from them a few months prior to when they would be returning home. Solis's vision was to work with workers and to build an organization that had a presence at each end of the migrant journey.

The towns in Hidalgo, Mexico, where most of the Farmingville workers came from, were very poor and rural. These towns lack many of the basics, including electricity and telephone service. The Farmingville workers were sending home a great deal of money. They wanted to do something to help their towns to develop but they wanted to ensure that the money was well spent. It was natural that they engaged in these discussions at the local worker center. In their work with the Workplace Project, they had participated in organizer trainings and discussions on the impact of globalization. Through these experiences, they gravitated toward the creation of a hometown association that would not only be in ongoing communication with their home communities in Mexico but would have an explicit political strategy for dealing with government officials informed by a deep knowledge of what was going on back home.

"When government officials from Hidalgo came to visit the community here during the anti-immigrant campaign, the workers realized that they had some level of power while they were here because of the money they were sending back home," said Solis. "They started to think about what they could do here to influence whatever happens back home. If a community needs a school, how could they make sure that the government official pays attention to that instead of putting down a road where it isn't necessary? It was interesting because many of them would say, 'We may not have much power here, but if we organize and get together, we have a little bit of power here and more power back home while we're here!' "

In May 2004, the Farmingville workers were focusing on the small town of Tenango in Hidalgo, which has a committee in the United States and back home. A worker who had been actively involved and then went back to Tenango from Farmingville got the committee started there and then came back and helped get it going in Farmingville. Working with the Tenango-based committee, they have been working to get phones and electricity in the town. Solis said, "We just got a call from Tenango last week, telling us that they've been to government officials and the officials are giving them the runaround. They want all of us here to call and put pressure on them and to send a letter from the center to the officials."

While there seemed to be little formal connection between hometown associations and worker centers, new models like the one the Workplace Project is discussing have the potential to create powerful transnational bridges that could operate effectively in both directions to assist workers in building power.

THE CHALLENGE OF MULTICULTURAL ORGANIZING, RACE, AND GENDER

Multicultural Organizing

As we have seen, for the New York Taxi Workers Alliance, ethnic networks already in place were a powerful source of connection. Drivers belonging to ethnically specific taxi driver associations worked with the alliance and organized via the citizens band radios in their cabs. But ethnic ties are also enormously complex and can also lead to division and exclusion. In describing some of the complexities of organizing among cab drivers inside of ethnic communities of northern Virginia, Mulgeta Yimer said: "I can organize my community, and talk to all the other communities to organize their communities. We have different communities and within them, different tribes. But the Afghan community is based on one tribe, the ruling tribe. The guy who is managing the Afghan community [in northern Virginia] is from the same tribe as the Afghan regime now, and he cannot cooperate with us because we are not supporting the ruling party. He has told us that if we are not supporting the same party he cannot help us."[28]

Organizing that brings together two or more distinct ethnic cultures that have different histories, traditions, cultural styles, and institutions requires tremendous thoughtfulness and patience. The language issues alone are immensely challenging. Staff meetings and membership meetings must be simultaneously translated into three languages, and written materials must also be prepared in each language. Many centers seek to hire immigrant workers who come from specific ethnic communities to work within those communities, but oftentimes they are not English speakers. Thus even staff meetings for small organizations require more than one translator, so that the Chinese organizer knows what the Spanish and English speakers are saying, the Mexican organizer knows what the Chinese and English speakers are saying, and so that the English speakers know what the Chinese and Spanish speakers are saying. This is an extraordinarily time-consuming proposition. Also, given the modest size of most worker centers budgets, the financial implications of translation issues are not inconsequential.

Worker centers have a very strong commitment to multiethnic organizing in the local labor markets and industries in which they work. For most, their motivations are both moral and practical, as Danny Park, executive director of KIWA, made clear about KIWA's decision to be multicultural from its inception. "Because we knew that Koreatown not only employs Koreans, but that each workplace is comprised of both Latino and Koreans. . . . working only with Korean workers or even organizing them wasn't possible. We felt that in order to do this kind of work we have to bring together all the forces and working with

other minority communities such as the Latino community was really important. That actually became one of the missions in our mission statement—
working with progressive minority groups in LA to raise issues that concern the
immigrant communities."

Early on, KIWA shocked mainstream Koreatown when it took the side of
three Latino workers against a Korean restaurant owner over an unpaid wages
dispute.[29] The organization's aggressive picketing and legal support sent a
strong message that the organization was serious about defending the rights of
all low-income workers in Koreatown. "We had done other boycotts before, but
they were with Korean workers, so the issue of ethnic solidarity wasn't a question until this one," said Paul Lee. "This was, again, kind of a public education
tool for KIWA to work on our political message overall, which was KIWA would
defend Latino workers against a Korean employer and do it publicly. It was very
controversial and a lot of people weren't supportive of this boycott. The sentiment was 'How can you go against one of your own for somebody that's not one
of your own?'" After a six-month campaign, the company settled with the
workers and paid them their back wages.

Worker centers that are struggling to build a base in industries where more
than one ethnic group is working must pursue two goals. On the one hand, they
must develop unique recruitment and leadership development approaches that
will work best for each ethnic group, while at the same time developing strategies for building a unified organization and encouraging interethnic understanding, cooperation, and joint action. They must do both these things in the
context of industries that often pit ethnic groups against each other, as Kimi
Lee, of the Garment Worker Center, described: "The garment workers, 75 percent are Latino and maybe 10 or 15 percent are Chinese. But when you look at
contractors it flips. So it's more likely that a Latino worker is working for an
Asian contractor. . . . There's stereotypes that get started because workers have
bad bosses and there's a high probability that they're Asian and so the Latinos'
only interaction sometimes with the Asian community is that they're the bosses
or the bad bosses."

As far as the Asian workers go, Lee says,

Many times they can't talk to the Latino workers, so the Latino and Asian
workers are kind of split in the factory based on language. We've heard
from workers what happens is that the workers can speak Chinese or Korean or Spanish, so the owners will set up the situation where they'll say
certain things so the workers think that the others are being treated better.
The Chinese workers think the Latino workers get treated better because
the Latino workers will protest and stand up if they get treated badly. The

Latino workers think the Chinese workers are treated better because they're the same race as the owners, so of course they're going to get paid more because they can talk more with the owner. In reality they're all treated poorly, but they all have these perceptions that the other side's being treated better.

When Latino workers come to the Garment Worker Center, on the other hand, they encounter a mostly Asian staff. "So the Latino workers for the first time see some Asians that are on their side . . . that initial dynamic is interesting because sometimes workers don't know what to think. Joann Lo is Taiwanese, but she speaks Spanish fluently, so then that breaks all their stereotypes that she's able to speak Spanish directly with them and that she is Taiwanese and that we're all here on the same side."[30]

In order to effectively combat tensions and bring workers together, the organizations must have a clear sense of each immigrant constituency and the positions they hold within the industry. Although many of the issues faced by Korean and Latino restaurant and grocery workers in Koreatown are similar, KIWA organizing director Paul Lee thinks that there are also important differences that must be taken into account. "The reality in LA is that Latino workers are more trapped from above in low wages and minimum wage jobs, whereas, Koreans and other Asian immigrants are trapped not only from above, but also from the sides by the bounds of their own communities," Lee says. He believes that Latino immigrants have more mobility and more of a sense of being part of a large-scale pool of low-wage Latino workers in greater Los Angeles because the Spanish-speaking population is so much larger. "You can start at a Korean restaurant and work there for a little while and then you can go to a Santa Monica restaurant or to construction. There's more mobility although it's very restrictive because they can't drive legally, and they're trapped from above because they'll never be able to get out of poverty and minimum wages unless they organize into a union."

On the other hand, in Lee's view, Korean workers are more confined to ethnic enclaves like Koreatown. "A Korean waitress can't go to a Filipino restaurant or a Vietnamese restaurant and be a waitress because the food is different, the clientele is different, and the language is different. A Korean cook is only going to know how to make Korean food. So they're limited to the boundaries of working for a Korean employer. They could move out of a restaurant and go to a grocery store or a liquor store or they could even start up a small business of their own, but they essentially don't leave the ethnic enclave."

In separate interviews, Helen Chien and Lupe Hernandez, the two worker organizers at the GWC put forth similar perspectives on the Chinese and Latina workers. Helen Chien said: "My main duty is to develop Chinese membership because you know Chinese workers aren't courageous and they don't dare to file claims against their employers."[31] Lupe Hernandez articulated the differences in the two groups as she has perceived them. In describing her own work experience, Hernandez believed that a Chinese manager at one of her jobs paid only the Chinese workers minimum wage. On the other hand, she saw the downside for these workers. "The Chinese bosses take the Chinese workers to work or take them home, so the workers have to wait until the factory closes or they have to be there in the morning when it opens. So often they work over twelve hours a day." Because of this close relationship, Hernandez also observed that the Chinese workers were more intimidated about speaking out: "The Chinese workers to us will say, 'Tell the boss,' because they can't defend themselves and they think that they'll lose their job. The little language that they know of ours is 'tu habla'—you speak, they are more afraid."

Lee and Lo believe that the differences in Latino and Chinese workers' attitudes toward speaking up have a lot to do with their previous political experiences in their home countries. Lee says, "For the Latino workers, many of them come from countries—Nicaragua, El Salvador—where there has been some type of political issue and many of them did come here because of that. So there is that reality that there are some workers that were politically active in their countries. Some of them were more involved with unions or involved in some other thing. There is that reality. On the Chinese worker side, it's less. The Chinese workers, from what we've found, don't have any direct experiences politically in China." According to Chien,

> Most of them don't speak very good English, so they are afraid to make mistakes and they don't know who they can go to for help. Some people [are] undocumented, so they will just take what they can get. Back home, when you work in the company, you are part of the union in the company. Those companies are mostly welfare companies, so they give you some benefits. The unions have really good positions in the companies. They are about the same as the director of the company. So in China they are not afraid of joining unions, but here they don't understand the legal system and they don't know about the laws, so they're afraid of joining any organizations.

At the Garment Worker Center, an enormous amount of thought and energy goes into conceiving ways of recruiting and then bringing workers from these radically different cultures together for common reflection and action. For example, GWC found that while word of mouth resulted in many Latinas coming into the center, much more intensive recruitment was required in order to reach Chinese workers. According to Organizing Director Joann Lo, "What we do with Latina workers and what we do with Chinese workers is different. With the Chinese workers, we have gone to factories and bus stops. Helen [the Chinese organizer] has gone to churches and supermarkets—all these different places to do outreach to workers because it's been much harder to attract workers to the center and to gain trust with the Chinese workers. With the Latina workers, we've only done a few leafletings outside factories around the garment district."[32]

Beyond recruitment, Lee and Lo have found that they also have to talk about the organization quite differently to the two groups. "For the Latino workers," Lee says, "we can do case management, while at the same time doing organizing and political education. Whereas with the Chinese workers we need to just break the ice and establish trust, so we emphasize the service side more with them. We don't go out and say, 'Come join the protest and become a member.' That doesn't sit well with Chinese workers. They don't want to walk directly out into a picket line. It takes a while for them to feel comfortable to do it." Instead, when talking with Chinese workers for the first time, GWC organizers ask questions such as "Are you being paid minimum wage?" "Usually that's the one thing that they answer 'no' to," says Lee. "Then you . . . explain that in this country there's minimum wage and overtime. It's connecting to them that we're here to help and if you haven't been paid properly, these are what the laws are, helping them with their cases, giving them some sort of direct benefit." From there, Lee believes that some of the Chinese workers will trust them and decide to work with them. "It's just a lot slower process. We do that with the Latino workers, but in a day. With Chinese workers, it takes maybe four months."

The situation with the ethnic media is quite parallel: the Chinese media has covered the center quite favorably, which Lee and Lo believe is because they have portrayed its mission in service and advocacy terms. They have been more explicit about the organizing mission in the Latino media.

GWC believes that it is essential for the organization to involve both Latinas and Chinese women in the organizing. That is why the board of GWC has guaranteed representation to both groups by designating six seats for Latinas and three seats for Chinese women workers (which is a reflection of their percentages in the industry). Monthly membership meetings are held in both languages as are all events. Workshops are generally taught separately, however, so that there is time for more interaction between trainer and participants. Within the larger worker leadership team of the GWC, efforts are made to have women learn about each other's countries and cultures as well as discuss common issues like the impact of globalization. The organization also sponsors parties and cultural celebrations as another way to encourage greater interethnic understanding and interaction. "To expose Latina workers more to Chinese culture, we had a Lunar New Year party last year, and it was a way to introduce Asian culture to them. Not just food but explaining to them about the lunar calendar and the Chinese horoscope. We thought maybe twenty or thirty workers would show up and eighty showed," said Lee. "Our general meeting last time it was Mexican Independence Day, so we had the workers talk about it, so the Chinese workers could know what it meant. There's actually this interest of not only the party kind of thing, but learning about each other and the opportunity to do that."

Immigrants and African Americans

Despite the fact that they share many issues in common, much more unusual among worker centers than multiethnic organizing is a focus on bringing immigrant workers together with African American workers. Most likely, labor market segmentation and racial prejudice together with the complications of language account for why this does not happen. Many centers are organized around a particular ethnic group or groups who are not English-speakers, and focused on particular industries that are often overwhelmingly comprised of immigrants. In answer to a question about who attends Workplace Project meetings, organizer Jaime Vargas replied: "All Latinos. The national origins are Central Americans, South Americans, Mexicans, El Salvador, Ecuador, Guatemala, Colombia." When asked "why no African Americans?" Vargas said, "This center is made to help Latino immigrants. Latinos tend to come from workplaces that are all-Latino, although when I say Latino, I define Haitians and Jamaicans as Latinos, too. So I am really talking about African Americans not being at our meetings."[33]

But there are also tensions between African Americans and Latinos. Some Latinos who come from cultures where darker-skinned people are treated as second-class citizens also hold racist views about American blacks. Vargas spoke bluntly about the problem of racism on the part of some of the Latinos in Long Island toward African Americans. "The Latino workers are racist. They don't like blacks. They talk about black people as if they were a completely different race and that's part of the consciousness that we have to work on." Vargas believes that some Latinos brought their racism with them from their countries of origin. "In some of the South American countries there aren't blacks like there are here. In Colombia and Brazil and Venezuela there's a big community. The discrimination here is the skin color.... Here and there. Whoever is slightly darker there they say is black."

Some in the black community hold immigrants partially responsible for black underemployment, unemployment, and declining wages. In South Carolina, Carol Bishop believes that some of the black middle-aged staff struggled within the organization when it began an aggressive campaign to recruit Latinos into the local chapters. "I think once the people were hired and the organization grew at a very rapid pace with Hispanics I noticed that some of the organizers had a big problem. There was a lot of tension that would build up in the staff meetings. A lot of people think working with Hispanics pretty much means we're planning for Hispanics versus planning together."[34]

When CAFÉ adopted a policy of switching off between holding meetings in English with Spanish translation and holding meetings in Spanish with English translation, "the black folks who were middle-aged left and said that they didn't feel comfortable because they thought people were talking about them." Day to day, Bishop says she hears a lot of blacks saying that jobs are being lost to Latinos.

> I don't think it's true because in this area here you will find people who just don't want to work. They think that if they can't find a job they want, then they're not going to do it, but if someone else comes along who's a different race, if that person is brown, then that's when the complaints start. It didn't start if someone white took their job. If the person is brown, they are assuming without knowing the person's nationality, that they're Mexicans. There's no problem with the Asians that work in this area. The Pakistanis, the Indians, there's no problem.

Bishop believes that Latinos are in jobs that blacks in South Carolina were no longer willing to do. "I think a lot of the jobs you will find Hispanics in . . . you'll find that black people aren't willing to work on the farm anymore. They're not willing to mop the floor anymore." Bishop also believes that blacks have exaggerated the numbers of Latinos moving into their neighborhoods. "When Hispanics moved into this neighborhood, there were only two homes that they lived in and there were a lot more houses on the street than that. What I kept hearing was that Hispanics are taking over the neighborhood."

Both the Tenants' and Workers' Support Committee and CAFÉ organize to bring Latino immigrants and African Americans together. In its tenant organizing work, TWSC brought Latino and African American families together to form a limited equity co-op and to fight to preserve other low-income housing. In its childcare work, TWSC has built a base of African Americans, South Asians, Haitians, and Latinos, and there are very explicit discussions about race and the need to come together as people of color.

In recent years, CAFÉ, a black-led organization, has staked out this territory as a central focus of work. They have defined the struggle of Latinos in the state as a continuation of the black civil rights struggle; at CAFÉ events, black leaders and staff often talk about the need to build "the black/brown coalition." Citing as examples the issues of racial profiling and housing discrimination, CAFÉ organizers and leaders have looked for ways to emphasize those things that both groups have in common rather than the differences.

Noting the skyrocketing numbers of low-wage Latino workers in the state, the organization decided to move aggressively into organizing Latino and black/Latino chapters and providing support to low-wage Latino workers in their individual and collective employment struggles. In the Pee Dee region of the state, the organization has targeted temporary employment agencies that place Latinos in jobs, pressing them to translate all materials into Spanish and to hire Spanish-speaking staff. After being contacted by CAFÉ, William Carroll, president of CSI Staffing, a temporary employment agency in Darlington, agreed to have information on health and safety printed and translated into Spanish for temporary employees. "Some of the Latinos work with acid and other hazardous chemicals, and because the instructions and safety precautions are in English they cannot protect themselves . . . and some injuries and deaths have resulted," said Roberta Benjamin, a volunteer and community leader involved with the temp project at CAFÉ. "Mr. Carroll is the only temporary agency in the state who we have approached about the health and safety of people of color that has taken it seriously and agreed to take action, which proves that safety comes first in his company," Benjamin said.[35]

In Greenville, Charleston, and other cities, CAFÉ has sponsored bilingual workshops on employment law, helped hundreds of workers apply for individual taxpayer identification numbers, and organized to bring in the Mexican consulate to provide passports and ID cards to Mexican nationals.

CAFÉ has also sponsored a series of discussions between blacks and Latinos, including one I attended in Darlington County. At the CAFÉ Youth Center, Latino youths and African American chapter leaders watched the video *Presumed Guilty* about racial profiling by the police and discussed it together afterward. One of the African American chapter leaders, Reverend Franklin Briggs, spoke passionately about the need for "black and brown" to work together, and about how Latinos were being targeted just as blacks used to be. All the leaders used inclusive civil rights language and were very explicit about blacks and Latinos making common cause together.

When IDEPSCA was working to open its very first day laborer center in Pasadena it was opposed by the African American community on the grounds that black neighborhoods were already disproportionately housing rehabilitation agencies and halfway houses. "They didn't want any type of agency that provides services," remembered Raul Anorve. Rather than blowing up into a conflict that pitted the African American and Latino community against each other, IDEPSCA initiated a dialog and eventually decided to seek alternative space. "They had reasons because historically the African American area of this city had been, as they described it, the dumping place for all the social services. No economic or self-determination projects were established for the African American community. So we respected that. We met with them and we dialoged and we decided to look for a project and a space across the 210 freeway."

Many neoclassical economists assert that immigration hurts low-wage African American workers and white workers. They often reach this conclusion through modeling rather than conducting empirical research in local labor markets. Economists, economic sociologists, and qualitative researchers have all looked at the question of whether blacks and immigrants are in competition for the same jobs. Econometric studies that have examined specific local labor markets have found little to no effect of immigrants on African American employment or wages. Economic sociologists have found that immigrants have an advantage in social capital that connects them to jobs that African Americans are not getting, but often fail to explain why African Americans don't move through similar networks, or whether they are just seeking jobs in other sectors. Nelson Lim's analysis of significant African American labor market niches in New York, Los Angeles, Miami, San Francisco, and Chicago in 1970 and 1990 showed an overall pattern of succession, as opposed to competition between African Americans and immigrants. Roger Waldinger also concludes that there is no direct evidence to show competition between African American and immigrant workers.[36]

So far the evidence suggesting that blacks and immigrants are competing for the same jobs seems modest but it clearly varies by geography and industry. Perceptions are important, however, and worker centers are engaging in important work in their communities to carry out that conversation constructively and to identify areas of common interest.

Gender Issues

Immigrant women in American society bear the triple burden of poverty, ethnicity, and gender, and they bear these burdens as workers as well, often working in low-wage industries that are segregated by gender as well as ethnicity. Worker centers also sometimes have to contend with the patriarchal traditions and practices men and women have brought with them. "Many Korean women workers," writes *Sweatshop Warriors* author Miriam Chang Yoon Louie, "have grown up under a harsh gender regime expressed in the proverb, 'The real taste of dried fish and tame women can only be derived from beating them once every three days.' Korea's traditional neo-Confucian ideology dictated women's subordination—first to father, then husband, then son, under the *Sam Jong Ji Do* (triple order instruction). Man was the *bakkat yangban* (outside lord) while woman was the *anae* (inside person) . . . women's ultimate role was to serve as *Hyun Mo Yang Cho* (sacrificial mother and submissive wife)."[37] Many worker centers, such as OTOC, had to deal with the fact that women members often deferred to men. "A lot of women are working in meatpacking plants," said Marcella Cervantes, "but they don't participate in this kind of movement because in our culture the people who decide these kinds of things are the men."

In addition, the centers have had to contend with the reluctance of the women themselves to see their housekeeping work, for example, as "real work." As sociologist Pierrette Hondagneu-Sotelo, who has studied domestic workers, writes, "Paid domestic work is distinctive not in being the worst job of all but in being regarded as something other than employment . . . many women who do this work remain reluctant to embrace it *as* work because of the stigma associated with it. This is especially true of women who previously held higher social status." Sotelo writes about one Mexican woman who used to be a secretary in a Mexican embassy who characterized her full-time job as a housekeeper and nanny as her hobby.[38]

Many of the women's committees and projects have strong consciousness-raising and confidence-building components because the centers understand that these issues have to be dealt with in order for their larger project of organizing women to improve their labor market positions to succeed. If they wanted to develop women's leadership, many centers talked about the need to create separate all-women spaces for discussion, as well as autonomous projects and committees. Some centers, such as Asian Immigrant Women's Advocates (AIWA) in San Francisco, GWC in Los Angeles, and the Domestic Workers Union, are entirely focused on women in female-dominated industries such as sewing and housekeeping, and they have an explicit language about gender and gender oppression in their work. Several centers, including CAFÉ and the TWSC, had specific leadership development goals and programs that were explicitly geared toward women of color. A number of the other worker centers have projects that are focused exclusively on women as well.

The Workplace Project created UNITY, a housekeeping cooperative that has grown from a handful of women in 1999 to eighty-one today. The co-op has its roots in the Project's women's committee, Fuerza Laboral Feminina, which was established early on in the organization's history (1994) after organizers observed that the women tended to keep quiet and defer to men in group meetings. Fuerza was created as a space where women could meet, discuss their lives, particular workplace issues they faced, build community, and plot strategy. Its first campaign targeted employment agencies that were charging usurious fees to women working as housekeepers.

The group decided to consciously stop using the term "trabajadores domesticas" (domestic workers) because the women had a very strong negative reaction to it. It evoked for them a sense of being members of the lowest of the low, going back to the way maids were perceived in their countries of origin. Instead, they decided to use the term "mujeres que trabajan en casa" (women who work in the home). Throughout that campaign and the development of the cooperative, UNITY meetings and activities have always mixed public action with personal support and sharing of stories and struggles, consciousness-raising, and confidence-bolstering. One of its most popular annual events is a Mother's Day party, in part designed to comfort women who are in the United States without their children.

During the successful ConAgra campaign, OTOC consciously built a worker committee that had a majority of women members. "That was a good experience for me to see how the women started working by themselves and got more involved in this organizing drive," said Cervantes. "Because women work hard in the company and then continue working in their homes with their kids and families. That was tremendous to see women realize that they can do things by themselves."

Gender issues have also come up within the staffs of worker centers. Recently the women on KIWA's staff organized an informal "women's caucus," the organization brought in a consultant to work with them on organizational development issues, including some that were gender-related, and this led to the development of a more participatory process for campaign strategy planning and decision-making.

CHAPTER 4

DELIVERING SERVICES ON THE FRONT LINES

Low-wage immigrant workers in the United States today are challenged on two fronts. As workers, they are badly treated and poorly compensated by employers over whom they have little leverage. As immigrants, and overwhelmingly people of color, they face racism and xenophobia and, if they lack documentation, the denial of many social services and the insidious threat of deportation by a hostile state.

Contemporary community organizing approaches have traditionally frowned on service provision, viewing it as "doing for others" as opposed to teaching them to do for themselves and putting band aids on deep social problems. Other American social movements have been less absolutist on the question of services. Some, in fact, such as the women's and civil rights movements, have even viewed service provision as an important extension of their social change work. Most worker centers have a long-term transformational social justice agenda, including more intermediate goals related to ongoing policy or organizing campaigns. But they are painfully aware that the changes they seek are not around the corner. Wins that will result from shorter-term campaigns are certain to be partial. Meanwhile, the workers they care about are having a very difficult time.

It is in the context of their dual oppression as workers and immigrants, the long-term nature of solutions, and pressing short-term needs that the majority of worker centers have come around to the necessity of service delivery.[1] Today, many of them engage in service provision as a central function. The provision of services is also a way that centers gain legitimacy with immigrant workers as well as the broader community. But while most centers do provide services, especially legal support for pursuing unpaid wages, they do so with great trepidation because they want to promote collective and systemic approaches to change. They want workers to see that the solution to their situation requires collective action to alter the relations of power and win concrete victories, and worry that helping workers individually cuts against that message and takes time and resources away from that work. They seek to address this dilemma in two ways: by delivering services in a way that empowers workers and by connecting service, as much as possible, to organizing.

THE RANGE OF SERVICES PROVIDED

Immigrant worker centers provide a wide range of different services to their members and constituents. These include direct services such as help with filing wage claims, ESL classes, and immigration-related assistance. It also includes indirect services such as referrals for health care and matching up workers with services provided by other agencies. While legal assistance and ESL classes are the most common services provided, individual centers tailor their offerings to specific needs of their local areas. Figure 4.1 provides a snapshot of the most common services provided by worker centers.

Most workers first come into contact with a center because they are seeking help with an employment-related problem. Sometimes the problem affects only that individual; other times it affects most of the workers at their places of employment. Whether or not the problem is widespread in a workplace, workers usually come in singly, and one of the things center staff members always try to do is get them to recruit their co-workers. The most common complaint by far is unpaid wages, which includes paying below the minimum wage and nonpayment or underpayment of overtime. For example, at KIWA, according to data accumulated by the legal clinic during ten years, 86 percent of all disputes were wage related.[2] Similarly, according to data collected during a four-year period at the Workplace Project, unpaid wages, at 31 percent of the total, was also the largest single category of cases.[3] Other common problems include health and safety violations, injured workers seeking help in filing for workers' compensation, sexual harassment, and racial or ethnic discrimination.

The balance of this chapter provides a more detailed look at some of the most common services provided by immigrant worker centers and the achievements and dilemmas presented by this important component of their activism. The sidebars shown here illustrate some of the problems and solutions offered by service centers to immigrant workers.

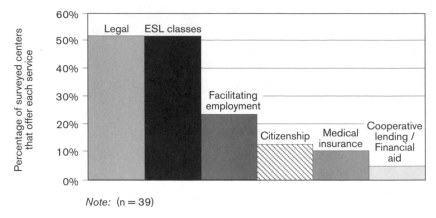

Note: (n = 39)

4.1. Worker centers: Major services

LEGAL CLINICS

Among the services currently offered at worker centers, legal help stands out. It is the one in greatest demand and also the most developed aspect of most centers' service work. In the operation of the legal clinics, one can see most clearly the challenges centers face, as well as their creative attempts to deal with the daily tug of war between service and organizing.

If you are a low-wage immigrant worker in the United States today, it is not that you lack employment rights, it is just that you probably do not know what they are or how to exercise them. While the violation of basic labor and employment laws is commonplace in immigrant-heavy, low-wage industries, the institutional mechanisms for informing workers of their rights and helping them to file claims are wholly inadequate.

Most workers are unaware of their rights and will not learn about them at their workplaces. They don't know the locations of the government agencies where they can go to seek help. Undocumented workers often don't go to them for fear of "outing themselves" and being arrested and deported. When they do find their way to these places, too often they confront workers who speak only English, or written material and forms that must be read and completed only in English, or they are frightened away by inappropriate and irrelevant questions about their legal status. Despite the fact that undocumented immigrants are covered by the same labor and employment laws as other American workers, federally funded legal service organizations are required by law to turn them away if they do come in seeking help.

WORKERS WHO HAVE REACHED OUT TO WORKER CENTERS

- Mrs. Lee, a restaurant worker and now organizer for the Restaurant Workers Alliance of Koreatown (an affiliate of KIWA), found out about her local worker center because "one day the employer's wife received a letter from KIWA regarding labor law seminars and asked the workers if anyone was interested in it. . . . I stepped up and said I was. . . . I was working twelve hours a day and receiving six hundred dollars a month. However, I had a large portion in tips, so I was taking home about two thousand dollars a month. Through the seminars I learned that the tips are from the customers, and the employer has the duty to pay you at least the minimum wage. So I took the six hundred dollars and calculated it into my work hours and I learned that I was making $2.15/hour at a time when minimum wage was $5.15. The following day I spoke to the co-workers who had been there a while before I had been working there. I set up a meeting with the employer. At the meeting, I told the employer that the wages were too low and I asked for at least the legal minimum wage."

- Helen Chien, a former doctor in China and now a garment worker and part-time organizer for the Garment Workers in Los Angeles first came to the center about a problem in the factory where she worked: "My factory was doing well, so they moved to a bigger site. In the beginning it was okay, but they decided to rent half the factory to other companies. . . . There is a lot of air pollution, and I was thinking about, because I was a doctor in Shanghai, what I could do and how I could improve this situation. I heard about the Garment Workers' Center on the radio station AM 1300. It's a Chinese radio station. I decided to call the center and they . . . contacted OSHA for me. This issue was resolved in only ten days."

- Mulgeta Yimer and many other northern Virginia cab drivers first came to TWSC when they heard emergency financial help was available after the crash in the travel and tourism industry in the aftermath of the September 11 tragedy. TWSC raised and distributed more than $250,000 to five hundred low-wage workers connected to the hotel and taxi industries who were laid off or lost their jobs permanently. Money went to help workers pay rent, utility bills, buy food, and deal with other basic needs.

- Marcello Lopez, who organized the first soccer team and league in rural Darlington County, South Carolina, first came to CAFÉ to help some migrant farmworkers. "I had a soccer team and one day they started to tell me that they've been working almost seventy hours a week and they're only getting paid for forty. . . . We started talking about it, and they started telling me about how they were treated. . . . They had them like prisoners there. After they told me, I talked with Carol [the executive director of CAFÉ] to see what we could do. Finally after three or four months, those guys got treated better—better housing."

In the communities in which they operate, immigrant worker centers are working hard to fill these information and representation voids. Centers have developed extensive workers' rights handbooks that centralize information about federal and state employment laws, and they publish them in many languages. For many immigrant workers, the employment rights they learn they have through these handbooks come as revelations. This was certainly the case among immigrant workers in Chicago who contacted the Chicago Interfaith

IDEPSCA DAY LABOR HIRING HALLS, LOS ANGELES

- Assist workers and employers in the negotiation of working conditions such as wages, transportation, and meals
- Help filing wage claims
- English literacy classes
- Classes in computer skills and technology
- Free medical and dental clinics
- Tool lending
- Free food and clothing distribution
- Recreation and sports activities (soccer leagues and marathon teams)
- Cultural celebrations
- Workshops on workers' rights
- Use of the telephone
- Use of on-site library
- Occupational training
- Translation and assistance filling out immigration and tax forms

KOREAN IMMIGRANT WORKER ADVOCATES, LOS ANGELES

- Community-based health clinic where members are served by a physician who speaks Korean, Spanish, and English, and a case manager who makes referrals to other health providers.
- Microloan project provides no-interest loans. Workers can borrow up to five hundred dollars and have six months to repay.
- Membership card.
- Check cashing.
- Worker Empowerment Clinic assists workers in filing cases for back wages and overtime.

Workers Rights Center. "In ninety-eight, we published the Workers' Rights Manual. We published it in both English and Spanish, and now we have it in Polish also. It's got the Department of Labor, it's got OSHA, EEOC, it's got all of these agencies' laws in it. . . . No one had ever thought to put labor and employment law into one simple format that workers can access. Every agency publishes their own law and that's it," said Jose Oliva, executive director. "We went

FARMWORKER ASSOCIATION OF FLORIDA

- Pesticide trainings conducted in English, Spanish, and Creole

- HIV/AIDS education

- Vocational rehabilitation program connects injured farmworkers with services so they can either continue in farm work or switch occupations

- La Campesina Ethnic Food Stores employ farm workers, offer ethnic foods, cultural music, international phone cards, and check wiring services

- Community Trust Federal Credit Union offers opportunities to farmworkers for saving and loans

NEW YORK TAXI WORKERS ALLIANCE

- In the summer of 2002 they organized a health fair for taxi drivers at a taxicab holding lot at JFK. Eighteen different health care institutions were present, and six hundred drivers were enrolled into Family Health Plus, given educational materials and referrals on HIV and AIDS, and screened for blood pressure, cholesterol, blood sugar, vision, spinal care, stress, asthma, hepatitis B, colorectal cancer, and tuberculosis.

- In the wake of September 11, they provided assistance with filling out Federal Emergency Management Administration mortgage and rent assistance applications.

- Website resources, "Know Your Rights" handbook, and links to helpful sites.

The alliance has arrangements with attorneys to provide discounted legal representation before the Taxi and Limousine Commission and the Department of Motor Vehicles regarding tickets and fines as well as other legal matters including criminal defense, personal injury and property damage, workers compensation, immigration, contracts, bankruptcy, medallion-related issues, and real estate closings.

out to different parishes all over the city and started talking to workers, and we sort of stood outside of the church and passed these out. And as a result of that, we got waves and waves of phone calls from workers who were completely mesmerized by, 'You know, it says here that I'm supposed to be paid forty, I'm supposed to be paid time and a half after forty hours a week. You know, that's not happening, what can I do?' "[4]

Typically, worker center walls and coffee tables are festooned with posters and brochures from the federal Department of Labor, Equal Employment Opportunity Commission, Occupational Safety and Health Administration, and Federal Department of Agriculture. Workers seeking help with employment-related problems find forms and brochures in their native languages and sympathetic bilingual staff able to explain the way the laws work and assist them in filing claims. For many immigrants afraid to come forward, some centers are the virtual equivalent of government offices, with two important differences: they will not ask about the workers' immigration status and they are structured to be responsive.

Worker center leaders and organizers throughout the country are quick to note the disparity between supply and demand in terms of available legal services. Offering help with unpaid wage claims, besides meeting a huge need in these communities, is also a very effective way to get workers in the door, and centers want to build as large a base of workers as possible in order to build political and economic clout. At the same time, the demand can overwhelm a small staff, the process is enormously time-consuming, and some workers will not stay involved after their claims have been resolved. Centers have experimented with different strategies for handling this issue, as discussed in greater depth below.

A minority of centers has full-time or part-time lawyers on staff. The D.C. Employment Justice Center is the extreme exception. It has created a legal advocacy model in which two hundred volunteer attorneys regularly donate hours, take referrals, and represent workers in wage and hour and other cases. In most centers however, workers are assisted by administrative and organizing staff and volunteers who are knowledgeable in workplace rights and employment law and highly adept in navigating government agencies and courts.

In an initial meeting, workers usually can find out whether or not the law has been violated in their case and what they can do about it. To facilitate this process, most centers have developed elaborate protocols and manuals to train staff and volunteers in employment law, how to calculate wages owed, and how the claims process works.

Centers usually first try to resolve unpaid wage claims and other disputes with employers through direct conversations with them. Sometimes, that is all it takes, as Pablo Alvarado of NDLON makes plain: "When the hiring hall coordinator calls an employer and tells them they need to, they pay. Otherwise they wouldn't pay. It's like eighty percent of the cases are resolved over the phone. When somebody calls them who speaks English it's a whole different story. For example, when someone says they're from CHIRLA, people end up paying. There's twenty percent that we've had to take to the labor commission."[5]

When they are unable to resolve the case via the first step of talking with an employer, center legal clinics help workers fill out wage claims and other complaints, gather the documentation they will need and help them file the claims at state and federal agencies and small claims courts. In instances in which workers have a choice between agencies to file and pursue a claim, centers offer guidance about which one is most likely to be sympathetic and efficient. Centers will then follow the progress of a case, keep the worker posted, and appear with them in state and court procedures when necessary.

The legal clinics fulfill two other important functions as well. First, when workers come in with problems, they provide the stories and, cumulatively, the aggregate data that centers can use in their advocacy work. With particularly egregious cases, the Workplace Project in Long Island, New York, has been able to generate front-page news stories about worker exploitation and the need for new laws. By keeping track of the data over time, KIWA and the Workplace Project have been able to document problems in processes and procedures of the state labor departments and bolster their claims that there are big abuses occurring in particular industries. In Los Angeles, the information collected by KIWA and GWC was analyzed in cooperation with the state Department of Labor and used to help develop new ways of monitoring enforcement with labor laws.

At the Workplace Project, nonpayment and underpayment of wages were by far the most common complaints received.[6] The project brought dozens of cases to the state Department of Labor only to be rebuffed.[7] Undocumented workers or workers working under the table were told inaccurately that they were ineligible to file claims, cases were taking up to eighteen months to be investigated, and a Spanish translator was available for only three hours every other week. The DOL had unilaterally decided to go back only two years in its investigations despite the fact that the law provided for up to six, and it was negotiating settlements with employers that allowed them to pay only 50 percent of what was owed and levied no penalties. Workplace Project staff and volunteers were appalled by the DOL staff's cavalier refusal to accept the claims of housekeepers, restaurant workers, and day laborers. Workers seeking assistance were instead subjected to lectures about illegal aliens not paying their taxes.

Beginning in 1993, the project began to systematically monitor the DOL's behavior with regard to its acceptance of cases, pursuit of those cases it did accept, the treatment of immigrant workers who went to the Long Island office seeking assistance, and case outcomes. Gordon summarized their findings: "Our computer database contained records of over nine hundred Latino workers who had sought help from our legal clinic over the previous three years. It showed that only two of the seventy-two cases that we had filed with the DOL over three years, or just 3 percent, resulted in even partial payment to workers. By contrast, over the same period, our office, with only one person working half-time on these cases at any one point, accepted 234 wage cases for representation and resolved seventy-one percent of them, winning over $215,000 for 166 workers during that time."

To respond to these problems, the Workplace Project began to take affidavits every time a worker and a lawyer or a volunteer returned from the Department of Labor complaining of mistreatment. These affidavits documented a pattern of flagrant disregard for the problems faced by low-wage immigrant workers. DOL investigators time and again turned away or tried to turn away immigrant workers on the basis of their own erroneous interpretations of state labor law. The database and the affidavits proved to be instrumental to cultivating members of the media at the *New York Times* and *Newsday,* in building alliances with Democrats in state government, and eventually in persuading even Republican legislators to pass the strongest unpaid wages law in the United States.[8]

In 2002, KIWA analyzed the data it had been gathering through its intake sheets and case logs and released a report to the *Los Angeles Times* and area ethnic media. The report provided a wealth of information about the nature of workplace violations in Koreatown and documented the impact of its ten years of legal representation to immigrant low-wage workers. The report also demonstrated just how challenging it is to file these cases and follow them through to a successful outcome.

The report found that a majority of the cases were from service industries, specifically restaurant, grocery, and janitorial workers, and that of the 1,861 workers who had sought assistance, fewer than 100 held jobs that had health insurance, sick leave, or other employment benefits. Most employers were out of compliance with California labor codes in terms of methods of payment, fulfillment of record keeping requirements, and tax deductions. While cases ran the gamut from racial or sexual discrimination, unemployment benefits and workers compensation, wrongful termination, collective action, and workplace abuse, the vast majority of the claims were wage-related and were initiated "as a result of unjustified termination."

KIWA staff had remarkable success resolving wage and hour disputes simply by sending a letter to employers: 40 percent were resolved in this manner, 21 percent were filed with the California Labor Commission, and 7 percent in small claims court. Of the 1,861 cases KIWA handled, 58 percent of all workers pursued their cases and ultimately received back wages. The other 42 percent either were dropped by workers, KIWA was unable to pursue for other reasons such as employer bankruptcy, or the organization had referred the worker on to another agency and did not know the case's final disposition. Over a ten-year period, the organization pursued 1,154 cases to the point of calculating the amount of wages owed to a worker. The total amount claimed was $8,829,677. The total amount pursued to the point of collection was $5,121,206. The total amount collected was $1,813,407. The average amount claimed per worker was $7,651, the amount pursued was $4,438, and the amount collected was $3,693.

There are several explanations offered for the lower percentage of wages reclaimed. First, even when workers win their cases, many employers refuse to pay, choosing to sell their businesses, file for bankruptcy, or move to another state. Second, wage settlements often involve parties negotiating and workers agreeing to a lower amount. "Unfortunately, after the time consuming claim process," the report authors summarize, "there is no guarantee wages will be recovered. In reality, the collection process is the most difficult process."[9]

This frustration with the collection process is what often leads from casework to grassroots organizing. Many of the centers engage in lively pickets of employers who have refused to pay what they owe to current or former employees. "We did the first picket with an employer that owed over sixteen hundred dollars and it had been over two years. We had won in court and the Department of Labor had also ruled in our favor. So we had the first picket at the employer's house. . . . The employer was not at home, but all the neighbors came out," Rhina Ramos, formerly of the Workplace Project remembered. "We had big copies of the judgment order saying this is the reason we are here and we had signs with the amount he owed. It was construction work." The following week the employer agreed to pay what he owed.[10]

Unlike government agencies or conventional legal clinics, most centers see their mission as empowering workers and aggressively look for ways to involve them in resolving their employment problems. If more than one worker has been affected by the problem, center staff encourages workers to go back and recruit their colleagues. If they do so, groups of workers are supported in filing class-action-type suits and in devising collective strategies for dealing with their employers.

In cases where workers are afraid to confront their bosses, many centers will organize a group picket of other workers and supporters at the workplace and seek to interest the media in writing about the story. "Last year, we did three demonstrations in Harbor City," said NDLON's Pablo Alvarado in 2004. "This really established business—a huge corporation—hired one of the workers and didn't pay him, as well as others. . . . So we took it really far and mobilized the day laborers and demonstrated in front of this business. We only did it three times and next Monday he paid them. We've never lost when we do that. We only do it when it involves claims over three thousand dollars."[11]

Sometimes the organizations stage multiple pickets or move on to a more elaborate campaign. They do so in a number of situations. These include when the amount of money at stake is significant, more than one worker is involved, or when the employer is a visible target who can be made an example of within a larger group of employers. They also do so when the organization knows that the same employers are operating under a new name in order to evade liability.

Group picketing, boycotts, and actions are quite successful when targeted at commercial employers who depend on strong foot traffic and maintaining a good reputation. However, many workers bring claims to worker centers that are individual in nature and not good prospects for collective action. Understandably, the workers involved still want to pursue them, especially in situations where they have won the cases they have filed, and employers have been ordered to compensate them but have refused to do so. The major challenge is for centers to devise efficient means for expeditiously filing and resolving these cases. Otherwise there would be no time for the advocacy and organizing work that is essential to transforming employment relations in these industries.

This is the central tension that most centers confront: providing needed services to people who often have no other means of accessing them versus engaging in advocacy and organizing that have the potential of impacting larger numbers. Helping workers file wage and other claims is the best recruitment and legitimating mechanism most centers say they have got and without a base of workers, they cannot carry out effective advocacy and organizing. Given that strategies for wider and deeper change in many of these low-wage industries remain hard to come by, it is hard to give up on something that, although time-consuming, works. Worker centers collect on average between $100,000 and $200,000 a year in back wages for workers. That is why some centers—even when there are alternative legal clinics to refer workers to—are ambivalent about discontinuing this service.

SNAPSHOTS OF FOUR LEGAL CLINICS

The Chicago Interfaith Workers Rights Center

The Chicago Interfaith Workers Rights Center has forged an unusual ongoing partnership with federal and state government agencies. Called the Chicago Area Workers Rights Initiative (CAWRI), this partnership brings nonprofit organizations and agencies together to improve monitoring and enforcement of employer compliance with state and federal labor and employment laws. Working with CAWRI, the center has developed three strategies for dealing with the time-consuming, resource-intensive nature of operating a legal clinic.

First, it worked with government staff at the Wage and Hour Division of the Federal Department of Labor, the Illinois Department of Labor, the Federal

Equal Employment Opportunity Commission, and Occupational Safety and Health Administration to devise one uniform complaint form and one central point of contact at the Wage and Hour Division. This contact receives the forms, determines which agency the complaint should go to, and ensures that when it gets there it is appropriately filed and investigated. Another important aspect of this program is that workers who want to file confidentially can do so by appointing a member of the worker center staff to represent them.

According to Connie Knutti, manager of field enforcement with the Illinois Department of Labor, which receives about eleven hundred minimum wage and overtime complaints and about ten thousand unpaid wage complaints a year, working with the Worker Center and other nonprofit organizations who are part of CAWRI made the agencies realize that having a way to come to them through a third party meant that more workers would file complaints. "Many of the federal and state statutes require a complainant," said Knutti. "So we tried to go back and look at our process."[12]

Second, to avoid backlog, it negotiated a system whereby those agencies would agree to move any complaints they received from the center to the top of the pile and to call the center within a few days of receipt of the complaint. "We came up with the Employment Report . . . it's a single page form. . . . And basically, all the information that every agency needs is here," said Jose Oliva. "And so, we started to . . . work out this process where we would fill this out, and send it to a clearinghouse person at the U.S. Department of Labor. They decide, they don't decide, they look at it and say, 'This is going to the EEOC or some other agency.' And the EEOC person calls us and says, 'I am the investigator on such and such a case, you can deal with me now.' So essentially, we worked out a way of doing direct action case service." After cases are submitted to the Wage and Hour Division, the CAWRI coordinator confirms receipt directly with the worker center director who is then able to parcel out the case to his network of volunteer advocates for ongoing coordination and representation. When questions arise, the volunteer knows exactly who to speak with at the appropriate agency. In addition to receiving and coordinating referrals, the Wage and Hour Division keeps tabs on the cases, holding regular interagency meetings to hear updates on each case.

Finally, the center recruited student interns as well as a corps of volunteers from among its networks of area churches and synagogues to be trained in policies and procedures and act as workers rights advocates, holding office hours at the center's two locations and helping workers to file claims. To maximize the efficient and strategic use of the legal clinic, they devised an action flowchart to help distinguish between different types of claims and choose the appropriate course of action.

In cases where a worker comes in with an individual problem, volunteers are asked to first make a determination about whether a law has been violated. If it has, they are instructed to file a complaint with the appropriate government agency. They are also encouraged to call the employer, notify them that a complaint is about to be filed, and see whether they can work out a settlement.

In cases that are group problems, the volunteer's first step is to set up a meeting between center staff and the group. If there is a union in the workplace, staff will contact the union, explain the situation, and ask how the center might help them resolve the problem. If the union is unresponsive, center staff will try to contact the union leadership and ask that they intervene. Also, they help the workers learn about the internal grievance procedure for the union and provide support to them as they use it. In most cases, there is no union, and center staff will help determine whether the job site is a good prospect for a union organizing drive. If it is a good prospect, they will identify the best union to represent the workers in the particular industry, contact them, bring the union and workers together, and provide active support during the organizing process. But there are other cases where, according to Oliva, "not only is there no union, but there is no possibility of an organizing drive." In these cases, in addition to filing legal claims, the center tries to organize direct-action pickets and demonstrations at the company.

Few worker centers have the kind of close working relationships and high level of trust with government agencies that CAWRI has facilitated. Knutti recalled the early days of the partnership: "There was a basic distrust when we started out and we had to improve ourselves as agencies and then the community and faith-based organizations had to prove themselves to us with valid complaints and background and information. They couldn't come up with assumptions. We wouldn't act on those. We needed more facts. We had a lot of growing pains. We've had a lot of successes." According to Knutti, both the state Department of Labor as well as the federal Wage and Hour Division in Illinois begin from the premise that workplace abuses like failure to pay minimum wage and overtime as well as unpaid wages are widespread, and that very few workers are filing complaints. The participating agencies say that CAWRI has helped them identify patterns in industries as well as problem employers and that the interagency work that it requires has resulted in stronger relationships between government agencies.[13] Most important, Knutti believes, "The best thing that probably came out of it was that we were actually able to service some workers who really would never have come forward. The worker center facilitates some things. They would have not had access to an agency. That was the best, but the numbers were small."

The Workplace Project

In its first several years of operation, the Workplace Project operated a legal clinic that was staffed by a lawyer, law students, and other knowledgeable volunteers. The clinic had established weekly daytime and evening office hours, helped workers fill out complaint forms and went with them to hearings. In exchange for providing assistance, and as a way of connecting individual casework to broader organizational goals, workers were required to take a worker's rights course and volunteer ten hours to the organization. At the time they took this step, it was widely viewed in the worker center world as a major innovation. In 1999, the organization decided that individual claims were still taking up too much of its time and keeping staff from being able to focus on organizing and advocacy. They concluded that tying acceptance of a worker's case to participation in the course often had not resulted in ongoing participation in the organization. They also felt that despite all the legal work that had been done, the well never seemed to dry up, workers kept right on walking in the door with the same problems the clinic had seen from the beginning.[14]

They decided to completely restructure the legal clinic. It is now called the Alliance for Justice. One-on-one consultations with project staff and attorneys were replaced with Friday night group orientation sessions for workers who had contacted the organization due to work-related problems. The groups are kept relatively small—eight or nine participants—and there is a focus on providing information to workers on the range of issues they are most likely to be walking in the door wanting to know about: unpaid wages, firing, workers compensation, health and safety, and negligent unions. According to Nadia Marin-Molina, executive director, the goal of the session, besides transmitting basic information about the next steps workers can take to resolve their own problems and answering specific questions, is to place the workers' individual problems in a broader context and "begin to develop consciousness about the need to organize." Workers who attend these sessions and express an interest in organizing are encouraged to join "industry teams" of other workers who are interested in organizing in their particular sector and can teach them how to file wage claims. There are now day labor, janitorial, and factory teams. The rule in place now is that workers new to the teams cannot immediately seek help with their particular workplace issue. They are required to attend three team meetings before they can bring their issue to the group. The teams are provided with technical assistance from the Alliance for Justice as well as from staff and a network of law students and pro bono attorneys. Not all workers who come seeking help with their cases join the industry teams, and not all workers who join the industry teams stick around long enough to get help on their cases. Nonetheless, Marin-Molina believes that the new structure has relieved some of the legal burden so that the organization can put the bulk of its resources into organizing and advocacy.

Garment Worker Center

In the winter of 2003, the GWC was in the process of restructuring its legal clinic. Alejandra Domenzain, the former case manager said: "When I first came, the system was pretty much workers come, we determine what issues they have and when it's a wage issue, which is 99 percent of the time, the Garment Worker Center would represent them in doing a wage claim at the Labor Commissioner's Office. . . . Doing case management is just incredibly time consuming and resource intensive. It ends up eating all of my time even though it's supposed to be half and it ends up eating parts of everyone's time. I've tried to make it a point for us to [ask the] question: What's our purpose? How's this tied to organizing? How much of our resources do we want going to this?"[15]

Workers with individual claims are now sent through a process that GWC calls "self help," in which they help workers draft and send a demand letter to the employer. Through this self-help program, workers who are trained to be peer counselors help the new workers through the process. "The organization couldn't handle the load of cases and we didn't want to drown in all the service" said Kimi Lee. "And so we have now trained about a dozen workers to be peer counselors who are paid to go through a training and paid for office time." The women put in fifteen to twenty hours per month. "I see them having become more confident as a result of being trained and prepared to answer questions from other workers," said Lee. "When they see new workers walk in now they go and greet them, they are taking on more responsibility as leaders of the center and clearly have more of a sense of ownership over the organization." Lee adds that they are also being trained in computer and wage calculation skills, which are also helpful in preparing them for other careers.[16]

Workers filing claims are asked to gather information that will be important to the pursuit of their case, which might include check stubs, "piece tickets," labels, and employer and manufacturer information. They are also asked if there are other workers from the same factory who may have an interest in filing a claim. During this initial conversation they are also informed that they will be expected to become a member of the center in exchange for help with their case. If they refuse to come to the orientation session or to become a member, they are referred out either to other free legal services or directly to the Division of Labor Standards Enforcement.

Often, employers will contact the worker and try to negotiate a settlement; if this does not happen within ten to twelve days, workers are asked to come back and a staff person or peer counselor from the GWC goes with her to the factory. If the factory owner still refuses to pay, a letter is sent to the manufacturer. When both of these strategies fail, a claim is filed with the Division of Labor Standards Enforcement but the worker is expected to represent herself at the hearing with help from a peer counselor. If the claim is decided in the worker's favor, the company is required to pay. If the worker wins the claim and cannot collect directly from the defendants, the money can be awarded from the Garment Fund, which was established by state government.

All garment contractors and manufacturers that register in the state of California are required to pay a registration fee, a portion of which goes into a statewide fund. However, the money awarded is only a portion of the amount owed, and those funds are limited so GWC only applies to tap into the fund selectively. Even when claims are successful, workers still struggle to collect the money owed because the state has no means for collection. As a result, a large percentage of claims go unpaid. Kimi Lee and others have discussed the possibility of creating their own collection agency to facilitate the process as well as to create an income stream for the organization.

Central Texas Immigrant Workers Rights Center (CTIWoRC)

CTIWoRC has pioneered an innovative approach to collection of unpaid wages through a partnership with the Austin Police Department (APD). In 2002, the APD agreed to utilize the "theft of services" provision of the Texas Penal Code to investigate charges of unpaid wages and prosecute offending employers.[17] Its policy statement reads in part: "The Austin Police Department is committed to thoroughly investigating all instances whereby an employer does not compensate an employee for services performed. If necessary, charges will be filed against an employer who does not reimburse an employee for services rendered." APD's adoption of this policy has meant that, for the past two years, CTIWoRC has been able to send out an unpaid wage demand letter to an employer which makes clear that, if there is no action taken, the APD will become involved. The letter reads, "This letter is a demand for payment of the amount [in dollars] in unpaid wages. Failure to pay the amount within ten days of receiving this letter creates a presumption of committing an offense and this matter will be referred to the Austin Police Department for Investigation." Between August 2002 and October 2004, thirteen employers were arrested by the APD under this statute, including six of the center's most notorious repeat offenders.

Julien Ross, coordinator of CTIWoRC, believes that the APD theft of service policy has "provided a tremendous boost to [our] ability to convince employers that unpaid wages could carry serious consequences." The organization realized, however, that additional steps were needed to make the policy more effective, including more closely aligning the APD with the County Attorney's Office, especially with regard to coming to a common set of criteria around what qualified as "intent not to pay." This was important because, while the APD had the power to make the arrests, the County Attorney's Office was responsible for prosecution. In addition, the organization discovered that the APD's implementation of the new policy was inconsistent. For example, workers who contacted the police department's nonemergency call center with complaints were sometimes told that unpaid wages were not a criminal matter and, according to Ross, "the effectiveness and expediency of each case depended entirely on which detective was assigned."

Some detectives aggressively pursued employers and issued arrest warrants while others gave the cases very little weight or complained that they should be dealt with in civil court. After prodding from the Austin City Council, the APD developed and implemented a "standard operation procedure" to clarify the theft of service policy department-wide.[18] Regardless of inconsistencies of enforcement, this policy seems to be having an impact. The specter of a police officer coming to arrest an unscrupulous employer for nonpayment of wages exposes them to the light of day and sends the message that local law enforcement, too often perceived as anti-immigrant, is on the workers' side. Some centers have been wary of this approach however. They have been concerned that involving the police might lead to workers being asked for their documents and also might have a chilling effect on contractors hiring day laborers.

IMPACT LITIGATION

Legal services are an extremely important part of what worker centers do in another sense: in addition to helping with individual cases, many centers look for strategic lawsuits that directly move the advocacy and organizing agenda forward through setting new precedents. The following are two pertinent examples.

In 1994, the City of Agoura Hills in Los Angeles County passed an ordinance that made it a misdemeanor offense to approach persons in moving vehicles for the purpose of being hired and Los Angeles County followed suit. "It was essentially an anti–day labor ordinance," said John Arvizu, of CHIRLA. "It was the city's response to not wanting to see day laborers on their street corners, so they armed law enforcement with this ordinance where they could ticket for stand-ing on street corners looking for work. People were getting arrested. Some of the workers were picked up and taken far away and dropped off and they'd have to take the bus back."[19]

Although the Agoura Hills ordinance withstood initial legal challenges, it touched off a flurry of litigation on the part of day labor advocates that ulti-mately proved successful. Pablo Alvarado recalled: "During that time the LA County Board of Supervisors enacted an ordinance to prohibit labor solicita-tion on public property so day laborers couldn't stand on the sidewalk or street. They could stand in the parking lot of local businesses but this got problematic because it was considered trespassing. But in California, businesses are obliged to designate a free speech area, so we used that avenue to tell them that looking for work is exercising free speech."[20]

In July 2001, after more than four years of litigation by CHIRLA and the Mexican American Legal Defense and Education Fund (MALDEF), the U.S. Ninth Circuit Court of Appeals issued its decision. It ruled that Los Angeles County's anti-solicitation ordinance violated the First and Fourteenth Amend-ment rights of day laborers to express their need for employment. On the basis of this decision, MALDEF sent letters to cities and towns in Los Angeles County urging them to repeal their ordinances. Another victory came when the Los Angeles County Sheriff's Department directed its deputies to cease enforcing the ban. As a result, government officials, civic leaders, and day laborers in a number of cities and towns have been compelled to sit down together and de-vise a collective approach to the issues surrounding day labor employment in their communities. "Once LA County had to dismantle the law, we began to do a lot of outreach and this is something that the National Day Laborer Organiz-ing Network (NDLON) has taken on as one of its primary responsibilities and also MALDEF—to approach different cities that have passed similar laws and that do not provide any alternative to the workers. That, I think, is a huge ac-complishment for the organization and for the movement," said John Arvisu. In 2004 and 2005, the statewide chapter of NDLON worked closely with MALDEF to get ordinances thrown out through a combination of litigation and organizing.

Los Angeles is also the site of another important worker center victory achieved through impact litigation. In order for conditions in the Los Angeles garment industry to be significantly changed for the better, advocates know that they must find a way to hold manufacturers and retailers responsible for the behavior of the contractors who sew for them. After ten years of advocacy, in September 1999 Assembly Bill 633 was passed by the California state legisla-ture and signed into law by Governor Gray Davis. The intent of the bill was to crack down on sweatshop abuses in California's $24 billion garment industry by holding retailers, manufacturers, and contractors liable for labor law violations.

The bill imposed a "wage guarantee" in the garment industry that required manufacturers and retailers who manufacture their own private label clothing to ensure with their contractors that workers are paid minimum wage and overtime. The bill also established successor employer liability so that garment factories could not shut down and reopen under a different name to avoid paying the wages of its former employees. If a manufacturer contracts with an unregistered factory, it becomes a "joint employer" and is then liable not only for its proportionate share of wages but all wages and penalties the employer is responsible for. It provided an expedited administrative process before the labor commissioner for garment workers to recover their unpaid wages under the guarantee and authorized the labor commissioner to revoke the registration of any garment manufacturer that fails to pay a wage award.

Assembly Bill 633 was so bitterly opposed by key industry players that it took until 2002 for its full implementation and even then many rules and regulations were still being worked out. The bill provides the GWC with a powerful tool to combat abuses in the garment industry that may some day lead to significant changes in the behavior of industry contractors, manufacturers, and retailers— at least that is the hope. So far, those wholesale behavioral changes have not taken place. This is where litigation comes in.

The organization achieved a major milestone in an unpaid wages case brought on behalf of garment workers Rosalba Garcia, Adriana Candelario, Andrea Beltran, and Juventina Ochoa against a contractor, manufacturer, and retailer. The labor commissioner ruled that Wet Seal, the retailer, along with the contractor and manufacturer, had to take partial responsibility for the actions of contractors who sewed for the label. The labor commissioner's decision read in part:

> A manufacturer is a person that contracts to have garment manufacturing operations performed. If a retailer by its actions comes within that definition it must register as a manufacturer and is subject to the wage guarantee. In this instance the evidence established that representatives were involved in monitoring the quality control of the work at DT Sewing. Such monitoring is typically a responsibility of the manufacturer. The evidence further establishes that employees of DT Sewing were aware of the presence of the monitors from the Wet Seal, Inc. The best evidence established a direct working relationship between the Wet Seal and DT Sewing. . . . In this instance the evidence established that the Wet Seal Inc. actions were sufficient to be deemed a retailer engaged in "garment manufacturing" and therefore . . . subject to the wage guarantee."[21]

This decision was historic because it was the first time that the California Department of Labor Standards Enforcement Division (DLSE) found that if a retailer was functioning as a manufacturer it could be held liable under AB633. This is critical because one of the biggest loopholes in the law is that when companies claim to be retailers, they are almost automatically let off the hook.

Wet Seal appealed the case in state district court but reached an agreement with the workers (after GWC organized several actions) in January 2004, in which it agreed to pay all the wages and liquidated damages that the labor commissioner had awarded the workers. In addition to the ninety-thousand-dollar payment, Wet Seal agreed to hire an independent monitor for all of its manufacturers and subcontractors, and to make quarterly reports of those monitoring inspections available on request. "This settlement was very important, because by settling, Wet Seal implicitly recognized its responsibility as a retailer to the garment workers that produce the clothes it sells, and is taking steps to assume that responsibility, steps that we can use to keep the company accountable to workers," said Domenzain. "This case is encouraging other workers to come forward to claim their owed wages."[22]

Despite some efforts by the federal Department of Labor to pursue garment manufacturers via new strategies of enforcement of the "hot goods" provision of the Fair Labor Standards Act, so far, GWC has relied on state rather than federal laws to pursue its strategy of holding manufacturers and retailers responsible. "Because our minimum wage is higher," said Kimi Lee, "and we have passed AB633, the wage claim process here in California is more defined, and there is a strict schedule that expedites the process, so we have found it is more efficient to go through the state process."[23]

In the fall of 2004, GWC, Sweatshop Watch, the Asian Pacific American Legal Center, the Asian Law Caucus, and the Women's Employment Rights Center were conducting an in-depth analysis of the successes and challenges to the implementation of AB 633, including recommendations for improvement. The results will be based on a review of a random sample of DLSE case files, as well as interviews with workers, advocates, and DLSE staff at all levels.

ESL AND OTHER CLASSES

After legal aid, the most common service offered by many worker centers is courses in English as a second language (ESL). Most combine teaching the English language itself with presenting information and fostering discussions that encourage participants to think critically and analytically about society and their own place in it. Classes often include curricula about the rights of immigrants and workers as well as organizing approaches and techniques. Some of the centers—especially those that work with day laborers and housekeepers—tailor their ESL classes to the development of particular industry vocabularies. Day laborer centers in Los Angeles, Maryland, and other places have negotiated with various local college professors to send student volunteers in to teach classes on a weekly basis. Casa Maryland, when told by community residents that they were willing to pay for high quality ESL classes, shifted from using volunteers to hiring paid instructors to teach the 1,200 people who sign up to take classes each year.

Since their capacities are limited in terms of size and scale, many centers use the classes as a means of getting to know potential members and leaders and to engage them in discussions of issues and strategies. There is a huge demand for ESL classes among the largely Spanish-speaking membership of the SEIU Local 615 janitors' worker center in Boston—and an ambition to be able to offer them on a much larger scale. But for now, the union uses the classes as a perk for deepening its relationships with potential shop stewards and other member-leaders. The learning of English is combined with lively discussions of union strategy.

Most centers provide extensive training in workers' rights and employment law. Many offer six- and eight-week-long courses in workers' rights and organizing, and a number of them require workers to take the courses before they are allowed to become members of the centers. CAFÉ continually sponsors day-long workshops across the state of South Carolina on a range of employment laws. These include the Fair Labor Standards Act minimum wage and overtime rules, workers' compensation, unemployment insurance, the Family and Medical Leave Act, Title VII, how to file a discrimination charge, and the rights of agricultural workers.

Some centers provide a range of other classes as well. Many offer workshops and trainings on organizing skills and the structure of their industries as well as political topics like the legislative process, globalization, and immigration reform. Several centers offer classes in computer skills and technology. A number of centers expressed interest in providing occupational training: some, including day labor and housekeeping cooperatives, already do.

HEALTH SERVICES

Immigrant worker centers offer three kinds of services related to health: workshops, ongoing programs and training in health education, referral services, and actual clinics. Examples include OTOC, which organized a one-day workshop on repetitive motion disorders that was attended by hundreds of meatpacking workers, and the New York Taxi Workers Alliance, which organizes an annual health fair at La Guardia airport. A number of the agriculturally based centers offer health and safety trainings and workshops related to the handling of pesticides as well as on HIV/AIDS prevention. CAFÉ and GWC refer workers to health clinics that will provide free and low-cost care, and KIWA, in cooperation with the Oscar Romero Health Center, offers a free care clinic once a week.

In addition to health programs, many centers are involved in campaigns to get employers to provide health insurance to workers. TWSC, for example, has pressed the City of Alexandria to provide health benefits to home-based childcare workers. It is also developing a campaign to press the state of Virginia to use a portion of the tourism tax, some of which is traditionally passed on to hotels for the purposes of advertising, to provide health insurance to hotel housekeepers. TWSC has also focused on getting hospitals to provide debt relief to low-wage workers, which by January 2005 had surpassed $1 million.

In conjunction with the services they directly provide, the centers engage in extensive "match-making" between immigrant workers and social service agencies in their local area. In the area of health services, GWC has a program to hook up immigrant workers with clinics that are looking to provide services. "There are tons of groups that do free medical services—there's clinics and groups that get money from the state or the government. Even though there [have] been budget cuts . . . these groups [still] exist," said Kimi Lee. The issue for garment workers is finding out about where they are, how much they cost, what their eligibility requirements are, and figuring out which ones have the language capabilities and services they need. "We created this whole referral system where we've been meeting with different providers to figure that out. We just got someone else to make a directory . . . so instead of just having workers go to emergency services all the time, here's a local place they can go," said Lee.

In the wake of the September 11 World Trade Center tragedy, thousands of low-wage workers in the tourism and hospitality industries became under- and, in many cases, unemployed. The New York Taxi Workers Alliance, Restaurant Opportunities Center of New York, and TWSC worked to identify programs that low-wage workers impacted by September 11 would be eligible to take advantage of, and helped them through the application processes. They also moved into advocacy and organizing when they felt eligibility requirements needed to be changed, as was the case with New York taxi workers who were not initially eligible for September 11 funds.

OTHER SERVICES OFFERED

Undocumented workers, prevented from obtaining drivers' licenses and seldom possessing passports, struggle to access services and programs that require some form of identification. Many centers provide laminated photo identification cards to members. A number of centers have helped workers open their first bank accounts by negotiating arrangements with area banks to accept ID cards and waive minimum deposit requirements. Some centers also offer no-cost check-cashing services to members, sometimes in cooperation with area banks.

Two centers, the Farmworker Association of Florida and Casa Maryland, have experimented with operating a check-wiring service for workers to send money home. A few centers make no-interest, short-term loans available to members. Centers routinely help workers file for workers' compensation and unemployment benefits. In addition, a number of centers, including CAFÉ in South Carolina, helped workers who did not qualify for social security numbers to apply for individual taxpayer identification numbers (ITINs). A few centers offer other kinds of group discounts such as reduced-rate membership in BJ's and other wholesale buying clubs.

The Coalition of Immokalee Workers in Florida set up a cooperative store for farmworkers in Immokalee, in an effort to create an alternative to local stores that were extremely expensive. The co-op sells staple foods and international phone cards at near-wholesale prices; it is governed by the membership and elected leadership and staff of the organization.

A number of centers have relationships with area agencies that provide them with free food and clothing for members in need, and a few have operated soup kitchens and food pantries for short periods. Some hold Alcoholics Anonymous and other self-help meetings on-site.

STRENGTHS AND WEAKNESSES OF THE WORKER CENTER SERVICE DELIVERY MODEL

Immigrant worker centers provide an essential service to their members and constituents with their provision of services. At the same time, they strive to deliver these services in ways that are as empowering as possible for the immigrant workers who receive them. In their legal work, for example, they insist that workers fully understand the process, appear on their own behalf when possible, and always make the crucial decisions regarding the pursuit and disposition of the case.

In this regard, they are very much in line with the thinking that guided the settlement house movement at the beginning of the last century. Settlement houses provided a range of services to immigrants, which included legal aid,[24] occupational training, housing, referrals for medical treatment, libraries, lectures, classes, and cultural events. The critical distinction between the services

provided by the conventional charities of their day and settlement houses originated in the latter's view of the immigrant workers they sought to aid and types
of services and methods of delivery that flowed from this perspective. Jane Addams, in the words of one biographer, aimed to "create citizens not manage
clients."[25]

At the same time, many centers strongly assert that they view the provision
of services as secondary to their central mission of winning systemic change
through political and economic organizing and advocacy. This is a dilemma.
Worker centers want to provide services as a concrete way of responding to the
urgent and immediate needs of their base and to recruit new members. They
want the form of service delivery they provide to reflect their ideology of empowerment but at the same time to be efficient, so that the bulk of resources are
left available for organizing and advocacy.

The debate over the extent to which immigrant workers centers should put
their efforts into service provision as opposed to organizing for systemic change
is not a new one. Echoes of this debate can be found in the development of immigrant fraternal organizations at the beginning of the last century and a number of important social movements of the 1960s.

Social movement organizations in the 1960s, including the United Farm
Workers Union (UFW), the women's movement, the Black Panthers, and Students for a Democratic Society, faced similar dilemmas in their efforts to combine organizing with meeting people's immediate needs. They all provided
services while grappling with how to do it in a way that empowered those receiving the help, was not all consuming of organizational staff and resources,
and built the power of the organization.

The UFW's farmworker service centers offered a wide range of services, including assistance with unemployment insurance, SSI or disability and food
stamps; medical and immigration problems; translation assistance and help
with tax forms; housing and other family problems, including illness, death, di-
vorce, childcare, and elderly relatives. The women's movement generated bat-
tered women's, rape crisis, and women's health centers. UFW organizers believed that the services provided by the centers legitimated the union in the eyes
of workers and offered something tangible to those working on ranches that
were not immediate targets of organizing drives. For the women's movement,
services were much more than a recruitment draw—the rape crisis centers, bat-
tered women's shelters, and abortion clinics were viewed as central arenas in the
struggle for social change.[26]

In looking at the way social movements in the 1960s approached the issue of
service provision, Ann Withorn argued that successful movement services must
provide "a utilized service" but also serve "the strategic needs of the move-

ment." Providing a utilized service, she argues, means that the service should address an important need, do so in a way that fosters self-determination and self-confidence among the receiver, and be consistently available over an extended time period to a targeted constituency group.

In Withorn's estimation, in order to serve the strategic needs of the movement, the service component needs to fulfill a number of criteria. It should be a draw for new recruits. It should enhance retention of existing members and give them opportunities to move into the service provider role. In both the content and structure of delivery, the service should reflect the ideology of the movement. The content of the service should "highlight injustices within the existing social order," and the structure of service delivery should "exemplify the ways in which the movement offers better patterns of human interactions and relationships." Finally, service provision should be viewed as a valid and valuable activity for movement members to engage in.[27]

Given how much worker centers have to do and how slim the resources they have do it with, to Withorn's first criteria, that of "providing a utilized service," let us add the proviso that centers should provide a utilized service that is not readily available elsewhere. To Withorn's second criteria of "serving the strategic needs of the movement" let us add the proviso that the service not crowd out the time and resources for organizing.

How do worker center legal clinics, as the most extensive service that they provide, fare when examined in the light of Withorn's criteria? It seems clear that with regard to the first—providing a utilized service consistently to a targeted constituency group—worker centers are indeed offering services that immigrant workers have displayed a strong demand for and that, unfortunately in the case of legal services, are often not readily available elsewhere.[28] In fact, as we saw in chapter 2, staff of GWC and Chicago Interfaith Workers Rights Center expressed dismay about having to limit the amount of broad worker outreach they do because of the overwhelming demand for help with legal claims.

As is the case with legal services, there is an enormous demand for ESL classes among low-wage immigrant workers. Although it was beyond the scope of this research project, there seemed to be wide variation between the cities in terms of availability of low-cost ESL classes. However, it seemed that while most centers offered some form of ESL classes, most were doing so on a relatively modest scale.

As for the financial services provided by worker centers, this is an area that holds enormous potential and is still not readily available elsewhere but is currently serving a small number of workers. While several have negotiated agreements with banks to offer help in opening checking and savings accounts, very few seemed to be engaged in aggressive marketing or recruitment. Similarly, check cashing is done ad hoc, by administrators at the centers for a relatively limited number of the most active participants. It is the same with loans. A few centers offer emergency loans but only to a small number of very active members. Check wiring, except Casa Maryland and the Farmworker Association in Florida, was virtually unavailable through worker centers.

Why hasn't this been an area of greater focus for worker centers? Most centers were founded by individuals and organizations that came out of the NGO or social justice sectors. They do not have a great deal of interest or experience with offering financial services, raise their money from foundations, and seldom devote much thought to potential fee-for-service activities. On the ground, there was no evidence of overlap between the worker center world and new social entrepreneurship networks and organizations.

Before the advent of the New Deal social insurance system and the rise of the commercial insurance industry, many fraternal organizations provided insurance programs to members and used the income from these programs to support other activities. Worker centers, because of the relationships and respect they have in immigrant communities, may be in a unique position to educate their members and others about financial matters. This includes talking about opening bank accounts as opposed to keeping money at home, helping them access debit cards, and wire money home safely and inexpensively. Providing these services themselves or entering into partnerships with banks to do so, could build the membership base of the centers while at the same time offering an important and ongoing means of financial support to the centers.

As can be seen in the examples above, worker centers today are struggling with the question of how to link service to organizing in general, and in particular with regard to the operation of their legal clinics. Most center legal programs are very self-conscious about offering support in ways that foster self-determination and self-confidence. Workers are not only treated respectfully by advocates who carefully explain the different options they have available to pursue a case, keep them up to date about the progress of the case, and consult them about any major decisions, they are really expected to be the leaders of their cases. Every aspect of a case is analyzed for opportunities for workers to deliberate and make decisions. In their descriptions of what they do, virtually all of the advocates placed the highest premium on providing workers with all of the information they needed in order to make their own informed decision about what to do.

Let us now turn to Withorn's other criteria for evaluation, that the service "serve the strategic needs of the movement." Certainly the legal programs fulfill her first requirement—they are probably the greatest draw for new recruits of any program or service offered by the centers. It should be noted however, that despite the extensive efforts that many centers make to require workers to take classes and fulfill certain volunteer commitments in exchange for legal representation, many still leave after their cases are resolved.

Some centers, certainly the Workplace Project and GWC, do use the programs in ways that enhance the retention of existing members and give them opportunities to move into the service provider role. Both place workers who have been through the process into the role of mentoring those bringing new cases. However, they are doing this primarily to conserve organizational resources for organizing and not because they view this particular role as a great one for carrying out leadership development.

For many centers, the trajectory to organizing begins with a legal case that escalates into a direct action campaign when an employer refuses to honor a judgment that has been brought against him. Many workers get their first taste of active participation via these pickets and other actions. On the other hand, there is a danger of too much of the organizing having its origins in individual legal cases. In some centers much of the organizing is reactive: it is initiated as a result of a particular worker or group of workers' having been mistreated or fired by an employer. The employer has often been found to have violated the law and commanded to pay a settlement to the worker and has not done so.

The centers initiate campaigns in order to help workers collect what is owed to them. These campaigns are great for visibility, media attention, and credibility with workers, but they are extremely time-consuming and pull the organization away from the development of a broader industry strategy. A strategic industry-based approach would be developed proactively with targets carefully selected as opposed to being chosen because they owe money to a group of workers. In this regard, it is clear that in certain situations, service provision— and even some of the organizing that is connected to it—can crowd out the time and resources for more strategic organizing.

Withorn suggests that the content and structure of the service reflect the ideology of the movement by highlighting injustice, exemplifying a humane and empowering model of service provision, and treating this work as worthy of doing. As we have seen, the legal clinics play an important role in highlighting injustice. Many of the cases they handle reflect clear violations of longstanding labor and employment laws. The message workers get is that they have rights and those rights have been violated—this is a powerful message for low-wage immigrant workers and their employers to hear. But it also resonates with the broader public and, as discussed above, the cases that come through the clinics offer opportunities to tell dramatic stories of worker exploitation in violation of the law. In this way, the legal clinics are playing a key role in supplying the grist for broader advocacy and organizing. Interaction with the legal system also contributes to a more critical understanding of the American justice system. While workers get the message that, at least in principle, the law is on their side, they see the harsher reality as well: long delays in the processing of cases, highly imperfect systems of enforcement, and occasionally, anti-immigrant bias on the part of government and judicial officials.

Centers seek to use the insights workers gain from their involvement in the legal system to move them into organizing. There are three principal ways they do this. First, they use legal services as a means of building the organizations by making receipt of them contingent on joining and participating in the group. Second, by bringing cases against targeted employers in specific industries they use them as a form of leverage intended to bring pressure to bear on key targets in support of larger organizing campaigns. Third, by strongly encouraging workers to talk to some of their co-workers, and by helping them mobilize allies to engage in direct action against employers, they look for opportunities to turn individual cases into larger opportunities to organize workers and expose their problems to the larger society. It is to this ambitious organizing component of worker centers that we now turn.

CHAPTER 5

ECONOMIC ACTION ORGANIZING

The advocacy and organizing that worker centers do above and beyond the services that they provide are what sets them apart from other immigrant agencies and organizations. As noted earlier, many centers were founded by individuals and organizations who believed that services alone would not be enough to achieve meaningful social change for immigrant workers. These founders always envisioned a new kind of organization that would make advocacy and organizing activities the priority. They understood the critical role of basic organizing: the need for creative direct action that can change institutions and build grassroots power.[1] Founders of other centers started out with more of a direct service model but backed into advocacy and organizing over time as they came up against the limitations of a "service only" model.

The organizing and advocacy work that workers centers now engage in can be grouped into five general areas:

1. Building a movement of low-wage workers: engaging in movement-building activities like leadership development, popular education, and acting in solidarity with broader international movements around globalization.

2. Publicizing the issues low wage workers face to the larger public framed in terms that will win them over: locating them within "human rights/ anti-sweatshop" frameworks as well as one of basic justice—"a fair day's pay for a fair day's work."

3. Seeking to enforce basic labor and employment laws, raise wages, and improve working conditions in low wage industries.

4. Working to stop racial and ethnic discrimination and normalize the status of immigrant workers.

5. Dealing with issues of immigrant access and incorporation and challenging institutional racism in: schools, housing, and healthcare.[2]

In terms of work-related issues, centers pursue these goals in a variety of ways. These include bringing direct economic pressure to bear on employers and industries (pickets, actions, boycotts, and more rarely, strikes and slowdowns), and through building political support for the passage of public policies that require employers and industries to change their behavior. These goals are also pursued through ongoing advocacy work that puts immigrant issues on the agenda and defends them from attack.

The primary targets of worker center advocacy and organizing work are private actors such as employers and industry-wide bodies on the one hand and local or state government entities on the other. Worker centers defend immigrants' rights and pursue immigration reform at the local, state, and federal levels. Although on the ground this work often blends together, for the purposes of analytic clarity, I will separate out two strands. Organizing work that targets private actors directly will be called "economic action organizing" and organizing work that targets governmental entities will be called "public policy organizing." The remainder of this chapter and the next will consider economic action organizing.

LOW-WAGE WORK AND IMMIGRANTS IN AMERICA TODAY

Low-wage work in America today is anything but homogeneous. There are industries that are dominated by super-sized employers and multinational corporations, others that have a mixture of large and medium-sized employers, and still others where small firms are dominant. There are enormous variations not only between these sectors but also within them. But competition on the basis of wages is a strategy common to all three, and subcontracting is a common method of achieving wage savings. Certainly over the past twenty-five years, production processes in many U.S. industries have become much more vertically disaggregated. In other words, in service industries such as health care and hospitality, and other sectors such as government, agriculture, construction, and manufacturing, steps in the production chain that were once performed by employees of a single large firm are often now performed by the employees of several separate firms.

In their book, *Divergent Paths: Economic Mobility in the New American Labor Market,* Annette Bernhardt and her colleagues argue that subcontracting and outsourcing are one of the least explored forms of restructuring "yet possibly the most important. . . . Subcontracting is redefining the very infrastructure of the domestic economy, with the emergence of complex supplier networks and the shedding of service functions previously performed in-house, such as custodial jobs, payroll and benefits management, data processing, and even entire units such as jobs in restaurants within the hotel industry."[3] The challenge for unions, worker centers, and community organizations hoping to organize workers and improve conditions is finding leverage points within these employment relationships and identifying effective strategies for bringing pressure to bear. It is even more difficult in the informal sector that functions in a range of industries. Some workers have no single stable employer while others may work for extended periods for individuals, families, or small businesses.

In low-wage industries that are more decentralized, it has always been more difficult for workers to organize to limit wage competition and establish broad and enforceable labor market standards and protections. It is in this context that centers function every day, seeing workers from across a wide swath of industries and trying to figure out approaches to establishing wage standards and labor market protections that will work and are enforceable and how to build enough power to accomplish them. A significant percentage of centers—more than 40 percent—don't do industry specific organizing at all. Of those that do, most organizations are doing their work on a fairly modest scale in terms of the numbers of workers they are reaching on campaigns, while some are devising ways of impacting much larger numbers.

Complex economic structures, though formidable, are not the only obstacles worker centers must overcome, and they are not the full explanation for why wages and working conditions are bad. The "color line" that W. E. B. DuBois famously described as the defining feature of American society, runs right through the low-wage economy: close to one third of all blacks and almost half of all Latinos, as compared to 20 percent of whites, earn poverty-level wages in America today.[4] Most of the workplaces and industries in which worker center members are employed and many of the communities in which they live are deeply segregated by race and ethnicity. The large number of undocumented immigrants who are working in the United States today represents a huge reserve labor pool for employers, who know that, because of their legal status, they can pay these workers less and hire them for this reason. Unfortunately, for many immigrant workers, lack of documentation is not a transitory position; many of them have been in the United States for five or ten years or even longer, have not been able to normalize their status, and have been stuck in low-wage employment.[5] That is why immigrant worker centers are likely to focus as much attention on organizing to defend the rights of immigrant workers and change immigration policy as they do around workplace issues. Worker centers cannot hope to significantly improve the economic fortunes of immigrant low-wage workers without confronting immigration policy and the legacy of racism and xenophobia in American employment and society at large.

In an effort to help workers gain some leverage over employers in the "brave new world" of twenty-first century employment relations, worker centers are experimenting with a host of strategies that are industrially, geographically, and policy based.

ECONOMIC ACTION ORGANIZING STRATEGIES

Immigrant worker centers deploy a broad range of approaches to compel employers to treat workers better and to push industries to improve conditions. These direct economic action organizing strategies fall into two broad categories: strategies that target a single employer or corporation; and strategies that target an entire industry.

Many immigrant worker centers conduct their organizing campaigns largely on their own or with the support of nonunion allies. These efforts have also included creating new structures and entities such as hiring hall systems,[6] small businesses, or worker cooperatives. Examples of these types of economic action organizing by worker centers are examined in this chapter. Other centers partner with existing unions to conduct sectorally based organizing drives or have experimented with founding independent unions. In chapter 6 I look at those types of worker center economic action organizing and present an overall assessment of the strengths and weaknesses of all types of economic action organizing strategies by worker centers.

TARGETING A CORPORATE EMPLOYER

In many low-wage industries in which corporations subcontract production it has become essential to unpack the production chain in order to identify the real powers-that-be in an industry and force them to take responsibility for their subcontractors' behavior. As discussed in the legal strategies section in chapter 4, organizers in the garment industry have undertaken a variety of efforts, from joint employer and "hot goods" lawsuits to legislation, to extend culpability up the production chain from subcontractors to manufacturers and retailers.

A good example of such efforts is the Garment Worker Center's (GWC) campaign against the Forever 21 label. The template for this campaign was a previous successful effort by the Asian Immigrant Women's Advocates (AIWA) in northern California against the celebrity retailer Jessica McClintock from 1992–1996.

Founded in January, 2001, within the first six months, nineteen workers from six different factories had come in complaining of unpaid back wages owed by contractors associated with the Forever 21 label, which is a major player in local garment production in Los Angeles. Other complaints included sixty-hour workweeks, short lunches, limited bathroom breaks, and an absence of basic amenities.

Forever 21 was based in Los Angeles and carried out 95 percent of its production in the city. More than a hundred contractors in LA's garment district were filling Forever 21's orders. "Here's a locally owned, locally producing company that isn't going anywhere," said Kimi Lee. "Part of it is that they do young women's fashion, which is the one area that will stay local because in garment production, you can't send something to China or Mexico, it takes a month or two to come back. With young women's fashion, you need something in like three days, so it's got to be local." Forever 21's formula, according to GWC's research, was based on a high-turnover strategy: "Every week, new stuff . . . Really cheap, sell it all, new stuff next week. They never repeat any orders," said Lee. GWC had been looking for a company to make an example of that would have a significant impact on thousands of Los Angeles garment workers, and Forever 21 seemed to fit the bill.

After reaching out to the company to no avail, GWC launched the campaign. Over three years, the campaign had the active participation of more than forty workers from twenty different factories that produce garments for Forever 21. "The owner of Forever 21 refused to recognize the work we did," said Lupe Hernandez, who had sewn for the label. "He said, 'I didn't hire these people' but to me, if it's in your name, then you are responsible. You have to check on the conditions under which your clothes are made."

From the initial lawsuit to early protests and pickets, GWC decided to escalate its tactics to include a national boycott campaign that would tap into the informal network of worker centers and anti-sweatshop activists to hold actions in front of stores in different parts of the country. Locally, the organization reached out to religious, student, and labor organizations, making one or two presentations a week. "The campaign gave us a vehicle for getting people to think about sweatshops and that their clothes are made in sweatshops," says Lee.

"Obviously we haven't been able to shut them down. They've actually grown and opened twenty new stores, but I think just the idea that we are out there is good," Lee reports. Unlike the McClintock campaign, which was able to take advantage of Jessica McClintock's high public visibility to shame her into reacting, Forever 21 is owned by a local Korean who had said that he would rather go broke than settle with the GWC. "He's spending millions of dollars on lawyers . . . we knew when we started the campaign that he had earmarked a few million dollars to do a whole media campaign and that never happened. So we think they put it into the lawyers," said Lee. Asked about what successful models GWC sees itself emulating with the Forever 21 campaign, Lee answered: "The only other example of a multiyear campaign that we've seen against a retailer is Jessica McClintock, so we knew it was going to take a couple of years." The organization started out conducting weekly pickets but reduced that to once or twice a month, sometimes more during the Christmas season. Some of the staff and leaders expressed some boredom and frustration with the pickets, "¿Otra protesta, que pasa?" they asked as they worried that the boycott was not working.

On the other hand, Lee and the other leaders of the GWC believed that the campaign was really helping to establish the organization within the community and within other organizations in Los Angeles. In addition, they believed they were having an impact on the industry. "In 2002, after only being open for one year, we were named by the *California Apparel News* as one of the most influential voices in the industry," says Lee. "In terms of workers, the campaign gave us an opportunity to recruit new workers and to give them a sense of solidarity so that even those who weren't working at Forever 21 were joining them on the picket line and have continued to do so for three years." The organization believed that the campaign also gave them an important tool to conduct intensive community outreach and education about the problems in the garment industry—without a specific target they believe this would have been less effective.

Lee cited the anti-defamation and loss of business lawsuit that Forever 21 filed against GWC as proof that their campaign was having an affect on the company. In the fall of 2004, the organization and the corporation became involved in settlement negotiations and on December 18, GWC announced it had reached a satisfactory settlement with Forever 21 and ended its campaign against the retailer. Although the terms of the settlement are confidential, it appears that Forever 21 resolved its back pay issues, committed to taking steps to ensure the clothes they sell are not made in sweatshops and to working with GWC on that initiative. Why had the corporation finally decided to negotiate? "We couldn't do as much as a national organization or an organization with a larger membership but what we were able to do did have an impact on the company," said Joann Lo, organizing director. "They didn't like the protests we were doing. They didn't like getting postcards from high school students saying 'we are going to boycott your clothes.' . . . During the five months it took us to negotiate an end to the litigation, we got the sense that the direct actions deeply bothered them and they wanted them to stop."

After three years of a David versus Goliath fight, Forever 21, against formidable odds, had been brought to the negotiating table. "This settlement with Forever 21 has broad implications," said Joann Lo. "It shows garment workers they can organize together, take on a multimillion dollar retailer, and gain positive changes from organizing."

Boycott campaigns are notoriously difficult to win—it is very hard to get to enough consumers of a product to make a noticeable dent in company sales and it is especially tough for local organizations to mount national and international campaigns. For this reason, the conventional wisdom in organizing has been to stay away from them except under extraordinary circumstances. Yet worker centers, and not just the Garment Worker Center, are having notable success.

In March 2005, after a four year national boycott of Taco Bell, called by the Coalition of Immokalee Workers (CIW) in Florida as a strategy to improve the wages and working conditions of tomato pickers, Yum Brands (the largest restaurant company in the world and owner of Taco Bell) agreed to pay a penny-per-pound "pass through" to its suppliers of tomatoes and to undertake joint efforts with CIW to improve working conditions in the Florida tomato fields. CIW compensated for its local base and extremely modest resources by going national and international—expanding the scope of conflict far beyond central Florida. The organization mounted an international publicity campaign that cast the issues faced by the tomato pickers in human rights terms that resonated strongly with opinion-makers. CIW worked with the federal government to expose latter-day slavery rings and super-exploitation, and publicized these stories in media outlets across the country. Major feature stories appeared in the *New Yorker* and the *New York Times*. CIW successfully recruited powerful allies to take up its fight: major Hollywood celebrities and national political figures stood with the workers at Taco Bell and Yum Brands shareholder meetings. At the same time, Oxfam America and U.S. Students Against Sweatshops mounted sophisticated internet and campus action campaigns in support of the boycott. CIW also demonstrated great strategic nimbleness, over the course of the campaign shifting the main target of its demands three times—from first going after local *rancheros* (the small contractors who sell their tomatoes to Taco Bell), then moving to Taco Bell and finally to Taco Bell's parent company, Yum Brands. In late May, when CIW announced that it was now turning its attention to other giants of the fast food industry including McDonalds and

Burger King, to pressure them to take the same steps as Yum Brands, the organization garnered major media attention.

In addition to succeeding at a boycott where so many others have failed in recent years, it is also of special significance that both the GWC and CIW succeeded in getting corporations to take responsibility for the wages and working conditions of their sub-contractors, after years of denying responsibility.

THE NATIONAL DAY LABORER ORGANIZING NETWORK AND HOME DEPOT

An interesting example of a worker center pioneering an effective strategy to go after a large corporation at the local level is in the day laborer community. As housing and small commercial markets have boomed across the nation, the Home Depot Corporation has sprouted new stores like mushrooms after a heavy rain. Every day, small contractors and homeowners visit the sprawling orange stores to pick up supplies, tools, and increasingly, day labor. Although the stores themselves offer carpet-laying and other services, day laborers in some communities gather in Depot parking lots and nearby in the hope of picking up a day's work.

"This is an issue for them because sometimes there are hundreds of men congregating in front of their stores," says Pablo Alvarado, an early day laborer organizer in Los Angeles and now executive director of NDLON. "So far their internal policy is that they don't endorse these types of commercial activities on their property. However, they've seen that they can't address it without involving advocates and municipalities. They can't get rid of the workers by utilizing security guards or by calling the cops to basically take care of the workers. They've done all that stuff and it never works. So they're looking into creating a different internal policy."

NDLON has been engaged in conversations with top executives of Home Depot Corporation to discuss the possibility of working together on siting day laborer workers centers alongside its busy stores. These conversations have been occurring on and off since the Instituto de Educacion Popular del Sur de California (IDEPSCA) and the Coalition for Humane Immigrant Rights of Los Angeles (CHIRLA) successfully intervened in the zoning process in Cypress Park. In 1999, after finding out that Home Depot intended to open a large store, the organizations contacted city councilor Mike Hernandez and developed a strategy to intervene in the siting process. "When Home Depot moves in, they always have to get the permit for operating the store and the permits for zoning, commercial use, [and other things]," said Alvarado. "We knew they were coming, so before they came in, we met with a councilman and told him what was going to happen. We met with some of the residents and leaders in the community. We told them we wanted them to pressure Home Depot to create the infrastructure within the premises. We didn't want it anywhere else because it wouldn't work."

The organizations found themselves on fertile ground. "The neighbors, local residents, and business owners were coming to city council meetings and saying, 'This is what is going to happen when Home Depot comes in,'" recalled Alvarado. "Not only will my business go out, but you guys are going to bring in day laborers." Working with residents and the day labor organizations, Councilor Hernandez was able to use his leverage to compel Home Depot, in exchange for a building permit, to agree to set aside space and create an infrastructure for the opening of a city-financed day labor center. Home Depot was very reluctant to set a national precedent by agreeing to the arrangement.

According to Alvarado, "It was something that they knew and in the headquarters they were really debating: 'Why are we going to have a day labor center in our facility?' And the answer was because the council member wanted it. That's the political power that we have. We had the power to make those changes." The company held out until a month before the store was supposed to open and then finally gave in after realizing that Councilor Hernandez was not going to budge. "In the end," Alvarado recounted, "we put together a lease agreement between our organization and Home Depot. That lease agreement is automatically renewed every year. The city served as a witness to that transaction. They signed that document as well, but they didn't want to."

"There were no day laborers here before," said Alvarado. "We just thought that they were going to come after the store opened. That's exactly what happened." Currently, the center serves between 130 and 150 workers each day. "It's very convenient," offers Alvarado, "because the employers buy the tools and materials and then they pick the workers up." Although another Home Depot in North Hollywood pays for a billboard that advertises a day laborer center that is four blocks away,[7] at present, Cypress Park is one of two day laborer centers in the country (both of which are in Los Angeles) that is located right in a Home Depot store parking lot. Plans are underway to open a booth for day laborers on-site at the North Hollywood store, and Alvarado hopes these two successes are only the beginning.

Home Depot is facing issues with day laborers in many other communities, not only in southern California, but in Arizona, Illinois, and Texas as well. Alvarado has met with the manager of external affairs of Home Depot Corporation and shown him around the Cypress Park site. According to an article in *Forbes* magazine, Home Depot is struggling to figure out an internal policy for dealing with the day laborers.[8] There are a number of issues involved. To keep unions out, the store has always maintained a staunch anti-solicitation policy. Home Depot also operates its own contracting businesses out of its stores; where local contractors make themselves available at the stores and are hired by customers to install windows, water heaters, and carpeting, day laborers may be seen as direct competition. In addition, the image-conscious corporation says it worries about running afoul of federal immigration laws against the recruitment or referral of undocumented immigrants for jobs. On the other hand, Latinos account for a significant percentage of American business consumption, and the corporation has just opened several stores in Mexico where millions of sojourners in the United States send home billions in remittances, so it cannot afford to offend an important customer base.

Alvarado and NDLON have proposed that Home Depot promulgate a code of conduct for its stores to follow, so that day laborers are treated fairly and not "criminalized" for seeking work. NDLON wants Home Depot to allow local day laborer centers to leaflet customers outside the stores about their services, to consider opening more day laborer centers on-site, like Cypress Park and to bring the organization in to help deal with the situation when day laborer issues emerge.

For several years Home Depot dealt with these issues in a decentralized fashion, but in the winter of 2005, it appeared that the corporation was moving in the direction of a coordinated national policy that would not look favorably on Cypress Park–type centers. While it is unclear exactly what will happen with Home Depot in the future, NDLON, because it is the umbrella organization for many of the most active day laborer organizations across the country, is in a good position to engage in a coordinated national campaign. In 2004, the organization established a national Home Depot subcommittee that meets regularly via conference calls.

TARGETING AN ENTIRE INDUSTRY

The restaurant industry has been a prime target of economic action organizing for a number of immigrant worker centers, as the following example illustrates.

By focusing on a single industry, Korean Immigrant Worker Advocates (KIWA) has been able to substantially increase payment of the minimum wage in the Koreatown restaurant industry in Los Angeles. Founded in 1992, KIWA launched the Restaurant Workers Justice Campaign in 1997. Prior to that, the organization had handled hundreds of claims from restaurant workers, accompanying many of them to one-on-one meetings with owners to try to achieve a settlement and holding pickets outside of certain noncompliant establishments.

They also filed suit against the Korean Restaurant Owners Association on be-half of a worker who had been blacklisted. In the litigation KIWA won not only back wages for the worker but more importantly a ten-thousand-dollar Work-ers Hardship Fund that could be used by workers who were unjustly fired for speaking out that the organization would oversee. When KIWA decided that the time was ripe for trying to organize an industry-wide campaign, restaurants were the obvious target.

"During our first five years . . . our records and data from all of our intakes and consultations were showing that restaurants were the biggest offenders," said Paul Lee. "It's a ten to one ratio of restaurant cases versus non-restaurant. It was an industry we couldn't ignore." The organization felt that the restaurant campaign would be a good first industry-wide campaign to build the capacity of the organization's leadership and its visibility and credibility in Koreatown. "The restaurant campaign was a good one because the violations were so obvi-ous. It was difficult to argue about paying the minimum wage," said Lee. "Espe-cially if you have the Department of Labor and the California Labor Commis-sioner's office doing raids and sweeps and coming out with these scathing reports that virtually 98 percent of the restaurants weren't paying minimum wage. You can't ignore that."

Over the course of the campaign, the organization picketed ten restaurants and targeted three for sustained boycotts. "The Korean Restaurant Owners As-sociation was a very powerful lobbying presence in the community, so taking on the industry meant taking them on as well," said Lee. Feeling that they had to send a message to the powers-that-be in the association, the organization de-cided to target Cho Sung Galbi, the largest and most profitable restaurant in Koreatown, which was owned by the vice president of the owners association. It also had a number of outstanding unpaid wage claims and unjust firings. "We took them on because they were the biggest fish. You build power by beating up on the biggest fish that you can find," said Paul Lee. KIWA began picketing once a week and then escalated to daily pickets during lunch and dinner hours. For nine days between Christmas and New Year's the organization even organized a hunger strike on behalf of one worker. At first, the Restaurant Owners Associa-tion turned out senior citizens and members of the association to counter these pickets, but then the united front began to fall apart. Eventually, this worker was reinstated and given his back pay.

Over the next two years, the organization targeted two other restaurants for sustained campaigns. Pequa Jong, its second target was significant for another reason: it was the first time that KIWA publicly went after a Korean owner for his treatment of Latino employees. When these workers filed unpaid wage claims, the owner threatened to call the INS. "That one was difficult and controversial because it was like now we were backing a Latino worker against a Korean business owner. We had done others before, but it was with Korean workers, so the issue of ethnic solidarity wasn't a question until this one," Lee recalled. The eight-month campaign ended when the restaurant settled and paid workers their back wages.

After Pequa Jong, KIWA organized a town hall hearing at the United Food and Commercial Workers (UFCW) union hall before elected officials, enforcement agencies, and key allies about conditions in the restaurant industry. It launched another high visibility campaign against the Elephant Snack restaurant where workers had been earning well below the minimum wage and some had been badly injured due to unsafe conditions.

Despite a blackout by the Korean ethnic press, the *Los Angeles Times* began to follow KIWA's restaurant campaign closely, and enforcement agencies working closely with the organization launched their own investigations and raids in Koreatown. "Publicity, enforcement agencies, community boycotts, consumer pressure, and things like that were what eventually drove the industry standards up," said Paul Lee. "Employers were beginning to accept it as a business practice, that just as you have to pay for anything else, you have to pay the minimum wage." Surveying workers who come to their offices seeking help, KIWA has been able to document a great improvement in the restaurant industry as more and more employers pay the minimum wage, comply with overtime, and fulfill workers compensation requirements. By the year 2000, based on a sample of more than one hundred restaurant workers, the organization estimated that the compliance rate of Koreatown restaurants with the minimum wage had gone from about 2 percent to more than 50 percent. Almost two thirds of the workers surveyed reported earning the minimum wage whereas only about a third said they had been receiving it two years earlier.

In 2001, KIWA decided to move forward with its restaurant work in two ways. It launched an aggressive informational campaign about California's new minimum wage of $6.25, blanketing restaurants with leaflets, and it formed the Restaurant Workers Association of Koreatown (RWAK). RWAK is an independent organization based at KIWA, which in the winter of 2004 had grown to about 350 members: 250 Latino men and 100 Korean women. "As our power and presence within the industry began to grow and compliance was starting to come up, the logical step was to help the workers build their own organization," said Paul Lee.

In 2004–2005, RWAK was seeking to build power in the industry by establishing a strong organization of restaurant workers that engages in direct action to improve industry standards. It had a staff of three organizers, all of whom were restaurant workers themselves. Members are required to pay five dollars a month and attend a seminar on labor law. The organization has received funds from the Catholic Campaign for Human Development, the LA Women's Foundation, and the California Wellness Fund. Its budget was about sixty thousand dollars, sixteen thousand dollars of which came from the members themselves who signed up for electronic transfer payments in order to hire and pay a third organizer. Every week, RWAK was conducting trainings on the minimum wage that generated mini-campaigns of workers going back to their restaurants and demanding it. "It is difficult to get restaurants to do more than is required by law," said Roman Vargas, one of the organizers. "The struggle right now is to just get them to do at least that."

Once a week, RWAK holds a protest outside a local restaurant and offers a seminar on workers' rights, education, or immigrant rights. In its effort to establish itself as a worker association that would operate as a quasi-union of restaurant workers, the organization offers a range of member benefits. It operates a free medical clinic for members only, and through KIWA helps members file claims for overtime, minimum wage, and lunch breaks as well as workers compensation. It gives members check cashing privileges (also through KIWA), helps them apply for individual taxpayer identification numbers (ITIN's) from the Internal Revenue Service, ID cards, or *matrícula consulars* from the Mexican consulate, and passports. It has an ESL component that teaches workers English they need to know in the restaurant industry as well as a vocabulary for organizing.

RWAK has about twenty-five to thirty people coming to meetings on a regular basis. "A lot of restaurant workers wanted to create a union," said Mrs. Lee, lead organizer. "But the reality is that the restaurants are really small, independent restaurants, so a union can't be established. Currently the idea is that RWAK will grow and will get powerful enough so that the association can meet with the owners association and create a policy and try to get rid of all the negative aspects of working in restaurants."[9]

CREATING DAY LABORER WORKER CENTERS

Worker centers in Long Island, Chicago, Seattle, Los Angeles, and smaller cities have achieved some significant successes through organizing day laborers in their communities. Most important, they have been able to establish minimum wages at the shape-up sites and day laborer workers centers where day laborers gather daily to seek work. But most found that before they could move into organizing proactively for a minimum wage, they first had to wage defensive campaigns to stop the harassment of day laborers. Pablo Alvarado, the first full-time day laborer organizer in California, remembered that in the early days, "They thought that by calling the INS, they were going to rid of the issue. There were some powerful communities here that would bring the INS and would carry out raids twice a month. The number of workers would decrease in those corners, but in two weeks it was up again. That didn't work."

As discussed in the section in chapter 4 on impact litigation, several municipalities in southern California enacted ordinances banning day laborer solicitation in public. "Now you don't see that as much as you did five or ten years ago. That's changed because we've been successful in challenging those ordinances in federal court," says Alvarado. "It was very common for restaurants to deny services to day laborers because of their physical appearance and backgrounds. Often we'd see Latinos standing out in bus stops waiting for the buses, and they were picked up because they were Latinos and the cops thought they were looking for work. Those things used to happen and it's not that they don't happen now, but not as frequently. Things are better off for the *jornaleros*. Now [in 2005] we have eight centers in LA. They were never here before."

Attempting to organize day laborers has led a number of worker centers to press for the formation of day laborer hiring halls. The most developed network of day laborer hiring halls so far has been created in Los Angeles. They are operated by CHIRLA and IDEPSCA under contracts with the City of Los Angeles, and workers meet in periodic general assemblies to set their wages. The workers at most of the day laborer worker centers have established a minimum wage for general helpers at between $7.50 and $8.00 an hour. This has been a major accomplishment, according to Raul Anorve, executive director of IDEPSCA: "You have to consider that day laborers are multifaceted and they can do anything, and you pay them five dollars and they'll be happy to get the five. They're that desperate. With the day labor centers, we've been able to move up their expectations of themselves to have some dignity about what they're worth in this society and have some pride behind it."

Hiring hall coordinators make sure that employers know that there is a minimum wage, which is only for general helpers. "The other jobs we have are painting, shoveling, masonry, and for that you can charge seven dollars or eight dollars an hour. When the contractor requires qualified skills, then we negotiate for more . . . if somebody owns their own tools, a framer for example, the business is different. Some of us go for ten to twelve dollars even fifteen dollars an hour," one day laborer said.

Day laborer workers centers have established systems for job assignments. They work by raffling the different jobs according to job classification or category. There are general helpers, painters, and carpenters and also people who possess an even broader range of skills. If a worker can speak English, he's given two tickets for the raffle, instead of one. Some centers ask contractors who hire the day laborers to sign written contracts which commit them to specific wages and conditions of employment.

One of the major problems IDEPSCA and CHIRLA face is that some workers prefer to stand out on nearby street corners and offer to work for less, instead of coming in to the day laborer worker centers. The Pasadena center was opened about three-quarters of a mile away from where the workers congregated originally. According to Pablo Alvarado, "The reason why it was opened here was because the whole community opposed having it there. . . . Right now, we are . . . considering the possibility of taking it back to where the workers are. It's more natural and that's where the majority of the workers used to be and where the largest concentration of workers is right now." Why do workers continue to go there rather than the center? "It has to do with supply and demand," said Alvarado. "There aren't many jobs here. There are only twenty-five or thirty jobs here. That's still not enough. Some people feel that in the streets they have more chances. Obviously in the streets there are also a lot of possibilities for abuse and all kinds of things."

When workers stand out in the streets offering to go to work for less money, it undercuts the minimum wage that has been set at the centers. Also, there are many more street corner shape-up sites than day laborer worker centers, and the organizations believe that there probably always will be. The organizations hope to deal with these problems by trying to move some of the existing day laborer worker centers closer to the optimal locations where day laborers gather and contractors are most likely to come. Their other strategy is to go out to the street corner sites and work with the day laborers there to establish their own systems for putting a minimum wage in place. "We're going to utilize . . . the resources that we have with contracts with the city to develop a regional strategy," said Anorve in 2004. "We want to make more of an impact on the wage scales of different corners that probably won't develop day labor centers. Now we know how to operate day labor centers. . . . We know how to organize them, how to set the rules, and how to negotiate with the police. We learned that from our experiences. Now we're going to step up to the next level. We want to bring in more day laborers than at the centers and bring up their minimum wages."

"In order to succeed," writes Mark Erlich, carpenter union leader and labor historian, "craft unionism in construction required firm and total control over the labor market. A local union's bargaining strength was directly related to the complete organization of the carpenters in its community. Unorganized skilled carpenters represented a serious threat to the union, an opportunity for contractors to staff their sites adequately with nonunion tradesmen."[10] Given the negative history of day laborers being harassed by the police and picked up by the immigration authorities, CHIRLA, IDEPSCA, and most of the day laborer organizers around the country are uncomfortable with the idea of engaging in any kind of coercive behavior to get the day laborers off the corners and into the centers. The Workplace Project, which worked with the mayor and Catholic Charities to set up a day labor hiring hall trailer in Freeport, on Long Island, faces the same issue. Organizers there have developed strategies that focus on compelling the contractors, rather than the workers, to use the site. "When it started, there were very few workers who were going. What we told the mayor was that we could try, but we need you to move those contractors and it's not just ticketing them once in a while when you feel like it," said Nadia Marin-Molina, executive director.

"At first it wasn't happening. Eventually they tried it and it worked. . . . It was having the police spend a few hours and when a contractor pulls up they say, 'I'm not going to give you a ticket right now. I'm going to show you where the correct places to go and pickup workers are. If I see you here again, I'll give you a ticket.' Then we had 90 percent of the workers and the contractors going. When you have the contractors going, the workers go." Morin says that they try to get the police to do this a few times a year, especially during times when jobs are more scarce and workers are most likely to stand out on corners. In addition, they are working with the town to explore the possibility of creating an entrance that is more visible and accessible from the city's main drag.

One strategy strongly under consideration among the day laborer centers in LA is to help some day laborers become contractors themselves. They would get contracting licenses, hire a crew out of the hiring hall, and carve out a niche in a particular subsector of the local construction labor market. According to Anorve of IDEPSCA, "We want to get contractors to hire day laborers from within the center and with a commitment of two years that only day laborers will go. There will be a lot of training and developing the skills so they can do a decent job." In addition, they will also organize for benefits: "At the same time we're going to push to have health insurance. Then if we can have a little more economic leverage we want to join the universal health movement that's going on." In 2004 and 2005, the organization had been in discussions with program officers in the economic development division at the Ford Foundation to fund a planning grant.

The organizations have also been engaged in discussions with the laborers and painters unions about bringing day laborers into their ranks. "Where do we want to be in ten years? We don't want to be day laborers, we want to get a full-time job with good wages and working conditions. People said they wanted union jobs. Folks are ready for that," said Alvarado. One project under discussion with the painters is for day laborers to do prevailing wage work with the

LA Unified School District. At present, when the district has to paint its buildings, the contractors it hires sometimes go to the paint stores and hire day laborers under the counter to do the work, which undercuts the union as well as the day laborer worker centers. The union has gotten the school district to agree to cease this practice and make sure that the contractors go to the painters union to provide the workers. The proposal that is under consideration is for CHIRLA and IDEPSCA to choose twelve day laborers who would go through a one-week paid apprenticeship program at the painters union and then be hired to do the painting. In addition, the painters union would assign an organizer to ensure that the day laborers were being paid fairly by the contractors. Although initially hopeful that the project could expand to hundreds of jobs, so far this has not happened.

ECONOMIC DEVELOPMENT

La Mujer Obrera (LMO), a first-wave immigrant worker center, was founded in 1981 in El Paso, Texas, by a group of Mexican women garment workers and their allies who were dedicated to organizing among low-income Mexican and Mexican-American communities in El Paso and close-by border towns in Mexico. Initially, the organization focused on leadership development, housing, education, political participation, and organizing to improve wages and working conditions for the mostly female workforce in the garment and textile industries in El Paso. A few years later the industry underwent fundamental restructuring. As a result, major manufacturers closed and were replaced by small subcontractors, many of whom paid poorly, violated overtime and health and safety laws, and went in and out of business with great frequency.

But as the organization grew to understand the industry, it began to distinguish between two types of small business entrepreneurs. In their view, the *barbajanes* (crooks) had no business plan or ethics and were just looking for a quick profit while the *empresarios* (entrepreneurs) were business people who had a business plan and cared about their businesses and the communities in which they were operating. In addition to grassroots organizing strategies of filing lawsuits, leading protests, and pushing the Labor Department to launch an investigation into the local garment industry, the organization also catalyzed a discussion with the El Paso city government and the business community around building the infrastructure for the city to establish itself as a cutting-edge garment production center. Mujer experimented with creating an industrial incubator, the High Fashion Institute, which opened in 1994 and focused on fostering the stability and growth of the *empresarios*. In each of its first two years of operation, the organization exceeded its original expectations, providing assistance to fifteen companies, helping close to three hundred workers to stabilize their employment. But the global changes set into motion by NAFTA dwarfed the consortium's best efforts.

As the organization worked to develop strategies for organizing in this context, it also bore witness, during NAFTA's first five years, to major plant closings as industry migrated to the *maquiladoras* across the border. A paragraph on its website tells the story,

> While the South Central was once booming with textile and garment manufacturing companies that employed thousands of women of Mexican descent, the area now bears the resemblance of a ghost-town. . . . The residents of South Central face a multitude of problems due to the lack of infrastructure. It is a neglected area. As a result, residents face substandard education for their children, and violence. The streets are torn from over-use and poor maintenance. Warehouses, which were once bustling with activity are now vacant and deteriorating.

LMO systematically documented the economic effects of NAFTA and became deeply involved as grassroots leaders in the global democracy movement, at one point helping to shut down the International bridge between El Paso and Juarez, Mexico. As El Paso experienced massive layoffs in the garment industry, Mujer worked to help displaced workers get through the torturous process of accessing retraining funds that were stipulated in the labor clause of the free trade agreement. But for many of the garment workers, the retraining programs failed to result in the acquisition of new job skills or new jobs.

It was in this context that LMO turned once again to an economic development strategy. In 1997, it launched El Puente Community Development Corporation, which focused on developing social service and training programs designed to meet the needs of the displaced workers and their families. El Puente created four programs. They included an economic opportunity center to "provide intensive outreach, recruitment and orientation of workers displaced by NAFTA and other local economic restructuring," and an entrepreneurial training center to help displaced workers and their families explore setting up their own small businesses. They also included a micro-enterprise incubator program to provide on-site legal and marketing services, help with financial management, facilitate access to suppliers and vendors for graduates of the entrepreneurial training program, and establish a revolving loan fund to be used by graduates of the training program as well.

It has established a number of "social purpose businesses" that provide eco-

nomic opportunities to displaced workers. The organization has created a successful day care center, restaurant, traditional marketplace for Mexican products and artisan crafts, and Disenyos Mayapan, a for-profit industrial sewing
business staffed by displaced garment workers that specializes in sewing uniforms, scrubs, aprons, and bags for restaurants, medical clinics, and hospitals.

COOPERATIVES

Cooperatives are another creative solution that worker centers have utilized as
part of their direct economic action organizing strategies. At the Workplace
Project, in Long Island, New York, discussion about launching a house-cleaners
cooperative began in 1998. It emerged out of frustration with earlier efforts by
the organization to improve the practices of the employment agencies, which
often charged exorbitant fees to place women in jobs and misrepresented the
nature of the job requirements as well. The Workplace Project already had
some experience with cooperatives, having launched a landscaping cooperative
in 1996. UNITY was initially composed of twelve immigrant women who spent
a year working with staff to develop the structure and marketing plan. Based on
market research; outreach to potential clients through local churches; organizational allies within close proximity to the town of Hempstead; and early media
coverage, ten families became UNITY's initial clients during January, February,
and March 1999, providing employment for all twelve members of the cooperative. With this initial client base, UNITY placed ads in a local newspaper and received a strong response. Now it gets most of its customers through word of
mouth.

UNITY sees its core mission not only as providing greater economic independence to house cleaners but also engaging in consciousness-raising and
leadership development. "The cooperative was founded for the betterment of
women in general, not just so women could have work, but also to give the
women self-worth," said Lillian Araujo, co-op director, former vice president
of the board of the Workplace Project, and former secretary of a coffee cooperative in her native El Salvador. "In each home, a woman suffers different kinds
of problems. The first thing we did was attract members and look for work.
Through that process we began to learn the problems that the women faced. We
have various trainings about domestic violence, health in general, so that the
women would be ready to deal with their problems," said Araujo.

There is a very strong emphasis on leadership development throughout the
cooperative's activities: there are frequent trainings, and members are also sent
to specific leadership development workshops. Through biweekly meetings and

other cooperative activities there are multiple opportunities to develop skills, from how to set an agenda and run a meeting to public speaking.

Members of the co-op go out and speak in area churches and other venues where they hope to find house cleaners and interest them in joining the co-op. Marketing the cooperative in the larger community through talks at congregations, community organizations, and in the media also raises the consciousness of opinion-makers, local leaders, and potential customers about the problems immigrant women workers face.

The women of UNITY were all required to participate in a special course developed by the Workplace Project on cooperatives and in one of the co-op's committees (finance, marketing, rules, and education), which meet every two weeks. Each committee elects a coordinator who serves on the central coordinating committee, and all the members vote together to elect a co-op president. The cooperative course that is a prerequisite for membership is now taught by co-op members. After participating in the first co-op class in 1999, members of the education committee engaged in an extensive evaluation, revised the curriculum, and have taught all subsequent courses.

The co-op developed a system for distributing jobs to members that is based on the level of each member's participation in the cooperative's activities. "The most active members are the first to receive new jobs. Subsequent jobs are distributed to members with decreasing participation. Once every member is assigned a client, the cycle starts anew from the beginning of the sequence."[11] Members earn twenty dollars an hour and contribute 10 percent of their wages earned through the cooperative to help cover operating expenses. In the spring of 2004, the cooperative had grown to eighty-one members. According to the Araujo, some members are able to work full-time through the cooperative, others are able to get two or three days of work a week through the co-op.

Several other worker centers are experimenting with cooperatives. IDEPSCA has a women's housecleaning and craft cooperative based out of its Pasadena, California, hiring hall. The Restaurant Opportunities Center (ROC) is opening a cooperatively owned restaurant in Manhattan and hopes to open more. Mujeres Unidas y Activas in San Francisco works with undocumented women immigrants and focuses on fighting domestic violence and immigrant rights. It operates the Caring Hands Workers Association as an economic development project that helps members get training and placement to work in home health care and therapeutic massage and then sets uniform rates and standards.

CHAPTER 6

RELATIONSHIPS WITH UNIONS

As discussed in the previous chapter, many immigrant worker centers conduct their organizing campaigns largely on their own or with the support of nonunion allies. Others, however, have a history of partnering with existing unions to conduct sectorally based organizing drives (see figure 6.1). Still others have experimented with founding independent unions. These forms of economic action organizing are the subject of this chapter, which also includes an overall assessment of the economic action organizing of worker centers.

In terms of organizing, worker centers have related to unions in a variety of ways. When approached by a group of workers who were interested in joining a union, some centers have followed a practice of helping them to find one that is interested bringing the two parties together and then essentially handing the workers off to them. Other centers have tried to maintain some level of involvement over the course of the organizing drive, although it is largely being run by the labor union. A smaller number of centers have participated in joint organizing campaigns with unions. In many instances, however, especially in cases of smaller workplaces, worker centers have struggled to identify a union that is willing to organize the workers.

OMAHA TOGETHER ONE COMMUNITY (OTOC) AND THE UNITED FOOD AND COMMERCIAL WORKERS UNION (UFCW)

OTOC is a faith-based organizing group affiliated with the Industrial Areas Foundation. In 1998, the organization began looking at the difficult conditions

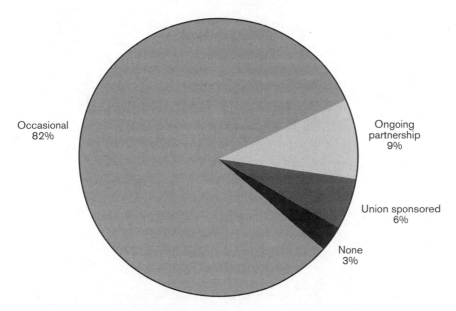

Occasional
82%

Ongoing
partnership
9%

Union sponsored
6%

None
3%

Note: While almost all worker centers report some contact with local unions, only
15% have an ongoing partnership or are union-sponsored.

6.1. Collaborations between worker centers and unions

under which the largely Mexican workforce was laboring in the meatpacking
industry in Nebraska. Omaha has been home to immigrants engaged in meatpacking work since the early twentieth century when conditions in the industry
were also highly dangerous and poorly paying. Still, what OTOC heard from the
workers shocked them. "They had no time clocks in plants, not nearly enough
bathrooms—people were having to go to the bathroom while they're on the
line, urinating in their pants . . . just terrible stuff," said Tom Holler, OTOC
lead organizer. "The speed of the lines was unbearable." In general, workers felt
powerless in their relationship to company managers.

Beginning in the 1930s, the CIO's packinghouse workers union and later its
AFL equivalent launched aggressive organizing drives in which ethnic churches
played an important role. By the 1940s the unions had nearly the entire industry
(95 percent at the peak) organized and for nearly two decades industrial unionism reigned in meatpacking. But beginning in 1969, the prevailing model of
production in the industry was fundamentally challenged by IBP (originally
Iowa Beef Products, now part of the Tyson Company). In the new system, virtually all the labor was done on quick assembly lines where each worker would

make the same cut hundreds of times a day (one of the reasons that repetitive stress injuries [RSI] have become increasingly common). Pursuing nonunion labor was a fundamental part of IBP's strategy to become an industry leader.[1]

Over the next twenty years, a new breed of packers led by IBP would dismantle virtually all the gains of unionization. Strike after strike proved unsuccessful in stopping the changes in the industry. The "new Big Four" (Tyson/IBP, Excel/Cargill, ConAgra, and National/Farmland) control around 80 percent of the market. New line packers continue to open and expand operations across the rural Midwest and have brought in a huge number of immigrants to fill the jobs. Several areas in Nebraska have seen their Latino population grow by ten thousand or more in just a few years.[2]

The OTOC leadership began holding meetings to discuss the meatpacking industry and conducted a series of meetings with workers where they heard firsthand about the problems in the plants. In anticipation of an organizing campaign, it hired Sergio Sosa, a talented organizer who had recently emigrated from Guatemala. At this point, with the exception of one plant that was struggling to get a contract, there were no unionized meatpacking plants left in Omaha. Over an eleven-month period, Sosa brought together Latino workers from a variety of plants and from other immigrant-heavy industries to discuss working conditions and possible organizing models and campaigns, including the creation of a multi-industry Latino worker center.

In 1999, OTOC organized a rally with twelve hundred people that focused on conditions in the meatpacking plants. In the fall and winter of that year, its efforts gained the strong support of the governor and lieutenant governor, who held investigations and promulgated a "meatpacker's bill of rights" in the first months of 2000 (see chapter 7). Also that year, OTOC's workers' committee began sponsoring clinics with meatpacking workers on how to prevent and seek treatment for repetitive stress injuries.

Initially OTOC considered building a workers' association instead of a union, but eventually decided they needed to work with an organization that had organizing experience. They decided to explore a partnership with the UFCW but with some conditions: "We're not going to say, like traditionally is done: 'We'll organize community support and you do the organizing,'" said Holler.[3] From an original list of 150 questions about the union, the group narrowed in on twenty-five to ask at a joint meeting between OTOC and the international union. After much deliberation, the workers' committee at OTOC decided to move in the direction of a union organizing drive in meatpacking. Over the next three years, the union provided financial support for OTOC to hire and train two organizers to work with Sosa and to open an office in South Omaha.

In June 2000, OTOC and the UFCW announced their plan to organize four thousand area packinghouse workers and launched the organizing in earnest. The Omaha Central Labor Council and the State Federation of Labor became involved in supporting the campaign and the national media began to write about what was happening. "*USA Today* did a big story on us. We were attracting a lot of attention to conditions in the meatpacking industry. This kind of became the defining fight," said Holler.

In less than two years, the partnership resulted in close to a thousand new workers being organized into the Omaha UFCW local. There was a very strong sense of momentum in Omaha about the drive. However tensions over the clash of cultures between OTOC and the UFCW had risen to the point where the partnership largely fell apart. While the drives had been dominated by the more personal organizational culture of OTOC, the contract negotiations and creation of union structures after the drive were dominated by the much more traditional union culture of the UFCW.

According to OTOC, plant leaders who had helped build strong participation in the organizing drives felt as though they were essentially demobilized by the union once the elections were won. There weren't any shop steward trainings or structures put in place. Workers who had voted for the union but who saw little immediate change felt betrayed. Sosa, OTOC, and the workers were extremely frustrated, not only with the UFCW's approach to organizing a drive, but to the work of building a union inside the plant once an election was won. "It's not worth it to keep on, to organize the next one and the next one and the next one because nothing's going to change," fumed Sosa.[4]

The union arrived at the plant with what OTOC organizers considered to be a boiler-plate contract which shocked workers who had expected to play a role in drafting it themselves. "When we organized ConAgra Beef . . . we developed strong leadership," said Marcella Cervantes, one of the organizers who worked with Sosa. "But when they started negotiating the contract, workers confronted something different. They were organizing because they knew what they wanted. When they started meeting with the union representatives, they found that the local union already had a different system. They presented them with a draft of their contract. They already formulated what they wanted to say."[5]

OTOC objected to the union's approach to soliciting workers' input into the contract: "They just gave the workers a survey to fill out and they didn't train workers on what the contract meant, how the contract works, and how to build something," said Sosa. "They are not addressing their work atmosphere, work rotations, workplaces. They are not addressing the immigration and the wording in the contract. Then the economics of it as well." Many active leaders complained that they could not get their phone calls answered by the local union leadership. "They are not addressing that workers belong to the community and they should be part of it."

The UFCW local did not understand the tensions in the same way. The union leadership felt that the partnership had been quite successful and that if there were tensions, that was largely because OTOC and the workers had no previous experience with unions. For example, to local president Donna Mac-Donald, circulating a survey was a perfectly appropriate way to solicit input into the contract and having a basic contract from which to work was standard operating procedure. "A lot of it's basic because it's pretty standard with the ADA, FMLA, a grievance and arbitration procedure, safety language, obviously wages that's the first thing they say they want. We put in a substantial wage increase in the contract and then we get into the economics and the verbiage first and then when we get to the bottom, that's where the economics are. Most people don't understand the way negotiations go. They have no clue. Even people who are unionized or have been unionized, if they haven't sat on a committee, they don't understand what you're doing."[6]

While MacDonald planned to hold an election of the entire plant for a four-person contract committee, she sensed that the OTOC organizers didn't understand that voting would be open to all: "Workers elect them. It's not just people who voted yes for the union who elect them, it's the entire bargaining unit."

Other UFCW union staff who had been close to the drive, had their own issues with OTOC, feeling that they were difficult to work with, had a very controlling attitude toward the campaign and a patronizing attitude toward the workers. "When I was interviewing witnesses and taking affidavits," one person told me, "the OTOC people acted like I had to treat the workers in a really fragile way, and that we should be grateful to them for having come all the way to the hotel to help us. Of course, I wasn't rude to the workers, but I didn't assume that they were totally removed from the situation and were there just to do the union a favor either—the case we were fighting was their struggle, and the union guys always understood that."

The problems experienced by OTOC and the UFCW in coming together to do a joint drive are quite typical. There is a dramatic culture clash between many unions and worker centers. Worker centers experience many local unions as top-down, undemocratic, and disconnected from the community; unions view many worker centers as undisciplined and unrealistic about what it takes to win. Unions have long-established patterns and routines for organizing and negotiating and set structures at every level of their organizations while worker centers are much more experimental and ad hoc. When a union proceeds to do things the way it has always done them, as in the example above, it is often interpreted by a worker center as a deliberate attempt to force an agenda. The union, because it is unable to step outside its own culture, is often not even aware that it is doing anything problematic. On the other hand, worker centers have their own entrenched cultural norms.

CHICAGO INTERFAITH WORKERS RIGHTS CENTER

On almost any weeknight, the staff of Chicago Interfaith Worker Rights Center, a project of the Chicago Interfaith Committee on Worker Issues, can be found presenting a workers' rights workshop to area ESL classes.[7] Through this outreach, the organization hopes to discover workplace situations that are ripe for a union organizing drive. But first they have to contend with what they say is predictable antiunion sentiment from many in the class. "At the workers rights workshops . . . there's always negative sentiment about unions from the crowd. It's because of experiences workers have had back in their home countries, and also some bad experiences here,"[8] said Jose Oliva, director of the center. Despite these initial sentiments, after Oliva's workshop he always gets workers who call to talk more about their workplace issues and explore unionization. Sometimes the center hands off workers to an appropriate union, although it prefers to play an active role in any resulting drive and often does. "If a group of workers come into the worker center and they have a problem in the workplace . . . we will go ahead and work with them to file a complaint with the Department of Labor, but we also give them the option of organizing into a union," said Oliva. If they choose to organize into a union, the worker center serves as a facilitator between them and the union they choose. However the center often struggles to find a union willing to take the workers on. Three stories illustrate how perilous and uncertain the road to union representation can be, even for those workers who are persuaded of its desirability.

In 2003, the center was involved in an organizing drive in which the Carpenters Union was seeking to organize workers who were employed by nonunion contractors, building thousands of housing units through New Homes for Chicago, the City of Chicago–sponsored affordable housing program. One campaign targeted Ansco, a contractor involved in doing residential rehabilitation. Several organizers on the union's staff conducted job site visits and house calls but encountered fierce employer resistance. "The fear factor was too great. The company was aware that the Carpenters Union was involved in an organizing drive almost immediately because we had been on job sites," said Dan McMann of the union.[9] "They bought off employees. They intimidated other employees. They fired other employees. They rewarded some. We were never going to gain

much worker support there, so we sat down with Jose Oliva." The union organizers recognized that they needed to try a new approach. Most of the workers
were Mexican, smaller numbers were from Central and South America. "We
thought the best way to go would be for them to have initial contact with the Interfaith Worker Rights Center."

Oliva began talking with the workers and pulled together a series of meetings
at the local Catholic church. At these meetings, Oliva and the union learned
that workers were earning six dollars to nine dollars an hour without benefits
and that safety conditions on the job were terrible. While they had been unwilling to speak with the union, large numbers felt comfortable attending the
church meetings. "We had as many as sixty-five to seventy people here, all
workers from the company, which is phenomenal in an organizing drive." A
few days later, fed up with working conditions and encouraged by what they
had heard at the meetings, about seventy workers spontaneously walked off the
job and showed up at the Carpenters' Union hall. "This district council here, I
don't know about anyone else, we haven't had sixty people walk off the job over
working conditions since the 1930s," said McMann.

The union and the worker center helped the workers elect a delegation of
workers to go back and negotiate with the owner. That delegation told him they
would return to work the next day, but demanded that he meet with them and
discuss the conditions of their employment. They went back to work but were
fired two days later. Over the next few weeks, the workers partnered with the
Carpenters Union and the worker center to put up a daily unfair labor practices
picket in front of the job site. McMann credited the Interfaith Center with the
drive's ability to garner extensive coverage in the Latino media. The center and
the clergy, as opposed to the union, were the media spokespersons throughout
the campaign and within a little more than a week, the company and the Carpenters' District Council were in negotiations, with the clergy at the bargaining
table.

Despite having reached a verbal agreement, Ansco reneged again, going back
on agreements and firing and reprimanding workers. The workers were back
out on strike a month later. Eventually worn down by all of the picketing and
negative press, the company signed an interim agreement with the union but it
was far from a happy ending, said McMann. "He says that he's going to go out
of business in 180 days because he can't afford the union contract." Although
they didn't get the company to sign on to the standard contract, McMann says,
"every other rehabber, and it's a close-knit group, is well aware of what is going
on at Ansco. The next time he resurfaces, he's really going to realize that he's
going to have to pay his workers a lot more money and treat them better so we

don't come back at him. It's all about that kind of shock wave that the Carpenter's union can put into the market."

While the union felt the campaign was a success because it essentially forced a nonunion contractor out of business, its own plans for organizing more low-wage rehabbers in the future were uncertain. "This campaign was costly for us. What these workers have under the interim agreement is union security, the ability to become members of the union, a modest raise. You've got to understand these workers are making six dollars to eight dollars an hour, when our journeyman wages are thirty-two dollars plus benefits and the first year apprentice is twelve dollars plus benefits. At this time we really don't know whether we want to spend the amount of time and effort and money that went into this campaign," said McMann.

While the workers in this campaign will all become union members, they also know that the company is likely to go out of business and that they will probably lose their jobs. They also know that the union will require them to go through apprenticeship training before they will be eligible for the journeyman's wage. "Obviously some of them aren't happy. Some of them would've liked to have seen a larger raise. . . . They're not seeing a lot more dollars in their pockets. It's all about the money," said McMann. "But they're going to have a union card. They're going to have membership in the union and at the end of the 180 days, we will do everything possible to keep them at work, to make sure they can come in here and actually be in the process of an apprenticeship." The interim agreement required Ansco to contribute forty-four cents an hour to the union apprenticeship fund, which the union intends to use to offer the workers "skill advancement" courses in carpet-laying, scaffolding, and framing.

In addition to the enormous wage differential between what nonunion rehabbers were earning and the journeyman's wage, McMann worried that the undocumented status of many workers would result in their being unable to participate in the union's program. "I think that the problem for us is that because of the low wages they are receiving at this time, it's the hardest to get them up to the union building trades scale. Our apprenticeship program, ourselves, and all the other building trades are covered by departmental labor law. So there's a lot of paperwork involved in that for every one of us in the building trades. They want to see birth certificates, social security cards, driver's licenses, and for the immigrant population, that's the toughest thing for them. Plus the fact that we have education requirements."

At the end of the whole process at Ansco, the workers, disenchanted with the union for not being able to deliver better jobs as well as with the worker center for having facilitated a relationship with the union that did not bear fruit, ended up pulling away from both organizations. This example demonstrates the complexities of bringing new groups of low-wage immigrant workers into a building trades union, even when the leadership believes strongly in doing so.

On a number of occasions, the Chicago Interfaith Workers Rights Center has been faced with a situation where groups of workers have contacted them but either were not in an appropriate setting for a union organizing campaign, or got frightened off when they began one and the employer retaliated. In cases where the center finds that union organizing has hit a dead-end, it implements other strategies. Oliva cited its work with a group of workers at Cicero Flexible Products in Sicily, Illinois, which manufactures plastic parts for cars. "They were basically willing to organize with UNITE. But when the organizing drive began, a whole bunch of them got fired, which is pretty common for a union organizing drive. The group of workers that had been fired wanted to continue organizing, but they didn't have a job. The workers that were in the shop were scared and didn't want to organize." The unfair labor practice charges that were filed were all dismissed and UNITE had decided to write off the campaign and move on. "We made the decision just because we had started the whole thing that we were not going to stop the drive. That's how we began to think more long term about what do we do in situations where there isn't the possibility of organizing a union."

Working with the workers who had been fired and the Chicago Interfaith Committee, the center organized a Workers' Rights Committee comprised of area religious and civic leaders in Sicily, based at a church that a number of the workers attended. The committee is a place where workers can bring their issues to a sympathetic group who then take responsibility to intercede with local employers and raise issues publicly. Oliva says that this is the approach that the organization is taking in other places where "there isn't the possibility to organize something specific with a union. The worker center will basically talk to whatever religious contact is in that community and figure out how to structure a worker's rights group in that church."

A related approach is the Worker Sanctuary Program, something the center has started together with Chicago Interfaith, the center's parent organization. It asks religious institutions across Chicago to sign up to become a worker sanctuary and pledge to intervene directly on behalf of workers with employers, as well as to participate in ongoing service programs and policy campaigns. Oliva believes that this structure "is giving us the reach that we needed citywide in order to create the infrastructure with the churches and religious bodies to have mini–worker centers in places that need them."

In Chicago as in many cities where worker centers are active, there are mixed feelings about them among union officials. Although the Chicago Federation of Labor (CFL) has been supportive of the Chicago Interfaith Workers Rights Center and Tim Leahy, the CFL secretary-treasurer, is a board member of Chicago Interfaith, he gave voice to the mixed feelings: "I just have concerns. I think what they do is provide a good service. If it provides a connection to the labor movement and apparatus, I think that's great. I get concerned to see the growth of labor centers when we should have the growth of the labor movement."[10]

Leahy worries that worker centers are often contacted by "hot shop" workplaces. These are places where there is unrest but which may or may not have good prospects for organizing and may or may not fit into the sectoral organizing agendas of the international unions that are trying to rebuild their density in specific industries. "What you get from worker centers as it relates to labor are hot shops. We're tired of hot shops. Those unions that are organizing strategically are growing. They're getting away from hot shops. They're going after the market. Like here, UNITE, I could send them a million hot shops and they'll say, 'We want Cintas [the large North America uniform supplier which is the target of a major organizing drive by the union], period.'[11] Our affiliates are changing the way they look at organizing. They're looking at what they've got and then where they need to be and how to get there. I don't know where the worker centers fit into this yet."

Notwithstanding union reservations, the Chicago Interfaith Workers Rights Center has also had some straightforward successes in terms of helping immigrant workers win a union at their workplace. In mid May 2004, the center was contacted by Crispin Torres, a worker at Berg Manufacturing in Wheeling, a suburb of Chicago. "It was a small shop, a little over sixty workers, and they came in complaining about a ton of things," said Oliva.[12] While workers were routinely working sixty-hour weeks, their paychecks reflected only forty hours. They were being paid in cash without the overtime premium for the other twenty hours. Workers were not provided any protective equipment, machines lacked guards or sensors, and one person had recently lost a finger. "When Crispin came in to the center, we did what we always do, telling him that we can file a ton of different complaints with different agencies, but if he really wanted to change conditions, the workers needed to organize." Torres went back and talked with his co-workers, returning with fifteen of them two weeks later who quickly decided that they wanted to pursue union representation. The center introduced them to the United Electrical Workers Union (UE) and the match was made.

"Our first step, always," said Oliva "is to let the employer know that this is what the workers want." Given the difficulties of going through the NLRB election process, "card check recognition" (in which the employer agrees to recognize the union without an election if a majority of workers sign authorization cards) is almost always the route favored by unions in recent years. To get it, they have to demonstrate enough community support and bring enough pressure to bear on the employer that it makes the decision to agree to forgo an election.

After the Berg workers signed authorization cards, Oliva called the company. The company ignored his calls for a while and when he finally spoke with the owner, the conversation was not a friendly one. Oliva organized a religious delegation, a common tactic used by the center, to pay an impromptu visit to the company, and they were able to sit down with the owner. "The religious delegation said we really think there are a number of legal violations here, including serious OSHA violations and we said that we were going to go ahead and file our complaints unless he was willing to sit down and talk union and figure something out." But at that point, the owner refused to negotiate and asked the delegation to leave his office.

Because of CAWRI, the Chicago Area Workers Rights Initiative, detailed in chapter 3, the center was able to move very quickly in filing charges against the employer. They talked with an OSHA investigator with whom they had a close working relationship, and she paid a visit to the company the very same day. That was enough to sway Berg Electronics to reach an agreement with the center.

"They didn't call the union back, they called us back," said Oliva. "We went back and met again and he changed his tone completely. . . . Some of the workers had been getting pressured, being told they didn't have documents so they can't join a union, they can't file complaints because then the INS will know where you are. Our number-one demand was to tell the workers they have the right to join a union if that is what they want and to sign a neutrality agreement." The owner immediately signed the agreement, the workers signed authorization cards and on June 20, just a little over a month from when the workers first walked in the door of the center, the UE local signed a first contract with Berg. "It was amazing," said Oliva. "It is not something that happens every year, but it is one of those stories that illustrates the power that a worker center and a union can have when they work together."

THE LABORERS INTERNATIONAL UNION'S EXPERIENCE WITH WORKER CENTERS

In its efforts to organize among asbestos workers in the Washington, D.C./ Maryland labor market, the Laborers International Union (LIU) initiated a relationship with Casa Maryland, an immigrant nongovernmental organization that was also operating a worker center for day laborers. "Although this center had been there a long time," said Yanira Merino, assistant to the president of the LIU, "the locals didn't know about it, and they were shocked to see the number of immigrant workers going there and not coming to our halls." In discussions with Casa Maryland, Merino learned that the workers were going to Casa, as opposed to the union halls because the unions were asking them for documentation. Also, there were no Spanish-speakers at the halls. The organizations negotiated a relationship whereby the union agreed to provide trainers and place those workers who completed the training and had the necessary qualifications at contractors who were signatory to the union agreement. However, the plan was never fully implemented.

Merino believes that the partnership foundered on two issues. First, Casa Maryland and the union could not agree about how membership would be structured. Casa was in favor of the workers becoming members of the union while also continuing to belong and pay membership dues to the worker center. The union favored a single membership. Second, Merino believes there were issues of trust, arising out of the sharp difference in organizational cultures between the two groups that were not able to be resolved. For a time relations worsened when Casa Maryland negotiated an arrangement to provide workers to Clark Construction, one of the largest nonunion contractors in the D.C. area.

Merino, the highest ranking Latina in the LIU, herself an immigrant and organizer from El Salvador who was recruited after leading a successful union drive in her own workplace, kept an eye out for other ways of working with day laborer worker centers. The opportunity came when she learned that the National Day Laborer Organizing Network (NDLON) was planning to hold its first national conference where organizers planned to discuss whether or not to form a day laborers union. "That raised a lot of eyebrows in my union and we said there are two ways to go: either we fight this and declare they are our enemies because they were establishing themselves outside of the labor movement, or do we understand that a number of them had been denied membership in our locals and had been forced to look to this type of organizing."

In the end, the decision was made to attend the national gathering, and although at first relations between the two groups were strained, NDLON made it clear that it wanted to have good relations with unions and did not intend to set itself up as an alternative organization. "But they expressed over and over again that they wanted to work with the labor movement under specific conditions like equality . . . that when we have conversations they didn't want us to act like a big brother who wants to call all the shots." Both parties agreed that it would be a good idea to hold the next national gathering within a labor institution.

Merino brought this message back to her union and the next year, the Laborers Union helped NDLON secure the national AFL-CIO's George Meany Center in Silver Spring, Maryland, to hold the conference. The Laborers Union endorsed the conference and also made a twenty-five-thousand-dollar financial contribution to NDLON to support the cost of the gathering. When General President Terrence O'Sullivan came to speak at the convention he was warmly received by the day laborers in attendance. O'Sullivan told Merino that he could see that these were workers who were ready to organize.

The union has struggled to turn these good feelings into joint organizing campaigns on the ground. "One of the necessities the day laborers had was training. The laborers [union] have sixty-seven training centers where we train people how to put up bricks, how to remove asbestos," said Merino. "How do we merge those two? How do we come out with a plan or system that allows us to work together but not to become one, or if we do become one, how to merge without losing the good parts of each? The union has been established for a long time, we have resources. The day laborers have their will, their participation, their democracy, their activism. . . . And that is where we are now, we are still trying to figure this out."

Another example of the LIU's experience with worker centers involves poultry workers in Morganton, North Carolina. Over a period of more than a decade, the LIU, working with a powerful leadership of Guatemalan workers, had engaged in a pitched battle with Case Farms to organize a union among immigrant Latino poultry workers in rural North Carolina. The union won a certification election, but five years later it was still trying to negotiate a first contract. "We went all the way to the Supreme Court with that organizing drive," said Merino. "We won the election, they filed charges, we went to the NLRB at the regional level and then to the appeals court and then to the Supreme Court trying to assert that the workers had won the election and the company needed to be at the table in good faith."

As the years wore on without a contract, and the LIU made a decision not to pursue organizing in the food processing industry, Merino felt strongly that the union could not just pull out of Morganton. "Making that transition it was clear to me if we were to leave and not keep fighting for these workers as we had promised, we needed to do something." Kim Bobo of the National Interfaith Committee on Worker Justice proposed that the union support the establishment of a worker center. "In a way, we were already doing it," said Merino. "We were not servicing inside that plant, we would go once in a while when workers had wildcat strikes, but we were mostly paying a lawyer to deal with grievances the workers had and getting them some help with immigration and housing issues."

Bobo and Merino envisioned a center that would take on the bread-and-butter issues of the workers, but would also take on broader community issues. "Once again, my view was that the worker center could be a bridge between the workers and the union. It was helpful to the labor movement and to the workers, and it was the best way out of the situation we were in. So the laborers union decided to sponsor that, at the same time they dropped the effort to get a contract." From Merino's perspective, the workers were glad about the center and did not feel that they were being abandoned. "In the South, everywhere unions have this practice, they go and try and if it doesn't work, they leave. . . . The Laborers didn't want this perception to be there, although the leadership felt they needed to get out of there because it is not the industry they wanted to keep organizing. That is how we decided to keep sponsoring the worker center so they were serving a good purpose for the union. That was a good experience."[13]

HERE AND YOUNG WORKERS UNITED

Another positive example of a close working partnership between a worker center and a union involves the former Hotel and Restaurant workers union (HERE) and Young Workers United (YWU), a non-immigrant specific worker center founded in 2002. YWU is an organization that targets young workers, regardless of sector or industry but in 2004, the group's focus was the restaurant industry. "Our analysis is not that unions aren't organizing low-wage workers in the restaurant industry because they don't want to," said Sara Flocks, an organizer with the group.[14]

> The way the industry is structured and the way the labor laws are written it is extremely difficult to organize for traditional unions because these shops are very small, it is major corporate chains, there is really high turnover, and people are part time. For a union they have to put in the same money and staff time to organize a twenty-person shop as they do for a five-hundred-person shop in many instances.

YWU sees its role as developing new structures and strategies for organizing in industries in which unions are facing significant challenges to organize, win improvements and raise the standards in the low-wage service sector. HERE Local 2 in San Francisco donates office space in their building, administrative support to the organization, and access to the union's legal staff.

While HERE has jurisdiction over restaurants, and the local has about a thousand members in San Francisco who work in them, it has made a decision in recent years to focus all of its energies on the hotel industry. "Because of everything happening with hotels now, Local 2 has made a strategic decision about where they are putting their energy," says Flocks, "but they obviously still want to see people raising standards in this industry and keeping the restaurant industry on its toes. They have said, do as much as you can in raising standards in the industry . . . but they have certain kinds of requirements. They don't want us to get into any kind of agreements with the restaurants that would undermine their contracts, and they also don't want us to get in a situation right now where they have to come in and negotiate our contracts."

HERE has been particularly interested in YWU taking on the restaurant industry trade association which, in the wake of passage of a citywide minimum wage in 2003, tried to lobby for an exemption for the restaurant industry. The Golden Gate Restaurant Association was trying to push through a tip credit that would allow restaurants to pay subminimum wage to tipped employees, and HERE encouraged YWU to build an organization of tipped employees to fight any legislation that might be put forward. "They asked us to do this and we said okay because we also wanted to get more into organizing restaurants. We wanted to find out whether people were getting paid the minimum wage and do some enforcement," said Flocks. "So basically we discussed what our strategy would be with them and went out to build this organization and through that our current strategy developed, which is using wage claims as leverage in organizing drives in restaurants."

YWU began working with the 250 employees at the Cheesecake Factory, a national chain with a very large restaurant in San Francisco. It started with a core group of workers there who had already begun to file claims after discovering they had not been given the breaks to which they were entitled. By October 2004, YWU, with the help of Local 2's legal department, had increased to 150 the number of workers filing claims worth more than $1 million. In addition to the effort to recover back-wages, YWU and HERE worked with the Cheesecake Factory employees to write a code of conduct, similar to a union contract, that they believe can be legally binding if signed by the corporation and designates a "special master" to resolve disputes. The code of conduct includes paid breaks, holidays and sick leave, and health benefits for employees who work more than twenty hours a week with employers paying 80 percent of premiums. It provides for employees to be accompanied by "employee leaders" to disciplinary meetings and for an appeals process when disciplinary action is taken and the employee believes there is not just cause.

YWU's goal is to build up a restaurant workers' association that will transcend individual workplace campaigns and mount a citywide policy campaign, possibly for paid sick days or "just cause" termination. "We don't get frustrated with HERE not turning this into a union drive," said Flocks. "We would love to have people be in a union but it is so difficult. Even if HERE did, it doesn't have the density it has in hotels. They have these contracts that they have held onto over the years. But we are interested in seeing [that] is there a new kind of organization that allows people to have portable benefits and membership from workplace to workplace, restaurant to restaurant."

YWU believes that while HERE is at least three to five years away from engaging in any serious restaurant organizing, its relationship with the union could evolve in a number of different directions over that period. "We have time to think about what our long-term relationship with them will be," says Flocks. "But there are a lot of different possibilities that range from affiliating with them, to becoming another local under HERE to spinning off an independent workers association and keeping our IRS 501(c)(3) status as Young Workers United." The organization is optimistic about the possibility that the union would come in and organize for representation building on the momentum of codes of conduct campaigns, and then perhaps turn over responsibility for day-to-day representation to it. "There are a lot of possibilities, and we are excited that we have this big ally," said Flocks.

CREATING INDEPENDENT UNIONS

While the foregoing examples illustrate the attempts of some worker centers to develop relationships with existing unions in order to advance economic action organizing strategies, other centers have sought to pioneer the creation of independent unions. This is most often the case among workers for whom a union does not already exist, such as cab drivers, or where existing unions are often reluctant to organize, such as small grocery stores.

The New York Taxi Workers Alliance

Historically, the American taxi industry has been notoriously difficult to unionize into traditional unions. However, the fact that industry structures, fares, and lease costs are set by public regulatory bodies presents important opportunities for organizing and some worker centers are having success in organizing drivers and mobilizing them to alter public policies.

In 2004, the New York Taxi Workers Alliance culminated a successful two-year campaign to win a fare increase for Yellow Cab drivers. It has managed to build an impressive organization of workers despite the large-scale restructuring of the industry in 1979 that established a leasing system and reclassified drivers as independent contractors. "We're a membership based organization. We're an advocacy group. Our drivers see us as a union. Technically because we're independent contractors we're not supposed to be union, but hey, there are many structures to unions besides what the AFL-CIO has in 2003," said Kevin Fitzpatrick, long-time driver and leader of the alliance.[15]

On March 30, 2004, the Yellow Cab drivers of New York City won an unprecedented 26 percent fare increase from the City of New York. It was the first fare increase in eight years. Most press coverage was sympathetic toward the cabbies as were many elected officials. In fact, during their deliberations, members of the Taxi and Limousine Commission (TLC) spoke repeatedly of the need for drivers to be able to earn a livable wage.[16] The current purchase price of a New York City medallion is about $400,000, placing ownership out of the reach of many drivers. As a result, fewer than 20 percent of those driving cabs own their medallion and taxi cab. The majority of drivers are lease drivers, who make either daily or weekly payments toward the use of the medallion, the taxicab, and fuel costs. A study conducted by the Brennan Center, which included extensive driver surveys, found that "it is not uncommon for drivers to spend 6 to 7 hours of a 12 hour shift paying off the significant deficit incurred daily from the lease cost." Salaries average twenty-five thousand dollars a year.

The leasing system that was put in place by the city council in 1979 transformed the industry. Under the old "commission" system, drivers were hired by medallion owners as regular, salaried employees who worked regular shifts and received wages, health insurance, vacation pay, sick leave, and had access to unemployment insurance if laid off. Under the new system, "the economic risk associated with operating a taxicab shifted from medallion owners to the drivers themselves. Medallion owners' profits were no longer dependent on the accumulation of fares because the owners imposed fixed leasing costs, ensuring a steady profit stream regardless of actual income from fare collection." Seven years after the deregulation of the industry, while medallion owners were earning 73 percent more on average, most drivers had seen their wages decline by 23 percent per hour, their benefits vanish, and their average work days increase by 15 percent.

Under the new system taxi drivers went from employees to independent contractors, so although they are often perceived as small businessmen and -women, their low wages and lack of benefits reveal them more accurately to be low-wage workers embedded in a subcontracting relationship. When the drivers were reclassified as independent contractors they also suffered a loss in terms of organizing and collective bargaining rights. As independent contractors, drivers are not covered under the National Labor Relations Act, which means that they have no legal recourse when owners attempt to block organizing activities or engage in unfair labor practices such as the termination of leasing arrangements. The shift in industry structure coincided with a shift in the demographic makeup of the industry toward immigrants from Asia (62 percent), the Caribbean (13 percent), Africa and the Middle East (7 percent).[17] "Basically we are a driver advocacy group," said Rizwan Raja, one of the Organizing Committee members.[18] "We cannot legally be a union because drivers are independent contractors, but we actually do everything a regular union can do. I tell them it is a union and we are for the drivers, and we are trying to change working conditions of the cab industry."

During the campaign for the fare increase, the alliance documented and publicized the financial hardships endured by most drivers and mobilized thousands of them for rallies, demonstrations, and hearings before the City Council and the TLC. Just as remarkable as the achievement of the fare increase has been the creation of a stable organization for cab drivers in New York City. Organizing the industry has always been a struggle. Since the 1900s, the Transit Workers Union, the United Mine Workers, the Taxi Workers Union led by Harry Van Arsdale, and the Service Employees International Union all initiated various union drives.[19] SEIU Local #3036 continued to have some fleet garages under contract even after leasing was allowed in 1979 but the last vestiges of unionization in the taxi industry disappeared in the late eighties.

The New York Taxi Workers Alliance was born independently of the established labor movement. The Leased Drivers Coalition (LDC) was started in 1992 out of the Committee Against Anti-Asian Violence (CAAAV), a pan-Asian organization that was begun by young Asian activists in New York City in the 1980s to create an organized voice for Asian immigrant rights.[20] CAAAV initially turned its attention to the taxi industry in response to violent attacks on immigrant drivers and had not intended to organize a separate cab drivers' organization, but over time that is what happened. Led by Bhairavi Desai, a fiery and talented first-generation young Indian woman, the organization ended up building relationships with some of the already existing ethnically based organizations among cab drivers and creating the LDC, an individual membership-based group of about seven hundred drivers that took on both safety and wage issues.

In 1997, the LDC split off from CAAAV, renamed itself the New York Taxi Workers Alliance, and rebuilt a membership base from scratch. The split was precipitated by differences between the staff and leadership of CAAAV and the LDC over issues of direction and accountability. LDC wanted to go beyond advocacy to building a mass membership organization of cab drivers.[21] Rather than answering to the staff and board of CAAAV, it wanted the organization to be governed by a board of taxi drivers. Despite its split from CAAAV, the alliance has not lost its racial justice focus. It has continued to place its work within the context of immigrants' rights and to link to broader social justice issues. It was the first labor organization to take a position against the Iraq War and organized sizeable antiwar rallies of its members.

Since 1997, the organization has built a membership base of more than five thousand drivers.[22] It first demonstrated its ability to lead concerted economic action in 1998 when drivers struck in response to drastic policies promulgated by Mayor Giuliani to quadruple fines on drivers and make it much easier for them to have their licenses revoked. "I thought, well, if we have 60 percent of the drivers off the road it's going to be a very successful strike," Kevin Fitzpatrick remembered. "In fact, 94 percent of the drivers didn't work that day. It was the most successful strike in taxi history." But while the strike was a success in terms of driver participation, it took some time before the alliance was able to achieve concrete changes in policy.

Over the next few years, the organization succeeded in softening some of the harshest rules and getting out the drivers' point of view in the media on issues like refusal of service. After a high-profile case involving the actor Danny Glover speaking out against drivers' frequent refusal to pick up African Americans, the alliance did not shirk the issue. It organized press conferences, appeared at public hearings and directly engaged the issue of refusal of service with leaders of the black community, at once asserting its opposition to the practice as well as explaining why drivers were doing it. It established itself with the media as well as the relevant governmental bodies as the leading voice of Yellow Cab drivers in New York City.

In 2002 and 2003, the organization developed a multi-pronged strategy to campaign for a wage increase. It partnered with the Brennan Center to produce research reports on wages and conditions in the industry, which provided the organization with a great deal of data to back up its claims to the media and government officials. By the time it began threatening to strike in the fall of 2003, the alliance had the attention of the major media, the City Council, and the TLC. Over the next several months, it was the major voice of taxi drivers in the media and the major player on the drivers' side that negotiated the fare increase.

As successful as it has been on the policy side, the alliance is still evolving as an organization and still working to develop a strategy for fully consolidating a union model within the context of the current industry structure. Desai and others have not decided whether to put all of their efforts into a return to the commission system, and they are not certain that it is something their members want. As difficult as the wages and working conditions have become, many drivers identify as small businessmen and -women; in addition, independent contractor status gives the large number of undocumented workers in the industry an ability to work without facing as many risks regarding documentation.

The KIWA Grocery Workers' Campaign

The goal of KIWA's market workers justice campaign, initiated in 2000, was to organize an independent union among the workers of Koreatown's seven grocery stores. KIWA felt that, unlike the restaurant industry in Koreatown, which was too diffuse with profit margins too low to sustain unionization, the ethnic grocery stores, with a combined profit of $100 million a year, could afford to provide benefits and pay higher wages. As with the restaurant campaign, KIWA leaders felt the best way to win was to convincingly demonstrate their power to the market owners. They decided the best way to accomplish this was to take on the largest of the ethnic markets first, and chose Assi Market for this reason. Over the years, KIWA had come into contact with many workers at Assi who complained of routinely being underpaid for the hours they worked. They had handled other cases of workers who had sustained serious injuries on the job, only to be denied the opportunity to file workers compensation and sent back to work. KIWA leaders made two other decisions early on: to organize an independent union rather than working out a partnership with an already established local, and to file for an NLRB election rather than pursuing card-check recognition.

The KIWA leadership decided to build the new Immigrant Workers' Union rather than working with the grocery workers local in Los Angeles, UFCW Local #770, because the organization had a vision of building a community-based union in Koreatown. "We have a community-based union idea as opposed to an industry-specific union idea," said Paul Lee, former organizing director.[23]

> The power of the union comes from the community. The workers are part of the community. The consumers and employers are part of the community. . . . The power not only comes from members of the union and the contract, but the ability to mobilize that community support and the public sentiment around the workers and the union. That is the idea of a community-based approach. In an industry-wide approach you line up all the employers in your industry and raise your guns. Density's also a factor for us, but it's also about "community density" and the ability to draw public opinion and support for the union and the workers.

The KIWA leadership, like a lot of worker center leaders, was critical of the politics and practices of mainstream American unions. They were excited about creating their own new type of union and disinclined to work with an existing local.

The organization felt that the UFCW lacked the knowledge of the Korean community essential to organizing a union drive. "This is an ethnic market, an ethnic employer who depends on ethnic customers—99 percent of the customers are Korean-American. It's very much part of the ethnic economy and tied to Korean economics and politics," said Lee. "Coming from the outside, you're going to have a hard time organizing the workers. Even if you hire Korean-speaking organizers and Spanish-speaking organizers, you'd have a hard time organizing the workers and winning a contract. Even if you did, it would be hard to represent the workers and renegotiate contracts and fight off whatever union-busting campaigns they do, unless you understand the ebbs and flows of the Korean community. That's why it started off independently, and the other is that the workers came to us."

Working with leaders from the Assi drive, KIWA staff painstakingly implemented the independent union idea. They drew up a constitution and put together a handbook for the Immigrant Workers' Union that offered a detailed explanation of the organizing process, including how the employer was likely to react and how union dues would work. KIWA leaders say that they met with the UFCW leaders, including the local president, made clear to them that they had no interest in organizing grocery stores outside of the ethnic enclave of Koreatown, and received the union's blessing to go forward with an independent union. However, they say that after KIWA began circulating authorization cards for a NLRB election at Assi Market in the fall of 2001, the UFCW changed its position and began circulating cards of its own. The union disputes KIWA's account of the facts. It took the position that ethnic grocery stores were a core part of the jurisdiction of the UFCW local and many in the local Los Angeles labor movement backed this position. In response to an argument about not being familiar with the community of Koreatown, local labor leaders expressed concern about KIWA's inexperience with union organizing drives and felt the organization was underestimating what it would take to win. This split within the progressive community undermined the organizing campaign.

Meetings between the two organizations were quite difficult. "We walked in and they said for us to give them the workers," said Lee. "We're open to partnership but the terms of what they presented to us were so unreasonable. They were saying that they would come in and negotiate the contract and they'd take the workers. They didn't talk about any resources they would consider putting down. They were saying: 'Why wouldn't these workers want our great benefit plan? So we'll have to negotiate the contract for you."

Well informed of the many pitfalls of following the traditional organizing approach of filing for an NLRB election, they considered following a "non-board strategy" of pushing for card check recognition of the union. But KIWA leaders decided that the NLRB election process, for their first union organizing campaign, would give them greater legitimacy in the eyes of the Korean community. KIWA hoped to tap into the Korean community's pride in the American legal system to bolster their campaign. "Given that it would be this very controversial new project and that obviously employers and the media and large business sectors of conservatives would be very much in opposition to it, the NLRB provided a way of utilizing this reverence toward the American legal system to win a union or to bring legitimacy to the fact that there is a process and right for workers to organize." KIWA's hope was that when they saw the organization working through the National Labor Relations Board process, employers would refrain from just reacting rashly and immediately firing people. But they were wrong.

The Assi campaign was extremely hard-fought. KIWA had not anticipated the sophistication of the antiunion campaign that was waged by Assi Market. "They immediately brought in a huge union-busting labor firm and delayed the election by a month and a half," said Lee. "They brought in a consultant. I think that was the one thing we hadn't quite known, to what extent these employers would go all out and how they'd put down in terms of money." Lee and the rest of the KIWA leadership were shocked that Assi had gone out of the confines of the ethnic enclave to hire one of the nation's largest and most renowned union-busting law firms. "Our experience had been that these employers get these shoddy lawyers."

For the duration of the ten-week campaign, Assi followed the textbook antiunion approach, engaging in daily captive audience speeches and one-on-one meetings with each worker. It had a lawyer going back and forth to the NLRB filing charges as well as a consultant and translator on-site full-time. Estimates in the community were that Assi spent approximately $250,000 to fight the union. While KIWA had a law firm working for it pro bono, it was less able to keep up a counter effort at the NLRB. On March 9, the campaign ended in an even split: 67 for the union and 67 against the union, with fifteen contested ballots, but the election was ultimately decided in the company's favor.

Mr. Park, one of the Korean workers who voted against the union but is now helping in a renewed union organizing effort at Assi, described the tactics the company engaged in.

I had been thinking about supporting the union, but Assi brought in people who told us that if the union comes in we'll have to pay high dues, but if they don't come in then the employer is going to treat us better and give us better benefits. About a month or two months prior to the election date the owner, Daniel Lee, would take us all out to these fancy restaurants and he would say that if we vote no on the union, then we would be helping him and in return [he] will help [us] by raising [our] wages and giving [us] benefits.[24]

Mr. Park said that he and the other Korean workers were susceptible to the Korean owner's appeals. "Myself and others when I heard promises from the employer I felt like maybe I could give the boss a chance. For a lot of Koreans because the boss is also Korean, he was earnestly convincing us. He would literally almost come to tears as he pleaded with us. He even blamed himself for the fact that things came to this point. So his pleading kind of changed our mind," Park recounted. In addition, managers tried to pit the Korean workers against the Latino workers. "He would say that KIWA was an organization that fronts for Latino workers. When the campaign first started, he would say that this is a fight between Koreans and Latino workers. With the Latino workers that were very up-front about being pro-union, I was told that Korean workers must also step forward in opposing the union." Park and most of his Korean co-workers voted solidly against the union, believing the owner's pledge that conditions would improve. But, "after the election and the union lost, everything was the same," said Park. "He didn't keep one of his promises. In fact he started harassing us more."

In July, Assi management presented no-match letters from the Social Security Administration to almost all of its Latino employees and a small group of Korean workers as well. On August 1, Assi market suspended almost all of its Latino employees and a small number of Korean workers in what KIWA regarded as an obvious case of retaliation against union supporters. According to one of the workers, "We received notice two weeks before the suspension that many of our names didn't match the administration's records and we would have to provide a new social security number. We knew that we could not do that for two reasons. First, we didn't have one, and second, if we did provide one we would portray that we were undocumented. So we just waited for the suspension." In fact, Assi Market was not compelled by the no-match notification to take action against the workers. According to the same worker: "Many of us got individual letters. The letters said that even though they're saying that our names don't match with their numbers, the employer cannot take action against the employee, not suspend or fire them. They decided to do it because they knew our condition as immigrants and they knew that we couldn't provide that information."

KIWA had not anticipated the mass suspensions and as a relatively small organization without deep pockets or a strike fund, did not have the resources to support the sixty workers. The day the suspensions began, KIWA and the IWU initiated a full-time picket line in front of Assi and organized a spirited consumer boycott in the Koreatown community. Many of the suspended workers spent all day every day for five months and most days for ten months, in front of the store. To provide financial support to workers, KIWA raised emergency funds from individuals as well as the California Wellness Foundation, Liberty Hill, the Unitarian Universalist Veatch Program at Shelter Rock, and the French American Charitable Trust. Eventually, many of the workers had to look for other jobs but some remained actively involved in the campaign.

In the winter of 2004, KIWA was in the midst of another intense organizing drive at Assi Market. It had a sizeable organizing committee of workers, including workers who were not involved the first time around, organizing staff who are former Assi employees, and a new strategy. Instead of holding another NLRB election, it planned to push for a "community election" in which workers vote in an election overseen by community leaders, or card-check recognition. Always told by workers that they were instructed by management to change the expiration dates on food, KIWA was working to deepen the consumer side of the campaign. A suit had been filed by a group of plaintiffs against Assi on food safety issues. KIWA had also assisted grassroots community activists in the organization of Healthy Fair Koreatown, a community-based organization that is mounting its own campaign on food quality, safety, and cost at Assi. In the wake of its last experience with Assi's union-busting campaign, KIWA was reconsidering the relationship between the IWU and the UFCW and had begun talks with the union about either direct affiliation or some type of joint affiliation. Although the organization was still concerned about losing control over the drive, there was greater recognition that to succeed, the organization may well need the resources and power of an international union. In 2005, KIWA kicked off a community and worker organizing campaign toward living wages and just treatment for workers employed at all seven Korean markets in Koreatown.

WORKFORCE DEVELOPMENT WITH UNION HELP

The following example illustrates a final form of economic action organizing that worker centers have undertaken—partnering with labor unions around issues of workforce development.

The fifteen-thousand-member Justice for Janitors local in Boston, which is a dynamic, immigrant-led union with limited financial resources, set up a worker center in 2003 as a "gateway for increasing participation and leadership development."[25] The Voice and Future Fund was able to raise foundation funds to develop education and training programs members wanted but the local had limited capacity to provide. Its ESL and computer classes have been very popular with members. Although a significant percentage of the industry is unionized and covered by a master contract, the industry in Greater Boston devolved a number of years ago into an overwhelmingly immigrant, overwhelming part-time workforce. Since new leadership took over the local in 2002, it has been the union's strategy to try to increase the number of full-time positions that offer health insurance. Workforce development strategies could fit in well with this goal.

In 2004, the local began working with ten employers on the Building Services Career Paths Planning Project to begin to create pathways, "of increasing skills, hours and economic rewards" for janitorial workers within the cleaning industry. The program was developed through a member-led process that included surveys and discussions with workers about what they wanted and long hours of deliberation among the leadership body of the worker center about how to structure it. Although the project is only at the planning stages, the center and employers have identified a number of potential industry pathways to better jobs. These include improvement of existing custodial jobs, going from custodial to higher-skilled building maintenance jobs, going from custodial jobs to owning small cleaning companies, going from custodian to custodial supervisor and pathways to other occupations via English classes or higher education.

The center believes that, while many of these jobs already exist, opportunities need to be provided for training and education as well as "mechanisms to make the labor market transparent and navigable" for their members to be able to access them.[26] The Boston Workforce Development Initiative requires a partnership between the union and employers, and has created the opportunity for the center to organize face-to-face meetings between the worker center leadership body and the ten participating employers. At these meetings, employers and workers talk through job quality issues and about the process through which hiring and promotion to supervisory jobs, something that has been largely mysterious to workers, is done. While the project was only at the very beginning stages when this study was being finalized, the center's intention to involve workers extensively in the development of the program and to link the workforce development to an agenda of restructuring the building services industry in Boston merits close observation.

GWC, as it contemplates the imminent expiration of the Multi-Fiber Agreement and the massive loss of jobs in Los Angeles's garment industry that are expected to result, also recently began exploring workforce development as a strategy to help workers transition to other employment.

STRENGTHS AND WEAKNESSES OF WORKER CENTERS' ECONOMIC ACTION ORGANIZING

The immigrant workers that are the subject of this study have little economic power. Given their immigration status, lack of English proficiency, the complex structures of many low-wage industries, and the fact that very few institutions have as yet been able to achieve large-scale economic improvements for them, how are we to judge the effectiveness of worker centers' economic action organizing?

In their classic work, *What Do Unions Do?*[27] Freeman and Medoff argue that unions have "two faces": a monopoly face, which corresponds to the economic power to raise wages above competitive levels, and a "collective voice/institutional response" face, which corresponds to the power to represent organized workers within firms. Although our subject is worker centers and not unions, with appropriate adjustments we can still make use of these categories to analyze and evaluate the direct economic organizing that they do.

We begin from the perspective that worker centers are not unions, not worksite-based, and do not have collective bargaining rights vis-à-vis individual employers, although some of the day laborer hiring halls do sign agreements with contractors. Also, while unions are struggling to organize workers in a wide variety of employment settings, worker centers are trying to organize workers who are embedded in firms and industries that are some of the most difficult to organize. For these reasons, by monopoly face, we will be evaluating whether or how effectively worker centers have been able to raise wages at a single company or across an industry. By collective voice/institutional response face, we will be looking at how effectively worker centers are able to develop mechanisms for worker expression within firms and within the larger context of industries and geographical labor markets.

The "Monopoly Face" of Worker Centers

As we have seen in this chapter and the previous one, worker centers are experimenting with a wide range of economic strategies for raising wages and improving working conditions. Some of the day laborer groups have had success in establishing a wage floor at day laborer workers centers, street corners, and co-ops. In Los Angeles for example, the organizations operate eight day-laborer worker centers and have an average of about 120 workers a day who seek employment. Of that number, during the busiest seasons they are able to put about 50 percent of workers to work each day. NDLON's Pablo Alvarado estimates that each hall sees between 1,500 and 2,500 individual workers per year.[28] But their abilities are limited by abundance of supply and a concomitant weakness of leverage. The old guilds and craft unions were able to build power in their labor markets by establishing a loose monopoly over a labor supply of skilled workers; if contractors refused to sign agreements, the unions could deny them access to the labor pool they needed to get their work done. Day laborers are attractive to small contractors not because of skill, but because of low wages and flexibility (you can hire them for a day at a time and don't have to take on the expense of an added employee). Given that there is an oversupply of workers, it is difficult to effectively deny contractors access to workers. In addition, while the building trades have historically engaged in coercive tactics to force workers not to undercut wage standards, the day laborer groups are philosophically opposed to doing so.

It is not clear whether craft union structures and strategies will ultimately prove successful. At the present moment, day laborer workers centers operate less like craft unions and more like humane shape-up sites. They are offering day laborers access to a community, very useful services, including help with recovering unpaid wages, rationalizing a chaotic hiring process, and establishing some expectations of the contractors who hire the workers. "Employers who come to the centers know that there is an infrastructure behind them so they don't repeat the same wage and hour violations," says Alvarado. They have been able to raise wages when there are jobs available, and Alvarado believes that the halls have attracted additional contractors and other employers who would not have gone to the corners. Still, in practice there are many instances where day laborers if they are able to find work at all, go to work for less money than the established wage floor and sometimes work fewer than eight hours a day.[29]

So far, direct public actions targeted at single employers on behalf of one or a small group of workers seem to be the most consistently effective way of reclaiming money owed. When workers engage in these tactics, employers often agree to pay the back wages. But these actions generally do little in terms of altering firm structures, raising pay scales, or changing business practices inside firms unless they are linked to an effort to create ongoing organization in a particular workplace or engage in a broader industry-wide campaign. In those instances, as we saw in the case of KIWA's restaurant campaign, individual restaurants were targeted with the larger goal in mind of using the threat of action to compel larger numbers of restaurants in Koreatown to pay minimum wage and overtime.

As the Forever 21 and Taco Bell cases demonstrate, local and national consumer boycotts, depending on the visibility of the target and the strength of the allies the center can recruit to support the campaign, can be a good way of expanding the scope of conflict, attracting public attention to an exploitative situation and compelling a company to take the first step in recognizing the worker center as an organization with which it must contend.[30]

Without a national campaign infrastructure or the resources to create it, boycotts that target large multinational corporations, even those that have become symbols for the contemporary antisweatshop movement like the Gap and Nike have proven extremely difficult to win. However, as Lee of the GWC points out, they provide important opportunities for organizational development and public consciousness-raising. In addition, these boycotts and others, such as those organized by United Students Against Sweatshops, have compelled large apparel retailers to respond. Some have agreed to "codes of conduct" and put systems in place for monitoring the working conditions of their subcontractors.

Unions like the SEIU and HERE have carefully analyzed industry structures in the health care, janitorial, and hospitality sectors and blazed new trails that have led to the organization of hundreds of thousands of low-wage workers. With some important exceptions—the New York Taxi Workers Alliance, Garment Worker Center, Restaurant Opportunities Center of New York (ROC-NY), and TWSC—even those centers that do industry-specific work often do not have the resources to engage in concerted industry analysis. While they are developing leaders and mounting creative campaigns, the volume of workers most centers organize is on a much smaller scale.

Many workers centers expressed a strong interest in labor unions, and a large number had at some point explored the possibilities for partnering, but there were very few joint campaigns taking place. There are several explanations for this. Many low-wage industries present unappealing targets for unions: they are characterized by loose labor markets, tight profit margins, subcontracting, small firm sizes, and shorter-term attachments between workers and firms. Given how difficult it is to win a union election in the United States today, the few unions that are actively organizing low-wage workers with any success are carefully choosing their targets. They mount cautious, strategic campaigns that focus on "building density" in a particular substrata of a particular industry and turn down other leads in order to concentrate their resources.

Because of the footloose nature of the garment industry, UNITE has essentially given up on garment workers and is focusing all of its efforts on Cintas. HERE by and large no longer organizes restaurants (unless they are attached to hotels or food service corporations). They focus on hotels, and within the hotel industry pursue their organizing campaigns extremely strategically, carefully targeting specific geographic areas and/or companies. They do not take on other targets. SEIU is organizing among a broad range of health care workers and has added a major campaign on security guards to its building services division (which is the home of the Justice for Janitors organizing work). But the union is very disciplined and focused with its resources and maps out its plans to move into new labor markets years ahead of time. For example, although the Building Services Department at SEIU indicated strong interest in working with the TWSC to organize janitors in northern Virginia, it told TWSC that, because of other commitments, it couldn't begin the campaign for two or three years.

The economic action organizing that worker centers are doing is much more reactive: workers walk out of their plants and into the center and want to do something immediately; a worker is injured or unjustly fired and the organization puts up a picket line. The two institutions become understandably frustrated with each other: the worker center wants the union to agree to help organize the workers, and the union wants the worker center to understand that not every "hot shop" is a good target for a union drive.

In many low-wage industries, existing union structures seem mismatched to firm structures. Efforts to build more general, craftlike unions of low-wage workers, organizations that would provide the stability and benefits that workers are not getting through their employers, seem more likely to sync with these workers, but so far, these efforts have been largely unsuccessful.

In summary, we can say that worker centers are currently struggling to fulfill "monopoly face" functions and are having only partial successes. Direct action on specific employers, especially those businesses that can be hurt by public picketing, has been successful in helping workers recover back wages, but very seldom reinstatement to the job, wage increases, or other improvements in firm-level practices. Industry-based worker centers vary widely in terms of impact: some have been successful in raising wages. However, impact has been limited to local or specialized labor markets because of the small scale of most organizing efforts.

The "Collective Voice/Institutional Response Face" of Worker Centers

Let us now turn to evaluating how effectively worker centers are able to represent workers within firms and within the larger context of industries and geographical labor markets. For Freeman and Medoff, "voice" means "discussing with an employer conditions that ought to be changed, rather than quitting the job." They contrast this to the "classic market mechanism of exit and entry which in the labor market context would mean quitting one's job or hiring new employees. Unions are the vehicles through which workers are able to have a voice as a group in communicating with management."[31] Although some have an episodically strong presence at particular worksites, most worker centers do not have a strong ongoing presence inside particular workplaces and do not aspire to.

OTOC, because it has organized majority unions in specific plants, does have the potential for ongoing structure and voice inside workplaces, but has not been satisfied with the state of UFCW Local 211's shop steward system. KIWA and the Restaurant Workers Association of Koreatown do not have worksite-level structures in place but do have the capacity to help workers develop collective voice and take action at specific restaurants at specific times. The New York Taxi Workers Alliance has ongoing structures in city garages, and the Domestic Workers Union maintains contact with domestic employment agencies. Perhaps of all the centers, the day laborer hiring halls and the role they play in placing workers with employers and negotiating with them on terms and conditions and when problems arise come the closest to some kind of on ongoing worksite presence.

The Workplace Project has occasionally had some ongoing structure at certain large employers and with unionized employers has been involved in several efforts to revamp the shop steward system and elect new worksite representatives. But in the course of this research, these were the handful of exceptions to a general rule: beyond the filing of individual wage claims on behalf of workers against specific employers, most worker centers do not represent collective voice for workers at the firm level. While the filing of a wage claim by a worker center staffer might be viewed as akin to the filing of a grievance by a union business agent, what distinguishes the two is that the union, by virtue of its collective bargaining contract, has potential for ongoing voice; the worker center has no formal agreement with employers and lacks the informal power to compensate.

It is really at the broader industry and local labor market levels that worker centers are able to represent something close to collective voice. The Workplace Project and its affiliated organization, United Day Laborers of Long Island, has created a gathering place for day laborers island-wide and in specific towns and villages. It represents a collective voice for day laborers within the larger communities in which they operate, including merchant and neighborhood associations, local government, and the media.

GWC has little ongoing presence in individual firms but organizes, offers assistance, and publicizes conditions in the Los Angeles garment district as a whole. It offers a place for garment workers to come together and speak as a collective voice to the industry, local and state government, and state and federal regulatory agencies. KIWA and RWAK have been able to play the role of a collective voice for restaurant workers. They have spotlighted abuses, negotiated with the employer's association to make improvements in standards, publicized the rise in California's minimum wage, and worked with government agencies to enforce wage, overtime, and safety standards. The New York Taxi Workers Alliance created a quasi-union entity in an industry that was considered "unorganizable" by the mainstream of organized labor after deregulation in 1979 made most drivers independent contractors.

As we will see in the next chapter, it is in the areas of advocacy and public policy change that worker centers are most effective in terms of their monopoly and collective voice/institutional response faces.

Improving the Worker Center/Labor Union Relationship

To play a role in effective, sector-specific union organizing, immigrant worker centers need more than just learning the tools of analysis and strategy that good union organizers know. They need to be connected to a larger institution that has membership and resources and can protect and support them when they are battling with employers. The best scenario would be for more of them to be in ongoing relationship with union partners who recognize their value and want to work together in a respectful, cooperative way. Unions have an established paradigm for organizing and representing workers, a capacity for industry analysis, and deep knowledge of labor law. In addition, they have experience with worksite organizing campaigns in the face of employer opposition and the financial and staff resources to support workers through organizing drives. Their membership numbers give them the political capacity and economic leverage that is essential to winning organizing campaigns.

Unions need, and can learn much from, immigrant worker centers too. Centers are mobilizing and organizing constituencies that much of the labor movement is currently unwilling or unable to organize, evolving new strategies, structures, and practices in the process. Working together with immigrant worker centers, and the communities in which they are active, can strengthen and help revitalize unions and reinvigorate organized labor as a whole. More unions need to recognize the potential inherent in such relationships and devote resources to cultivating better ties to sympathetic worker centers.

To organize on a massive scale again, the labor movement must be perceived as speaking on behalf of the whole. As labor economist Richard Freeman has shown, the American labor movement has always grown in great spurts as opposed to slow accretion.[32] It grew the most in the 1930s, during the height of popular unrest over the economic crisis. What today's unions need in order to succeed is the moral legitimacy that immigrant worker centers have demonstrated they have in their successful worksite and public policy campaigns.

Today's unions cannot easily take in new members and cannot accommodate low-wage workers who work in industries comprised of small employers and subcontractors. In order to be able to do so, organized labor needs to make room for new organizational structures of membership and affiliation. But at present, the major debates in the labor movement are unfolding over a different set of issues. The watchword of the most aggressive organizing unions today is "density." These unions believe strongly that in order to rebuild, individual international unions must focus on their core industries and work strategically and aggressively to organize them. They reject reactive organizing—disparaging the "hot shop" approach in which unions respond to shops that reach out to them whether or not they fit within the union's core industry—and stick to a proactive strategy to increase density within their industry.

Most of the worker organizing that takes place within the worker center context is "hot shop" organizing. Frustrated workers spontaneously walk out of their workplaces, or go as a group to the worker center seeking help with organizing, and they become frustrated when they are unable to find a union interested in taking them on. On the one hand, it is true that, given how difficult a union drive is to win these days, these workplaces are often not the most promising prospects for success. On the other hand, common sense would dictate that there has to be room in any labor movement to respond to hot shops because they involve workers who are at a prime moment for organizing.

Unions need have flexible approaches that enable them to initiate strategic campaigns and respond to angry workers who really want to join. Labor's arsenal must reflect the varieties of the terrain on which workers struggle—industrial strategies must not be pitted against geographic ones. Unfortunately, as discussed earlier, those unions that are the most adept at organizing in low-wage industries choose their targets with tremendous parsimony and then focus exclusively on those campaigns. This leaves out a lot of the low-wage immigrant workers who have allied themselves to worker centers. Some of these workers are at employers that might be of interest to unions if they had the time, resources, and strategic flexibility. Others work in highly competitive industries characterized by small employers and subcontractors, and are viewed as almost impossible to organize. To address this, unions need new models of organization that enable them to do for low-wage workers in decentralized industries what craft unions have traditionally done for construction workers. They need to create models of permanent organizations that bring workers into membership across a multitude of employers and provide the voice, stability, training, and access to benefits that they cannot get from their employers.

Key constituencies within the low-wage workforce have been unable to unionize within current union structures. For example, there are sizeable concentrations of day laborers in a number of cities and suburban areas, and a number of worker centers have set up hiring halls and helped to overturn anti–day labor ordinances at the local level. Yet none have evolved into union hiring halls, and so far only one or two of these day labor projects have been approached with concrete proposals to organize their members into the construction unions.

There are several reasons for this. First are the jurisdictional issues surrounding day labor. Unlike the construction unions, day laborers engage in a variety of construction-related activities. When they walk into a day labor hiring hall, workers may be sent out on a wide variety of projects. This is different than, for example, the immigrants who were successfully organized into the Roofers Union in Phoenix, who were already working for nonunion roofing contractors and could be organized into the roofers union in a straightforward way. Second, most day laborers are working in residential and small commercial construction—these are segments of the construction market that have been or have become almost entirely nonunion in most local labor markets. For unions to bring them into membership without a plan to go back into the residential and small commercial markets would mean that they would be taking on more mouths to feed without expanding the work available. Finally, asking day laborers for documentation and requiring them to enter traditional apprenticeship programs is not effective.

"There is no use bringing members into your union if you don't have work for them," said John Martini, the international president of the Roofers Union, who has strongly supported bringing day laborers into his union, organizing 65 percent of residential roofers in Las Vegas and 30 percent in Phoenix. "Everybody wants to join a union but what good is it if you don't have work for them. . . . If you have a lot of work then you can do it, but in a situation where we had one contractor signed up with us, we needed to organize workers at nonunion contractors and bring the contractors in to the union."

The local union in Phoenix has grown from fewer than thirty members to more than seven hundred by organizing immigrant day laborers in residential construction. "We never had a worker organized in residential construction until a few years ago, and everyone said it couldn't be done, but they were wrong," said Martini. "If you go out and talk to workers you find they are looking for help, they have gone on strike a few times and done things my own members haven't done." The union's approach was to target the workers at nonunion roofing contractors. In house visits with groups of workers, organizers learned about the workers' problems with being underpaid for their work and helped them to file a class-action lawsuit against one of the contractors. In the end, the lawsuit was settled by the contractor who agreed to pay workers the wages owed and to sign a contract with the roofers union. "We have organized three or four contractors in Arizona the same way," said Martini. "Two we threatened with lawsuits and they signed on. Some were underpaying, cheating workers out of their rightful fees, charging for safety equipment—if they wrecked a truck they had to pay for it—all kinds of things."

In both cities, Martini's local unions worked with affiliates of Interfaith Worker Justice to bring area clergy into an alliance in support of organizing. "I know they are undocumented," says Martini. "You couldn't build a house in Texas, Arizona, or Southern California without undocumented workers—the whole thing would fall apart. . . . But that is not my business. If they are out there working they deserve to be treated fairly."

Finally, some construction locals have demonstrated anti-immigrant biases that found expression in opposition to the opening of day laborer centers. For example in 1993, IDEPSCA ran into difficulties with the IBEW and the Operating Engineers. The organization had identified an empty lot north of the 210 Freeway and worked out an arrangement with the City of Pasadena to put up a trailer that would operate as a loose hiring hall. "The unions went berserk," Raul Anorve recalled. "They claimed we were in competition with them and that by establishing a day laborer center between these two buildings we were undermining their efforts to organize."

The two unions ended up suing the local American Friends Service Committee (AFSC), which had been acting as IDEPSCA's fiscal agent, on the grounds that the trailer didn't meet building standards and were ultimately successful in intervening in the zoning process to stop the project. "I think the unions are a force to reckon with," said Anorve. "I know the history of unions, I studied them and I know they have done some good work, but on a practical level in dealing with us who organize the most disenfranchised in our society, they don't seem too open."[33]

Taxi drivers, considered to be independent contractors in most cities and thus excluded from coverage under the National Labor Relations Act, have been for the most part considered to be off-limits by unions for this reason, despite intermittent interest and activity on the part of groups of drivers. The New York Taxi Workers Alliance decided to organize cab drivers despite their being contractors, and they make clear that they consider themselves a union no matter what the National Labor Relations Board might say. Just as SEIU is now moving into organizing security guards, who for years were thought to be unorganizable, there needs to be similar efforts in other areas.

In addition to these structural tensions, there are issues of traditional union culture: unions often do not translate contracts into other languages, have shop stewards who speak Spanish, understand the vast differences between Spanish-speaking communities, and know immigration law. While these union practices are obviously problematic, other culture clashes between unions and worker centers are more constructively understood as misunderstandings. For example, IDEPSCA, on discovering that workers at their Kal Kan company ESL classes were unionized, decided to have everyone read the union contract as a text for teaching literacy. Expecting the union to respond enthusiastically to this idea, it was instead viewed as a hostile act by local union officials. They felt that IDEPSCA, in focusing on the written contract, was attempting to foster a literal interpretation of what was written there and stir up trouble with members. IDEPSCA was astounded by the union's angry reaction to what the organization considered to be an act of solidarity.

As we saw in this chapter, unions, based on years of experience, usually have a set way of going about union organizing campaigns. But these approaches, as was the case with OTOC and the UFCW, can sometimes make immigrant activists who bring their own organizing traditions with them from their home countries feel that there is no room for their own ideas and approaches. These activists often feel that unions are too formulaic and too top-down in their decision-making structures. The most common complaint I heard from many worker centers was that they could not get unions to engage with them—phone calls and letters went unanswered.

A certain percentage of the workers that go to worker centers are union members seeking help because they feel their union is not providing it or because they are dissatisfied with the shop steward at their place of employment. Centers take many of these cases on, contacting the union on the worker's behalf and helping groups of workers to learn their rights and organize to elect new shop stewards. Unions feel that the worker centers always assume that these workers are right and also perceive the centers to be meddling inappropriately in their internal business.

This lack of trust between the parties can result, as it has in the case of SEIU, Local 32BJ, and the Workplace Project, in a total unwillingness on the part of the union to work with the worker center. This in spite of the fact that the center could have been a very valuable resource for the union's janitorial organizing drive on Long Island. Unions need to be sophisticated enough, as they are in so many other relationships, to work with worker centers on campaigns and is-

IMPROVING UNION/WORKER CENTER RELATIONSHIPS

The first step in moving forward is to sponsor national, regional and local dialogs between worker centers and unions. These will enable both sides to hear more about how each approach their work, visit each other's headquarters and tour each other's projects. It will help identify the tensions that exist, create a set of guiding principles and ground-rules for working together and most importantly, to look for concrete projects on which to partner. What follows is a set of suggestions about what those projects might be:

- Development of an ongoing system of communications between worker centers and unions, perhaps identifying liaison people who will take responsibility to trouble-shoot when necessary, perhaps creating an organizing committee where worker center and union organizers would meet jointly to share the status of their campaigns, see how they can help each other and explore joint work

- Organizing reciprocal local and regional tours and discussions between day laborer organizers and leaders with construction union organizers and leaders where in-depth orientation and discussion about the operation of hiring halls could take place

- Seats on central labor councils for worker centers as some CLC's have begun doing for Jobs with Justice and ACORN

- CLC's and local unions sharing space and other kinds of administrative and legal support with worker centers targeting key industries or employers

- Leadership and organizing schools, such as those that are put on by university labor centers, that include union and worker center leaders so that they can develop relationships directly, share information and strategies and push each other on issues like dues and union models, in the case of the worker centers, and leadership development in the case of the unions

- Joint training sessions between worker centers and unions on labor and immigration law so that unions feel that worker centers are more steeped in labor law and worker centers feel that unions are more steeped in immigration law especially with regard to the rights of immigrant members whose status is challenged

- Expanding the NELP and National Low-wage Worker Task Force list serves or replicating them at the local level so that organizations can get answers to their questions in real time, coordinating legal strategies and sharing legal resources at the local level including those that are union-based, especially with regard to cases that might be precedent-setting either with respect to labor or immigration law

- To promote reciprocity and improve relations, a formal commitment to joint solidarity work similar to the Jobs with Justice pledge: worker centers supporting union drives and unions supporting worker center campaigns

- Shared research and structured deliberation about targeting low-wage immigrant industries for organizing, anticipating the issues that are likely to come up, brainstorming the structures for organizing, membership and representation that stand the best chance of success

- Local construction unions taking day laborers into their membership, working out ways to deal with questions of documentation, language and education requirements in the apprenticeship programs

- Cooperative development of ideas for new union structures of membership and representation that can more fruitfully accommodate low-wage immigrant workers who are working for sub-contractors or more frequently moving between jobs.

- Include repeal of Hoffman and multi-employer bargaining in Employee Free Choice Act and other pro-organizing legislation. Single employer and single establishment bargaining are of little value to the many low-wage workers who work in small, scattered worksites or for employers in highly competitive industries. To raise their wages and improve working conditions, these workers need multi-employer bargaining on a geographic/industrial, or chain of production/ business network basis.
- Cooperating on the design and implementation of a joint organizing drive. Developing a set of principles, clear governance structure, organizing model, division of labor and time-line for organizing a set of workers into an existing local which includes a dues-sharing arrangement, specific steps the local will take regarding leadership development and on-going representation (putting a shop steward structure into place, etc.)
- The national AFL-CIO or international unions giving local union charters to a worker center, or a worker center industry-specific project as a new local, explore relationships with Working America
- Working together on strengthening minimum wage and overtime enforcement and monitoring via legislation and creating coalitions with government agencies
- Working together on immigration reform including federal and state legislative issues such as amnesty, driver's licenses, student financial aid and in-state tuition

sues of common concern even as they are dealing with tensions in other areas of their relationship. They also need to recognize that the worker centers, unlike some other progressive organizations, come out of a different history and conceptual framework. They are not automatically going to defer to the unions just because they are larger and more established.

Worker centers also need to do more to avoid polarizing the situation; when workers come with problems with their union, the centers need to recognize that the individual worker is not always right and the union always wrong. They also need to acknowledge that in many cases, unions are not losing because they are stupid or bad at what they do, but because the laws are completely stacked against them. They need to recognize that unions often know more than they do about labor law and union organizing and that they need that kind of help in order to win organizing drives. Independent union organizing efforts, such as KIWA's immigrant workers union effort among grocery workers in Koreatown, reinforce a union perception that worker centers are sometimes overconfident about their ability to succeed where unions fail and insufficiently prepared for the level of opposition they encounter in organizing drives.

CHAPTER 7

PUBLIC POLICY ENFORCEMENT AND REFORM

Worker centers are struggling to enforce standards, raise wages, and improve working conditions in low-wage industries and to normalize the immigration status of the workforce. As discussed previously, they do this in part by bringing direct economic pressure to bear on employers and industries and in part through campaigns to influence and change public policy. In this chapter and the next, we turn to this other component of advocacy and organizing work.

Worker centers' public policy organizing and advocacy takes a variety of forms. They include partnering with government agencies to enforce existing labor laws and regulations, working with them to strengthen compliance and improve enforcement, and organizing for the passage of new legislation to raise wages and improve working conditions of low-wage workers. In general, worker centers and other contemporary low-wage worker organizing projects have had their greatest impact on wage enforcement and raising wages through government action and local and state public policy initiatives. These campaigns will be discussed in the present chapter. In the next, we will look at centers' advocacy and organizing work aimed at defending or expanding the rights of immigrants and other people of color and waging other campaigns that promote a broad "social justice" agenda.

FEDERAL AND STATE LABOR LAWS AND THE LOW-WAGE WORKER

The primary regulatory foundation for the economic rights of the working poor (including undocumented workers) is the Fair Labor Standards Act of

1938 and state wage and hour laws. The FLSA abolished child labor in manufacturing, guaranteed a minimum wage, and established the forty-hour workweek as the national norm. But the FLSA was the product of compromise between New Deal liberals and a powerful conservative southern power bloc. As a result, it was a limited reform that pegged the minimum wage to the low-paying southern textile and lumber industries and excluded agriculture, domestic service, retail, and the restaurant trades from coverage.

Over the years, the FLSA has been intermittently amended—coverage has been expanded to previously excluded occupations,[1] and the minimum wage has been raised many times to its current level of $5.15 per hour, but it is no longer enough to lift workers out of poverty.[2] In addition, the FLSA only covers businesses whose annual gross volume of sales made or business done is not less than $500,000 and that put goods into the stream of interstate commerce. On this precarious foundation nothing else of comparable effect has ever been built. The FLSA, passed almost seventy years ago, and contoured to an economy that has undergone profound transformation, is still the signature statute on which the hopes of millions rest.

At the federal level, there are a number of ways in which the minimum wage requirement of the FLSA is enforced. First, a worker or group of workers who have not received minimum wage or overtime pay can sue the employer for their unpaid back wages and an equal amount in liquidated damages (double the amount owed). Second, the Wage and Hour Division (WHD) of the Department of Labor can inspect a firm's payroll records and sue the employer for unpaid back wages, overtime, and liquidated damages if FLSA violations are found. Third, the secretary of labor can levy a fine of up to a thousand dollars per violation against employers that "willfully" or repeatedly flout minimum wage and overtime requirements. Fourth, the Department of Justice can bring criminal cases against employers, but this is rarely done. In the end, most enforcement of the FLSA is carried out through inspections by the Wage and Hour Division and lawsuits brought by the Department of Labor, which settles most claims out of court.[3]

Even though, owing to the growth of the workforce and the expansion of coverage, the number of firms and workers covered by the FLSA has grown, enforcement resources of the Wage and Hour Division have become, in the words of one analyst, "steadily more inadequate throughout its existence."[4] The number of investigators per thousand covered employees has consistently declined. In 1939 it was 0.05, while in 1988 it fell to about 0.01. As a result the share of firms that WHD inspected fell from 9 percent in 1947 to 2 percent in 1979 and 1987. Throughout its history, WHD has initiated most investigations in response to worker complaints (as opposed to initiating them without a specific complaint from a worker).[5] Thus while the system is premised on workers bringing complaints, immigrant workers and low-wage workers, in general, are often either too fearful to do so or unaware of their rights.

Most states have their own wage laws as well as state-level departments of labor, which sometimes also have procedures in place for workers to bring unpaid wage and overtime complaints. Some states also have minimum wages higher than the federal minimum wage. State laws are very important for immigrant workers because the FLSA, which only covers businesses that put goods into the stream of interstate commerce or have gross sales of $500,000 or more, does not cover many of those working for smaller employers. The division of labor between the federal WHD offices in states and the state departments of labor varies from state to state, but often a worker center can choose between the two agencies in terms of filing a complaint where they feel the case has the best chance. Some state attorney generals' offices also have labor law enforcement divisions, and this provides another avenue for centers to pursue cases.

The Sisyphean task of compelling enforcement of the FLSA and state labor laws has fallen in no small measure to worker centers and other community-based organizations. The centers' relationships with workers mean they frequently hear about egregious problems with employers. The trust they have earned means workers are more willing to file cases through their legal clinics. Center staff and volunteers walk workers through the wage claims process, help them file claims, gather evidence, and appear at hearings.

Through the cases they file every day in their legal clinics and the impact litigation they pursue, and through their public policy advocacy and organizing, worker centers are making a real difference for their constituents. In Illinois, California, New York, and the eighty communities in which they currently operate, centers have worked closely with government agencies to make industry monitoring more effective and streamline the process of filing wage claims. They have lobbied for legislation to increase the number of wage and hour inspectors, and to double the fines on repeat violators.

In addition to the FLSA and state wage and hour laws, worker centers attempt to make use of a range of other labor and employment laws. The centers help workers (who are often told they are not eligible for coverage) file workers' compensation claims.[6] Many centers work closely with the federal Equal Employment Opportunity Commission (EEOC) and its state counterparts and have filed numerous lawsuits under Title VII of the Civil Rights Act of 1964, which prohibits discrimination on the basis of race, sex, national origin, religion, or disabilities.

Worker centers have also made use of the Age Discrimination in Employment Act of 1967 and the Americans with Disabilities Act of 1990. But employers have repeatedly tried to seek court rulings that exempt undocumented workers from coverage, and some courts have ruled in their favor. In 1998, the Fourth Circuit Court of Appeals held that an undocumented job applicant was not covered by Title VII because he was not eligible to be employed in the United States. In 2001, the Fourth Circuit also ruled that a Mexican national applying for a job via the H-2A guest worker program was not protected by the Age Discrimination in Employment Act.[7] States covered by the Fourth Circuit (Maryland, Virginia, West Virginia, and North and South Carolina) are constrained by these rulings, but not the rest of the country. In spite of these rulings, worker centers continue to bring cases under Title VII and these other laws. The Mississippi Workers Center for Human Rights, for example, works to identify cases of racial discrimination and use the Title VII framework to mount organizing campaigns and legal challenges against employers in the healthcare, poultry, manufacturing, and retail industries including Tyson Foods, the University of Mississippi Medical Center and Wal-Mart.

All centers make use of the Occupational Health and Safety Act of 1970, which requires employers to provide safe and healthy working conditions. Often centers find that safety violations march hand in hand with racial and ethnic discrimination, when workers of color and immigrants are more likely to be placed in harm's way. Those who work with agricultural workers make use of the Migrant and Seasonal Agricultural Worker Protection Act (AWPA) of 1983, which requires employers to provide advance disclosure of work terms and conditions, compliance with work arrangements and wage obligations, transportation and housing safety, and licensing of farm labor contractors. Many agricultural worker centers have used AWPA to bring charges against contractors.

The centers also utilize the National Labor Relations Act (NLRA) of 1937 to assist workers who are fired for engaging in concerted action—when two or more employees act together to protest an unfair job condition. The language in the act can provide rights to private-sector workers even when there is no union or formal labor organization. However as discussed in chapter 1, the NLRA has become significantly less effective in protecting the right to organize, and the Supreme Court has ruled that while undocumented immigrants have the same rights they have fewer remedies under the Act than other workers.

In the Hoffman Plastics decision in 2002, the Supreme Court held that undocumented workers were not entitled to the remedy of back pay under the NLRA.[8] For a short period, after the Hoffman decision, the EEOC rescinded its guidance on remedies available to undocumented workers but then issued a statement reaffirming its commitment to protecting undocumented workers from discrimination. In September 2002, it settled a $1.5 million sexual harassment and discrimination complaint brought by a worker center and its legal allies on behalf of a group of immigrant workers, some of whom were undocumented, with DeCoster Egg Farms in Maine.

Many labor and employment laws are increasingly mismatched to the structure of the contemporary postindustrial economy. Most American labor-market, social insurance, and labor law policies at the federal and state levels passed in the 1930s were premised on assumptions about structures of employment and employment relations that have changed enormously, especially for low-wage workers, and have increasingly become less relevant for many white-collar workers as well. These New Deal–era programs and labor laws assumed long-term, stable employment at a single firm.

Today, workers move between employers more frequently and many are not able to access health benefits, pensions, and job training through their employers. In addition, while the total number of firms has grown, average firm size has shrunk, in part because of the growth of subcontracting, which means that while there are more workplaces to be monitored and inspected than ever before, fewer resources are available with which to carry it out. It is not uncommon for federal and state departments of labor to have four or five inspectors who are expected to cover hundreds of thousands of workplaces. Furthermore, penalties for breaking the law are minimal.

The National Labor Relations Act was also premised on the assumption of a long-term stable relationship between a worker and her employer, and it was tailored to a fairly large, industrial workplace. Today's reality is that millions of workers in the new economy find it difficult to organize a union under its provisions. In addition to the fact that an extremely high level of employer opposition is tolerated, there is the same structural mismatch between the approach to union organizing specified by the Act and the approach that makes sense for workers in the low-wage economy.

The NLRA, like social insurance policies, was designed with large, stable employers and worksites in mind, which unions, it was presumed, would organize and bargain with on a single-employer basis. But many low-wage workers have small and diffuse worksites, and they are employed by businesses in highly competitive industries who very often cannot act on their own to raise wages and improve working conditions because they would be at a severe competitive disadvantage. In these situations, low-wage workers need multi-employer bargaining on a "geographic/occupational, geographic/industrial, or chain-of-production/business network basis."[9] As we will see, mismatches between the structure of the economy and the structure of labor and employment policies condition the terrain on which worker centers and unions act and the strategies they choose.

PARTNERING WITH GOVERNMENT TO ENSURE ENFORCEMENT OF EXISTING LAWS AND REGULATIONS

In some powerful cases, worker centers have found it possible to develop partnerships with federal and state governmental officials and agencies in their efforts to ensure that existing labor and employment laws and regulations are fully and fairly enforced to the benefit of low-wage workers. The following three examples demonstrate the variety and range of these partnerships.

Omaha Together One Community (OTOC) and the "Workers Bill of Rights"

It is arguable that the union organizing drive of the Omaha meatpacking industry would never have been possible were it not for an unusually strong intervention by the state's Republican leadership. Indeed when OTOC began its work by calling attention to conditions in area meatpacking plants in 1997 and 1998, it faced formidable odds. The organization was up against a very powerful industry, a deeply conservative city power structure, a Republican-controlled state government, and a daily newspaper that had been editorializing against the organization from the day it came to town.

In one early action in 1997 by OTOC congregations and their emerging base of immigrant workers, Omaha city council candidates were asked to commit to holding hearings on the industry if elected. The next day, the editorial page of Omaha's only daily paper, the *World Herald* thundered, "Where's the Beef?" arguing that wages and working conditions in the meatpacking industry were set by the laws of supply and demand, not government regulation, and that the city council should not intervene.

After two years of several hard-hitting exposés and public actions, Governor Mike Johanns, a second-term Republican, agreed to launch a probe of the meatpacking industry. "I'm not accusing anyone of anything," he said, "but the claims made in my judgment are serious claims and . . . remind us of the days when workers worked in an atmosphere of involuntary servitude."[10] Johanns appointed his lieutenant governor and labor commissioner to conduct the investigation. The two were charged with visiting the plants, talking with community groups, meeting with workers, and then reporting back to the governor on what they had seen.

In the summer and fall of 1999, Lieutenant Governor David Maurstad made a number of scheduled and unscheduled visits to plants and held a series of offsite meetings with meatpackers from each of the large plants, organized by OTOC. After the four-month probe, Maurstad presented his findings in a report to the governor in which he documented unsafe and unsanitary working

conditions, abusive language and discrimination by supervisors, and inadequate training and communication of company policy. One of his greatest concerns, Maurstad told the *Lincoln Journal Star,* was that workers were not willing
to take their complaints to regulatory agencies. "We need to assure them," he
said, "that you're protected if you complain."[11]

In January 2000, Governor Johanns issued a ground-breaking "Workers Bill
of Rights." It included, "the right to organize, the right to a safe workplace, the
right to adequate facilities and the opportunity to utilize them . . . the right to
adequate information . . . the right to existing state and federal benefits and
rights, the right to compensation for work performed and the right to seek state
help." He asked that each plant post the Bill of Rights and asked the legislature
to create a new position within the state department of labor of meatpacking
industry worker rights coordinator. In February, the conservative Republican
said the following to the *Lincoln Journal Star:* "My preference is always that industry self-regulate and that government steers clear, but if that is not happening, my recommendation is that we set, in the form of regulations, what the
workplace should look like and proceed to enact and enforce them." At a meeting that same month organized by OTOC and covered by the *Journal,* Johanns
"urged workers to organize and promised to stand with them if they encounter
reprisals at work."[12]

As discussed in chapter 6, working together OTOC and the UFCW reopened
the union organizing question in Omaha. They have had some major successes
organizing in the meatpacking industry—something that was unthinkable for
many years. Donna MacDonald, the local UFCW president believes that Johanns's support was critical to the successes that have been achieved. "It actually gave workers the courage to come forward . . . knowing they had laws behind them. Governor Johanns said, 'Yes, we need to do something for the
packinghouse workers,' . . . telling the people, 'I'm the governor of your state
and you have the right to organize.'"

MacDonald says that all of the plants, even the notoriously antiunion Nebraska Beef, have posted the meatpacking Bill of Rights. However, given the
weaknesses of contemporary labor law, there are limits to what even having the
support of your governor can do. Asked whether workers have been fired by
employers during organizing drives since the Bill of Rights was promulgated,
MacDonald replied: "Always, in every campaign."

CIWA and the Office of Low-Wage Industries

During state budget hearings in 2000, four worker centers in low-wage industries in Los Angeles came together to create a unique coalition, the Coalition of

Immigrant Worker Advocates (CIWA).[13] Its mission was to advance labor law enforcement in the targeted low-wage industries of garment, restaurant, ethnic market, day labor, domestic, and janitorial work. As Lilia Garcia of the Maintenance Cooperation Trust Fund described it, "We all identified similar complaints and frustrations with the regulatory agencies and similar challenges our workers were facing. What was common in low-wage immigrant industries was non-established employers who were flight risks, workers who were monolingual Spanish-speaking with high illiteracy even in their native language, and no presence of enforcement in these industries. Yet, we were trying to make these agencies work for these industries."[14]

Garcia and other worker center directors found that too often, when it came to trying to claim more resources for enforcement, their industries were often pitted against each other in meetings with labor department officials on enforcement issues. With CIWA, they began to speak as a united front. Over the next two years, CIWA worked to develop a series of specific recommendations on changes in labor law enforcement and to forge close working partnerships with key actors within the state labor bureaucracy.

From its inception, CIWA took forceful public action in support of budget increases for the enforcement division of the state Department of Industrial Relations. Garcia recounted the coalition's early work in this regard. "We all testified at senate hearings in 2000 and held a significant action outside of Governor Davis' office . . . where we refused to leave until they agreed not to cut the budget for these enforcement agencies . . . which are the only light of hope that most of these workers have in these industries." This was an unusual step for advocates who were often mistrustful of government agencies, and one that was appreciated by the California secretary of labor, who initiated a closer working relationship.

The coalition's first significant accomplishment was the state secretary of labor's establishment of a low-wage worker advisory board, which was made up of CIWA's member organizations. The advisory board met quarterly with the labor secretary advising him on enforcement issues. In addition, CIWA began to work quite closely with Henry Huerta, senior deputy labor commissioner and a twenty-four-year veteran of labor standards enforcement in California. Huerta began managing the Wage Claim Adjudication Office in downtown LA in 1996 and then went on to manage a Bureau of Field Enforcement unit in Southern California. He became a key ally in CIWA's efforts to improve enforcement. "I tried to work with them . . . to develop a better working relationship between advocacy groups and the agency because traditionally it had been very hostile. . . . Some things were attitudinal. Investigators were putting the burden on low-wage immigrant workers to complete their claims without considering the level of education and the workers' fear of dealing with a government agency."[15]

Huerta also believed that state inspectors, caught in a dysfunctional system that made it impossible to sensibly prioritize, were saddled with huge caseloads compared to their federal counterparts. "If you ask people in any federal wage and hour office in California how many cases they work on a yearly basis they will say between forty and fifty. Ask a deputy labor commissioner in the State Labor Commissioner's office how many cases they work on, and it is two to three hundred. Do the math, it is not possible to do an adequate job, to work that many cases."

Huerta worked with CIWA to implement a number of changes that included the development of publications such as *Los Derechos de Trabajadores* in an easy-to-read format and a partnership with the groups around workers' rights training and education. Huerta believed that his efforts to work with advocates and listen to their suggestions paid off. "We started seeing better claims come in to the office, workers were more educated on how to handle their complaints through the process, and they had more success in proving their claims."

State officials and CIWA had another common self-interest: tax fraud. As Huerta saw it,

Sometimes we as a society look at the workers as the problem, we say they are the ones undercutting wages, working for cash, not reporting their income, setting lower standards, and taking good jobs away from working people, but we have to flip this over. We are targeting the wrong people. We need to look at those that are undercutting legitimate operators, not paying their proper taxes, and in reality are not playing on a level field with those that are complying with all statutory requirements. This is not only a worker issue, but a societal issue, and a legitimate employer issue.

Lilia Garcia, whose Maintenance Cooperation Trust Fund had been set up by unionized employers in the janitorial industry to abolish illegal practices by nonunion employers that were giving them an unfair advantage in the marketplace, agreed. "Workers are used to create an unfair advantage for employers . . . when you have worker exploitation you have an unlevel playing field created as well as serious tax fraud at a time when public funds are so scarce." Both Garcia and Huerta cited similar statistics: $3 billion lost to the state of California due to employer tax fraud, $1 billion in Los Angeles County alone due to employers operating in an underground economy in which payroll taxes were not deducted.

The efforts of CIWA and its allies in state government got a significant boost in June 2001 when the California Works Foundation released a damning study documenting the radical decline in enforcement of state labor laws. The study found that as of 2000, the Division of Labor Standards Enforcement, the agency charged with primary responsibility for enforcement of state labor laws, had a 36 percent lower ratio of inspectors to the working population than it had in 1980. While the number of workers in California had gone from 7.6 million in 1970 to 16.2 million in 2000, the ratio of inspectors per million workers had gone down. In 1970, there were 29.1 inspectors per million workers, while in 2000, there were 26.7.

The Bureau of Field Enforcement made 19 percent fewer investigations in 2000 than ten years earlier, and the number of health and safety inspections conducted by California's Division of Occupational Safety and Health had declined by 47 percent between 1980 and 1999. The study also cited federal Department of Labor statistics on California industries that were even more dramatic, including an overall level of compliance with minimum wage, overtime, and child labor laws in the garment industry of just 33 percent. A federal sweep of forty-three restaurants in LA's Koreatown, catalyzed by KIWA, uncovered labor law violations in all but two of them, and 80 percent of the state's grape industry was in violation of the state's agricultural labor law.[16]

In 2002, a consensus emerged among the group about the need for an office of low-wage industries within the state's newly consolidated and powerful labor department, the Labor and Workforce Development Agency, which was created through the merger of several previously separate agencies. The Office of Low Wage Industries (OLWI) was proposed in 2002 and established in March 2003,[17] and it continued a relationship with the low-wage worker advisory board.[18] In this capacity, CIWA worked to plumb the organizations' collective experiences to develop very specific recommendations for operational changes in the approach to low-wage industry enforcement.

As Alejandra Domenzain of the Garment Worker Center described it, "Labor law is written with certain assumptions that just don't apply in our industry—that there's a set workplace, that you know who your employer is, that it's a stable thing and its not going to close up shop because you file a wage claim and move down the street, which is what everyone does. In our industry, there's cash payment, subminimum wages, and little documentation. There's subcontracting, there's people afraid to speak out, and language issues." Domenzain believes that these differences are why CIWA has been so critical. "It just kind of calls for a whole different strategy for how you do things. That's what the Low Wage Industries office has been able to do: to look at these industries and come up with enforcement strategies that are appropriate for these realities."

Labor groups interested in the Low-Wage Office recommended the establishment of daily scheduled intake clinics where deputies would lead workers through the process of filing wage claims. Labor representatives argued that this would result in more effective use of deputies' time and would help larger numbers of claimants. Combining the wage conference and hearing would expedite resolution of wage claims and alleviate the backlog of cases. Giving workers their hearing date at the same time that they file their claims as well as translating all forms into multiple languages were also key recommendations.

In terms of enforcement, CIWA groups also put forward very specific proposals. They suggested the development of a system for prioritizing cases according to how many violations an employer had and how many workers were impacted. They also suggested that a training, mentorship, and certification program be created that would train investigators in the internal dynamics of specific industries and the most effective enforcement and investigation strategies. New personnel could then be partnered with an experienced deputy. Perhaps most significantly, CIWA recommended strategic changes to how industry sweeps were to be conducted. "What can you do to enforce things in these kinds of industries? You need to be flexible and creative, to authorize staff to go out at two and six in the morning," said Garcia. "We must work with staff to train them in how to have confidence-building interviewing techniques where they don't isolate or intimidate the worker."

Garcia believes that, instead of immediately asking for names and facts, inspectors need to *establecer confianza* (establish confidence) so that workers feel comfortable talking with them. "We are talking about approaching workers [who], according to the federal government, are engaged in an illegal activity by working in this country. . . . They are being approached by a representative of state government who wants them to give information on their employer as to the illegal activity their employer is doing by employing them and not enforcing minimal standards. That is very overwhelming ask." Garcia and others pointed out that the department is often unable to provide adequate job protection to those workers who do speak to investigators.

In response to CIWA's proposals, the OLWI created a low-wage industries task force to take a new approach to monitoring and enforcement. Huerta's perspective is that the worker centers were critical to the establishment of the task force and to changing prevailing approaches to enforcement. "The worker centers were very important in making this happen. The coalition made a recommendation that there needed to be a refocus of resources to low-wage industries and that program needed to target employers that had a number of low-wage workers that were being exploited and multiple violations."

Significantly, the task force developed another criterion for its choice of targets:

That there be some relationship with a third party group and that is important because traditionally in the agency people are less likely to file complaints or pursue complaints on their own initiative. The system becomes too complex, there are language and educational barriers. But an advocacy group, if it does have a large group of workers, can provide for workers at a hearing or educate them on the process of what they will encounter.

Huerta estimates that 30–40 percent of complaints filed in the 100,000-person-plus Los Angeles garment industry came through GWC.

Huerta and the advocates shared a similarly critical view of traditional approaches to enforcement in which industry sweeps lead to large numbers of citations but little investigation or follow-up after that. "Statistics generated from some industry sweeps can be misleading," Huerta says. "We need to look at the actual results. How many inspections resulted in citations and penalty assessments and whether those assessments were collected." Garcia adds that "they will say 'we did 1,000 inspections' but ask them how many citations were issued and how much in wages were collected and the number will drop significantly."

"What happens is government agencies are so used to running on enforcement activities that do not correct noncompliant activity that it has made them ineffective," Garcia continued. "For business it is a cost of doing business. They know there is a nine out of ten chance they won't get caught and if they do get a citation, they appeal it. It is really, really astonishing, the clearest display of ineffective government." Together, Huerta and CIWA developed a proposal in which the inspectors would conduct two-day sweeps and then have another two and a half days to do the follow-up. To learn about the best way to police the industry, inspectors would have to participate in an industry-specific certification training program.

In March 2003, LWIO launched its first revamped industry taskforce that targeted the garment industry, with Huerta in charge. The new strategic "complaint" or "lead-driven" approach of working closely with advocates to zero in on the worst employers resulted in a much greater number of citations. In just two months, May and June, the organization conducted 239 inspections and issued 263 citations, compared with the 1,600 inspections and 900 citations for all of the previous year.

According to Huerta, "the low-wage industries task force increased activity in the garment industry, increased the number of citations, increased the number of penalty assessments and penalty collections." The only decrease was in the number of inspections "because we were really targeting those employers who needed our attention." In an internal and informal assessment, the agency estimated that $1.6 million more was assessed in tax liability than in the previous year. In the wake of these successes, the Office of Low Wage Industries laid plans to expand the program to create four specialized investigation units by industry.

In addition to the garment industry task force, between 2002 and 2004, the Office of Low Wage Industries implemented many of CIWA's other proposals. These included establishment of an intake clinic, working with advocates to get the most important forms translated into multiple languages, and persuading the Department of Labor Standards and Enforcement to adopt the prioritization checklist for cases against employers. Unfortunately, after passage of the recall of Governor Gray Davis and the subsequent election of Arnold Schwarzenegger, the future of the Office of Low Wage Industries was in jeopardy. After a new investigation was launched but then discontinued, people were instructed to return to their original units and the office was slated for elimination but this did not occur. As of November 2004, the office was still in existence but only actively working in the garment industry. The low-wage advisory board was also still in existence but with the position of labor commissioner vacant for more than a year, the organizations decided to suspend their meetings, according to Garcia because "the agency would not commit to any action, hiding behind the reason of no chief."[19] CIWA expected to resume their meetings once a new commissioner was appointed.

The Harris County AFL-CIO and Interfaith Worker Justice in Houston, Texas

Richard Shaw, secretary-treasurer of the Harris County Central Labor Council, AFL-CIO, became extensively involved with day laborers in 1999. Since then, he has helped to build important bridges between the immigrant community and local unions. When Shaw and the Central Labor Council (CLC) began an effort to strengthen prevailing wage enforcement on public works jobs in the construction industry, they were made aware of all the problems of nonpayment and underpayment of wages. The vast majority of cases, according to Shaw, were among Latino, largely undocumented workers. "The building trades were saying that no one is enforcing prevailing wages so our contractors can't compete. I started looking at their payrolls and all I saw were Hispanic surnames and I said this is discrimination. Not only do you have prevailing wage violations but you have blatant discrimination."

The CLC organized to bring the EEOC to Houston to hold a hearing and put together a research report entitled *Houston's Dirty Little Secret,* which documented the widespread underpayment of wages in the construction industry. "It was so bad," said Shaw, "we could take any TV station to any prevailing wage worksite and find workers not getting paid correctly. That makes a real dramatic image on television when you have the contractors sticking their hand in the camera and shutting the door so you can't get into his trailer and ask for wages to be posted."

After the hearing, the organization worked with Interfaith Worker Justice, local unions, and government entities to create the Low Wage Earners Taskforce to investigate abuse and exploitation of immigrant workers in other areas of employment. They worked with the mayor of Houston to establish an office of Immigrant and Refugee Affairs, which hired a well-respected immigrant advocate to take on employment issues and three day-labor sites were created by the city.

Within a few years, the taskforce evolved into the Justice and Equality in the Workplace Program (JEWP). It consisted of the EEOC; Department of Labor; the CLC; the Mexican-American Legal Defense and Education Fund (MALDEF); the Catholic Diocese of Galveston-Houston; the Houston Interfaith Committee for Worker Justice; the Mexican, Colombian, El Salvadoran, and Guatemalan consulates; the City of Houston; the Department of Justice; and eventually OSHA. JEWP worked to set up a hotline for workers and created a "one-stop grievance procedure." The idea, according to Shaw, "was to set up a mechanism where complaints from the Latino worker committee could go through one central place: the Mexican consulate. From there, the complaint would be routed to the appropriate agency." JEWP also created an aggressive outreach program that makes regular presentations at day labor centers and other community meetings and even sent union leaders out to visit contractors and talk with builders about "nonpayment of wages" cases.

As a result of the work the CLC was doing around the issue of low-wage worker exploitation, workers began coming to it, asking for help with wage claims. "We started getting workers just coming in the front door asking for help. The majority were in construction, not so much in commercial and industrial but residential, where none of the work is union and is all mainly being done by immigrants," said Shaw. Since beginning its work in 1999, the CLC has witnessed an enormous change in the attitudes among building trades unions. "I am not saying that there still aren't ill feelings toward immigrants . . . but the leadership of the building trades came out strongly against the cheating of immigrant workers, brought on Spanish-speaking staff, and began organizing them." The apprenticeship programs are aggressively recruiting immigrant workers, and while there are still language issues, most, according to Shaw, have stopped asking for proof of citizenship.

Shaw believes that growth of the labor movement in Houston will come through organizing immigrant workers. "There has always been a large Hispanic population in Houston but the new growth is immigrants coming due to the devastation in their home countries. In terms of union organizing, unions know where their bread is going to be buttered. They know where this union movement is going to grow, where the new democrats are going to come from. In Houston it is really tough to avoid all that. It is hard to take an anti–undocumented immigrant stand if you want to be a growing union movement."

When Shaw and the president of the council were elected in 1995, the Houston labor movement was at about 1 percent density of the local workforce. "We were faced with turning out the lights on this movement or moving forward. So I see moving organizing among immigrants as the major focus of my work." In June 2002 the CLC sponsored an immigrant organizers conference that brought together union organizers with the immigrant community.

> We did a two and a half day retreat, the first of its kind, and the idea was to give union organizers more of an in-depth look at the immigrant community and their issues. We covered everything from immigration law to EEOC stuff, things organizers just don't know, and we also covered immigration issues. We tried to do some sensitivity training around those issues because the biggest problem our organizers have, even those who speak Spanish, is understanding the immigrant community and where they are coming from, not knowing what they face, particularly those who are undocumented.

Shaw is now working with Interfaith Worker Justice to raise the funds to open an immigrant worker center.[20]

WORKING ON POLICY CHANGES TO STRENGTHEN COMPLIANCE WITH EXISTING LAWS AND IMPROVE ENFORCEMENT

While partnerships with governmental entities to enforce existing labor laws are often useful, worker centers have frequently found that they are not enough. Enforcement policies and regulations are often inadequate, and absent policy changes, state and local governments may be unwilling to take the necessary steps to protect immigrant worker rights. The following examples illustrate how worker centers have organized to advocate for policy changes to strengthen compliance with existing labor laws and/or promote more effective enforcement.

The Workplace Project and New York's Unpaid Wages Law

From the first day the Workplace Project's legal clinic opened its doors to immigrant workers on Long Island, nonpayment and underpayment of wages were by far the most common complaint it received.[21] Although state and federal laws require all workers, documented or not, to be paid the minimum wage, enforcement of the law in relation to low-wage immigrant workers is generally nonexistent and the penalties for violators ineffectual.[22] The New York Department of Labor (DOL) had approximately one investigator per seven thousand private workplaces; employers found not to be paying the minimum wage were subject to only a 25 percent civil penalty and repeated nonpayment of wages carried only a misdemeanor, not a felony conviction.

For an immigrant workforce in search of enforcement of the law and due process, Long Island was a Wild West of exploitative employers and hostile, or at best, ineffectual regulatory bodies. The project took dozens of cases to the state Department of Labor (DOL) only to be rebuffed.[23] Undocumented workers or workers working under the table were told inaccurately that they were ineligible to file claims, cases were taking up to eighteen months to be investigated, and a Spanish translator was available for only three hours every other week. DOL staff often refused to accept the claims of housekeepers, restaurant workers, and day laborers, instead subjecting them to lectures about illegal aliens not paying their taxes.

In the summer of 1996, the organization voted to mount a campaign to pursue passage of a law its own leadership had drafted called the Unpaid Wages Prohibition Act, during the 1997 state legislative session.[24] The act increased the maximum civil penalty the commissioner of labor can impose on the worst wage offenders from 50 percent to 200 percent of the amount owed and it raised the criminal penalty for repeat violating employers from a misdemeanor to a felony, doubling the maximum penalty to twenty thousand dollars. In addition, the bill prohibited settlements of less than 100 percent of what the worker was owed unless the worker agreed, and it required regulators to continually update workers about the status of their cases. Finally, the law shifted the burden of proof from workers to employers, in cases when employers have failed to maintain proper records.

The members of the Workplace Project believed that only by dramatically increasing the penalties would unscrupulous employers be compelled to change their ways. As the organization saw it, employers were engaging in illegal practices because they not only thought they had a good chance of getting away with it, but also because the penalties if caught were so minor. They reasoned that the imposition of higher fines and criminal penalties would mean that employers might desist from these practices or, if caught, would be much more inclined to pay than to fight. While the organization knew that passing legislation was an extremely remote possibility, it viewed the campaign as a way to publicize the problem of unpaid wages and to provide major learning opportunities for members and leaders.

The Workplace Project succeeded in getting the two most important small business associations on Long Island to endorse the bill. They also received the endorsement of a large assortment of religious organizations, unions, central labor councils, and community organizations. Over the course of the winter and spring of 1997, the project organized numerous meetings with legislators. Over the objections of the twenty-seven-thousand-member New York Farm Bureau, the bill's biggest opponent, eventually ten Republican senators signed on as cosponsors of the bill, including five from Long Island. Surprisingly, several of the senators that sponsored or cosponsored the Unpaid Wages law had been at the forefront of efforts to pass virulent anti-immigrant legislation. Some were the chief architects of a New York bill that was nearly identical to Proposition 187 in California. Others had earlier championed an English-only campaign in the Senate.

The organization got tremendously good press. *Newsday* ran a front-page story about the plight of immigrant workers on Long Island. It featured a full-page picture of a worker who came to the Workplace Project for help after being paid approximately 30 cents a day for working twelve hours a day, seven days a week for fifty-seven days and eventually sleeping on the floor of the freezing restaurant at night. The article featured the unpaid wages bill and contained a boxed section that listed the names of Long Island employers charged with violations of the state wage and hours laws.

To the amazement of virtually everyone involved in the campaign, the bill moved through the assembly unimpeded and fared similarly well in the senate. On July 1, it passed both chambers unanimously, and on September 17 Governor Pataki signed the Unpaid Wages Prohibition Act into law.

The Workplace Project has been disappointed in the bill's implementation under Republican governor George Pataki. According to an investigative piece written by *Newsday* reporter Jordan Rau, "Fines against errant employers during Pataki's tenure have amounted to 8 percent of all the recovered wages . . . which is two thirds lower than the amount assessed during 1994, Governor Cuomo's last year in office."[25] The fines were lower, despite the fact that the Unpaid Wages law quadrupled the maximum fine the agency could impose, to 200 percent of wages owed.

As a result of the administration's lighter penalties and longer delays in settling complaints, the Workplace Project, despite drafting and successfully shep-

herding the Unpaid Wages law, seldom refers cases to the state labor department, instead advising workers to pursue their claims in small claims court. In
addition, worker centers in New York have increasingly turned to the state Attorney General's office, which has aggressively targeted low-wage industries, including green grocers, laundries and dry cleaners, and day labor employment
agencies in recent years, cracking down on worker abuses and winning large
settlements.

Deborah Baumgarten, a member of Attorney General Eliot Spitzer's labor
law enforcement bureau, believes that worker centers have been very important
to their work in low-wage industries. "Anyone in the public who brings us a
complaint, we can look into," Baumgarten said. "And worker centers are in an
excellent position to be garnering complaints because they are places where
people with employment problems go." Baumgarten believes that beyond helping to identify cases, the centers provide the support immigrant workers need
in order to feel comfortable filing complaints. "All you have to do is walk into
any small business, there is massive under-enforcement. We do work with primarily low-income recent immigrants. They don't just walk up to government
and make a complaint. That's why organizations in the community are so important. With those relationships workers are less likely to be scared."[26]

Domestic Workers United and the Domestic Workers Bill of Rights

In June 2003, Domestic Workers United (DWU) succeeded in getting the New
York City Council to adopt the Domestic Workers Bill of Rights, the first citywide legislation in the country that protects the rights of domestic workers. Domestic workers brought together by the Committee Against Anti-Asian Violence's (CAAAV) Women Workers Project worked together to develop a
standard contract that was modeled on one in use in Hong Kong. Many of the
Filipino domestic workers were familiar with it, having come to the United
States after first migrating to Hong Kong to work as domestics there, and were
shocked by the lack of regulation of the industry here. Using that contract as a
base, they developed their own model.

At a summit of domestic worker organizations to discuss the idea of building
power among the more than half a million city domestic workers in an
industry-wide way, they presented the contract, and two immigrant women's
organizations, Andolan and CAAAV, decided to work together on an industry-
wide organizing strategy. CAAAV is largely Southeast Asian, and their Women's
Workers Project was largely Malay and Filipino. Andolan is largely South Asian,
with women from India, Bangladesh, Sri Lanka, and Pakistan. When the workers hit the parks and playgrounds to talk to domestic workers, Caribbean and

West Indian domestic workers, who had for generations been involved in domestic work in New York City, became involved as well.

As organizer Ai Jen Poo recalled, "They kept saying 'we need a union, we need a union.'" The groups started holding meetings all over Brooklyn. "The word of mouth was unbelievable, news of the contract spread like wildfire. At the first meeting there were twenty women and at the next one there were ninety."[27] The women took their model contract to sympathetic city councilors, several of which had worked as domestics or had members of their families who had, and the Immigrant Law Project at NYU helped them draft the legislation.

According to Brian Kavanaugh, chief of staff to City Councilor Gale Brewer, who was the main sponsor of the legislation, "Working at the city level, we had to look for whatever legislative authority we had to support our involvement in this, since most hard core labor and employment law is set at the state and federal level."[28] While Kavanaugh and Brewer concluded that the city did not have the authority to create broad new protections for domestic workers, they felt they did have a role in publicizing and enforcing existing laws. However, since the state does delegate authority to regulate employment agencies to the city, via the Department of Consumer Affairs, the city did have the standing to require them to make some concrete changes.

The bill requires employment agencies that place domestic workers to do two things. First, it requires them to make sure that the terms and conditions of employment are spelled out in writing when workers are placed in a job. Many domestic workers at the DWU describe a "bait and switch" situation, where they are told one thing by the agency when they are first given the assignment, only to discover a much different and usually more difficult arrangement when they arrive at the employer.

Second, the bill mandates the agency to get the signature of the employer who is hiring the domestic worker on a statement that lays out the state and federal rights that protect domestic workers and keep it on file and available for inspection. If an employer refuses to sign the statement, the agency is not supposed to place the worker with them. While domestic workers are excluded from the National Labor Relations Act, they are covered by other state and federal labor and employment regulations, including wage and hour laws under the Fair Labor Standards Act, but most employers are unaware of their obligations under these laws.[29]

The council's leverage was in the licensing process. "Essentially, we used what we could . . . employment agencies are licensed and their licensing is reviewed periodically," said Kavanaugh. "So the theory is that that if you are a licensed agency, you are required to keep certain records on file and the Department of Consumer Affairs inspects the records. While some of the agencies came in and said it was too much to expect of them, our thinking was that if you are a licensed agency, you are not going to jeopardize the legal standing." Status as a licensed placement agency was something they would want to protect because it is a comparative advantage in the domestic worker placement marketplace. Again, according to Kavanaugh, "A lot of folks want the legitimacy and cover of an agency, they don't want to recruit someone off the street to watch their children. They go to an agency and they want the deal to happen, and they will be told that they can't get a worker without signing the statement."

While the City Council was limited in what it could require, councilors passed a companion resolution to the legislation, which called on the state and federal governments to enact and enforce broader protections. It also called on employers to agree to standard contractual terms proposed by the DWU, which include notice of termination, severance pay, annual paid vacation, overtime after forty hours of work, paid sick days, and paid national holidays.

DWU, in coalition with a range of other worker centers and immigrant rights organizations, is now working to pass legislation at the state level. The legislation calls on the state of New York to establish a living wage for domestic workers and require employers to pay it along with providing health insurance, paid vacations and holidays, sick and personal days, and severance pay. The bill also calls for changes to existing state and federal laws that have excluded domestic workers, including the Family and Medical Leave Act and the National Labor Relations Act. Finally, it also calls on the federal government to allow employers of domestic workers to pay unemployment, disability, and workers compensation insurance on an annual, rather than quarterly basis.

The organization felt that the legislative campaign provided a great opportunity to build a strong membership base of domestic workers. "Every month actions were called and workers had many activities they could participate in, from rallies and marches to calls to city councilors. There was always a way for the rank and file to engage," said Poo. The campaign also provided many opportunities to develop the skills of the domestic worker leadership, and workers were always at the table when they met with city councilors.

The Tenants' and Workers' Support Committee and Childcare Workers

TWSC studied the childcare industry closely and researched a wide variety of public policy campaigns to improve conditions and protections for low-wage childcare workers working under contract for the City of Alexandria. By federal law a state is required to conduct local surveys every two years to determine the market rate for childcare before setting the amounts it will pay, and the rates then go to the federal government for approval.

TWSC found that Alexandria's reimbursement rate had lagged behind those of neighboring jurisdictions for years and petitioned the city to correct this inequity. It also mounted and won a campaign to get the city of Alexandria to go back to its original payment system so that the childcare workers would get paid on time at the end of their workweek. When the city stopped providing certification training for Latina childcare providers in Spanish, the organization circulated a petition and successfully lobbied the city council to restore it. The city agreed to hire a bilingual person to provide the trainings. TWSC also won a set of grievance procedures for home-based childcare providers that the city's Social Services Department must follow before it terminates one of their contracts. Most recently, the organization has been trying to get the city to provide health insurance to the childcare workers.

ORGANIZING TO PASS NEW LAWS TO RAISE WAGES AND IMPROVE WORKING CONDITIONS

In addition to fighting to improve enforcement of existing labor laws and policies, immigrant worker centers have been at the forefront of organizing efforts to pass new laws that would benefit low-wage workers. These include living and minimum wage campaigns and campaigns to strengthen laws protecting employment rights.

Living and Minimum Wage Campaigns

Community-based worker organizing projects have been involved in living wage campaigns from the start of the contemporary movement to pass local ordinances. In 1995, Solidarity, the joint organizing project of the Industrial Areas Foundation, and the American Federation of State, County, and Municipal Employees (AFSCME) pioneered the strategy in Baltimore, where the targeted low-wage worker population was largely African American (although there has been an influx of Latinos in the past few years). That ordinance, which took wages from $4.45 to $6.10 and built in incremental increases over the next four years, raised wages by 44 percent for an estimated four thousand workers. By the spring of 2003, 103 communities had adopted local living wage ordinances, and more than 80 others were pending. Worker centers were involved in many of these campaigns.[30]

In June 2000, TWSC led the drive to pass a living wage ordinance in Alexandria, a town of 130,000. The law required contractors for food services, parking attendants, and janitors to pay a minimum of $9.84 an hour. After the law was passed, the Alexandria business community tried to block it at the state level and got the Virginia State Legislature to pass a measure banning local living wage laws. But spurred on by the TWSC, the Alexandria City Council appealed to the legislature to allow local control, and the living wage law was preserved.

In San Francisco in 2003, the Chinese Progressive Association (CPA) and its affiliated Worker Organizing Center along with Young Workers United led a community/labor coalition that mounted Prop L, a successful campaign to pass a citywide minimum wage of $8.50, the highest rate in the nation. The law, like the federal minimum wage law, applies to all employers, not just those doing business with the city, and affects an estimated 54,000 low-wage workers and 29,850 of their children. These workers gained on average, about two thousand dollars annually.[31] CPA cochaired the coalition's steering committee and mobilized hundreds of Asian-American workers over the course of the campaign.

While local unions strongly supported the effort, the Worker Organizing Center and Young Workers United, because they were actively engaged in organizing among low-wage workers, were able to provide spokespersons who would be the direct beneficiaries of the proposition to talk about how difficult it was to make ends meet. These workers were central to the effort to persuade a majority of San Franciscans to vote yes. In the belief that local government would be more vigilant in enforcing the law, Prop L also placed the authority for wage enforcement in the hands of the City of San Francisco and local county government, as opposed to the state or federal government. In the spring of 2005, the city was in negotiations with CPA and other grassroots organizations on contracting with them for community-based wage enforcement services.

Through work stoppages and a thirty-day hunger strike, the Coalition of Immokalee Workers succeeded in forcing wages up statewide when the agricultural industry in Florida was compelled to follow state minimum wage requirements. Not all living wage campaigns have been successful. In Omaha, OTOC worked with the Central Labor Council to pass a very modest ordinance, only to have it repealed with the election of a new mayor and city council.

Job Rights Campaigns

Some worker centers have broken new ground in bringing key employment-related issues to the forefront even when they do not always win them. CAFÉ, which explicitly defined itself as a union for nonunion workers in a Right to Work state, held what it called "job rights" workshops across the state during the eighties and involved itself in a range of employment issues. In 1986, it won passage of a legislative measure that made it more difficult for employers to fire injured workers. In South Carolina, during the 1990s, CAFÉ was the central organization documenting the rise of contingent and temporary employment and proposing legislative measures to address a variety of inequities. The measures did not pass but brought a previously little acknowledged issue into the center of public inquiry and debate.

CAFÉ was one of the first organizations in the country to launch a campaign around a specific code of conduct for temporary agencies and began its work by targeting state government which, at ten thousand workers, turned out to be the largest employer of temporary workers in the state. It has been part of a national campaign to get Manpower to sign onto a similar code of conduct.

Over the past several years, CAFÉ has mobilized with the South Carolina AFL-CIO and other organizations to block numerous attempts that have been made to pass a version of workers' compensation reform that would greatly limit the amount of money someone can collect if they have a recurring injury. In 2004, it was part of a campaign to mobilize grassroots activists to defeat a state bill that would have nullified protections to the employment termination grievance procedure detailed in employee handbooks of individual companies, if these protections accorded workers more rights than the state's employment-at-will doctrine.

Campaigns to Raise Taxi Fares and Wages

As discussed in chapter 6, in March 2004, the New York Taxi Workers Alliance won an unprecedented 26 percent fare increase for the forty thousand licensed cab drivers of New York City. During the campaign for the fare increase, the alliance documented and publicized the financial hardships endured by most drivers and mobilized thousands of them for rallies, demonstrations, and hearings before the City Council and the Taxi and Limousine Commission.

Just as in New York City, the taxi industry in Alexandria is highly regulated, and it is possible to enact policy changes that will have a tremendous impact on wages and conditions of work. TWSC has organized the six hundred taxi drivers into AUTO, an organization that has been targeting the Alexandria city council to change the rules and regulations that structure the medallion and leasing systems. TWSC's proposal would give the drivers more negotiating power by granting the ability to switch companies and transferring control of the medallion certificates from the cab companies to the owner-operators of cabs.

CHAPTER 8

IMMIGRANT RIGHTS AND SOCIAL JUSTICE

As noted in the previous chapter, worker centers' public policy organizing and advocacy takes a variety of forms. In this chapter we look at their public policy campaigns that fight for immigration reform and immigrant rights, against racism and for a broader social justice agenda. The chapter ends with an overall assessment of the strengths and weaknesses of worker centers' public policy campaigns.

FEDERAL AND STATE IMMIGRATION POLICIES AND THEIR IMPACT ON IMMIGRANT WORKERS

Poverty, global economic inequalities, and the development and trade policies that have exacerbated these problems have catalyzed enormous numbers of immigrants to seek higher-paying employment in the United States. Federal immigration policy and enforcement is creating a huge reserve labor pool of workers whose status as undocumented immigrants leads them to work for low wages, make few demands on employers regarding other conditions of work, and resist going to government agencies for help. The issuance of "no match" letters by the Social Security Administration (SSA), which alerts employers to the disparity between a workers' reported social security number and the SSA's records, has given employers an additional powerful tool for control over the workforce.

At the state level, other restrictions on immigrants have been imposed. These include requiring social security numbers in order to obtain drivers' licenses, which has a very direct impact on employment prospects, as well as denying in-state tuition and college loans to the children of undocumented workers not born in the United States. Following the September 11 terrorist attack, there has been a general government crackdown on immigrants and a dramatic increase in xenophobia and local anti-immigrant attacks. Given that local police forces have been encouraged to cooperate with the INS and now with the Department of Homeland Security, undocumented immigrants and their families are often fearful of calling the police for help. In October 2004, for example, there was a string of brutal attacks on immigrant laborers in Plainfield, New Jersey, including one murder. Newspapers reported that these attacks had been taking place for several months and were widely known in the immigrant community, but workers did not go to the police out of fear of being asked for their papers and arrested.

Many worker centers view their work as much through a social justice frame—championing the rights of immigrants and people of color generally—as they do through a workers' rights frame. They view immigrant workers' employment, housing, and health care experiences as having as much to do with their ethnicity and status as new immigrants as it does with their class position. The same is true for centers that came out of the African American community, which views blacks' experiences in the labor and residential housing markets and public school systems as having at least as much to do with race as class. As a result, many centers view struggles against xenophobia, racism, and discrimination, and for immigration reform, as just as central to improving the lives of their members as any of the wage or enforcement issues highlighted in the previous chapter.

At the centers themselves, immigration and employment struggles are almost always intertwined. When local residents, businesses, or municipalities move to restrict day laborers from seeking employment, or police make arrests at shape-up sites, references to them as "illegal aliens" and claims about their immigration status are always a major part of the public conversation. As the debate on immigration reform becomes more contentious, centers are often called on as the local spokespersons of a pro-immigrant point of view, speaking in opposition to anti-immigrant policies and practices and discussing the unfairness of the current immigration system. The dramatic personal stories of their hard-working members help to illustrate the problem and evoke public empathy with their plight. This establishes a foundation on which a local campaign of support for federal immigration reform, and one that draws support beyond the "usual suspects," can be launched.

Worker center public policy organizing and advocacy campaigns on these issues have taken a number of different forms that are examined in this chapter. They include countering anti-immigrant policies in local communities and fighting for immigration reform at the national and state levels. They also include struggles against racism and discrimination in housing, education, and the allocation of social services that build bridges between immigrant workers, African Americans and other communities of color, and other poor and marginalized groups in American society.

COUNTERING ANTI-IMMIGRANT ATTACKS AT THE LOCAL LEVEL

The fight against attacks on immigrant workers in local communities on Long Island is perhaps the best-known example of a worker center public policy campaign, thanks to the movie *Farmingville* that appeared on many Public Broadcasting Service stations. The focus of these attacks—day laborers and the shape-up sites at which they gathered—enabled the Workplace Project to link economic struggles to defense of immigrant rights and immigration policy reform at the local level.

Shape-up sites have been a feature of the Long Island landscape since the mid 1980s as large numbers of newly arrived Central American immigrants became the area's chief source of flexible labor in the landscaping and construction industries. Beyond their labor market functions, shape-up sites are also symbolic of something much larger. In their communities, they are the most visible symbols of the new immigration and have been lightning rods for discontent, discomfort, and outright xenophobia. This is, in part, why the Workplace Project and so many other worker centers engage on the issue.

The Workplace Project has been involved with day laborer struggles since its founding in 1992. Since that time, Long Island's day labor shape-up sites have grown dramatically in number and size, and they have attracted increasing amounts of attention from the media, elected officials, local businesses, police, churches, and other civic organizations. The organization has worked closely with elected officials and civic organizations to develop constructive solutions that balance the right of day laborers to seek employment with the needs of local commercial businesses and residents. Outcomes have varied, as we will see in the following two stories of Farmingville and Freeport.

During the mid 1990s, Mexican immigrants, chiefly from the state of Hidalgo, began migrating to the small town of Farmingville on the eastern shore of Long Island. As Connie Hornick, of the Church of the Resurrection recalled, "I've been the outreach coordinator for the past eleven years. In that time, I've watched the immigrant population grow from about twenty-five people on the street corners to hundreds." Hornick estimates that all together, more than six hundred workers gather each day to seek work at the four day laborer corners.

Beginning in 1999, Farmingville became a national point of convergence for anti-immigrant activists.

After a local woman was tragically killed in an automobile accident in which the driver was a day laborer, a local anti-immigrant organization started gaining steam. The Sachem Quality of Life Committee, working with national anti-immigrant groups, staged direct confrontations with immigrant day laborers and narrowly lost an effort to have the Suffolk County legislature pass a law that would have required county government to become more involved in pursuing and prosecuting undocumented immigrants. The measure proposed that the county sue the Immigration and Naturalization Service on the grounds that it was not doing enough to stem the tide of illegal immigration.

Anti-immigrant forces also succeeded in defeating an effort, initially supported by a majority in the Suffolk County legislature, to establish a day laborer center in Farmingville. After two Mexican workers were horrifically beaten in 2000, Hornick helped found the organization Brookhaven Citizens for Peaceful Solutions (BCPS) in the hope of identifying middle ground. "The major complaints of the community were that, (a) they couldn't walk in the streets because the men were in huge masses and (b) that there were too many people in the houses. There was between twenty to thirty people in a house. These were their complaints and they were legitimate complaints." Hornick and other BCPS leaders felt that centralizing the shape-up would help with community tensions. "What would you logically think was the answer to this? Well . . . you think shape-up. It's the logical way to get them off the street."

BCPS and the Workplace Project worked very closely with Paul Tona, a Republican and the presiding officer of the Suffolk County legislature, who believed that "these immigrants are working and doing real shit jobs that no one else will do. They're doing it quietly and professionally. And all they want is to be treated with a little dignity and respect." Initially, Tona was able to use the considerable power of his office to organize the legislature to vote in favor of the day labor site.[1] "What we did was, we created in the budget an eighty-thousand-dollar fund that would support the creation of a shape-up site. I don't want to use the phrase hiring hall because it really wasn't a hiring hall. It was just a shape-up site. . . . The idea was just to get them off the streets and out of the community's eye and get the contractors to go there so people aren't getting beaten up."

In 2001, in the face of increasingly virulent, organized anti-immigrant activity, BCPS and the Workplace Project worried that the day laborers were physically at risk and organized a major legislative campaign in support of the shape-up site. Both Hornick and Tona were repeatedly threatened over the telephone and in person during this time. Sachem Quality of Life activists began to charge the Church of the Resurrection with having recruited the Mexicans to come to Farmingville: activists slipped notes in the collection plate that read "when you close the borders, I'll give you money."

But the Long Island Association, the island's largest and most powerful business association got behind the measure, lobbying for its passage. After initially passing in the Suffolk County legislature, it was vetoed by the Suffolk County Executive. The other Republican legislators who had initially supported the idea, reversed their positions, which made an override impossible. "When the bill failed to override, it was crushing," said Hornick.

Tona believes that his efforts were derailed, in part, when another legislator who was sponsoring the bill referred to the site as a hiring hall. "The big problem was that it spelled psychological permanence to the Farmingville community," said Tona. "They think the INS is going to finally come in there sooner or later, roll in with tanks and helicopters and round all these people up and send them back to their country of origin. I'm not kidding. That's the only acceptable measure and when you say you're going to build a hiring hall it spells infrastructure, a building, and permanency."

Hornick also believed that Farmingville residents were fearful of the shape-up site because "they said 'if you build it, more will come here.' They said they're taking jobs away from Americans, but we know that's not true because we can't get other people to do those jobs. That's the thing that kills me . . . I don't see a teenager on earth that would do the jobs they do with the pride that they do it with."

During the hearing process, Tona worked closely with the Workplace Project. Tona repeatedly touted the organization's professionalism and commitment to ensuring that the day laborers themselves participated directly in the debate. "They helped make sure that people were articulate and organized and they helped the day laborers feel that they're part of an organization where there's a community that's supportive of them and Americans are supporting them. The other thing that was good was that you had English-speaking Latinos who were citizens, which took a lot of the wind out of their sails." From Tona's perspective, the Workplace Project functioned as "an ombudsman for this community that had no voice prior to them" and helped fortify the immigrant community to organize themselves and fight back through constructive means.

During the past few years, despite the fact that the two day laborers were severely beaten and the house of a Mexican family was burned to the ground in 2002, the Latino immigrant community has never responded in kind. "From a public safety standpoint, I think the Workplace Project has had a lot to do with the fact that you don't have any major complaints about crimes or anything like that with day laborers," said Tona.

As things heated up, Farmingville became a national symbol of anti-immigrant fervor and xenophobia in the United States. Hornick feels that the town has been vilified in the media and she believes that while the issue has been tremendously polarizing, the majority of local residents are much more middle-of-the-road in their views. The anti-immigrant activists were always outnumbered by the hundreds and, at certain points, thousands of social justice activists who came out from across Long Island and the New York metropolitan area to show their support for the immigrant community. But they have still managed to block any efforts to create a hiring hall. "As I see it now, when I look at this whole series of events over the past six years," said Hornick, "the town is frozen literally, because there is no government that will come and help and no government that can. The county tried at one point, and 'no' was the answer."

During the same period that Farmingville became a national battleground over immigration, things unfolded quite differently in the next county over, as the Village of Freeport grappled with similar issues. Freeport, a town of forty-three thousand, has long been a highly diverse community. Currently, blacks, Latinos, and whites each comprise about a third of the population; the local government says that sixty-four different cultures are represented in the local community, including people from many parts of Latin America, Asia, and Africa. Day laborers had been shaping up near one of Freeport's busiest intersections since the mid 1990s. By 2001, their numbers had grown to between fifty and one hundred workers, traffic issues had worsened, and after September 11, 2001, local police had begun to take a much more aggressive approach to dealing with them.

"What happened in Freeport was that the police just started to push the workers around, the workers came to us, we started to organize them in little meetings, and then Carlos was handing out fliers and the police arrested him," Nadia Marin-Molina, the Workplace Project executive director recalled. After Carlos Canales, the project's day laborer organizer was arrested for solicitation, the organization hired an attorney and got the charges dismissed. They also began getting the day laborers to go out and do presentations to local churches and other organizations to garner support and bring groups of day laborers and allies into Village Hall to meet with local officials. The project approached Catholic Charities and William F. Glacken, the mayor of Freeport, to try to negotiate the establishment of a day laborer site.

"It's one of those things where the bureaucracy says, 'No, we'll never set up a site,' but once we sat down with the Mayor, he liked the idea," said Marin-Molina. "He has control of the village; in fact, we said to him, 'Are you going to have to have public hearings or something?' and he said, 'No, this will pass,' and it did." The mayor and his economic development director worked closely with the Workplace Project to organize the day laborers and with Catholic Charities to administer the site. "I thought that since it was more than just matching contractors with workers, there are a lot of support services that are necessary, literacy problems, health problems, immigration problems—that's the reason for Catholic Charities existence. They've had a 150-year history of doing this. If we brought an organization in like Catholic Charities to work with the Workplace Project, we felt that we wouldn't have to reinvent the wheel."

The two government officials hoped that, while Catholic Charities would see to the day-to-day operation of the center, the Workplace Project would take charge of recruiting, organizing, and developing the leadership of day laborers. Carlos Canales works on recruiting day laborers and contractors to use the site. He also works to involve them in decision-making at the center in terms of how the hiring process works and to involve them in the Freeport chapter of the United Day Laborers of Long Island (a Workplace Project–organized, day laborer–led group).

"Some people would stop short or pick up or drop off people right on Sunrise Highway where you've got tractor trailer trucks barreling down. We recognized that there was a problem that needed to be dealt with," said Mayor Glacken. "What was happening was that people were gathering and blocking sidewalks and spilling over into the streets."

Although anti-immigrant activists tried to stir things up in Freeport, sending a few people to public meetings to speak out, they were not able to establish a local foothold. "We certainly didn't have the level of outright hostility that we saw in Farmingville. We went in exactly the opposite direction than Farmingville," said Glacken, a life-long Freeport resident who was elected eight years ago as the candidate of the Home Rule party, a coalition of registered Democrats, Republicans, and Independents. "I think the main difference between the way we've handled the problem is that we have dealt with it not as a social problem. We didn't make more of it than it actually was. We never looked at this problem as if it were an immigration problem. We looked at is as if it were a traffic and public safety problem. If you're going to have these trucks, they should be loaded and unloaded off of the street."

Ellen Kelly, director of the Freeport Community Development Agency, who has played a central role in getting the site off the ground, also viewed the issue as one of economic redevelopment. "Part of my daily job is to work on the downtown revitalization and the growth of the commercial core. We've got new construction coming in and rehab going on. So it was definitely to the advantage of sprucing up our downtown to find a more appropriate site than the corner." The Village of Freeport contributed a municipally owned parking lot for the site, a construction trailer, and ten thousand dollars in federal Community Development Block Grant money to the effort.

Glacken's view was shaped in part by his belief that the laborers were working for local contractors and local residents. "A lot of the trucks represented local contractors, because the laborers worked for local contractors. They weren't working for corporations, and incidentally they were also working for private residents." As a young man, Glacken worked with migrant farmworkers in Suffolk County as an employee of the Office of Economic Opportunity (OEO) and believed strongly in their right to unionize. He also sympathized with the plight of the day laborers: "In many ways, I think the day laborers are the migrant workers of the twenty-first century. They have similar problems." Responding to a question about the impact of day laborer employment on the local labor market, Mayor Glacken responded, "I don't believe that these day laborers take jobs away from other citizens . . . these jobs that they are filling is a need that others do not want to fill."

With regard to the issues of tax collection and illegal immigration, Glacken's public position was that local government did not have a role to play in either one. "I look at it basically as who's responsible for what. The IRS and New York State Department of Taxation and Finance are responsible for the collection of taxes. That is not the responsibility of the Village of Freeport. My responsibility is to bring and maintain peace and order. If the IRS wants to pursue these contractors, that's their prerogative." As far as the workers are concerned, "I think they should pay taxes. I don't see any reason why they shouldn't, but at the same time, if they're here and if they pay taxes, they should get benefits."

Ellen Kelly pointed out that the day laborers have also stimulated the local economy: "The contractors are all a bunch of small business people as well. It has created this whole second layer of the economy where entrepreneurial small business people, contractors, roofers, [and] landscapers have taken advantage of the day laborer force." While she believes that these contractors, by and large, are not paying taxes, "They're building businesses and employing workers. When I look at it, it seems that the money being spent is in the U.S. economy."

Glacken believed that the shape-up site would never be able to fulfill its function if workers avoided it out of fear of deportation and instructed the Village of Freeport police not to conduct immigration raids at the site. "I don't work for the INS," he said. But his views on immigration policy went beyond questions of the role of local government.[2] "I think that the immigration policy that this country has is insane because we pretend that we want to do something about illegal immigration, but we really don't do anything serious about it," he said. "If we want to have people come in and do manual labor that citizens are unwilling to do, then it should be something that's organized. They're here, they're not going to go away, they're providing a service. At the same time, I don't see any problem with charging them taxes or with contractors having to report their taxes. Give these people legal status to be here so they don't have to come here surreptitiously."

While the mayor believes that the village has found a successful solution to the problem of day laborers congregating at busy intersections, he hopes the site continues to grow in terms of the number of day laborers and contractors who use it. "I'd like to see every day laborer at the center. That's not entirely the case. There are still people who hang out on the street corner because they think they might have an edge. I look at that as something they can do to improve. I think we've given the site a chance to succeed, but in order for it to do so, they've got to go out and organize. They have to show the day laborers that this is a better way to get steady work."

This victory would not have been possible without the Workplace Project. "What has happened so far, and the way I see things going forward," said Ellen Kelly, "is a very close continued partnership in the effort to make the Freeport site successful because the Workplace Project has been involved since day one. . . . Having a functioning trailer with a paid manager has been critical, but the Workplace Project is the one who can go out and be on the site in the morning trying to move men to the new site and working with them in a labor organizing way."

FIGHTING FOR IMMIGRATION REFORM

Most of the worker centers interviewed for this study are active participants in national and state immigration reform coalitions. They have worked with the National Council of La Raza, the National Immigration Forum, the National Network for Immigrant and Refugee Rights, the National Immigration Law Center, the National Farmworker Justice Fund, the American Friends Service Committee, and many other groups. NDLON has made immigration reform an important component of its advocacy and organizing work, conducting a national discussion among day laborers and within the larger immigrant rights community about the type of reforms that would be the most helpful.

In 2003, many immigrant worker centers participated in the historic Immigrant Workers Freedom Ride sponsored in large part by the Hotel Employees and Restaurant Employees (HERE), which helped to organize hundreds of local events across the country and culminated in a very large national rally in New York City. Many of these groups are now involved in the Fair Immigration Reform Movement (FAIR), a new national coalition for immigration reform that is being coordinated by the Center for Community Change. FAIR is also working as part of the New American Opportunity Campaign, the immigration reform effort that grew out of the Freedom Ride.

Notwithstanding these efforts at the national level, most of the campaigns of worker centers on immigrant rights are focused on changing policies at the state level. Laws and administrative rules limiting the rights of immigrants to obtain drivers' licenses are one of the most frequent targets.

Until 2004, California was one of approximately sixteen states that require people to show a social security card in order to get a driver's license. MIWON, the coalition of immigrant worker centers in Los Angeles, has been a central organizing hub for immigrants' rights, coordinating an annual march for legalization that has mobilized thousands and playing an active role in the state driver's license campaign. The organizations succeeded in getting Governor Gray Davis to sign SB60 in September 2003, which allowed all California residents, regardless of their immigration status, to apply for a state driver's license or identification card. The bill eliminated the "lawful presence" requirement and modified the Social Security number requirement for California residents who applied for a license, allowing those who did not have one to use an individual taxpayer identification number (ITIN) instead. All California residents, regardless of immigration status, would have been eligible to obtain a license provided that they passed the driving and written tests, submitted proof of identity, and complied with other licensing requirements. The bill was scheduled to take effect on January 1, 2004, but was repealed by the legislature after Arnold Schwarzenegger was elected governor and threatened to place it on the ballot.

After the events of September 11, in which seven out of nineteen of the terrorists involved were shown to have had Virginia drivers' licenses, sweeping changes were passed by the legislature there, which made it very difficult for immigrants and refugees to obtain licenses. Tenants' and Workers' Support Committee (TWSC) became one of the major organizations fighting to change the law and helped to pull together and staff a statewide coalition.

TWSC took the position that all persons regardless of immigration status should be eligible for drivers' licenses and argued that the Department of Motor Vehicles should not be in the business of trying to enforce federal immigration law. TWSC won over some powerful allies in the DMV and law enforcement, who believed that the new requirements were a detriment to public safety but were not able to reverse the restrictions.

In May of 2005, states lost their autonomy in terms of setting standards for drivers' licenses, when Congress passed and President Bush signed, the REAL

ID Act. The act established strict national provisions for states regarding the issuance of drivers' licenses and state identification cards. It requires proof of the person's social security number (SSN) or verification that the person is not eligible for an SSN.[3] In addition to federal immigration and statewide driver license campaigns, some worker centers, such as Wind of the Spirit in New Jersey and the Brazilian Immigrant Center in Boston, have worked on statewide campaigns to allow the children of undocumented workers the chance to pursue higher education with in-state tuition.

At the local level, because immigration status is such a central fact of life for so many of the workers that worker centers organize with, campaigns often have an immigration angle to them. As we saw in the Suffolk County case discussed above, day laborers are often the "canaries in the coal mine" for the local immigration debate. Although the issue of street corner shape-up sites is most often framed in terms of how workers pose a public safety hazard, often for the local groups opposing them, the presence of large numbers of immigrants is the real issue underlying the conflict. In some cities and towns, there has been a dramatic increase in the immigrant population in a relatively short period of time. For example, between 1980 and 1990, the Latino population in Long Island increased by 78.8 percent in Nassau County and 49.7 percent in Suffolk County. The Workplace Project, through its advocacy, organizing, and public relations work, has played a major role in "introducing" Latino immigrant workers and their issues to the larger public and working to engender a positive perception of them on Long Island.

During union drives in heavily immigrant workforces, employers very often threaten to "call the INS" (although it is now called the Department of Homeland Security), and unions and worker centers in the course of soliciting community support for the drives are once again called to engage the issue. In addition, a number of centers, including Centro De Derechos Laborales in Minneapolis, have worked to pass local city council ordinances to ban police from cooperating with the INS or DHS. Sometimes the issues are much more "nuts and bolts"; over the course of building a base among immigrant workers in Omaha, OTOC mounted a campaign to enlarge the waiting area at the immigration office so that during the winter months people didn't have to queue for hours in the cold.

The constituencies with which the centers work put them in the front lines of the local immigration debate in their communities. In their role of representing low-wage immigrant workers and advocating on their behalf, these centers have emerged as important actors as communities struggle to come to terms with changing demographics.

FIGHTING FOR RACIAL AND ECONOMIC JUSTICE

As should be clear by now, many worker centers do not focus exclusively on labor and employment issues—or immigration issues. Their broad "social justice" agendas mandate that they also organize around racism and domestic violence, education and youth, housing and development, and health care issues. Taking on these issues enables centers to champion the rights of a broader constituency—not just immigrants but all workers, people of color, and the poor and marginalized in American society. The following are a few examples of this most challenging area of worker center public policy organizing and advocacy.

Tenants' and Workers' Support Committee

TWSC has always been a multi-issue community organization. Its stated mission is "to develop the collective power of Northern Virginia area low-income tenants and workers—particularly immigrant and African American working class women—and to fight institutional racism, develop collective ownership and control of community resources and build multi-racial understanding and collaboration." This is a broad mandate that results in the organization's involvement in a range of issues. As Jon Liss, long-time executive director describes it: "In terms of worker organizing, community organizing, there was a vacuum in northern Virginia. So, if someone dies, the collection can comes through here, someone gets beaten up by the police Saturday, on Monday they're sitting here in our office. . . . Partly because we were the only organization and in many ways still are the only organization that is organizing immigrants."

As mentioned in chapter 1, TWSC started out in 1986 as a tenant organizing project that worked to stop mass evictions and saved about two thousand units of affordable housing. The campaign was well publicized, involving a number of national celebrities including Martin Sheen, the television and film star, and the late Mitch Snyder, former director of the Center for Creative Nonviolence. During its early years, the organization established a three-hundred-family limited equity cooperative that it has continued to work closely with, sitting on its board of directors and holding an ongoing contract to provide translation and youth services.

Since 1986, the organization has worked with residents of the Arlandria section of Alexandria, a neighborhood that became overwhelmingly Central American during the 1980s and 1990s, on a host of issues. On public education, TWSC has organized African American and Latino parents to create a model dual-language elementary school program, and prevented the busing of hundreds of low-income Latino schoolchildren. It also pushed the school district to enact a model suspension/expulsion policy and to take action on the minority achievement gap in the Alexandria public school system.

The TWSC organized a Women's Leadership Group to discuss community concerns and women's issues particularly. Concerned with the lack of recreational facilities and park space, the women mounted and won a campaign for the establishment of a neighborhood playground. TWSC has also worked with youth in the community to develop a number of programs, including after-school tutoring, mural projects, and the establishment of a youth or social center. In fact, TWSC raised the money to buy a building in 2004 that will house the center. Another program, Communidad Salud/the Healthy Community Project, established in 1996, mobilizes the Latino community to increase access, regardless of income or immigration status, to "culturally competent healthcare." By January 2005, the organization had worked with low-wage families and area hospitals to forgive more than $1 million of medical debt.

In the past few years, the Arlandria neighborhood has been threatened by gentrification and a redevelopment plan put forward by the city that TWSC believed would be detrimental to current residents and businesses. "The proposed buildings are geared to certain types of businesses, which in turn generate certain kinds of jobs and customers, which in turn has profound implications on the affordability of nearby housing, which impacts who will actually live in the surrounding neighborhoods," TWSC's critique of the plan reads. The organization has worked, not only to counter the city's proposal and put forth one of its own but also to organize a local small business association, Arlandria Community Businesses.

Carolina Alliance for Fair Employment

In addition to its focus on expanding the labor and employment rights of nonunion workers in South Carolina, CAFÉ has pursued a broader agenda of issues in the cities and towns in which it has active chapters. The organization's fourteen grassroots chapters have taken up domestic violence, students' rights, and racial tracking in the public schools.

After becoming aware that the state of South Carolina ranked third in the nation in 2002 in domestic violence and the number of women killed by men, CAFÉ kicked off a statewide series of "Domestic Violence is Real" workshops in observance of Domestic Violence and Sexual Assault Awareness Month. The organization partnered with county sheriffs' offices and domestic violence agencies and featured survivors of domestic violence speaking about their own experiences of abuse.

In 2003 and 2004, CAFÉ's Florence chapter in the Pee Dee, a largely working class and black area of the state, took up the issues of school expulsions and suspensions. Many CAFÉ activists felt that school officials were expelling and suspending students in a discriminatory manner. While disciplinary officers claimed to be following the state's "zero tolerance" policy and asserted that they were not able to exercise discretion in making decisions about expulsions and suspensions, CAFÉ leaders demonstrated that they were in fact doing so, often in a racially and ethnically biased manner.

Instituto de Educación Popular del Sur California (IDEPSCA)

IDEPSCA, in Pasadena, California, was founded in 1987 as a grassroots organization that marries popular education to community organizing for social and economic justice. The organization works to consciously link community issues with literacy skills development. IDEPSCA operates a host of programs and projects, including a public education watchdog group, a Latino Neighborhood Association, a women's federation, a youth organization, several day laborer centers, and a computer technology training program. By teaching participants to engage in critical analysis as they learn to read and write, IDEPSCA explores critical issues with its members, and they often move into action.

"I found out that this work of popular education is like a mirror where you facilitate a process where people can see themselves and their reality and then they want to do something about their conditions," says executive director Raul Anorve. For ten years, IDEPSCA operated as an all-volunteer group, organizing literacy circles, pushing for improvements in the Pasadena school system, and taking on other community issues until it formally incorporated in 1997. All told, the organization has spent eighteen years organizing literacy circles and developing popular education programs that involve low-income Latino immigrants and their families, teaching literacy in the context of economic, social, and racial oppression, and working with them to organize for change.

In the nineties, IDEPSCA organized a group of Latino parents, and for the past several years, the organization has intensified efforts to improve the Pasadena public schools, electing a Latino school district representative and taking on the district's approach to school reform. IDEPSCA has focused its efforts on developing the leadership of public school parents so that they are able to play an active role in advocating for their children's education.

Although IDEPSCA operates day laborer hiring halls, it backed into that work as a result of the literacy circles it was organizing among low-wage Latino workers, many of whom were day laborers. The organization became involved when some of the students in the literacy circles talked about the difficult experiences they were having in Pasadena when seeking work. "They were harassed by police, employers would hire them and not pay them, residents would throw bottles at them," said Anorve. The day laborers organizing led the City of Pasadena to agree to open up a day laborer center and contract with IDEPSCA to administer it. The organization now operates eight day-laborer centers in southern California and played a central role in the formation of NDLON.

STRENGTHS AND WEAKNESSES OF CENTERS' PUBLIC POLICY ORGANIZING AND ADVOCACY

Based on the research conducted for this study, it seems clear that so far worker centers have made their greatest strides in the "monopoly face" area of improving wages as well as the "collective voice/institutional response face" of representing workers, in the public policy arena. Organizations have been able to win economic improvements for low-wage workers by moving government to act in ways that have required employers to raise wages and improve conditions of work. In addition to these monopoly face achievements, collective voice achievements have also come via public policy. Organizations have so far been most capable of forcing improvements in employers' treatment of workers via catalyzing government administrative action and public policy change.

The "Monopoly Face" of Workers' Centers

Unionized workers generally enjoy higher wages and better working conditions than other sectors of the work force. In 1999, union workers earned 32 percent more than nonunion workers, according to the Bureau of Labor Statistics. Unionized women earned 39 percent more than nonunionized women, unionized African Americans 45 percent more, and unionized Latinos 54 percent more.[4] As such, while union organizing is arguably the most effective antipoverty strategy for low-wage workers in the United States today, the climate for union organizing has become extremely difficult. Employers routinely fire workers for organizing and engage in other illegal tactics in order to break the back of organizing drives.

To try to counterbalance the enormous power of employers in recent years, unions have increasingly sought the help of elected officials to send a message to employers that they will protect workers' right to organize and to take affirmative steps to control the antiunion activities in which employers may engage. These actions are especially important for immigrant workers who have tremendous fear of employer and government retaliation and persecution.

As we have seen in the case of the Omaha meatpacking industry, the actions of the governor and lieutenant governor paved the way for the city's first successful union organizing drives in several generations. Although it was ultimately through collective bargaining campaigns that wages were raised, these organizing drives may never have succeeded without the clear public support of the state's highest elected officials. The Meatpacker's Bill of Rights, although not a wage-related document, stated clearly that workers had a right to organize and many statements by the governor and lieutenant governor communicated the same message.

Similarly, actions taken on behalf of day laborers by local governments in Los Angeles, Long Island, and elsewhere to oppose anti–day laborer ordinances and create and sustain permanent shape-up sites have protected the livelihoods of these workers. These actions have also made it possible for day laborers to begin to engage in collective action to set higher wages. Worker centers and especially unions have even more opportunities to raise wages in cases of those who work for public sector employers (although very few immigrants do) or in highly regulated industries. In fact, in recent years, the Service Employees International Union (SEIU) has made some of its greatest and most innovative organizing strides in industries, such as homecare and mental health, that have been privatized but are still supported through government funds. For worker centers that work with a primarily immigrant constituency which is not employed in what can be called the public sector, this is harder to do.

However in highly regulated industries such as the taxi business in New York City, in which immigrants are represented in large numbers in the workforce and where government essentially sets wages, worker centers such as the New York Taxi Workers Alliance have been able to win important victories. They were able to organize cab drivers for collective action and target the government entities that had the power to grant fare increases. As a result, they were able to win a very significant wage increase directly through government for forty thousand workers.

Living wage efforts, where worker centers have been able to raise wages via local ordinance for those working for employers holding contracts with the municipality, do this on a much smaller scale. Depending on the extent of privatization that has taken place in a local city or town, and how expansive the ordinance is in terms of how many businesses are covered, these ordinances cover fairly modest or larger numbers of workers. But by altering the terms of debate about economic development strategies, the nature of low-wage employment, and the responsibilities of low-wage employers to their workers, they have opened a whole new front in the struggle to improve conditions for low-wage workers.

Some living wage ordinances, such as those pioneered by the Los Angeles Alliance for a New Economy (LAANE), have specific language that makes it difficult for frequent labor law violators to receive city contracts and rewards union employers and those who agree to card-check neutrality. Pioneers of the living wage movement in Baltimore were also strongly motivated by the desire to halt privatization, which had resulted in the loss of thousands of comparatively decent-paying, overwhelmingly unionized blue-collar, public sector jobs. By taking wages out of competition, some ordinances have taken some of the percentage out of contracting out. Some have even resulted in a return to the public sector, or "re-publicization" of jobs that had been contracted out. But these gains have been limited.

Of course, minimum wage campaigns like the one in San Francisco that covers all private sector workers, not just those with public sector contracts, are much more sweeping. Where worker centers and other advocates have the power to pass them, they are exciting opportunities to raise wages for many thousands of people. However, in many communities and states minimum wage activists don't have enough power, and the forces of opposition make it very tough to win.

State-based efforts that bring workers excluded from the federal minimum wage under the protection of state minimum wage laws, as the Coalition of Immokalee Workers was able to do for agricultural workers in Florida, are interesting policy ideas and have the potential to impact large numbers of low-wage workers. Again, there is the question of having enough power to win. Efforts that target local government bodies on which a sizeable number of representatives are sympathetic have so far worked best. TWSC was able to pass a strong living wage ordinance and improve wages for home-based childcare workers under contract to the City of Alexandria because, working with allies, it had enough power to win over a majority of the council.

The TWSC's efforts to get the Alexandria City Council to provide health insurance for childcare workers and hotel housekeepers, while demonstrative of great imagination, are also illustrative of some of the limitations of worker center policy efforts. The fact that, in 2005, fewer than 50 percent of private sector employers now offer health insurance to their employees is indicative of a spectacular national problem. Efforts to attack this problem at the individual state level through government-provided services via the expansion of the federal

Child Health Insurance Program (CHIP) and Medicaid have definitely helped millions of low-wage families but they have not addressed the underlying reason why so many workers are without coverage: cost.

More and more employers even in non-low-wage industry sectors are asserting that they cannot afford to shoulder the cost of health insurance premiums and are calling for an overhaul of our health care system. Employers in many low-wage industries either do not provide health insurance or offer plans that are so expensive (and usually so inferior) that workers do not opt to take them. In this context, although it is certainly to their credit for trying to do something and for calling attention to the problem, it is difficult to imagine worker centers being able to substantially increase the number of workers with health insurance through local public policy initiatives. But they could be important components of a broader national movement for national health care reform.

The "Collective Voice" of Worker Centers

Immigrant worker centers are mediating institutions for low-wage workers that provide opportunities for collective voice as well as collective action. Today day laborers, domestic workers, taxi drivers, garment workers, and so many other low-wage immigrant workers exist within industries in which there are no unions or other organizational vehicles through which they can speak and act. The Domestic Workers Union in New York City has created a collective voice for the 600,000 housekeepers and nannies who, despite their numbers, have had no ongoing mechanism for advocacy and organizing. The Domestic Workers Bill of Rights has given them a means of intervening in their industry and forcing some changes in the way that employment agencies operate. Their work on development of a standard contract gives domestic workers a means of improving conditions at the level of the individual employment relationship.

Worker centers provide mechanisms through which low-wage workers can speak and act on their own behalf to employers, industries, and government about issues of concern. They are doing their work in industries where noncompliance with the Fair Labor Standards Act, OSHA, and many other laws has become the norm and where strategies for effective enforcement are few and far between. By giving workers an opportunity to file claims and take direct action against employers, worker centers offer one of the few mechanisms for collective voice that low-wage workers have to pressure their employers.

Endeavoring to fill the monitoring vacuum is another way to understand the

work of the legal clinics—the individual and group cases they file and use to analyze overarching industry trends are an important way in which ongoing monitoring and regulatory intervention goes on in these industries. When KIWA
saw the large numbers of restaurant workers seeking help at its legal clinic, it
was able to pinpoint an industry in which noncompliance was commonplace,
tell this story to government and the media, and through its advocacy and organizing activities, take steps to improve the situation.

As we saw in the case of CIWA in California, immigrant worker centers in
Los Angeles have created the institutional mechanisms through which reform
of government enforcement procedures in low-wage industries has been aggressively pursued. Worker centers, because they see workers every day and hear
about their experiences, have built up enormous knowledge about what works
and what doesn't work in terms of inspection and enforcement.

In addition, as is the case both with CIWA and CAWRI in Illinois, through
their work helping thousands of workers file claims, they have been able to see
clearly the strengths and weaknesses of administrative processes and to imagine
alternative systems that will work better. They have example after example and
the data to identify overall industry patterns that spotlight the problems. They
can bring out real workers as opposed to advocates, who can tell their own stories, and they have the institutional resources to develop ongoing relationships
with government inspectors.

At the Workplace Project, the staff and workers leading the Unpaid Wages
campaign came to the conclusion that the key to lessening the problem of employers not paying wages and flouting settlements lay in making penalties stiff
enough to act as deterrents to illegal behavior in the first place. The organization deliberated carefully over development of a law that would accomplish this
deterrence and then, because it was an organization that represented the workers being harmed, was able to have these workers go out and sell the law to
elected officials and other key constituencies. Although the organization could
not intervene in the relationship between these workers and their employers,
through the legislative initiative it was able to represent the voices and interests
of these workers to larger industry and business groups who supported cracking
down on businesses that were competing on an unlawful basis.

In all of these cases, the organizations were able to provide a means of collective representation in the public policy arena for low-wage workers. As we can
see in the New York and Nebraska cases in which Republican officials became
key allies, the presence of the workers themselves in the storytelling and advocacy lent important moral legitimacy and standing to these efforts. On issues
from public education to day labor to living wages to immigration reform,
these organizations, by showing the impact of current policies on flesh-and-

blood workers and their families, have changed the policy climate in their local areas by injecting new ideas and principles into old debates.

As we will discuss in greater detail in chapter 11, this moral power that the groups have built is an important way of understanding how they have been able to accomplish what they have in the policy arena, but also their limitations. Most immigrant worker centers have little direct political power. Most centers do not have well-developed electoral or voter participation efforts, and it is not clear that they could, given that a significant percentage of their members are not voters. Their power comes from their ability to cast issues in moral terms and capture the sympathy of constituencies that have more political power.

The Workplace Project, because of its strong moral claim, was able to win over elected officials, editorial boards, and other organized constituencies such as organized labor who had more political power than the organization had, and this was key to winning passage of the Unpaid Wages law. On the other hand, the law has not proven to be an effective deterrent to employers, in part because there has been so little enforcement under the Pataki administration. Its effort on behalf of day laborers in Suffolk County was never able to win over a majority of legislators, and because of this, it lost.

At the present moment, limited economic power keeps worker centers from being able to win significant wage increases or establish permanent institutions like hiring halls or unions. Limited political power has an impact on the proposals worker centers put forward in the first place and their ability to win the campaigns they do initiate. But there are few other organizations that are currently trying or have figured out how to accomplish these things for the vast majority of low-wage workers. Even in cases where unions have been successful, models of organization and representation for workers at smaller employers who may have no or limited ties to larger corporate entities have yet to be perfected.

As the debate on immigration reform continues to unfold, worker centers have a unique role to play in ensuring that the reality of the country's deep dependence on low-wage immigrant workers and the conditions under which they work, is forcefully presented. The presence of these groups in the discussion helps to hold up a mirror to an American society that is in a collective state of denial about just who is cleaning and constructing their homes and offices, caring for their young and elderly, harvesting their crops, tending their gardens, sewing their clothing, cooking and serving their meals. If we are ever to construct a more sensible immigration policy, the "dirty little secret" of American business and family dependence on undocumented immigrants must be told.

Engagement with immigration policy also makes clear for low-wage immigrant workers that their problems stem from a larger, systemic issue that cannot be solved at the local level alone.

In addition to labor market and immigration policies, the immigrant rights and broader social justice agendas the centers pursue provide their constituencies with unique opportunities to engage other issues of major importance to them and their families, such as public education, housing and health care. Engagement with a broader agenda also provides a means to transcend local struggles and become part of larger movements for social change in the United States.

CHAPTER 9

THE INTERNAL LIFE OF WORKER CENTERS

In chapters 5 through 8 we looked at the external activities of worker centers. In this chapter and the next, we shift to an examination of internal organizational features. As we saw in previous chapters, most worker centers take the long view of what it will take to achieve economic and social justice. Because of this and because they have a more comprehensive and transformational approach to social change, they are often not as "campaign-oriented" as many unions and community-organizing groups.

This same perspective also leads them to a strong focus on the internal life of their organizations and the development of their members as among the most important "products" of their work. For these reasons, understanding the inner life of worker centers is essential. In this chapter we will explore the organizational landscape of worker centers under five broad topics. These are (1) developing activists and leaders; (2) popular education; (3) membership; (4) staffing and decision-making; and (5) budgets and financing. In the next chapter we will examine networking among worker centers and evaluate the strengths and weaknesses of their internal organizational structures and processes.

Immigrant worker centers provide a striking counterpoint to the status quo in an era during which *Bowling Alone,* Robert Putnam's description of a hobbled civil society in which fewer and fewer Americans are actively participating, became a bestseller.[1] In contrast to national trends, they are engaging healthy numbers of people on an ongoing basis. In addition, while political scientists Verba, Schlozman, and Brady highlight the increasingly upper-class skew to civic participation, these organizations are involving thousands of people of very modest means.[2]

DEVELOPING ACTIVISTS AND LEADERS

A major activity of worker centers is identifying and developing activists and organizational leaders from within the ranks of low-wage immigrant workers. This effort has a number of components. It involves developing their capacities in a number of different areas, including public actions and campaigns, planning and organizational development, and internal governance. Centers devote considerable resources to training individuals to represent themselves before the media, public officials, and employers, and hold debriefings afterward to discuss and bring out lessons about power and politics. They also train members to recruit and lead other workers, to choose issues, develop and implement campaigns, and to critically evaluate what works and what does not.

In addition, many worker centers strive to create a culture of democratic governance and decision-making. In place of just making decisions themselves, staff works not only to put deliberative processes in place but to foster expectations on the part of workers that decisions will be made consultatively and collectively. "We create moments, when we organize events or conferences," said Raul Anorve of IDEPSCA, "where we teach people not only *how* to plan but to *understand the logic* of planning—the difference between objectives, goals, and activities, how these are tied together and how we take responsibility."

For many worker centers, developing activists and leaders also means transforming the way that workers see themselves. The building of a day laborer movement in Los Angeles is a good example. According to Pablo Alvarado, the Spanish word for day labor, *jornalero,* had long been used as a pejorative, not only in the United States but in Latin American countries as well. "Being a *jornalero* is the lowest you can be not even just here, but in your homeland." Alvarado and Victor Narro, a former CHIRLA organizer, and their nascent day labor movement reappropriated the term, transforming its connotation. "I think we shifted the understanding of what a *jornalero* is. We developed collective profiles of who a day laborer is in the centers . . . and replaced the old negative stereotypes with who they really were."

Printed on T-shirts and posters, sung out by the nation's first Day Laborer Band, "somos jornaleros" ("we are day laborers") was asserted as a positive identity, an expression of pride in one's work and even though perhaps a transitory category, one's occupational community. "There is a parade here in the park every Cinco de Mayo and when we talk to the workers and we ask them if they want to participate in the parade, they say yes," said Alvarado. "When we ask them how they want to do it, they say they want to take their helmets and tools and march along with the floats. They march on the streets with their tools and people applaud."

Developing activists and leaders is a continuous process, and centers recognize that structures need to be created to enable individuals to actively participate in their work. While most centers provide a variety of venues for participation and offer different levels of participation—from coming out once in a while to an event, to taking a course, to serving on a core committee or on the board—they all have strong cores of active participants.

- "There's a collective of about twenty-five people who are at the heart of the organization," said Tom Holler, lead organizer of OTOC. "There's a functioning strategy team of another twenty-five people. Then there's a steering committee of about sixty people. There's also a clergy caucus of about twenty. Then you have the initiatives. There are probably about thirty people in and around this work strategy [the meatpacking organizing drive with the UFCW]. Then there [are] twenty-five people who've done a lot of work on youth strategies." The largest turnout OTOC has ever had at a single event has been 1,100.

- The Workplace Project is run by a seven-member board of directors elected entirely from the ranks of the membership. In addition to the board, the organization has four standing committees related to worker organizing. These are the UNITY co-op of housekeepers (which has eighty-one members and requires all of them to serve on one of four possible committees); LOVELI, a committee of janitors that has between twenty and forty members; MILI, a committee of factory workers with ten to fifteen active members; and the United Day Laborers of Long Island, which has chapters in Freeport, Brentwood, Farmingdale, and Farmingville with a leadership base in each that ranges from five to twelve. In 2003, the organization graduated its thirty-first and thirty-second workers' rights classes, which average twenty-five pupils per class. The largest turnout the Workplace Project has ever had at an action or event has been three hundred.

- TWSC has a thirteen-person board and three low-wage worker organizing committees: Pa'Adelante for northern Virginia hotel workers, UNITY for Alexandria childcare workers, and AUTO for Alexandria taxi drivers, which each have about ten to fifteen leaders. It also has three geographically based local chapters, two in Fairfax County and one in Arlington County, which average about twelve to fifteen core leaders. Finally, it has four community organizing chapters: the Campaign for Uninsured Access to Health Care, Education Project/School Reform, Alexandria United Teens/Youth Organizing, and the Arlandria-Chirilagua Housing Cooperative, each of which involves an average of seven to fifteen core leaders. In addition, the organization staffs the Northern Virginia Jobs with Justice chapter and helped start a local business organization in the Arlandria-Chirilagua neighborhood. The largest turnout TWSC has ever had at an action or rally (besides the annual cultural festival it sponsors) has been six hundred.

• "The board is nine plus two alternates, so it's eleven," said Kimi Lee of the GWC. "Initially, we had five committees, but only two or three actually functioned. The finance committee has two to three people, it talks about the worker membership dues, where should it go, the worker loan program, and that kind of stuff. There's a recruitment/retention committee of ten to fifteen workers. These people help with membership because we know that a lot of times a problem with worker centers is that workers come in when they have problems and then they leave once it's fixed. Also to help with retention, we have stewards. We have stewards who are members who then are assigned other workers to help outreach to them and bring them in and make sure they're connected. That program just started last year. Our biggest committee is our campaign committee which has about twenty to thirty." The largest turnout the organization has had for an action or event has been sixty members.

Worker centers engage in extensive training with other volunteers as well as board and committee leadership. POWER in San Francisco, which works with a diverse base of "workfare" recipients, has a leadership development and political education curriculum that has various levels based on different levels of participation. There is an initial orientation, which provides information about the history and mission of the group and ongoing political-education sessions that teach about current events. The leadership development course provides a more extensive history, a detailed explanation of the organization's programs, and lays out systematically the ways in which leaders play roles in the organization.

Over the course of conducting the research for this study, dozens of workers said that before they had become involved with the worker center, they had never gone to City Hall, met with government officials, or spoken publicly. Many said that they had never really felt they knew "how things worked," or that they could affect them, until they met up with the worker centers, and that they had been very isolated in their own small communities. Many said that they had never been asked to join an organization or asked their opinion about anything in the "public realm" until they came into contact with the worker center.

Andrea Davis, an African American leader of TWSC said that what she had got-

HOW IMMIGRANT WORKER CENTERS PROMOTE LEADERSHIP DEVELOPMENT

- Working with board and committee members.
- Developing critical thinking skills in workshops and trainings.
- Teaching members to run meetings and organize events.
- Involving leaders in the development of organizational strategies and strategic planning.
- Overseeing the organization, making decisions in terms of budgeting, hiring, monitoring, and evaluation.
- Taking part in various types of actions, holding elected officials and others accountable.
- Meeting with policymakers and testifying at public forums.
- Public speaking and developing media spokespersons.
- Working with members to learn how to recruit others to the organization ("leaders have followers").
- Negotiating with employers, industry representatives, elected officials, government agencies, and other public actors.
- Participating in formal trainings as learners and presenters.

Most important, the leadership that is developed through worker centers has ripple effects throughout communities via hometown associations; home country politics; civic organizations; social, cultural, and athletic organizations; tenant organizing groups; schools/parent-teacher associations; and civil rights and immigration reform bodies.

ten out of her experience working with UNITY, the childcare organizing project, was "working with different people, getting to know different countries, being able to talk to people, cause I'm shy about talking to people so now being able to, if I have a problem, I could be able to talk." Asked whether she had ever been involved in political action before, Davis said, "No, I never really did it too much."

As a young leader with OTOC, Alejandro Garcia was one of a group of packinghouse workers who met with Republican governor Johanns to describe the conditions in the industry. "We were in the basement of Guadalupe Church," he said.

I walked him to the door and told him it was nice he was there. . . . I said, 'I expect to see you some other time.' At that time we were planning on doing a rally three weeks after that day. We were expecting somewhere around five hundred to a thousand people, and we wanted to make sure he would come. He said he's going to do the best he can to be there. . . . Some people were worried about what we were going to give him to drink or they wanted to treat him like a king, but we all said he's going to come with workers and see how we live. We just gave him water in a plastic glass. If you're going to be with the people, we just treated him like everyone else.

When the Workplace Project mounted a statewide campaign for a new unpaid wage bill that members drafted themselves, the organization believed that passing legislation was an extremely remote possibility and viewed the campaign as a way for members and leaders to gain experience. Maintaining organizational leadership and control over the campaign became key—only in that way could Workplace Project leaders, members, and staff really maximize their learning about the whole political process. Maintaining leadership over the campaign meant having the immigrant workers themselves, and not the English-speaking staff or well-meaning allies, take the lead. The staff designed trainings for the workers that included diagramming the entire legislative process in Spanish, and setting up role plays so that workers could anticipate arguments that would be made against the bill.

Over the course of the winter and spring of 1997, the project conducted fifteen meetings with legislators. They held these meetings in lawmakers' Albany or district offices, unaccompanied by any allies, in Spanish. "We visited with a Republican Senator," Jennifer Gordon recalled.

We walked into his district office in Rockville Center with twelve immigrant workers, a box full of translation equipment, more people than they had room for and no one speaks English. And we say "Hello, Senator Skelos, here's your headset." And the meeting takes place, and Senator Skelos, because we have translation, is hearing from all these articulate people who he normally sees on street corners. Here they are in their best clothing giving good arguments that show a clear understanding of how the political system works and his place in it and his needs and things like that, and this is a big deal.

The Workplace Project members who went on these visits absolutely loved taking part in them, often taking time off from work or paying someone to work for them, just to be able to participate.

POPULAR EDUCATION

To many staff of worker centers, real participation begins with the inculcation of critical thinking skills. A number of the centers utilize a popular education approach that is associated with the Brazilian educator Paolo Freire. Work-

OMAHA TOGETHER ONE COMMUNITY

We teach people to become effective leaders, explore their legitimate issues, do solid research, engage in sometimes tough but always respectful public discourse, hold elected officials accountable, and create positive change through collective action. Through the practice of these skills, people build relationships of trust and, by acting collectively, become part of solving their own problems rather than expecting someone else to take care of them. . . . This is OTOC's 'iron rule': never do for others what they can do for themselves. Community organizing demands time, talent, discipline, and commitment. Those willing to do the work experience personal growth and transformation.

Source: OTOC's organizational brochure, "What is Omaha Together One Community?"

shops, classes, and discussions are designed to get workers talking and thinking not just about the way things are, but how they got that way. As Raul Anorve, whose organization has deep roots in the Salvadoran literacy movement of the 1980s describes it: "People do not look at the structure of this society, they look at the issues. They go by the branches not the roots of the tree. We look at the roots of the tree so we don't get lost in the branches . . . we also need to look at the forest not just at the tree!"[3]

The Workplace Project, like most of the centers, offers a worker's rights course in which workers learn about U.S. labor and employment laws. The classes explain basic information about how U.S. labor and social welfare laws work. For example, immigrant workers learn that minimum wage and overtime laws apply to all workers, regardless of whether they have legal working papers. Workers are also taught that organizing at the workplace is protected under the law, and that it is illegal for workers to be fired for it, whether they are documented or undocumented.[4] But they also learn the difference between what is "on the books" and what is actually enforced.

In each class, speakers are brought in from government agencies such as the state Department of Labor and OSHA, as well as from unions, worker centers, and local universities. All class sessions follow a popular education pedagogy and wherever possible draw insights and opinions from the students themselves. The project always works to point out the discrepancy between theory and practice, between the law on the books and what happens to workers in reality. They always connect these disjunctures back to the need for organizing. The classes are structured so that before the students hear from the "experts," they identify their own experiences with a topic, such as occupational safety and health. They are asked to draw and discuss hazards at their own workplaces and learn about the laws that are on the books in this context.

By the time the "experts" arrive, students are primed to put the tough questions to them, and not just to accept their presentations at face value. In this way, the organization consciously follows a "Frierian" pedagogy aimed at developing the students' critical thinking skills. As Anorve describes it: "This work of popular education is like a mirror where you facilitate a process where people can see themselves and their realities and then they want to do something about their conditions. That is what happened in Pasadena with day laborers who then fought to successfully establish a hiring hall."

For many centers, political education is another component of developing the critical thinking skills and capacity to act of members. Many of the centers have worked to develop curriculum that provides members the tools to talk about complex issues. The idea is to give them information and help them formulate questions, as opposed to telling them what they should think.

In 2005, the Multi-Fiber Agreement (MFA), which established quotas on the amount of garments and textiles that countries could import to the United States, is going to be abolished. The GWC expects about fifty thousand workers in the Los Angeles garment industry to lose their jobs as a result. At the GWC, members are learning about the structure of their own industry and how it is affected by global trade rules, and they are encouraged to debate the issues around free trade as well as immigration policy.

"The whole MFA issue is enormously complicated because on the one hand, our members might lose their jobs, but on the other, their own home countries might benefit from the abolition of the MFA when U.S. tariffs are abolished," said Kimi Lee.

> Because it is so complex what we're doing is just educating people about it and trying to tell people what it means and what's going on. What we're doing then is we're having several globalization workshops with the workers. We've talked about the MFA. We've talked about all the different free trade agreements. We've done workshops on NAFTA, on the [Central America] free trade one [CAFTA]. There's all these different free trade agreements, so we've been doing different sessions with the workers. That's kind of where we're at and that's enough to try to deal with—educating the workers about globalization.

MEMBERSHIP

Most worker centers began without a developed idea of membership requirements. While they have grown more sophisticated in recent years, for many centers the issue of membership size and membership requirements remains

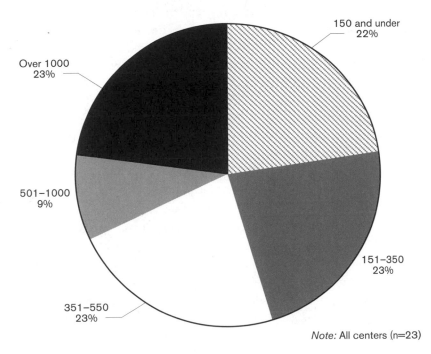

9.1. Worker center membership sizes

problematic. As can be seen in Figure 9.1, 68 percent of worker centers have memberships of 550 persons or less.

How are we to interpret the relatively small formal membership bases of immigrant worker centers? Although they have moved from service and advocacy into organizing, most do not have a well-developed metric for measuring organizational power in general, either because they do not think in those terms, or because they feel they are not yet strong enough for it to be a relevant question.

Based on survey responses and case studies, many centers did not view membership size as a central measurement of organizational strength or power. This lack of emphasis on building up large numbers of formal members is in part a reflection of the organizational origins of the centers; most do not come out of union or community organizing traditions that place a high premium on membership enrollment. As we saw in chapter 1, most centers come out of organizations that were service providers, ethnic non-governmental organizations, or social movement organizations. In addition to the question of origins is how worker centers understand their current organizational models. The sharpest distinction is between those that engage in industry-based organizing and view themselves in part as some type of labor market institution, and those that are engaging in work that may or may not be industry-specific but view themselves more as social movement organizations. Many organizations combine elements of both and do not fall neatly into either grouping.

Some centers simply do not have a membership-based organizational model. For others, modest membership size seems to be more a reflection of the most active members than of how many area workers use the centers or come out to actions and events. Most worker centers believe that workers have to earn membership; it is not conferred automatically. But even when membership is conferred, centers have enormous trouble keeping up-to-date records.

The majority of worker centers treats membership as a privilege that workers attain through participation and is attached to specific responsibilities and duties. Membership is not automatically extended to anyone who attends an event, comes in to the center, or receives a service. Many believe that it is better to have quality rather than quantity and that large numbers do not guarantee power in cases where most of the organization's members are inactive. Centers often require workers to complete a course on workers' rights, participate in other trainings, serve on a committee, or volunteer a specified number of hours over a certain period of time as a condition of becoming a member.

A number of years ago, the Workplace Project board, which requires workers to take an eight-week course and commit ten hours of volunteer time before they can become members, had a very intense debate about easing the pathway to membership. The majority of board members strongly objected to doing so. To them, membership in the Workplace Project was something that had to be earned, and they passionately objected to any attempts to build numbers by making it more "automatic." Nevertheless, the organization has created an "associate membership" category that has less stringent requirements, but also denies workers a vote in the general membership meetings, the body that elects the board and makes other important decisions.

Among the case studies, OTOC, the New York Taxi Workers Alliance, TWSC, and KIWA stood out as exceptions to the rule on stringent membership requirements. All of them have industry-specific projects but TWSC also has a neighborhood organizing component that actively solicits memberships. As an affiliate of the Industrial Areas Foundation, OTOC follows an institutionally based model, which means that individuals do not join, institutions such as churches, unions, and schools join, and requirements of membership include substantial financial as well as organizational participation commitments.

It is also important to note that many centers are able to turn out groups of workers many times larger than that of their formal membership base for specific activities and economic and political actions. The New York Taxi Workers Alliance has a thousand dues-paying members, but an additional 4,500 drivers who are non–dues paying members, and via the economic actions they have taken, the organization is widely regarded as representative of many more drivers than the five thousand drivers. The TWSC has about 850 formal members, but is the primary sponsor of an annual cultural event that draws 10,000 immigrants and their families.

STAFFING AND DECISION-MAKING

Leadership development and popular education are also important to worker centers as a source for recruitment of new staff. A number of the worker centers that were visited as part of this study had a trajectory in place for leaders to become staff members. At several of the centers, former leaders were now long-time members of the staff, a good sign that the difficult and often unsuccessful transition from volunteer to staff, or leader to organizer, had worked. In fact, some of the organizations operated as all-volunteer groups for several years before getting to the point of hiring staff. IDEPSCA operated as an all-volunteer organization for the first ten years of its existence.

At most of the centers there were a majority of immigrants and people of color on staff—as well as a diverse staff in terms of class composition. Organizers and others have been hired directly out of the constituency bases the centers were working with, something that is much more unusual among most union and community organizing groups. Here are a few examples.

- At TWSC, ten of eleven staff were immigrants and people of color; several who had started out as volunteers, had been there for a decade or more. Most of the staff has been hired out of volunteer ranks.

- At GWC, in addition to short-term, part-time jobs for unemployed members, there are two permanent "worker organizer" positions, one for the Latino workers and the other for the Chinese. Lupe Hernandez, a volunteer who had been hired on the staff about six months earlier told me: "When I was working in a factory, when I would come home, my body would hurt. But now, my head hurts. I'm in this class on community power analysis and economic development. I'm learning English. I'm trying to learn everything here. Also I'm learning the computer and how to carry an unpaid wage case and the wage calculations. I'm just trying to fit everything into my head!"

- Most of the restaurant and grocery organizing staff at KIWA started out as leaders in local campaigns in Koreatown. Mrs. Lee, the lead organizer of the restaurant workers, became involved with KIWA while she was a waitress in a local restaurant. Max Mariscal, worked stocking shelves at Assi Market, the largest grocery store in Koreatown, and was fired for his union organizing activity. Now he is one of the lead organizers on KIWA's grocery organizing campaign.

- At the Workplace Project, all of the staff positions are held by Latino immigrants or the children of immigrants, and historically many of the organizers have been former board members or volunteers. The UNITY housekeepers cooperative is staffed by Lillian Araujo, a former domestic worker as well as board member for four years, and one of the founders of the co-op.

On the staff of many worker centers one can readily find, not just first- or second-generation immigrants, but people who have recently emigrated, have worked in local industries, and become involved in the centers as volunteers. A large number of the top staff of immigrant worker centers are first-generation immigrants who arrived as children and grew up in the United States. Their parents arrived in the same ways and held many of the same jobs as the workers they now seek to organize. As the middle-class, college-educated children of immigrant parents they have grown up with a foot in each world: they feel part of their ethnic communities while also having achieved a level of personal and professional comfort in the wider world. But it is clear that they are drawn to the work out of deeply personal commitments; their own histories link them to the low-wage workers they see every day. Here are some examples:

- Nadia Marin-Molina, executive director of the Workplace Project: "Before I entered kindergarten, my mother used to take me with her to clean houses in the wealthy suburbs of Boston. More than twenty years later, she is working two jobs every day instead of one. One is in a school cafeteria and the other is in a department store fitting room. She is being paid slightly more than the minimum wage, but has no complaints except about the kind of gloves they give her in the cafeteria—'too thin' she says."

GARMENT WORKER CENTER

When I came to the center I saw they were all young people—especially a lot of American-born Asians—and they speak good English and they have very good educations, but they were still willing to sacrifice their time. Maybe they could have gotten a better job, but they are willing to speak for the common workers. I thought, as a common worker myself, I should come out and speak for other workers, and help them.

Source: Helen Chien, Garment Worker Center, garment worker and part-time organizer. (Ms. Chien was a physician before emigrating from China.)

• Jose Oliva, executive director, Chicago Interfaith Workers Rights Center: "My family actually came here in 1984. I was thirteen. . . . My mom was a student teacher. She worked in the western highlands in Guatemala. She was involved in a couple of organizations outside of the school in which she was doing organizing to get running water and electricity inside the schoolhouse and it got her in a lot of trouble with the government, and we went into hiding in Mexico for a while. We went back to Guatemala and my dad, a student, was . . . captured and tortured. And when he was released, which was actually something that didn't happen all that often in Guatemala. . . . one of the things that they told him was that we're only letting you go so you could tell your friends what's coming. So we left and came to the States."

• Irma Solis, Organizer at the Workplace Project: "I was born in Mexico and was brought to this country at the age of four. . . . As a single parent, my mother has worked at a sweatshop garment factory in Brooklyn, six days a week, eleven hours a day since she first arrived in the United States. I recall spending my afternoons sitting by my mother's sewing machine while she worked because her weekly pay was not enough to pay for a baby sitter."

• Cindy Cho, organizer, KIWA: "I didn't know that my parents had been undocumented until just this year. I was talking with my mom. Apparently my father came like a lot of Korean immigrants do with a visiting visa and overstayed it and became undocumented that way. My mom came in and she didn't have any sort of visa and she got caught. Luckily because we had family here, she was able to get an immigration lawyer, got out, and got sponsored through a church because she had gone through seminary in Korea. That's how we got our status, but it could've very easily have gone a different way."

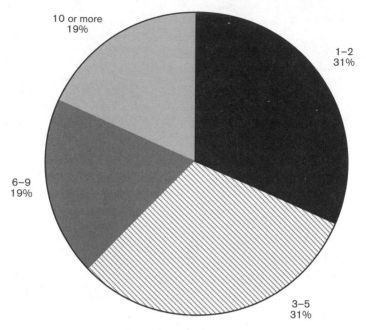

9.2. Worker centers: Size of staff

As can be observed from figure 9.2, most worker centers have very small staffs. Sixty-two percent of those surveyed had between one and five employees. Often the executive directors handle all administrative and fund-raising responsibilities as well as carry out programmatic work, sometimes including the provision of services like the legal clinic and acting as a chief spokesperson for the organization. There is sometimes another administrative support person. Other common positions are linked to the legal clinic, ESL, or other services and organizing. Given how small they are, center staff often operate as "Jacks of All Trades" doing a bit of fund-raising, a bit of administrative work, a bit of legal work, a bit of organizing, and a bit of advocacy.

A number of center staff talked about how much they liked being able to build an organization from scratch, as opposed to working within long-established structures and routines. Many spoke freely of "making things up as they went along." Kimi Lee, who is the daughter of a garment worker, explained that "part of why I wanted to do it was because I had worked for the ACLU and a union, which is very top heavy. It's these national bodies telling you what to do. Many times I disagreed because I felt like people of color, immigrants, and woman usually kind of get left out from that. This was a very interesting dynamic where there was this new center and we'd have the run of the place and figure out what to do and it could be worker oriented. That's why I wanted to do this."

The second person hired at GWC was Joann Lo, who had been working at the SEIU Justice for Janitors local in Los Angeles. "For me, one, it was nice because the organization was just starting and it was exciting to be part of something new and to help shape it and feel like my input would be taken into consideration. I felt like at the union it was a big organization and both of the campaigns I was on, the International had a big hand in directing it and telling us what to do. I felt sometimes frustrated that the organizers who were in the field weren't really listened to."

When Jon Liss helped found the TWSC in 1986, he worked as a volunteer organizer for the first three years, supporting himself as a courier. In 1989, he began to get paid for ten hours a week, at which point he was able to incorporate the organization and begin to raise foundation money. TWSC, like most of the other worker centers, was not connected to a larger network of community organizations with an existing practice around organizing, nor was it connected to a union or an existing social service infrastructure. "We were making up all that stuff as we went along . . . there might have been conferences and stuff that we'd stick our head in and whatever, but largely we were just making the stuff up. So . . . to really conceptualize, you almost had to painfully experience every bad thing you could do or wrong turn and then make a decision not to do it."

Most executive directors I interviewed, especially those who were the founders of their organizations, had been drawn to the work by their desire to help immigrant workers to organize for better conditions; they had strong entrepreneurial leanings, but little prior administrative experience. As their funding bases have grown, they have had to learn to put systems in place for staff supervision, organizational planning, fund-raising, and financial reporting.

Bhairavi Desai, who has been lead organizer of the New York Taxi Workers Alliance and its predecessor the LDC for almost a decade, talked about what it was like to go from being a one-person show to director of a small staff. "I think what happened is that for a long time I was the only staff person and then in 2001 we had two other staff people join pretty much at the same time." Developing relationships with colleagues while at the same time playing a supervisory role, was a challenge for her, she reports. As she explains it, "When you work 70 hours a week and have to balance the focus on a broad political vision and the minute details of your work, you put yourself on autopilot just to keep sane while being productive. And then, all of a sudden, you have to shift gears when new staff comes in and you have to delegate, build organizational memory, and create new processes for decision-making."[5]

Just as the directors were often new to their work, most of the centers' volunteer leadership, including boards of directors, also had little prior experience in belonging to organizations and usually none in overseeing organizations. Many directors recounted stories of tensions between leaders and paid staff of the centers. Kimi Lee realized that the garment workers on her board had no idea what was involved in running a worker center. "The board . . . didn't know what the staff was doing and part of it had to do with we were training the board and trying to explain all the pieces of the organization and we hadn't gotten to staff," she said. "To a garment worker, working in an office all day is like we're just sitting around. What are you doing? Explaining . . . grant writing or coalition work or general stuff that we do or even just explaining how much time it takes to do the cases and the paperwork and the calls and the visits [is really hard]."

Most of the organizations talked about having had very little time to focus on the internal lives of the organizations for the first several years they were in operation. A small number, including OTOC and the Chicago Interfaith Workers Rights Center, are part of national networks that provide ongoing training and strategic support. But the majority of centers are not. In the last few years, a number of the others have begun working with organizational development consultants, sometimes funded by long-time, anchor foundations interested in their long-term sustainability.

The New York Foundation (NYF) has many immigrant worker centers in its portfolio and has a highly developed infrastructure around providing capacity-building technical assistance to the groups it funds. "The signature NYF grantees are small organizations operating with a tiny staff, few resources, and enormous expectations," said Maria Mottolla, executive vice president. "Their goals are huge in comparison to the resources they have available to achieve those goals. A grant from NYF is often the first large grant an organization receives. . . . Our reports are likely to be the first time a group has put down on paper what their accomplishments are, or what their projected budget will be."

The foundation offers a series of monthly workshops for grantees on topics ranging from fund-raising and media techniques to social policy topics. "We never require people to come, there are occasions where we will strongly suggest that a group take advantage of technical assistance, but we keep it confidential," said Mottolla. "We want people to feel they can talk to a consultant or go to a workshop without feeling there's a report card at the end or a funder breathing down their neck. We feel this is like therapy and it won't work unless it is confidential." For ongoing technical assistance, organizations are able to specify their needs and choose the person they want to work with from a pre-screened and approved roster of consultants.[6]

The New York Taxi Workers Alliance has been able to make productive use of this technical assistance support to look at its administrative and staffing issues. In the past year, KIWA and GWC both began working with a consultant on organizational development, strategy development and implementation, and staff communication issues. CAFÉ in South Carolina expressed strong interest in ongoing training and technical assistance but had been having trouble identifying someone local to work with on an ongoing basis.

BUDGETS AND FUND-RAISING

As can be seen in figure 9.3, worker centers have very small budgets: 51 percent have annual incomes of $250,000 or less, and only 9 percent exceed $500,000 annually. Like most nonprofits, the vast majority of their funds go to paying modest staff salaries and center overhead. With the exception of a few trailers, few of the centers own their own buildings. The Chinese Progressive Association in Boston has recently undertaken an ambitious capital campaign for this purpose; TWSC and the Anti-Displacement Project (ADP) in western Massachusetts own sizeable buildings they are rehabbing for use as hiring halls and work and meeting spaces. Some use office space donated by religious organizations but the majority of centers are not in subsidized situations.

The New York Taxi Workers Alliance, credited with winning the first fare increase in eight years for the city's forty thousand licensed taxi drivers, has an annual operating budget of about $160,000. "Maybe with the three staff people we were at about $180K," said Desai. "We'd like to have a minimum of five staff people. We give stipends to the Organizing Committee members for coming to meetings so they don't have to pay for their lease out-of-pocket. Right now it's at ten active driver organizers. We'd like to increase it to twenty. We think we need about $225,000."

CHIRLA operates three day-labor hiring halls that help hundreds of workers every month negotiate employment in addition to operating ESL and computer classes and helping with legal claims. For this it receives $150,000 per site per year from the City of Los Angeles, through community development block grant or CDBG funds. "About eighty-five percent of our money goes to hiring staff and benefits," said John Arvisu. "The rest of the money goes into the operation of each center." Here are some additional examples.

• The Workplace Project is the only organization solely dedicated to assisting the 325,000 plus Latinos on Long Island with their employment-

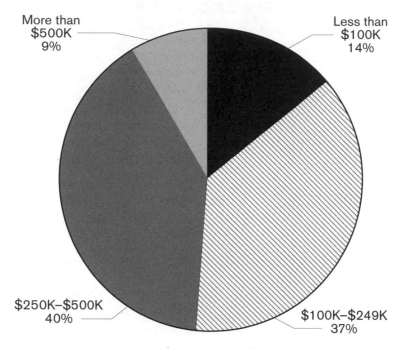

More than
$500K
9%

Less than
$100K
14%

$250K–$500K
40%

$100K–$249K
37%

9.3. Worker centers: Budget sizes

related issues through a mixture of service, advocacy, and organizing. Its total operating budget in 2003 was $398,072.

- GWC, the only organization of its kind that is dedicated to organizing, advocating, and providing services to the 100,000 women who work in the Los Angeles garment industry, has an annual operating budget of $393,000. GWC has gotten more than $1 million in back wages awarded to workers.

- In 2002, the Chinese Worker Organizing Center in San Francisco helped 240 low-wage Chinese workers collect more than a $1 million in back wages. Its annual operating budget is approximately $175,000.

Immigrant worker centers raise the majority of their funds (61 percent) from foundations. According to a survey of worker center funders that was conducted for this study by the Neighborhood Funders Group (NFG) Working Group on Labor and Communities, the vast majority of foundations are funding the organizing and advocacy work that is done by the centers.

Centers have helped workers recover hundreds of thousands in unpaid wages, apply for individual taxpayer identification numbers, receive free medical care, open bank accounts, cash paychecks, and take out no-interest emergency loans. Every month, they refer scores of workers to health clinics, legal services, and family counseling. Most worker centers do not charge any fees for their services, although some ask for small donations. Despite their increasing role as gateway institutions for newly arriving low-wage immigrants struggling to navigate the world of work, immigrant worker centers are not packaging their service programs to foundations and are not raising money for the services they provide.

Those foundations answering the NFG survey who were not funding worker centers were funding a variety of programs and services that included ESL, literacy, and legal services, suggesting the possibility that centers could be raising more foundation money for service-related activity. Those foundations answering the survey who were funding worker centers expressed the challenges they often face in framing support for advocacy work to their boards. These funders also worried about the long-term sustainability of worker centers, given their tremendous dependence on foundation support.

Some centers have received funding for their service-related activities, but struggled with the expectations of foundations accustomed to dealing with very large providers. Former executive director of the Workplace Project, Jennifer Gordon, cautioned about thinking of service provision as a revenue stream that could help support the overall work of the organizations. "When we got money for legal services . . . we had to put in place all sorts of data bases and record-keeping and filing. . . . They are used to funding these huge social service agencies so their reporting requirements are onerous. It is not just a matter of worker centers needing to figure out what sources can support services, but foundations understanding a different approach to service, otherwise if centers ramp it up, it could swallow everything else."[7]

Angelica Salas, executive director of CHIRLA, also cautioned about the organizational compromises involved with contracting with government to deliver a service, as is the case with the organization's operation of day laborer centers for the City of Los Angeles. "Although city councilors always understood our interest in developing the leadership skills of day laborers and working with them to organize for better treatment, we were repeatedly reprimanded by city administrators for integrating these activities into our work at the day laborer centers."[8]

One of the most difficult issues that worker centers face in terms of budgets and financing is the issue of membership dues. Of the minority of centers that began their work with the notion of a need for dues, most did not have, and have still not developed, a systematic means for collecting them. The GWC is fairly typical of these groups. "Very few people have checking accounts. So they come here and pay," said Joann Lo. "Generally it's when they come to a meeting or a protest, if they can pay, they do."

Forty-eight percent of worker centers surveyed said that they had a system of membership dues, 3 percent said they were planning to develop one, and another 13 percent indicated that the larger organizations to which they were attached collected dues. Dues in most instances were five to ten dollars per month, although in some cases they were considerably lower—ten to twenty-five dollars for the year. Thirty-six percent of centers surveyed said they did not have a system of dues collection. My survey and case study data indicate that most centers have not systematized their dues collection and report that payments are irregular. Most centers are not worksite-based and do not engage in collective bargaining. As a result, they do not have a system in which dues are deducted from workers' paychecks by employers like unions do, and they have not yet figured out other mechanisms for reliable dues collection.

Belief in the need to have a dues-paying membership base in the worker center world can be best understood on a continuum. It runs from those who either do not view it as important or see it as unfeasible to those who feel very strongly that it is critically important and have made efforts to expand and consolidate it or plan to. Hence there are three very different reasons why centers are not further along in having sizeable dues-paying membership bases. Some groups aren't sure they believe in it on principle, some groups just don't think it is feasible, and others believe in it but haven't figured out how to do it consistently. Here are some examples.

- The New York Taxi Workers Alliance separates the issue of dues-paying from the issue of membership entirely. In August 2004, it claimed a membership of fifty-four hundred, but a dues-paying membership of around a thousand. "To become a member, you just have to fill out the membership form. Then you join our membership list. Each of the people that joined has had to participate in some kind of activity to get the form. Out of that base, would be our dues-payers," said Bhairavi Desai.

- Workers who participate in TWSC's industry-specific organizing projects are asked to pay dues. AUTO, the cab driver organization of about six hundred drivers is organized by nationality: each ethnic group has its own leadership representatives. The leadership of each one collects the dues, gives receipts, and brings the money into the TWSC office. According to Jon Liss, about 100 of the taxi drivers pay ten dollars a month. The hotel workers pass the hat at meetings, and out of 150 childcare members about 80 paid dues at one point, and then it dipped down to about 25 and they are now building it back up. In addition, the geographically based chapters are also required to raise five hundred dollars a year to contribute to the organization. TWSC charges twenty-five dollars a year per individual or forty dollars per family, has 850 dues-paying members, and asks for weekly reports from staff about how recruitment is going.

• The KIWA-sponsored Restaurant Worker Association of Koreatown, as we saw in chapter 6, is collecting enough dues and contributions from its membership base of about 340 people to pay sixteen thousand dollars to support one organizer's salary.

Although there are exceptions to the rule, the vast majority of worker centers did not view membership dues as a central component of their budgets or as a major strategy for achieving greater financial self-sufficiency. Also, very few of the centers surveyed or those who participated in the case studies talked about dues giving workers a sense of ownership over their organizations. In fact, most of the worker centers that participated in the case studies manifested a profound ambivalence about requiring dues as a condition of membership. Their reasons can be grouped into five categories:

1. They believed that members were too poor to be asked: "The issue of collecting dues is a pretty big tamale for day laborers because their job isn't steady. It's not something where they have a guarantee of work. . . . You see the influx of guys coming in and going out. All of those issues make it a lot more complicated. The issue of having to send money back home. All of those realities we try to take into account. We don't want to impose like, 'Let's collect dues,' and then all of the new people coming in would they understand that reality? Would they also agree to it? What sort of education has to be ongoing in order for people to really buy into an idea of paying into a center?"

"The board and the worker leaders agree that a lot of people can't pay and we don't want them to feel too pressured. It helps when you explain that the membership money goes to help members work here when they're unemployed, so people feel this is a good reason to pay dues. We don't say that if you don't pay dues, you can't be a member and we won't help you."

2. They worried that charging dues in order to access services was extortive and that workers who had already been "ripped off" in the United

States or back home would just get turned off. They were more comfort-able having the conversation about fund-raising separately from mem-bership dues: "A lot of the times we don't want to impose this dues pro-cess on the day laborers. We're really taking an approach where it can't be done if we're saying, 'In order to do this, you have to pay into it.' That takes a long time. It's a very complicated process."

"The workers do give a lot to the center in terms of money, but they do it almost on a volunteer basis. Or, and this is very small time fund-raising, but if we ever need to pay for a certain event that's happening, we orga-nize fund-raisers. We do raffles and different things. The workers are able to give part of the money that they have, but they also feel like they're a part of that drive. It's just that we don't have a mandatory dues process."

3. They did not believe they were offering enough services to "charge" for membership, or feared they would not be able to deliver services satisfac-torily if they had an influx of new members: "There was a member that said that we should do a big march downtown so more workers know about the center and come out and that he could hand out booklets. I said, 'If a whole lot more people come, we don't have the capacity to deal with all the wage claims that they would bring.'"

4. They were concerned about sacrificing quality for quantity, and that if membership was easily attainable it would not mean anything: "We don't want people to come just for the sake of coming, becoming a member and filing a claim. We want to be able to develop people's commitment to the center and to organizing and fighting. To me it's important that the mem-bership increases, but at the same time I think it's important to have a quality in membership. The numbers won't mean anything if the people aren't involved and participating."

5. They rejected the making of a financial contribution as a measurement of commitment, arguing that participation was a better way to measure it: "Members have to participate somehow in the activities of the organiza-tion and this is more important than dues. . . . We are moving toward a membership based organization and will be starting ten-dollar monthly dues; however, membership will really be based on commitment and not money. Members must attend ten of the twelve collective meetings and volunteer ten hours a month."

While some centers did view membership numbers as a way of evaluating their strength or power, many said that they had just not been able to devote the time to development of an effective system of dues collection. "We are on the side of folks [who believe that they] should support their own organizations financially. You've got to be able to get to scale so that the organization's power becomes real," said Gihan Peirera of the Miami Worker Center.

> The organization has had a couple thousand sign up as official members, but we have an active membership of about two hundred. The organizers and staff don't collect the dues, our leadership collects it and keeps track with pen and paper. One of the leaders has a ledger book and keeps track of collecting it month to month at meetings. So, while two thousand or so people came to meetings and applied to be members, we, like the rest of the worker centers, don't have any mechanism to collect dues. I know from my work with unions that having automatic dues deduction through check-off is huge in terms of sustainability.[9]

Bhairavi Desai thinks the organization has had trouble putting a system in place because it keeps going from campaign to campaign. "Really it's like you have to look at dues collection as a campaign of its own. We've just not had a period of time where we could take six months out of our political work to just concentrate on building the dues system. So the dues payers that come to us are one-by-one on their own." The New York Taxi Workers Alliance is working on shifting to a system of charging seventy-five dollars per year to workers but dreams about the possibility of one day being able to collect dues automatically at the garages, as the old union once did, or when they go to the Taxi and Limousine Commission to renew their licenses.

The issue of dues collection and its implications for fund-raising and organizing is further discussed in chapter 11.

CHAPTER 10

NETWORKING, STRUCTURES, AND PRACTICES

In the previous chapter we looked at a number of features of the internal life of worker centers. In this chapter we will look at some of the networks that worker centers have created to enhance their power and end with an evaluation of the strengths and weaknesses of worker centers' organizational practices, structures, and activities.

Although there is no one single overarching national network or association that brings together all 137 worker centers under a single umbrella, more than fifty of them belong to one of the three major national networks of centers. The centers are also imbedded in a variety of national, regional, state, and local networks and coalitions. A few of these are sector specific, but most bring groups together around specific issues such as labor and employment law and wage enforcement, immigration reform or contingent work. A small number are explicitly focused on providing a range of technical assistance to members.

NETWORKS OF WORKER CENTERS

The network that brings the largest number of organizations in a sector together is found among the day laborer organizing groups. The National Day Laborer Organizing Network (NDLON) was founded in 2001 and has twenty-nine day-laborer organizations as affiliates. Prior to the founding of the formal network, organizations in California, Washington State, and Oregon began working together in 1998 under the auspices of CHIRLA and IDEPSCA. Their decision to bring workers together was catalyzed by the realization that many of the workers were part of the same migrant rotation and that they were struggling largely with the same issues in every community. For the next few years, organizers and leaders traveled between the centers sharing ideas.

Since 2001, NDLON has brought together day laborer centers from all over the country to share experiences, increase the participation of day laborers in the operation of the centers and organizing work, and help set up new centers. In 2004, the organization grew from one to five staff members. NDLON now provides a wide range of technical assistance to affiliates. These include challenging anti–day laborer solicitation ordinances in federal court,[1] assisting in the process of transitioning informal corners to structured worker centers, strengthening the processes of discipline at worker centers and corners, and educating and building relationships with public officials. They also include resolving conflicts with other groups, building relationships with Home Depot, connecting member organizations with potential funders, and creating a leadership development curriculum. The organization maintains a website with a "members-only" section where member groups can contribute to and access a shared pool of campaign, legal, and fundraising materials.[2] As the basis for its training and technical assistance work, NDLON has convened discussions and worked with affiliates to develop a model of the ideal day labor center.

Decision-making is carried out through the organization's national convention to which all affiliates send voting delegates and where major matters of organizational policy and governance are voted on. NDLON member organizations host the conventions where the expectation is that "the national convention must have a significant political and organizing impact on the lives of day laborers in the metropolitan areas where it is held" and "where priority is given to cities or regions where day laborers are under attack."[3] Host organizations must be willing to organize a large-scale demonstration as a condition of the national convening taking place there. There is a national coordinating committee that guides the organization between conventions.

In 2001 and 2002, the organization convened thirty-five roundtable discussions with day laborer groups across the country about what national legislation might look like. It worked with Congressman Luis Gutierrez (D-Chicago), the National Employment Law Project, Sweatshop Watch, and the Mexican-American Legal Defense and Education Fund (MALDEF) to draft comprehensive protective employment legislation, the Day Labor Fairness and Protection Act, and has organized members to lobby for its passage. In addition to its annual convention, NDLON convenes monthly national conference calls with affiliates as well as local, statewide, regional, and national trainings, assemblies, and strategy sessions. During 2003–2004, the organization held eight regional conventions that brought together day laborer organizations in California, the

Washington, D.C., area, New York/New Jersey, Arizona, Chicago, Texas, and Washington/Oregon. Following the conventions, NDLON put a system of monthly conference calls in place for each regional grouping.

Beyond the day laborers, there is not a single network that brings together most immigrant worker centers. During the 1990s, there were two or three efforts to bring together a national consortium of worker centers that did not succeed in building anything long-lasting. The efforts broke down over political differences between the groups. In the summer of 2003, *Labor Notes,* the magazine and think-tank for worker activists from union and community organizations, brought together sixteen worker centers from across the United States and published a series of articles that profiled various centers. In the summer of 2005, the Center for Community Change convened thirty-five worker centers for a conference on strategies for membership building, dues collection, and income generation.

While there are several cities that are home to a cluster of worker centers, only a few have strong ongoing networks. For a time, San Francisco had a loose network of worker centers and unions called LION, the Labor Immigrant Organizing Network. In 2004, Chicago Interfaith Worker Rights Center was in the process of bringing together a worker center network that would be comprised of its two worker centers and three others. There is a small informal network of worker centers and allies in Miami. New York City has a high concentration of worker centers, and there are close working relationships between small groups of them, but no citywide network that encompasses all or most of the centers.

By far the most mature and vibrant local network of worker centers and their allies is in Los Angeles. The network is comprised of CHIRLA, which is twenty-five years old, and KIWA, which is ten, who both have helped found a number of other organizations, including the Filipino Worker Center and the GWC. In addition to the informal contact they have with each other day to day, the collaboration has spawned two important citywide organizations to address the two most pressing problems for low-wage immigrant workers.

The Coalition of Immigrant Worker Advocates (CIWA), which was discussed in chapter 5, works on labor law enforcement in low-wage industries. The Multiethnic Immigrant Worker Organizing Network (MIWON) is a coalition of worker centers that work together on legalization issues. The group has worked on legalization of undocumented immigrants at the federal level, the statewide level through efforts to regain access to drivers licenses, and the local level through work coordinating support for the specific campaigns and boycotts of the individual centers. The organizations jointly raise money for MIWON and then each dedicates staff to work together to build a grassroots legalization movement in Los Angeles. For several years, MIWON, now a coalition of KIWA, CHIRLA, the Filipino Worker Center, and the GWC, has organized a march for legalization on May 1, International Workers Day. The first march in 2000, initiated by KIWA, brought out several hundred, the next year a thousand people participated, and in 2002, the march grew to fifteen thousand.

After the national mood about immigration reform changed so drastically in the wake of September 11 and discussions at the federal level about amnesty and legalization stalled, the Los Angeles City Council voted to adopt MIWON's workers rights platform. The resolution called for legalization, greater protection and enforcement of labor and employment laws, voting rights, access to health care, higher education and financial aid, and drivers licenses for all immigrant workers. In 2003, in addition to numerous rallies, marches, and vigils, the network organized a Town Hall meeting that was attended by fifteen legislators and four hundred workers. That same year, MIWON was also central to the organizing efforts of a statewide coalition that after several years succeeded, during the height of recall mania, in getting Governor Gray Davis to sign a drivers license bill that eliminated having a social security number as a requirement. As discussed in chapter 8, that bill was repealed by the legislature a few short months after Governor Schwarzenegger took office and threatened to place repeal of the law on the ballot.

In 2003–2004, MIWON, with support from the Immigrant Funders' Collaborative, coordinated a national multiethnic worker center exchange that allowed eight immigrant worker centers to visit each other for several days and to come together to share models and experiences. There is also a strong network of legal and policy advocacy organizations that provide support to the Los Angeles worker centers. It includes CHIRLA, which in addition to its worker organizing projects has always had a strong legal and advocacy component, and the Asian Pacific American Legal Center of Southern California, which was very involved in the landmark El Monte Slave Labor case and in the founding of the Garment Worker Center. It also includes Sweatshop Watch, which was the GWC's fiscal sponsor and continues to work closely with the organization on state, federal, and international policy issues, and the Downtown Labor Center at UCLA, which has organized workshops and forums on topics of interest to the centers.

OTHER NETWORKS THAT INCLUDE WORKER CENTERS

ENLACE, a network of local low-wage worker organizing projects in the United States and Mexico, brings together twenty-six unions and community organizations, including ten worker centers, and provides training specifically tailored to community-based worker organizing projects, ongoing technical assistance, national conferences, and other networking opportunities. The organization has created a powerful ongoing solidarity network between groups in the United States and Mexico. Through its contacts and campaigns, a number of worker centers, including GWC, the Workplace Project, KIWA, and CAFÉ, have been introduced to union organizers and leaders in the *maquiladoras* and have undertaken several international campaigns.

Through ENLACE, Mexican and U.S. organizations pool their knowledge on multinationals in different industries and have coordinated activities on joint targets. Its signature focus is on trainings and technical assistance promoting "organizational regeneration" maintaining and expanding a healthy leadership core team inside of each group.

In 2004, ENLACE won a signal victory in a campaign against the Sara Lee Corporation. Sara Lee—the world's largest producer of women's intimate apparel—had been locked in a bitter battle with workers seeking to organize an independent union in its Monclova II *maquiladora* in Coahuila, Mexico. Key to ENLACE's success was forging a global network of organizational allies in Mexico, Canada, France, and India as well as unions, community organizations, and worker centers across the United States. This network deployed a strategically sophisticated set of tactics including synchronized actions in cities around the world, from Los Angeles to Paris, Mumbai, Mexico City, London, and Montreal.

In October 2004 Sara Lee agreed to employer neutrality and freedom of association for its Coahuila workers—the *first* labor neutrality commitment by a major corporate entity in Mexico to date. Sara Lee also agreed not to retaliate against these workers for union activities and to rehire 210 union activists and other workers who had previously been laid off at Monclova II.

The National Alliance For Fair Employment (NAFFE) is a network of national, regional, statewide, and local organizations that take on issues relating to nonstandard work arrangements, including part-time, temporary, and contingent work. The organization provides technical assistance, conducts research, maintains an online clearinghouse, convenes conferences and workshops, and brings its members together to work on joint campaigns. It has sixty-eight member organizations in its network and fourteen worker center members, including NDLON.

The most common national networks that were mentioned as coalition partners by worker centers in the survey were the Center for Community Change, Jobs with Justice (JwJ), and the National Organizers Alliance (NOA). JwJ has forty labor, faith-based, community, and student coalitions in twenty-nine states and an organizational membership structure. JwJ has provided a range of support to worker centers in communities across the country. In its hey day, NOA had hundreds of individual organizers as members across the country and thousands more it brought together in its annual gatherings, regional trainings, and local discussions. Several worker centers are members of their city or state Jobs with Justice organizations and many also sent organizers and leaders to NOA regional and national gatherings. Many organizations also mentioned two other national advocacy/funding organizations as frequent partners at the local level: the American Friends Service Committee and Catholic Charities.

The Center for Community Change provides research and ongoing technical assistance to community organizations across the country. It worked with a wide variety of low-wage worker organizations through its National Campaign on Jobs and Income Support and has had an ongoing low-wage work team in which more than a dozen worker centers have participated. More recently, it has started two new initiatives that include worker centers: a national network of local grassroot organizing groups to participate in the national reform effort and a worker center support project as a follow-up to this national study.

Several national organizing groups founded a subset of worker centers, which do a lot of their networking and receive much of their technical assistance from these networks. By far the largest and fastest growing, Interfaith Worker Justice (IWJ) has nine worker centers that are directly affiliated with it, three more under development, and several others that have attended events and trainings. In recent years, the network has been growing fastest in the South, working closely with the Equal Justice Center. IWJ provides ongoing organizational development, organizing, and legislative and fund-raising support to its affiliates. It has played a leadership role in the fight to raise the federal minimum wage as well as in forming coalitions with state and federal government agencies, including working closely with the federal Department of Labor Wage and Hour Division on wage enforcement issues. IWJ has excellent relations with the National AFL-CIO and many international unions and works closely with them in support of organizing campaigns. Its signature contribution is organizing among national denominations and local faith communities in support of organizing drives and other labor-related campaigns.

The Solidarity Sponsoring Committee in Baltimore and OTOC in Omaha are both affiliates of the flagship Industrial Areas Foundation (IAF) community organizing network which provides trained organizers and ongoing training and technical assistance to organizers and leaders. In addition to supporting and participating in conventional organizing drives, several IAF organizations have long experimented with new organizational forms and strategies for worker organizing and improving the labor market prospects for low wage workers. Using a broad-based organizing approach whose building blocks are local faith-based institutions, they have also worked closely with various unions locally and nationally, including the SEIU, HERE, and AFSCME.

ACORN, Associated Communities Organized for Reform Now, is a very successful national community organizing network with chapters across the United States that focuses on low income people. During the 1970s, building off of its welfare rights and unemployed worker organizing, and frustration with the lack of union organizing taking place among low-wage workers, ACORN began experimenting with community-based worker organizing models in many places including Detroit, New Orleans, Boston, and Chicago. Several of these projects blossomed into innovative organizing campaigns. ACORN's United Labor Unions (ULU) formally affiliated with the SEIU and went on to pioneer work in organizing homecare and other industries. For almost twenty years in Illinois, Local 880 of the SEIU, originally an ACORN union, worked to organize the homecare industry, and won collective bargaining rights from the state for 29,000 workers in 2004.[4]

The National Employment Law Project (NELP) works very closely with dozens of immigrant worker centers across the country, providing legal and public policy support and technical assistance. NELP has prepared a host of policy reports on a range of topics, including unemployment insurance models for low-wage workers, state legislative models for advancing immigrant workers rights and labor law reform, and a report on the impact of the Hoffman Plastics decision. NELP's immigrant employment rights and contingent worker listserves are indispensable resources that lawyers and advocates across the country make use of and contribute to on a daily basis.

The National Immigration Law Center (NILC) also works very closely with many immigrant worker centers and focuses on immigration law and the employment and public benefits rights of immigrants. It conducts policy analysis, impact litigation, and provides technical assistance and training to legal aid agencies, community organizations, and pro-bono attorneys. NILC has been extremely involved in tracking and challenging decisions that have arisen in the wake of Hoffman Plastics and in proposing federal legislation that would overturn the original decision.

GWC is working closely with Sweatshop Watch, an international watchdog group based in the United States, to develop relationships with garment workers in other countries. "Sweatshop Watch has been establishing relationships with garment organizations throughout the world. Hopefully next year we're going to do an international garment worker strategy meeting," said Kimi Lee.

Because of Sweatshop Watch we're able to put a foot in that, otherwise there's no way we could handle all that international stuff. We've already had a few meetings with garment organizations and women's organizations in other countries, but we're trying to actually push toward some kind of collective strategy. How do we deal with it? The only way to address the vicious cycle of globalization is to have international connections. We can't just do it here and toot our horns and say, 'It's about the US workers,' because it's not.

STRENGTHS AND WEAKNESSES IN THE ORGANIZATIONAL LANDSCAPE OF WORKER CENTERS

Still relatively new, the structures and practices of most worker centers are continually evolving. Currently, however, it is possible to step back and observe certain organizational cultures, structures, habits, and patterns of behavior.

In general, worker centers are a mixture of the formal and the informal, of organization and movement. On one hand, many have their own nonprofit tax status, boards of directors, full-time staff, programs, services, classes and training, and conduct sophisticated foundation fund-raising. These are all formal activities conducted by formalized, structured organizations. On the other hand, they have limited formal membership structures, no reliable and consistent systems for dues collection, loose networks, and, for the most part, minimal infrastructures.

Another characteristic that worker centers share is their emphasis on the role of their constituency in leadership and decision-making. Many worker centers are strongly committed to having the organizations be led by low-wage workers. While leaders certainly emerge organically during social movements, there is seldom a structure in place or an orientation toward deliberate leadership identification and development. Worker centers place great emphasis on identifying and developing grassroots leaders. Organizational culture and structures emphasize participatory processes that provide opportunities for volunteers and leaders to learn how to think critically and strategically and to be part of the decision-making about organizational direction. This is also evident in the strong commitment to popular education. For these organizations it is not just a methodology, it is a stance. It is a way of having organizational practice reflect the way they would like society at large to function.

As we have seen in this chapter, most of the organizations have very healthy leadership and volunteer bases. In my visits to worker centers over the past two years, I have been continually struck by the number and quality of the volunteers who have gravitated toward them. Not all of them stay, of course, but also striking was many of the organizations' track records at retaining volunteers and leaders over a period of several years. This was also evident in terms of staff retention. Community organizing networks often struggle to recruit and retain organizers, and especially organizers of color, but worker centers did not seem to suffer from this problem. It seemed that founders and executive directors worked hard at developing a participatory approach among staff as well as leaders and in grounding the organizations in the culture and practices of the communities they were seeking to work with. There was a strong sense of ownership over the organization on the part of staff at all levels and less of a distance between organizational culture and the social, cultural, and political orientation of individuals hired to work at them.

Some of the achievements of worker centers in the areas of leadership development and staff recruitment and retention flow out a belief that building the organization and ensuring a rich internal life, rather than winning a particular campaign in the short-term, is primary. This stands in marked contrast to more campaign-driven organizations for whom driving toward the goal is the primary focus and cultivating the internal life of the organization often gets less attention. There are a number of reasons for the focus on internal dynamics among worker centers, but a major one is political orientation. Since the organizations are striving for systemic change in American life, and they know this is a long-term proposition, they view the work of consciousness-raising and developing leaders as the most essential parts of what they do.

As we have seen, formal membership for many worker centers requires active participation in the organization on the part of workers. Formal membership sizes are modest and very few worker centers have established reliable and consistent mechanisms for dues collection. While some centers were setting membership recruitment quotas and actively struggling to regularly collect dues, most of them, even those who said they believed formal membership to be important, were not making it a priority.

This is in strong contrast to leadership development, which most of the organizations placed a very high priority on, actively discussing, evaluating, and adjusting their practices often and "counting" leaders inside their organizations—taking stock of the numbers they were developing and thinking about how to grow. Lack of attention to building a large membership base could be viewed as at odds with the strong public claim made by these groups that they are democratic organizations that organize low-wage workers in their communities to speak for themselves. The low membership numbers have implications for organizational legitimacy and power as well as financial sustainability. Dues are one important way that people demonstrate a strong commitment to an organization and make clear by their actions their sense that the organization is needed. Dues-paying members demonstrate that the constituency itself, and not just outside sources, is supporting the organization. When an organization is completely or overwhelmingly supported by outside money, it is at greater pains to demonstrate that it has grown from a strong demand on the part of the community.

As a measure of power, worker center membership sizes must be viewed as a weakness. In doing their advocacy work, it is harder for the organizations to claim to be speaking on behalf of a significant base: this can undermine their legitimacy in the eyes of elected officials, other opinion leaders, and the media. Elected officials may be less compelled to support the groups' public policy proposals because they know they are organizations with few members and they may question the organization's claim to be speaking on behalf of immigrant workers in their community.

Worker centers, by not institutionalizing a system of dues collection, miss out on substantial financial support and over rely on foundation support. This is problematic because of the unpredictable nature of foundation support and also because foundations measure future organizational viability of centers by looking for internal revenue-producing strategies. When these strategies are not in place, which, as we have seen, is the case for most centers, organizational stability is always at risk. To be fair, with the exception of organized labor, this same critique applies to the vast majority of organizations on the progressive side as well as many other nongovernmental organizations. Even ACORN, the IAF, and other faith-based community organizations, while they collect significant contributions from individual and institutional members, rely on foundations for a substantial portion of their funding. But these groups are in the constant and unenviable position of worrying about losing their funding.

In fact, many have mythologized the existence of a large dues-paying membership among low-wage workers in previous eras of labor history. For example, although the United Farm Workers union has been understood to have built a significant dues-paying base in the years prior to negotiating contracts with growers, in truth it never did. As the following quote from Cesar Chavez makes clear, the UFW never figured out how to systematically collect dues until after contracts were signed.

> At a farmworkers' convention, we told them [the workers] we had nothing to give them except the dream that it might happen. But we couldn't continue unless they were willing to make a sacrifice. At that meeting, everyone wanted to pay $5.00 or $8.00 a month. We balked and said "no, no. Just $3.50. That's all we need." There were about 280 people there and 212 signed up and paid the $3.50 the first month. 90 days from that day, there were 12 people paying $3.50. By the time the strike came . . . only a small percentage of the workers were paying dues. But it was ingrained in them that they were going to have a union come hell or high water.[5]

When looking at low-wage worker organizing in the immigrant community, it is important to be cautious about measuring organizational vitality by the size of the dues-paying membership base. There are other ways in which a community may demonstrate its support for an organization that are independent of payment of membership dues. Also, the mechanical difficulties involved in collecting dues on a regular basis without access to payroll deduction or bank drafts are formidable and will have to be addressed in order for things to improve appreciably.

On the other hand, organizers who hesitate to ask for dues because they think their members are just too poor also need to be challenged. Again, in the words of Cesar Chavez,

> No matter how poor the people, they had a responsibility to help the union. If they had $2.00 for food, they had to give $1.00 to the union. Otherwise, they would never get out of the trap of poverty. They would never have a union because they couldn't afford to sacrifice a little bit more on top of their misery. The statement "They're so poor, they can't afford to contribute to the group" is a great cop-out. You don't organize people by being afraid of them. You never have. You never will. You can be afraid of them in a variety of ways but one way is to patronize them.[6]

Some low-wage worker organizations have been able to institutionalize grassroots fund-raising and a dues system.

New Labor, an immigrant worker center in New Brunswick, New Jersey, worked with its leadership to develop a creative and successful grassroots fund-raising program and dues collection system. During its first two years when it had no external sources of funding, member contributions were enough to support an office and an infrastructure including telephones, a DSL line, and copying machine solely from money generated by members. "I think our staff was reluctant to ask members for money, but for us, we went to our governing council and asked them how to raise money and they suggested a slew of ideas that involved members and their monies," said Rich Cunningham, one of the group's codirectors.[7] "The price for all goods that New Labor sells and what we sell, ninety percent begins as an idea from a member." Along with ESL, computer and occupational safety and health classes, the organization has a very popular computer lab that has ten iMacs, which members use to send e-mail to family members back home, access the web, and do instant messaging with friends. Its grassroots fund-raising includes selling cans of soda, blank CDs, and T-shirts.

El Comite, the governing committee of the center, set annual dues at fifty dollars a year, and in its four years of existence, has collected that amount from about a thousand people. Cunningham estimates New Labor's renewal rate to be about 30 percent, "and we average new members every year which means we generally generate three hundred to four hundred dues payers in a year at fifty dollars." The organization recently made a decision to also ask for a twenty-five-dollar initiation fee from new members when they join. "We are strict with dues and renewals," says Cunningham. "There are no free riders at New Labor. You don't pay, you can't play or stay. We can do this because of our services, which people see as vital and cannot access anywhere else for the rates we charge, not in spite of them." The organization's soccer team is also self-sufficient, raising the eight-hundred-dollar inscription, and the cost of uniforms on its own.

Casa de Maryland, an ethnic NGO that grew out of the Central American community and evolved into a workers' center, is still developing membership and dues structures, but has developed important supplemental revenue sources. Gustavo Torres, the organization's executive director, has placed a high priority on developing income generating projects and also believes strongly that people are more committed to the organization when they pay something for services received. The organization issues ID cards that are accepted by area banks, public schools, and public safety authorities. Casa charges fifteen dollars per card and raises an average of $50,000 a year. The organization also operates eight different kinds of classes including ESL, literacy, vocational education, computers, and citizenship. The ESL classes are the most popular, about four hundred people sign up for each fifteen-week cycle for which Casa charges $100 (although scholarships are available). The classes yield about $100,000 a year, but most of this just covers the cost of renting classroom space and paying professional instructors. In Torres' experience, constituents have been quite willing to pay for classes and other services, as long as the quality was good.[8]

The Chicago Homecare Organizing Project (CHOP) was founded in 1983 as a community-based worker organizing project by ACORN and "specializes in providing support for organizing low-wage workers that traditional labor unions have not supported." The organization, affiliated with Local 880 of SEIU, focused its work on organizing the low-income home care workforce in the Chicago area, and in 2003 it won state legislation that established collective bargaining rights for home care workers.

Today CHOP has twenty-nine thousand workers under collective bargaining agreements. It gets a small amount of grants but 98 percent of its budget comes from membership dues. During the years that CHOP worked toward winning the legislation, it organized thousands of home care workers and asked that each one pay a one-time five-dollar "joining fee" and join the organizing committee. Organizers focused on collecting the joining fees rather than ongoing dues from these workers because they knew that they were working toward a collective bargaining agreement that would have payroll deduction.

In the past few years, the group has moved into organizing childcare workers as well as home care Medicaid workers who are not yet covered under collective bargaining agreements. They have found that, especially when it comes to recruiting very small (three or fewer) "licensed-exempt" home childcare providers, there are certain neighborhoods where there are so many providers, organizers can literally go door to door to find them.

In one zip code, Field Organizer Myra Glassman noted, there were close to eighteen hundred. For these workers, rather than a one-time joining fee, CHOP is trying to get as many as are willing to agree to pay monthly dues via "bank draft," which are deducted automatically from their bank accounts. Local 880 has been collecting authorization cards and getting memberships from large numbers of these workers. "It's just like any other 'ask,'" said Glassman. "We tell people that we have an organization to run, that this is what the dues are, people are signing up and here's how you join . . . and at least 50 percent will sign a bank draft."[9]

Glassman estimates that close to one thousand of the newly targeted home care Medicaid workers, licensed home childcare providers, and licensed exempt home childcare providers are now on bank draft. Dues have averaged about $18 a month and are now yielding about $100,000 a year in income to the organization. "If they have a bank account, the monthly dues can be deducted automatically," said Glassman. "You have to get the form with their signature and language saying 'I authorize my bank to deduct this amount of money, by the fifth of each month, payable to CHOP.' . . . They give a voided check and it gets sent into the bank and shows up on their monthly bank statement."

While immigrant worker centers sometimes say that their members don't have bank accounts or don't have them in places that would allow "bank draft," Illinois ACORN is having success not only with African American workers but also with low-wage Latino workers, regardless of their immigration status. In Little Village, the organization's major Latino chapter in Chicago, out of fifteen hundred members, five hundred are on bank draft. "In any community that has a lot of undocumented, the self interest of the banks has superceded any other principles," said Madeline Talbott, lead organizer. ACORN organizers have negotiated agreements with several banks to accept the *matrícula consular* (the

Mexican ID card) or an Individual Taxpayer Identification number as sufficient to open up bank accounts. "We can make the case to banks about these issues and then as we are recruiting people to join, we try to get them to go with us to the bank to open up an account, or send them to banks that will do accounts with *matrículas*."[10]

These banks also offer an extra ATM card that can be used in Mexico," Talbott added. In addition, the banks have agreed to allow workers to open accounts with very small initial deposits. "We tend to go with a more aggressive political approach in our recruitment, because you end up with more committed members who are in it for the long haul," said Talbott. "All low and moderate income people get it. Immigrants really get it. It is a very straightforward conversation, not everybody is ready to pay the dues, not everybody is ready to make the commitment, but they all get what it will take to build an organization," said Talbott. "It is not enough of the budget yet . . . we are not anywhere close to self-sufficient for the amount of resources we are spending on immigrant organizing, but we can see that we can get there . . . as long as we keep making progress in that direction it is a good thing," said Talbott. "We have been a dues-paying organization forever because we have always believed that is the way to go because at some point external sources of income dry up."

Talbott believes that the reason more community organizations don't aggressively collect dues is because staff members don't like to do it. "The job description is what people are opting out of. Asking for money is not the job that people come into this work to do. They want to help, to build, to fight, but they don't really want to ask for money. The job description is just plain hard—you have to ask a lot of people, it is harder to hire and retain people in that job description."

On the other hand, doing membership recruitment and asking members to sign bank drafts can be tremendously energizing. "The newer cities that have started on this have watched it grow exponentially," says Talbott. "It can grow exponentially up to a certain level and then it becomes more regular and slowly increases over time. But when you start, you get to see these dramatic increases every single month. You get the money you signed up last month plus this month, three months ago plus two months ago plus one month. That is an amazing thing."

Ginny Goldman, ACORN's lead organizer in Houston who previously worked in Chicago with Talbott developing the Little Village system, says that out of about 2,000 members, 530 are currently on bank draft. Dues collection without bank draft says Goldman "is a haphazard nightmare."[11] Every three months Houston organizers make a round of calls to members to ask them to become current on their dues, they also collect dues at membership meetings. Goldman works with organizers, and leaders try to get people to go beyond monthly dues to paying three months or six months worth, and eventually getting them on to bank draft. "I try to get organizers to update their lists every month and get members to update their dues, but it is hard to get organizers to do this every month when they are rocking and rolling with their exciting campaigns. At the beginning of the year, I try to do this 'happy new year time to get on bank draft' rap . . . I talk about wasn't last year great and this year we are going up against some even bigger targets and you know how much money they have so we need to have the resources to take them on."

Goldman estimates that the organization is bringing in about forty-three hundred dollars a month in dues in Houston, which is about a quarter of the budget. Goldman compared asking members to pay dues to tithing to the church: "Our members are used to paying money at church—they are committed to their church—it is their church and they are paying for it. It is not a foreign concept to low-income people . . . I think people really do feel it is theirs when they pay for it. They feel they can demand more out of the organization and it keeps us more accountable." ACORN does believe that outside money is key to supporting organizations while they are getting the system going and has been the recipient of grants and loans that were specifically for this purpose.

Both Glassman and Talbott strongly asserted the importance of membership dues not only for financial self-sufficiency but also as a measure of commitment on the part of members. "You have to build a dues-paying membership base because then people have a stake in the organization, they feel more like it is theirs," said Glassman. "People know that it costs money to run an organization and they know that if you are paying to help run an organization then it is linked to power. If people aren't paying something it is somewhat a measure of their investment in wanting to organize. They can say 'I support this or that' but when they put their money down, that is commitment."

"Unless you charge dues, you can't build an organization that can win. You are an advocacy organization, which is fun to do and in the absence of alternatives is a good thing," said Talbott. "I love being an advocate and I love providing service. I see the attraction of it. But I also love being in the driver's seat and that is what you get to do if you are at an advocacy organization, no matter what you say, nobody can tell you what to do. In organizations where you allow yourselves to become dependent on the dues that poor people pay, they don't have to outvote you, or fight with you, they can just take a hike."

Devoting this much attention to the problem of dues collection should not be read as a blanket criticism of worker centers. The issues of membership, financing, and sustainability are enormously challenging and not unique. As centers develop and evolve, they will no doubt find creative responses to them. But it is important for them not to be afraid to frankly address thorny problems like consolidating a membership base.

ISSUES OF STRATEGIC ALLIANCE BUILDING AND NETWORKING

In general, immigrant worker centers are terribly overburdened with the day-to-day work they are trying to do. As a result, some are fairly isolated and struggle to engage in strategic alliance building and coalition organizing. Most commonly, centers respond to organizations that reach out to them, but less often are proactive about which prominent individuals and organizations they ought to try to get on their side in a particular campaign. As we have seen, race and ethnicity are the central constitutive categories for worker center recruitment, and mobilization and the racialization of the economy is the central lens through which many centers view the problems workers face and possible solutions to them. This perspective also conditions the types of alliances and coalitions many centers decide to pursue and prioritize.

Many focus on building coalitions with other worker centers and organizations of people of color, especially those working with low-wage immigrant and African American workers. While this work is essential, it is also important for centers to consider other types of strategic alliance building across race and class lines with constituencies whose power could be extremely important to winning a particular campaign. Feminist historians have shown, for example, that without the intercession of Jane Addams and the white, middle-class women reformers of Hull House to support immigrant workers, the Amalgamated Clothing Workers of America would never have gotten its first contract with Hart, Shaffner, and Marx. Who are the Jane Addamses and the Hull Houses of today who might join with immigrant worker centers to effectively pressure employers and elected officials?

When we look at the Workplace Project's outreach to key business organizations, OTOC and the Chicago Interfaith Workers Rights Center's work with religious institutions, and the Coalition of Immokalee Workers' enlistment of prominent persons, we can see important examples of the power of this kind of broader alliance building. But perhaps the best examples of strategic alliance building in the worker center world are the day laborer centers. Centers know that to win an equitable solution for day laborers in a given community, they must identify the interests of a range of stakeholders, including local police, area businesses, and neighborhood associations. The organizations know that they cannot win without building relationships with these constituency groups.

Given that centers have, as one of their major activities, enforcement of labor and employment laws, partnerships between worker centers and government agencies are also extremely important. The Los Angeles centers have done tremendously impressive work in this regard. So have the Interfaith Worker Justice centers, in their case not only state by state, but also in terms of the relationships they have developed in Washington, D.C., with the Wage and Hour Division of the Department of Labor as well as other federal agencies.

Other organizations communicate sporadically with government agencies. They invite them to address their members, but are less involved in ongoing partnerships. Also striking is that while worker centers are dealing with low-wage workers and their issues on a daily basis, many develop and carry out their work largely in isolation from local unions and central labor bodies in their areas. This means they are not able to share information, pool resources, or coordinate activity. It also leads to hard feelings when one organization does not know what another is doing, has not had the opportunity to hear about it ahead of time, or to voice an opinion or provide information that might have influenced the strategy. Many centers acknowledged this problem but some said that their efforts to work in partnership with organized labor had been rebuffed.

At present, worker centers are under-networked at every level. Local networks such as MIWON and CIWA in Los Angles enable worker centers to aggregate their resources and magnify their impacts. They enable centers to work together on labor market strategies as well as immigration reform and other public policy campaigns. In cities like New York, Chicago, and San Francisco, no such local networks of worker centers currently exist. There are informal relationships between far-flung centers that share strategies and ideas (such as is the case with POWER in San Francisco, the Miami Workers Center in Florida, and TWSC in Virginia). However, more geographically proximate networks have the greatest potential to lead to economic and political success because worker centers can coordinate action on common economic and political targets.

At the statewide and regional levels, in most parts of the country the same vacuum exists: organizations may come together on driver's license or other campaigns, but they are not working together on an ongoing basis. Day laborer centers, however, through NDLON, have been pulling together statewide and regional conference calls and meetings around the country. However, in some states, centers approach moving forward with the creation of these types of networks with caution. In discussions about the possibility of creating a statewide network in California, several reasons emerged for the centers' caution.

First and foremost, many of them felt they had their hands full just trying to do their day-to-day work and simply did not have the time or resources to participate in a network. Second, a number of the groups felt that before a statewide network went forward, a northern California regional network needed to be put in place. Third, although largely unspoken, it was clear that there were issues of trust and that the organizational history between some of the groups made them wary of working together. What was striking about the discussion about participation in a network was how universally it was viewed, because of the time involved, in terms of detracting from local work. Potential positive effects of a network, such as enhancing the work through staffed technical assistance, sharing of strategies, multiplying power through coordinated campaigns on common employers or public policy, or helping with fundraising, were largely absent from consideration.

On the other hand, a gathering of midwest worker centers organized by the Center for Community Change, Interfaith Worker Justice, and NDLON in May, 2005 was extremely well-attended and well received by participating groups. Many organizations spoke about their desire to coordinate strategies and share ideas and strongly supported the establishment of a midwest network of worker centers.

The lack of a comprehensive national network outside of the day laborer groups is problematic for several reasons. First, when invited to national convenings, individual worker centers are unable to project a national presence. They often feel marginalized by the AFL-CIO and other national entities. However, when national groups are looking for someone to represent the day laborer centers, they can contact NDLON. When NDLON sits at the table it makes clear that it speaks on behalf of thirty-plus organizations around the country. But most worker centers are not part of NDLON, they are only representing their own local organization but are sitting at the table with national organizations whose power and influence derive from having many subsidiary affiliated organizations.

Second, many funders hesitate to try to fund at the local level and to develop capacity to distinguish between individual local organizations. They often seek heuristic tools such as regional or national intermediaries through which they can make their grants. To the extent that worker centers do not have such intermediaries, they may miss out on funding opportunities. Third, there is rich learning that could be taking place between worker centers. Some have spent many years working hard to perfect a model legal clinic, others an ESL class on workers' rights, successful fundraising strategies or a method of matching up low wage workers with health services. More important, some may have developed innovative labor market strategies or public policies and could be coordinating work that targets common employers across local and state lines. The absence of a national clearinghouse means that outside of the day laborer centers, most centers only hear about these models and ideas episodically.

It is not clear what the best approach is to building capacity at the national level. One approach would be the formation of a new encompassing national organization of worker centers that would undertake some technical assistance/clearinghouse, fund-raising, political coordination, and representation functions. Creation of a new organization, however, creates another "mouth to feed" in a context of scarce resources. It would require an intensive organizing effort to bring groups together and may well not succeed.

An alternative approach might be to strengthen the capacities of the cluster of existing organizations that are already working with worker centers. For example, as we have seen, NDLON is doing important work with its day-laborer organizations; might it be strengthened to allow it to provide more hands-on technical assistance or to open its membership to an even larger number of organizations? ENLACE provides technical assistance to its member organizations on internal issues as well as strategy and organizing, but due to limited resources it usually does so either in times of crisis or during specific campaigns. Might ENLACE be strengthened so that it is able to provide steady ongoing support to its member organizations, possibly take in new groups, and establish more of a national presence? In addition, the organization has been pioneering strategic international campaigns on transnational corporations by coordinating actions between low-wage organizing groups in the United States and Mexico that in some instances have also involved activity on the part of allied organizations in several other countries. Perhaps ENLACE could be resourced to refine and strengthen this work.

Interfaith Worker Justice has its own network of nine worker centers. In addition to enhancing its ability to provide hands-on organizing support and technical assistance, support could be provided to enhance the organization's excellent work at the national level with religious denominations, international unions, and government officials. This includes collaboration with the Wage and Hour Division and other federal agencies, its advocacy around increasing the federal minimum wage, opposing Bush administration proposed changes to overtime regulations, proposing a pilot federal living wage bill for nursing home workers and working with the United Food and Commercial workers to launch a poultry industry organizing strategy in the South.

In terms of ongoing support, the National Employment Law Project is the centers' closest ally in terms of rapid response to legal issues and providing research that is finely calibrated toward meeting their advocacy, policy, and legislative needs. Many low-wage worker organizations rely on NELP's legislative models and policy expertise. The National Immigration Law Center (NILC) works closely with NELP as a linchpin of legal support on immigrant-worker-related issues in particular. NELP could be a natural home for an online clearinghouse not only on policy questions but also on enforcement issues and approaches to delivering legal services.

The clearinghouse function could be carried out very well by NELP, which has strong web and listserve capabilities and a special understanding of the needs and interests of these groups. NAFFE has specialized in issues of contingent work and has worked with several worker centers on these issues as well.

As these networks and alliances further develop and expand, they will undoubtedly affect individual worker centers and the way they see themselves and their roles. Working together more closely may also influence whether or not centers move in the direction of a common organizational form. The nature and possible future direction of worker centers is the subject of the next chapter.

CHAPTER 11

A HOLISTIC ASSESSMENT OF THE WORKER CENTER PHENOMENON

In contrast to previous chapters, in which I have looked at particular aspects of worker centers, in this chapter I will present an assessment of worker centers as they have emerged, evolved, and become an integral part of their communities.

WHAT EXPLAINS THE RISE OF WORKER CENTERS AND WHAT DOES THEIR EMERGENCE SIGNIFY?

Immigrant, Latino, African American, and other workers in communities across the United States today, in the face of widespread exploitation, low wages, and scanty health benefits, are in desperate need of help and opportunities for self-organization. The difficult conditions under which low-wage immigrant workers currently toil are the result of a "perfect storm" of labor laws that have ceased to protect workers, little effective labor market regulation, and a national immigration policy that has created a permanent underclass of workers. In addition to the problems posed by outmoded labor laws and labor market regulation, low wage African American workers face a legacy of racism in structures of education, employment, and housing. In their tripartite efforts toward labor market policy change, worker organizing, and immigration reform and confrontation of institutionalized racism, worker centers are attempting to address all three of these inclement conditions.

In part, worker centers have emerged because of the void in representation that has been left by the decline of organized labor and the institutional narrowness of the contemporary labor movement. If workers still had a meaningful right to organize in this country, and unions were able to enact labor laws and create union structures that more accurately reflected the realities of the new economy and the low wage workforce, many more of the industry-based centers might well be unions. However, it should be noted that many of the centers organize within very low-wage, loosely organized labor markets inhabited by day laborers, housekeepers, hospitality workers, and agricultural workers, who have always been underrepresented within the ranks of organized labor.

Just as worker centers have been conditioned by the absence of accessible unions, they have also been strongly affected by enduring xenophobia and racism in labor markets and employment as well as other areas of community life such as education. During the last twenty-five years a "raced" community organizing practice, which places race and ethnicity squarely in the center of its analysis and strategy, has emerged. Most worker centers strongly identify with this approach. Immigrant worker centers as political actors seeking to enact laws more favorable to immigrant families are also a reflection of the decline of local immigrant-based political party organizations and the rise of a new generation of community-based organizations who pursue political change outside of political party structures. Finally, many of the centers strongly identify with the global justice and democracy movement, which has a very strong anti-sweatshop program and works to link student, community, and worker organizations internationally.

More generally, as we discussed in chapter 1, many of the institutions that once comprised an infrastructure of immigrant incorporation in addition to unions and parties, such as mutual aid/fraternal organizations and settlement houses, have either ceased to exist or have declined in size and strength. Immigrant worker centers are a piece of the newly emerging infrastructure of immigrant incorporation that is based in the country's growing "third sector" of nonprofit civic institutions.

As we have seen, although immigrant worker centers address a common set of problems, their origins lie within a diverse set of institutions, including immigrant nongovernmental service organizations, legal aid agencies, and faith-based groups. These organizations, despite their differences, have embraced common organizational forms and strategies in order to address the pressing needs of low-wage workers in their communities.

LOCAL LABOR MARKET INSTITUTIONS OR SOCIAL MOVEMENT ORGANIZATIONS?

In previous chapters we have looked at issues of membership, participation, and economic and political action, but ultimately how we understand the role and effectiveness of worker centers today has a lot to do with the lens through which we view them. If we view them as labor market institutions, we might expect to see more of a hiring hall model in which the organizations focus on providing benefits and pensions, job training and placement, and undertake efforts to organize workplaces and negotiate with employers. We might expect a much narrower public policy focus and less in terms of community organizing or mobilization.

If we view them instead as social movement organizations (SMOs), or "local movement centers" that focus on issues of work (because employment is such a central area of exploitation for immigrants and native-born people of color), our expectations would be different.[1] Then we might expect to see more community organizing, mobilization, and a broader public policy focus and less job training, placement, benefits provision, and workplace organizing.

A local movement center, according to civil rights movement scholar Aldon Morris, is an organization "within the community of a subordinate group that mobilizes, organizes, and coordinates collective action aimed at attaining the common ends of the subordinate group." Morris argues that a movement center can be said to exist when the community has developed "an inter-related set of protest leaders, organizations and followers who collectively define the common ends of the group, devise necessary tactics and strategies along with training for their implementation and engage in actions designed to attain the goals of the group."

As examples, Morris cites three local civil rights organizations: the Montgomery Improvement Association (MIA), the Inter Civic Council (ICC) in Tallahassee, and the Alabama Christian Movement for Human Rights (ACMHR) in Birmingham. Earlier scholars of the civil rights movement, Morris argues, often "reached erroneous conclusions about the origins of the civil rights movement" because they underestimated these movement centers as "weak and incapable of generating mass collective action." But he argues that, despite the loose membership structures and limited financial resources of these groups, they were quite central to the organization of civil rights movement activities in their cities and across the South. Scholars tended to focus on their difficulties, including repression and fear among members of the subordinate group, struggles devising effective strategies and tactics, and meager financial resources. But while the problems described were certainly accurate, Morris argues that scholars overlooked these organizations' important strengths and capabilities.[2]

Perhaps a parallel situation exists today in the case of critical perspectives on worker centers. The centers work with constituencies who live day to day with tremendous fear. They struggle to identify tactics and strategies that will be effective for workers who have very little economic and political power, and they have much looser structures than the more established organizational bureau-cracies of labor unions. They have not yet figured out how to formalize mem-bership and many may never do so. On the other hand, like the local movement centers of the civil rights era, the organizations are strongly based in local com-munities, they have impressive cadres of leaders and an ability to mobilize fol-lowers. They are important hubs in local and regional low-wage worker, anti-sweatshop/globalization, and immigration reform networks. Furthermore, they initiate strategies and campaigns, and have figured out how to raise money from outside sources.

In the advocacy and organizing work they do, worker centers have been able to cast the struggles of low-wage immigrant workers in moral terms, alter the terms of debate in their communities about how these workers are treated, and win some important local policy and worksite victories. If we view them through the lens of social movement organizations, we may understand that some will be impermanent organizations that will fulfill certain critical func-tions at an important moment in time but may or may not go on to institution-alize themselves for the long haul.

If we view the organizations through the lens of local labor market institu-tions, our expectations are for a larger, more formal, dues-paying membership base, greater efforts at economic self-sufficiency, targeted industry-specific or-ganizing campaigns and strategies, and contracts with employers. But as we have seen in chapter 9, most of the worker centers have small formal member-ship bases. And as we saw in chapters 5 and 6, while they certainly engage in firm- and industry-specific campaigns, and some even operate day laborer cen-ters, the vast majority do not create firm-based structures or negotiate con-tracts. Most victories at the firm level come through lawsuits and direct action and at the industry-wide and geographic level through direct action and public policy change.

Most worker centers, even those with a strong industry-specific focus, have not yet become full-blown unions. But perhaps a better way to understand today's industry-based efforts of worker centers is that they are functioning as "preunions" that are laying the groundwork for a more systematic union or-ganizing effort. Some of the day laborer organizing efforts might be seen is this light as well as the TWSC's organizing efforts among hotel housekeepers, and the work of ROC-NY, KIWA, and Young Workers United among restaurant workers.

It is not yet clear whether immigrant worker centers will follow a trajectory toward social movement organization, labor market institution, or a new orga-nizational form altogether. It is certain that the different centers will not all evolve in a single direction but will follow different organizational paths: some toward new union forms, others toward social movement organizations. While it is tempting to leave the discussion here and say that the organizations will evolve organically, a few cautionary words are in order.

Over the course of reviewing drafts of this manuscript, some organizations took sharp exception to my efforts to categorize them and strongly resisted categorizing themselves. Are categories important? To the extent they help centers to focus in on a specific set of strategies, I think they are. Without a clear strategy and model that defines the range and focus of activities a center will undertake, the risk is that they will try to do it all. As a result the numbers of workers they reach and campaigns they win will be modest, and funders and outside observers will hold them accountable for perhaps an unrealistically broad set of programs. For centers to get to the next level of efficacy and power, it may be important for them to face up to questions of focus and capacity in their work and develop metrics for measuring success.

With this framework in mind, we now turn to a summary of worker center strengths and weaknesses.

THE GREATEST STRENGTHS OF WORKER CENTERS

The greatest strengths of worker centers include their successful leadership development programs and their successes in winning improvements in the employment situations of low wage workers. Their strengths also include providing a collective voice for low wage workers to express themselves and an openness to organizational change and experimentation.

Leadership Development

Survey data and case studies indicate a very strong commitment on the part of paid staff to the organizations for which they work: many directors and senior staff have been at their organizations for several years. Most of the organizations did not have high staff turnover. In most community-based organizations, consistency of staffing is an essential component of increasing effectiveness over time. In many social justice organizations, staff turnover, along with retention of people of color, are serious problems, but these are much less in evidence in the worker center world. In addition to the stability of the staff, most of the case study organizations had long-time leaders who had been participating on the board and in the advocacy and organizing work for several years.

For most of the case study organizations, leadership development, including development of a leadership body to whom the organization would be accountable, was a central focus. Staff understood their work to go beyond representation of low-wage immigrant workers to developing the capacity of those workers to speak and act for themselves. They devoted much of their time to activities that would further this development.

Direct participation in the ongoing life of the organization via boards and committees was where the centers really evinced strength—there is a vibrant leadership core at the heart of these organizations. Numbers ranged between sixteen and twenty-five in terms of the core leadership teams, but most organizations could point to a range of seventy-five to a hundred individuals who had strong ongoing affiliation and participation as volunteers. In addition to the numbers of active participants, as we discussed in chapter 9, some organizations have held quite sizeable events and actions that have numbered in the hundreds and even in the thousands. Others have not ever put more than sixty of their members in a room at the same time. In terms of picket lines, actions, and ongoing activities, my impression was that the numbers ranged from fifteen to thirty workers turning out at a time.

Providing Vehicles for Collective Voice/Altering the Terms of the Public Debate

Although they are present in greater and greater numbers in a growing number of communities, immigrant workers are still to a large extent invisible to the larger society. While companies and individuals rely on their labor on a daily basis, there are few mechanisms for these workers to speak for themselves and make their needs and opinions known publicly. Sometimes, public discussions of immigration and other issues surrounding low-wage immigrant labor are conducted at the abstract level, without the voices of immigrants themselves represented in the debate. Other times, debates are not at all abstract, and immigrant workers, especially those who seek employment in visible public places, are the focus of intense community discussion. In either case, immigrant workers are talked *about*, rather than talked *with*. New immigrant communities are in the process of developing vehicles for collective voice that give them opportunities to speak for themselves. Worker centers represent one vehicle through which the representation of the interests and expression of a low-wage immigrant point-of-view is taking place.

Worker centers have been quite successful at interjecting a low wage worker point-of-view into public debates about economic development, employment, and immigration issues, and this perspective has been quite influential. In an earlier project in which I tracked local newspapers of record, I documented how the media framing of economic development altered drastically after the

Solidarity Sponsoring Committee and its sister organization, Baltimoreans United In Leadership Development (BUILD) began its work in Baltimore. In Long Island, New York, coverage of immigrant worker issues changed dramatically after the Workplace Project entered the conversation.[3] Part of the power of worker centers derives from their ability to organize a base of the working poor to speak from their own experiences. This enables them to "reframe issues," proposing fresh analysis and policy ideas, casting employment issues in starkly moral terms, and often altering the terms of the debate in a community.

Through this work, worker centers do not just operate within what Lukes and Gaventa have called the "first face of power," working toward immediate and medium-term political goals. The groups also work in the "second face of power," expanding what is on the political agenda and building coalitions and alliances, and the "third face of power," redefining issues so that they are viewed as appropriate arenas for public policy intervention. Worker centers may not win all their campaigns in the short and medium term, but by mounting them, they are altering the terms of debate and changing the way that people understand the world around them.[4]

Effective Enforcement of Minimum Wage and Other Employment Laws

While American employment laws require employer compliance, enforcement largely hinges on individual workers knowing their rights and taking action. In low-wage America today, violations of wage and hour laws are commonplace. Centers provide an effective means for workers to learn their rights and to obtain redress from employers. They know the laws and procedures and have systems in place for workers to file claims and recover back wages. Beyond legal expertise, the groups encourage workers to organize their co-workers to act collectively and support them when they do so. They also use individual cases and the statistics compiled over time to publicize in the media and to policymakers the problems low-wage workers are facing. As we have seen, these organizations are well-positioned to see what is and is not working in terms of enforcement of minimum wage, overtime, and occupational safety and health regulations, and to work with government agencies in developing improvements to existing regulatory regimes. Some are deeply engaged in these partnerships, others are more limited in their thinking about strategic alliance building. The organizations are working to set legal precedents that assist low-wage workers in holding employers accountable and to set aside others that do not.

Pioneering Campaigns for Improving Conditions in Low-Wage Industries

Many of the workers who contact worker centers are in industries that are increasingly characterized by small, diffuse firms and subcontractors. Others, while they may still work for a subcontractor, are really at the tail end of supplier chains that connect to very large multinational corporations. In the first instance of small and diffuse firms, the difficulty lies in uniting workers across many separate workplaces, launching multi-firm or market-wide campaigns so that wages can be raised across an industry and employers can be united into an entity that can be meaningfully bargained with.

In the second instance of large multinational corporations, added to the collective action problems associated with diffusion of employers and workplaces is the enormous economic power these companies bring to bear on workers when they attempt to organize. Even international unions, which have enormous resources in comparison to worker centers, struggle to exercise effective leverage on large multinationals. It is not yet clear what set of strategies will result in significant and lasting improvements for large numbers of low-wage workers. It is in this context that worker centers have developed campaigns and devised some very creative and effective strategies.

As discussed in chapters 5 through 8, the greatest strength of the economic action campaigns is in providing a vehicle for collective voice. The greatest accomplishment of these campaigns to date are at the level of compelling individual employers to repay back wages to workers and at succeeding in setting minimum wages at day laborer shape-up sites. Other campaigns that have targeted firms or industries to alter their behavior (as opposed to "paying up" one time) are distinguished by the creative approaches they have taken but have been harder to win or to sustain gains that have been made over time. It is important to point out, however, that, as in the cases of the Taco Bell and Forever 21 boycotts, there have indeed been successes, and these have come in part because of the organization's strategic use of organizational allies as well as the law.

Many centers have been able to compel employers to settle complaints, change their behavior, and in some instances, even drop their opposition to a union out of fear of the organizations' ability to generate bad publicity as well as to file OSHA violations, unpaid wage claims, discrimination suits, and other legal cases. Worker centers have made their greatest strides both in the "monopoly face" area of improving wages as well as the "collective voice-face" representing workers in relationship to individual firms, industry sectors, and geographic labor markets in the public policy arena. Organizations have been able to win economic improvements for low-wage workers by moving local government to act in ways that have required employers to raise wages and improve conditions of work. In addition to these monopoly face achievements, collective voice achievements have also come via public policy. Organizations have so far been most capable of forcing improvements in employers' ongoing treatment of workers via catalyzing government administrative action and public policy change.

Experimentation/"Bottom-upness"

In explaining Hull House's approach to its work, Jane Addams once wrote, "The one thing to be dreaded in the Settlement is that it loses its flexibility, its power of quick adaptation, its readiness to change its methods as environment may demand."[5] Contemporary business school prevailing wisdom is that the most effective firms are those that operate as "learning organizations" constantly evaluating their work, sizing up shifts in the business environment, learning from their mistakes, and shifting gears and approaches. In conversations with the nine case study organizations, I was struck by the willingness of the leadership to acknowledge what they did not know and by their openness to trying new approaches. In a context in which it is still not clear what strategies will prove most effective, this openness to rethinking is critical. On the other hand, it is important to stick to strategies long enough to give them time to work.

WEAKNESSES OF IMMIGRANT WORKER CENTERS

The major weaknesses of immigrant worker centers are their relatively small memberships, the limited capacity they have for deep industry-based research, and problems with their financial sustainability.

Numbers/Scale

Pulling together facts and observations about services, membership, leadership development, and organizing, the composite view of worker centers is that, while their advocacy and organizing work is clearly having an effect on the wider low-wage worker community, total numbers of workers directly participating are still modest.[6] When asked about these numbers, many center leaders resisted the idea of measuring them as an indication of organizational, political, or economic power. Several leaders argued that there were many ways to create power and that power was not "just big numbers of people" and that "sometimes it is better to have quality rather than quantity." Others argued that while their formal membership numbers might be modest, the "contact networks" connected to active members, as evidenced by turnout at events, add up to substantial numbers.

As we have seen, with 77 percent of centers surveyed reporting formal membership numbers of one thousand or less, formal organizational membership is modest. Most centers treat membership as more of a privilege bestowed on an individual after she demonstrates her commitment to the organization than as an indication of organizational muscle. As discussed above, how serious an issue formal membership size is depends on our expectations and the lens through which we are viewing and evaluating worker centers. If we see them as social movement organizations that focus on issues of work because employment is such a central area of exploitation, than formal membership may be less important than their ability to mobilize a base that takes visible action and draws allies into the fight. But if we see them as labor market institutions that are attempting to impact firm and industry behavior directly and provide representation and services to members, then the size of formal membership becomes a much more important measure of organizational effectiveness.

Economic and Political Research/Strategy

When asked the question "What is your strategy?" I was most likely to get an answer about the organization's mission or goals. Most of the organizations in the case studies did not seem to have had the resources to engage in thorough economic and political research in their communities. Nor had they asked themselves what kind of power and how much of it they needed to build in order to have significant labor market or policy impact. In surveys and case studies, it was clear that most organizations had not set specific numerical goals for the levels of participation or membership they were striving to reach and did not correlate this with building power.

Although centers believe strongly that they are engaging in power analysis, there was very little "working back from impact" kind of thinking, in terms of what kind of numbers it would take to impact the local labor market, a subsector of the local labor market, or the local or state policy environment. For example, although some organizations used terms such as *labor market,* they could seldom answer specific questions about overall numbers of workers or employers or more fine-grained questions about relative firm sizes and the numbers of workers employed in individual firms in a given local industry. Without this information, it is difficult to calibrate how many workers at how many firms an organization would need to be able to mobilize in order to have an impact on a local labor market in a specific industry.[7]

Similarly, although some organizations used terms such as *political power,* they could seldom answer questions about overall numbers of voters in a district, or more fine-grained questions about the margin of victory of a specific city councilor or state representative they were seeking to influence. Without this information, it is difficult to calibrate how many sympathetic voters one would need to be able to mobilize in order to persuade an elected official to support a particular position. Some groups understood the questions, had a frame of reference for them conceptually, but seemed to think that these workers were so vulnerable and these organizations so weak that such questions were, for the moment, irrelevant.

Finally with regard to research and strategy, there was a substantial gap among some of the centers when it came to delving into the historical record with regard to models of worker organizing in the United States, especially earlier union efforts. Day laborer organizers had very little knowledge about earlier efforts to organize construction workers or longshoremen and historical or contemporary hiring hall practices. Assertions of "no one has ever tried to do this before" were common, as opposed to beginning from the premise that perhaps others have, and there might be some useful things to be learned from those efforts.

Sustainability

As we saw in chapter 9, 61 percent of worker center income derives from foundation funding, 21 percent from government, 16 percent from earned income and grassroots fund-raising, and 2 percent from dues. Government funds go primarily to day laborer worker centers, which means that for the non–day laborer centers, the proportion of total budgets coming from foundation income is even higher. Over-reliance on foundation funding is problematic for several reasons. First, when organizations begin with a model that is funded from outside sources, they are not forced from the beginning to ask for significant commitments from members or to develop income-generating strategies. This is reflected in the small percentages that dues, grassroots fund-raising, and earned income contribute to worker center budgets. If foundation funding were not available, would centers have been less resistant to asking members for money and charging dues and would they have worked harder to develop a system of dues collection? Might the day laborer hiring halls that are now funded by foundation support and government grants have evolved a model more closely resembling craft union hiring halls?

Second, foundations are unpredictable: their priorities change and the amounts they give out sometimes vary with the performance of the market in a particular year. When income is unpredictable from year to year, planning and implementing for the longer term is difficult. Even those foundations that are very reliable usually have a time limit regarding the number of years in a row they will fund the same organization. Some of the strongest worker centers in the country are now in that situation—at the peak of their effectiveness they are now contemplating having fewer resources available to do their work.

Third, centers are forced to constantly be on the lookout for new foundation sources of support, sometimes taking on programs to make them eligible for particular grants whether or not adding the new activity makes sense. Finally, without asking for more significant support from the workers themselves, worker centers never have to face up to the question of how deeply situated in their communities and valued by their constituencies they really are. It is worth thinking about how a new center might constitute itself and what it might ask from workers if it began from the premise that it was never going to allow foundation support to account for more than a certain percentage of its overall budget.

Questions of sustainability and member support are relevant whether or not centers see themselves as social movement organizations or labor market institutions. While unions are known to collect dues from members, movement organizations have also received significant financial support from their constituencies. Morris's research on the civil rights movement documents that despite the low incomes of many of the participants, the majority of financial resources for local movement centers were generated from local blacks via church collections.[8]

POLITICAL, MORAL, AND ECONOMIC POWER

Central to any discussion of organizations dedicated to social change are questions of power. How much do they have, how effectively do they deploy it, and what do they have to do to gain more of it? We now turn to an examination of worker centers in terms of political, moral, and economic power.

Given the small number of constituents who are voters, immigrant worker centers, even if they were focused on building numbers, would wield very little *direct* political power. How can non-voters overcome this problem? The political power of immigrant worker centers derives from three sources. The first source is relational power that is created through the initiation and multiplication of relationships.[9] Worker centers have alliances with organizations in the

faith, labor, and immigrant advocacy communities that do have political muscle and, even when they do not make an issue their top priority, are often willing to lend some support.[10] In addition, if elected officials perceive that an important part of their constituency base will be sympathetic to low-wage
immigrant workers, this is an indirect but important source of political power
as well. As Republicans and Democrats increasingly move to woo the Latino
vote, they will look for ways of demonstrating fealty to this constituency. Supporting legislation that treats low-wage immigrant workers more justly is a way
for elected officials to demonstrate concern and support for Latino voters
whose own family members, friends, or acquaintances may be undocumented
or in difficult work situations.

For example, while the Workplace Project's majority non-citizen base had no
direct political power, it had organizational allies on Long Island who did. In
addition, the number of Latinos who were registered or eligible to vote was certainly growing on Long Island, and politicians could have felt that this was a
way of showing support for the larger Latino community. In terms of the Unpaid Wages campaign, it won powerful Long Island and statewide interest
groups to its side. Both *Newsday,* Long Island's newspaper of record, and the
New York Times provided strong editorial support. It is a plausible assumption
that The Workplace Project was able to translate its high visibility and strong
moral standing into voter sympathy that extended beyond the membership
bases of its closest organizational allies and that elected leaders knew it. On the
other hand, with a few exceptions like Casa de Maryland and Voces de la Frontera in Milwaukee, few worker centers have developed focused voter participation programs and very few, despite their pursuit of public policy change, have
undertaken detailed electoral analyses of their communities and developed
strategies on the basis of this information.

The second source of political power is moral. Worker centers, through their
legal, organizing, and advocacy work, have been able to cast the struggles of immigrant workers to organize for better working conditions and wages in
straightforward "right" against "wrong" terms that have piqued the interests
and pricked the consciences of opinion-makers, elected officials, and the general public. For poor people's organizations, the ability to claim the moral high
ground is critical to persuading allies to join the fight. The third source of power
is through the direct activities of the workers themselves. Whether they can vote
or not, non-citizen immigrant workers are still engaging in political work. They
are knocking on doors, circulating petitions, organizing rallies, meeting with
legislators, and testifying at hearings.[11]

Most centers do not believe workers have much labor market power to bring
to bear on their employers. Of course, there are some situations where they have

been able to do this, principally when they have been able to compel employers to resolve unpaid wage disputes by mobilizing against their business. This has most often occurred by publicizing a business's wrongdoing in the local media, erecting picket lines in front of businesses that rely on foot traffic (restaurants, grocery stores), or by organizing boycotts and publicizing them through local and national networks.

There are other examples as well. These include the day laborers, who have sometimes been able to set minimum wages at their shape-up sites and especially their hiring halls, where they have also affected contractor behavior by requiring them to submit to a formalized hiring process and to comply with the minimum wage and workday hours. Other examples are the New York Taxi Workers Alliance, whose members believe that their leverage came from their ability to threaten to withhold their labor, and the union drive in Nebraska. But most centers believe that they have little economic power and either tend toward reactive campaigns that target specific employers to pay up, or toward advocacy and organizing around public policy change.

Over the course of conducting the study, I was struck by how little worker centers utilized the potential economic power of low-wage immigrant workers themselves. In order for low-wage workers to have direct labor market impact that is not attained via public policy, they must have the power to leverage changes in employer behavior. Organizations hesitate to move workers directly into economic action because they fear that workers won't participate because they will be too fearful of being fired or deported, or that it is irresponsible to ask them because it might result in their being fired or deported. Do centers believe that economic action is off the table for low-wage immigrant workers? If they do, are they correct in thinking so? If they are, this would suggest that perhaps there should be an even stronger focus of resources and organizing by the centers on federal immigration reform.

While termination and deportation are the most extreme possible consequences, I sensed other reasons centers hesitated to ask workers to engage in economic action. They were afraid workers would say no, either because they were not that deeply unsatisfied with their situations, unwilling to risk having to return to their home countries, or viewed their situations as temporary and for that reason, tolerable. There are a host of reasons why immigrants might be reluctant to engage in direct economic action at the point of production. The slowness in developing strategies to overcome them is a continuing weakness of the worker centers.

On the other hand, it has always been difficult for workers at the bottom of the labor market, especially in the private sector, to exercise economic power. For workers to have a direct labor market impact, worker centers must be able to affect labor market dynamics either through supply or demand strategies. Supply strategies based on gaining control over entry into the labor market are difficult to carry out when low-wage immigrant workers are available in large numbers and operate largely outside of licensed professions. Other supply strategies, such as providing job training and placement support, are difficult to implement on a large enough scale to have an impact.

Demand strategies—moving significant numbers of workers into collective action at particular employers or concentrated within particular industries—are even more difficult to implement, for several reasons. The first set of reasons has to do with the situation of the workers individually. First, this would be asking very low-wage workers to make difficult economic sacrifices that may be impossible. Second, for those workers who are undocumented, there is fear of being caught, fired, or deported. Unfortunately in the United States today, retaliation against workers who take collective economic action is now the norm and not the exception. In addition, since the Hoffman Plastics decision, back-pay awards for discharged workers are unavailable to undocumented immigrants illegally fired because of organizing campaigns.

The second set of reasons, as we explored in earlier chapters, has more to do with structures of employment relations, firms, and industries, especially the rise of subcontracting, which often separates immediate employers from the real powers in these industries. It is often unproductive to go after immediate employers to raise wages because they lack the ability to do so, and it requires a much more sophisticated and expensive campaign to move up the corporate food chain.

With such limited economic power and the barriers to building it so high, it makes sense that immigrant worker centers have succeeded most at public policy. As Gary Marks has argued in attempting to explain variations in economic and political strategy among unions, those workers less able than craft workers to control the supply of labor into their occupations were historically more likely to pursue "open" unionism strategies like industrial unionism. They were also more likely to turn to public policy in order to accomplish through politics what they could not achieve through economic organizing. While he asserts that both craft and industrial unions "politicize the labor market by introducing power relations in place of the impersonal logic of market competition," it is the "open," or industrial unions, that have "had to introduce political considerations in a more explicit way, by force of numbers rather than by controlling the supply of labor, and this has led them to support extensive political regulation of the labor market."[12]

In order to alter the labor market dynamics of a particular sector of the low-wage service economy, a significant number of individual workers and workplaces have to be organized, but in order to win on a public policy issue, a community organization often just needs to mobilize a dedicated minority. For a community organization that is pursuing a strategy of passing public policy to alter labor market dynamics—at least in many cases—far fewer recruits are necessary to win. Given the generally low level of participation in politics in America, as evidenced by low voter turnout and low levels of active political engagement, well-organized minorities are often capable of mounting successful campaigns in the public policy arena. There is an often unspoken multiplier effect at work when legislators are contacted by constituents: when a legislator receives fifty phone calls, the assumption is they are representative of a much larger number.

Worker-friendly public policy is essential to improving the lives of low-wage workers. In the United States today, individualized approaches to raising wages simply won't do the job. Broader public policies that require firms to pay living wages, provide health insurance, deal with contingent workers more equitably, and honor the right to organize may well need to come first. In addition, in recent years, labor market policy has increasingly been set via immigration policy, trapping immigrant workers without legal documentation in dead-end jobs and depressing the wages of all low-wage workers. To raise wages and improve working conditions, immigration reform is essential. In recent years, the success of municipal living wage and statewide minimum wage campaigns demonstrates that, given the opportunity, the public may well support policy initiatives that begin to put a new social compact between business and society into place.

Historically, many of the most significant labor market interventions benefiting low-wage workers came via public policy. Frequently, these policies began at the state and local level, eventually becoming national policy. During the Progressive Era, in state legislatures across the country, reformers fought to strengthen labor regulations, enact unemployment insurance, old age and widow's pensions, disability and workers' compensation laws. Sometimes these efforts began locally, as in Massachusetts, where between 1915 and 1916 eight cities overwhelmingly approved old age pensions by popular referenda.[13] The Fair Labor Standards Act, passed in 1938, which mandated a nationwide minimum wage, outlawed child labor in manufacturing, and established the forty-hour work week by requiring employers to pay time and half for hours worked above that number, was the culmination of many local and statewide efforts.

In thinking about the current economic power of low-wage workers in general, it is tempting to accept as a given the categories of "skilled" and "unskilled" rather than understanding them to be socially constructed. An essential strategy for increasing the labor market power of workers currently considered to be unskilled must involve a deeper societal debate about the values underlying our decisions about which types of jobs and industries are accorded high and low levels of market power and respect. Does it make sense that childcare providers who care for millions of the nation's toddlers are viewed as unskilled and compensated so poorly? Does a society with a rapidly aging population and a nursing home industry now larger than auto and steel combined really want to label as menial and compensate accordingly the work of caring for our country's elders?[14] This is precisely the kind of question that immigrant worker centers have the moral standing to pose. It is also a question that may well need to be posed first via politics and public policy before direct labor market intervention can succeed.

As the national AFL-CIO and international unions expand their "Right to Organize" campaigns to educate the American public about the need for federal labor law reform and greater respect for labor in general, it would do well to heed the lessons of history and work more closely with worker centers. Because, although the federation has tremendously strengthened its electoral work in order to mobilize labor's resources and membership to support candidates for office, to succeed in labor law reform, the right to organize must be cast in moral terms. One concrete step the federation can take to indicate its desire for an alliance with worker centers in this work is to include the reversal of the *Hoffman* decision in its agenda for labor law reform.

PUBLIC POLICY REFORMS

By shining a light on the working poor and forcing the issues to be debated, worker centers are laying the groundwork for new national policies on low-wage work and the rights of immigrant, Caribbean, Latino, Asian, and African American communities. In so doing, they are catalyzing Americans to feel a moral stake in supporting a wide variety of labor and immigration law reforms. To greatly simplify this complex field, we can say that policy reforms in five broad areas are needed: immigration, labor law, minimum wage, social insurance, and new approaches to labor market regulation.

Immigration Reform

Labor market outcomes for low-wage immigrant workers of uncertain status cannot be substantially improved without immigration reform. As stated earlier, our country's immigration policy is now the single most influential labor market policy we have. The following elements of a new immigration policy are from the Fair Immigration Reform Movement (FIRM), a project of the Center for Community Change, which is led by low-income immigrant and nonimmigrant grassroots community organizations working for immigration reform and immigrant rights:

Provide a Path to Permanent Resident Status and Citizenship for All Members of Our Communities. Our immigration policy needs to be consistent with reality. Most immigrants are encouraged to come to the United States by economic forces they do not control. Immigrants bring prosperity to this country, yet many are kept in legal limbo. Legalization of the undocumented members of our communities would benefit both immigrants and their families and the U.S.-born, by raising the floor for all and providing all with equal labor protections.

Reunite Families and Reduce Backlogs. Immigration reform will not be successful until we harmonize public policy with one of the main factors driving migration: family unity. Currently families are separated by visa waiting periods and processing delays that can last decades. Comprehensive immigration reform must strengthen the family preference system, by increasing both the number of visas available both overall and within each category. In addition, the bars to re-entry must be eliminated, so that no one who is eligible for an immigrant visa is punished by being separated from their family for many years.

Provide Opportunities for Safe Future Migration and Maintaining Worker Protections. With respect to worker visas, we need a "break-the-mold" program. Such a program must include: legal visas for workers and their families; full labor rights (such as the right to organize and independent enforcement rights/the reversal of the *Hoffman Plastics* decision); the right to change jobs; and a path to permanent residence and citizenship. A regulated worker visa process must meet clearly defined labor market needs, and must not resemble current or historic temporary worker programs. The new system must create a legal and safe alternative for migrants, facilitate and enforce equal rights for all workers, and minimize the opportunities for abuse by unscrupulous employers and others.

Respect the Safety and Security of All in Immigration Law Enforcement. Fair enforcement practices are key to rebuilding trust among immigrant communities and protecting the security of all. Any immigration law enforcement should be conducted with professionalism, accountability, and respect. Furthermore, there should be effective enforcement of laws against human trafficking and worker exploitation.

Recognize Immigrants' Full Humanity. Immigrants are more than just workers. Immigrants are neighbors, family members, students, members of our society, and an essential part of the future of the United States. Our immigration policies should provide immigrants with opportunities to learn English, naturalize, lead prosperous lives, engage in cultural expression, and receive equitable access to needed services and higher education.

Labor Law Reform

Labor market outcomes for low-wage immigrant workers cannot be substantially improved without meaningful access to unions. The Employee Free Choice Act, introduced in Congress in 2004, includes a provision for "card check recognition" that would give workers the right to sign cards for union representation. It would provide mediation for first contract disputes and establish much stronger penalties for violations of employee rights when workers seek to form a union as well as during first contract negotiations.

In addition to the Employee Free Choice Act, workers in low-wage industries need access to multiemployer bargaining. To raise their wages and improve working conditions, these workers need multiemployer bargaining on a geographic/industrial, or chain of production/business network basis.

Provisions for multiemployer bargaining must allow unions to seek certification through an election conducted among all of the workers in a geographically based industrial sector, in which a union would become the exclusive bargaining agent of all workers in a sector if it receives a majority of votes from that sector's workers. New legislation should also allow the NLRB to combine existing bargaining units for purposes of collective bargaining, either on its own initiative or on petition and majority vote of each of the affected units. Finally, similar to the Davis-Bacon Act for the construction industry, new legislation should extend the basic economic terms of an existing collective bargaining agreement throughout an entire geographic/industrial sector if the agreement covers a significant percentage of workers in that sector.

In addition to multiemployer bargaining, the National Labor Relations Act should be amended to allow any employer to sign a "prehire" agreement with a union, under which the parties would agree that the union would represent all workers that the employer subsequently hires. Prehire agreements make collective bargaining possible in sectors where jobs are unstable; currently these are only permitted in the construction industry.

Finally, the Taft Hartley provisions of the National Labor Relations Act that banned the use of secondary economic pressure (pressuring one firm in order to achieve recognition from another) should be repealed.

The Minimum Wage, Fair Labor Standards Act of 1938 (FLSA), and State Wage and Hour Laws

For those industries in which union organizing is very difficult to accomplish there ought to be the option of legislating industry-specific minimum standards concerning wages, overtime, benefits, and conditions of work at the local, state, and federal levels.

According to the Economic Policy Institute, minimum wage employees working forty hours a week, fifty-two weeks a year, earn $10,700 a year, which is close to $5,000 below the poverty line for a family of three.[15] The federal minimum wage needs to be increased substantially and then permanently indexed to inflation. States and cities can take the lead by enacting higher minimum wages or living wage measures.

Guard against misclassification of employees as independent contractors at the state and federal levels.

States should work to provide additional coverage to low-wage workers whose overtime rights were diminished by actions of the Bush administration.

Given the rise in subcontracting, FLSA should include a "joint liability" section in which manufacturers and retailers can be held legally responsible for the actions of contractors. The definition of "employer" in the FLSA should be amended so that it explicitly includes successors (in cases where contractors close and re-open under another name) and the largest shareholders of a corporate employer.

Section 15(a), the "hot cargo" provision of the FLSA, should also be strengthened by allowing for "hot goods" injunctions to force retailers and manufacturers to take responsibility for actions of contractors in terms of minimum wage and overtime compliance and allowing workers and worker organizations to sue. The 1949 statutory provision that exempts from the "hot goods" provision any firm that relies on a contractor's written assurance and lacks notice of a contractor's violation should be repealed.

The FLSA should also contain a section on contingent worker parity that would require equal pay for part-time and other nonstandard workers doing the same work as permanent employees. It should also prevent discrimination in benefits against workers in part-time and other nonstandard work, and require states to set standards for service contractors employing nonstandard workers. As is the policy in France, it should insist on wage and benefits parity between temporary workers and regular workers of a user firm, include requirements to notify workers in advance of the duration of an assignment, and ban temporary work in some dangerous workplaces.

To improve compliance with the FLSA, congress should enact a Federal Unpaid Wages Bill, which would make it a felony, not a misdemeanor, not to pay workers; quadruple civil fines on employers who don't pay workers; and make it possible for workers to use multiple venues to pursue cases. The bill should also clarify that punitive damages are available for retaliation under the Fair Labor Standards Act, require the DOL to seek liquidated damages in all minimum wage and overtime cases that it litigates, and eliminate the court's discretion to reduce or not grant these damages to workers in FLSA lawsuits brought by the DOL.

New Paradigms of Enforcement and Monitoring

The system of monitoring and enforcing compliance with federal and state labor and employment laws is broken.[16] Just as existing labor laws must be amended in order to accommodate the needs of low-wage workers in highly decentralized industries, so must there be new approaches to monitoring and enforcement.

The Department of Labor's Wage and Hour Division at the federal level, and state departments of labor as well, should establish offices of low-wage industries, similar to the one that was created in California, which would have designated staff liaisons with worker centers, unions, and other legal aid organizations.

These new offices, in consultation with the worker centers and others, would have responsibility for the development of an entirely new system for assigning priority to cases according to how many violations an employer has and how many workers are impacted. They should also create training, mentorship, and certification programs that would train investigators in the internal dynamics of specific industries and the most effective enforcement and investigation strategies and partner new personnel with experienced deputies. They should also work to establish cross-agency cooperation, similar to the one in place in Illinois, as the norm, which includes a uniform complaint system and close cooperation with community partners.

Because timely access to information about who is breaking the rules is key to improving compliance with minimum wage and overtime, these new approaches at the federal and state levels should provide for a formal role to those organizations with the greatest knowledge of the industry: worker centers, unions, and competing businesses.

- Low-wage immigrant workers are much more likely to bring cases when they are part of a group. Therefore, the FLSA should be amended to allow groups to bring cases. All lawsuits that can be brought by individual workers under the FLSA should also be allowed to be brought by representatives designated by those workers, which could be worker centers, unions, community organizations, or informal groups.

- To facilitate horizontal monitoring between firms, rule changes should allow firms to complain to WHD about the behavior of competitors and to sue other businesses for damages that result from a defendant's violations of the FLSA. Also helpful would be changes that would allow agencies to impose injunctions against falsifying records.

- Provisions must be made for the establishment of local industry committees that include representatives of employers, workers, and the public, as exists in Canada. The Ontario Industrial Standards Act and Quebec's Collective Agreement provide for union and employer participation in both setting and enforcing minimum employment standards on a local industry-wide or occupation-wide basis.[17] If petitioned by a sufficient number of workers or unions or worker centers representing them, and a sufficient number of employers in a geographic/industrial sector, the WHD could be authorized to establish a local industry committee consisting of equal numbers of representatives of employers, unions/worker centers, workers, and the public. In areas of high wage and hour violations, establishment of these committees should be mandated by state and federal departments of labor. Unionized workers, worker centers, nonunion workers, and employers would each elect their own representatives. The committee would be given authority, at a minimum, to hire its own inspectors, conduct its own complaint-driven and regularly scheduled inspections, and report violators to the DOL.

- There should be elected multiemployer consultative committees that would have the authority to consult with employers regarding all federally mandated basic labor standards, including minimum wage, overtime, occupational safety and health, and family and medical leave. Committees of elected worker representatives would have the authority to consult with the employer regarding all federally mandated basic labor standards, including minimum wage, overtime, occupational safety and health, family and medical leave. These would be mandated within a specific geographic or occupational or geographic/industrial sector on petition by a certain percentage of the workers in the sector. As an alternative, especially for workers in unstable jobs or small worksites, a worksite monitoring role would be built into the law for designated worker representatives who are not collective bargaining representatives, like worker centers or central labor councils. These representatives would be designated by the WHD or state department of labor either on its own initiative or through communitywide elections of workers.

Social Insurance Laws

All employers should be required to provide health insurance or to pay into a joint employer fund in low-wage industries in which individual employers cannot afford to provide health insurance without being able to participate in a larger group.

Portable Health Insurance and Pension Benefits

Provide unemployment insurance for cumulative work under the same rules for part-time as full-time workers. Strengthen the definition of employment and identify and prosecute employers who misclassify employees as independent contractors to avoid paying payroll taxes and providing benefits.

FINAL THOUGHTS

Worker centers are providing critical assistance to the growing low-wage immigrant worker population in the United States. They offer a critical mix of services: advocacy to meet some of the immediate needs of these workers and place their problems on the public agenda, and organizing to empower workers to take collective action on their own behalf. These centers are an important component of the newly emerging gateway infrastructure that is providing support to what has numerically now surpassed the Golden Era as the largest influx of foreign workers in the nation's history. New economic structures, a profound absence of labor market regulation, and an immigration policy that banishes so many to the shadows all pose formidable challenges to these developing institutions.

While worker centers are struggling at the moment to build the monopoly power that Freeman and Medoff attribute to unions, they are succeeding at providing an ongoing vehicle for collective voice to workers at the very bottom of the wage scale. As we have seen, most of their successes at broad labor market intervention have so far come via public policy rather than direct pressure on firms and industries. Worker centers have clearly not obviated the need for massive unionization of low-wage immigrant workers. But most unions today are also struggling to succeed at broad labor market intervention, particularly in scattered site industries that do not rely on public sources of funding.

Through their advocacy and organizing work, we have seen that worker centers excel at working in Luke's and Gaventa's second and third faces of power. They are helping to redefine issues so that they are viewed as appropriate arenas for public policy intervention. They are altering the terms of debate, changing the way people understand the world around them, the problems they face, and the possibilities they see for change. This work is instrumental to a brighter future for immigrant workers in the United States.

As Frances Fox Piven and Richard A. Cloward write, "If the distribution of power simply reflected other structured inequalities, then political challenges from below would always be without effect. The realm of power and politics would inevitably reiterate other inequalities. . . . If people without wealth or status or technical skill sometimes prevail, then they must have some kind of power."[18] The histories of the labor and civil rights movements tell us that they are right.

"People have potential power, the ability to make others do what they want," Piven and Cloward go on, "when those others depend on them for the contributions they make to the interdependent relations that are social life. Their power, the power of people we ordinarily consider powerless, derives from the patterns of interdependence that constitute social life, and from the leverage embedded in interdependent relations." The challenge for immigrant worker centers is to clearly identify the leverage that low-wage immigrant workers have, develop a consciousness about that leverage within their organizations, and implement strategies that take full advantage of it.

ORGANIZATIONS SURVEYED FOR NATIONAL IMMIGRANT WORKER CENTER STUDY

- Alliance for Workers' Rights—NV
- Brazilian Immigrant Center—MA
- Casa Latina—WA
- Casa of Maryland—MD
- Central Texas Immigrant Worker Rights Center—TX
- Centro de Derechos Laborales (Resource Center of the Americas)—MN
- Chinese Progressive Association Workers Center—MA
- Chinese Worker Organizing Center (Chinese Progressive Association)—CA
- Citizenship Project—CA
- Coalition of Immokalee Workers—FL
- Community Voices Heard—NY
- DC Employment Justice Center—DC
- Domestic Workers United—NY
- Farmworker Association of Florida—FL
- Filipino Worker Center—CA
- Fuerza Unida—TX
- Instituto Laboral de la Raza—CA
- Maine Rural Workers Coalition—ME
- Malibu Community Labor Exchange—CA
- Mississippi Poultry Workers Center—TX
- Mujeres Unidas y Activas—CA
- New Labor Worker Center—NJ
- North Carolina Occupational Safety and Health Project (NCOSH)—NC
- NW Arkansas Interfaith Worker Rights Center (NICWJ)—AK
- Oscar Romero Day Laborer Center, Gulfton Area Neighborhood Organization—TX
- People Organized to Win Employment Rights—CA
- Philadelphia Unemployment Project/Unemployment Information Center—PA
- Pilipino Worker Center—CA
- Pineros y Campesinos Unidos del Noreste—OR

- Pomona Economic Opportunities Center—CA
- Restaurant Opportunities Center (ROC)—NY
- San Lucas Worker Center—IL
- Southwest Center for Economic Integrity—AZ
- Southwest Public Workers' Union—TX
- Steel Valley Authority—PA
- UNITE for Dignity—FL
- United Workers Committee—RI
- VOZ—OR
- Wind of the Spirit—NJ
- Working for Equality and Economic Liberation—MT
- Working Today—NY

COMPLETE CONTACT LIST OF WORKER CENTERS AS OF JANUARY 31, 2005

ARIZONA

Central Arizona Shelter Services (CASS),1209 West Madison, Phoenix, AZ 85007-9974; Phone: 602-256-6945 Fax: 602-256-6401; Website: http://cass-az.org; Contact: Mark Holleran, CEO; Email: mholleran@cass-az.org

Primavera Workers, P.O. Box 41972, Tucson, AZ 85717; Phone: 520-882-2165; Website: www.economicintegrity.org; Contact: Karin Uhlich, Executive Director; Email 1: info@economicintegrity.org; Email 2: karin@economicintegrity.org

Tonatierra, PO Box 24009, Phoenix, AZ 85074, Phone: 602-254-5230, Website: www.tonatierra.org; Contact: Salvador Reza; Email 1: tonal@tonatierra.org; Email 2: srza@aol.com

ARKANSAS

Northwest Arkansas Workers' Center, P.O. Box 2392, Bentonville, AK 72712; Phone: 479-544-2421; Contact 1: Lucia Hernandez; Contact 2: Steve Striffler

CALIFORNIA

Asian Immigrant Women Advocates, 310 Eighth Street, Suite 301, Oakland, CA 94607; Phone: 510-268-0192; Fax: 510-268-0194; Website: www.aiwa.org; Contact: Young Shin; Email: info@aiwa.org

Central American Resource Center (CARECEN), 2845 West 7th Street, Los Angeles, CA 90005; Phone: 213-385-7800 x143; Website: www.carecen-la.org; Contact 1: Jeronimo Salguero; Contact 2: Amilcar Osegueda; Email 1: salguero@carecen-la.org; Email 2: aosegueda@carecen-la.org

Centro Laboral de Graton, P.O. Box 362, Graton, CA 95444; Phone: 707-318-2818; Contact: Darvin Cardenas, Organizer; Email: carlo1023@hotmail.com

Centro Legal de la Raza, 1001 Fruitvale Avenue, Oakland, CA 94601; Phone: 510-437-1555; Fax: 510-437-9164; Website: www.centrolegal.org; Contact: Patricia Loya; Email 1: info@centro legal.org; Email 2: p.loya@centrolegal.org

Chinese Worker Organizing Center (Chinese Progressive Association), 660 Sacramento Street, Suite 202, San Francisco, CA 94111; Phone: 415-391-6986; Fax: 415-391-6987; Contact 1: Gordon Mar; Contact 2: Alex Tom; Email: gordonmar@yahoo.com

Citizenship Project, 931 East Market Street, Salinas, CA 93905; Phone: 831-424-2713; Fax: 831-424-1309; Website: www.newcitizen.org; Contact: Paul Johnston, Executive Director; Email 1: citizenship@newcitizen.org; Email 2: paul.johnston@newcitizen.org

Coalition for Humane Immigrant Rights of Los Angeles (CHIRLA), 2533 West 3rd Street, Suite 101, Los Angeles, CA 90057; Phone: 213-353-1333; Fax: 213-353-1344; Website: www.chirla .org; Contact 1: Angelica Salas, Executive Director; Contact 2: Tony Bernabe; Email 1: info@chirla.org; Email 2: asalas@chirla.org; Email 3: tbernabe@chirla.org

Day Worker Center at Calvary Church, 1880 California Street Mountain View, CA 94040; Phone: 650-903-4102; Fax: 650-938-1915; Contact: Maria Marroquin; Email: distancia5@ hotmail.com

Domestic Workers Home Care Center, United Domestic Workers, 3737 Camino Del Rio South, Suite 400, San Diego, CA 92108; Phone: 619-263-7254; Fax: 619-263-7899; Website: www.udwa.org; Contact 1: Fahari Jeffers, Treasurer and General Council; Contact 2: Ken Seaton-Msemaji, President; Email 1: unionheadquarters@udwa.org; Email 2: faharijeffers@ aol.com

FOCUS/Filipino Community Support, 525 West Alma Avenue, San Jose, CA 95125; Phone: 408-297-1977; Fax: 408-297-1978; Website: www.focusnow.org; Contact: Jay Mendoza, Executive Director; Email: focus@focusnow.org

Garment Worker Center (GWC), 1250 South Los Angeles Street, #213, Los Angeles, CA 90015; Phone: 213-748-5866; Fax: 213-748-5876; Website: www.garmentworkercenter.org; Contact 1: Kimi Lee; Contact 2: Joann Lo; Email 1: klee@igc.org; Email 2: jlo@igo.org

Hermandad Mexicana Latinoamericana, 611 West Civic Center Drive, Santa Ana, CA 92701; Phone: 714-541-0250; Fax: 714-541-2460; Website: www.hermandadmexicana.com; Contact: Nativo Lopez, National Director; Email: info@hermandadmexicana.com

Iglesia San Pedro; 450 South Stage Coach Lane, Fallbrook, CA 92028; Phone: 760-728-7034; Contact: Father Edward Kaicher; Email: msa9703@yahoo.com

Instituto de Educacion Popular del Sur de California (IDEPSCA), 1565 West 14th Street, Los Angeles, CA 90015; Phone: 213-252-2952; Fax: 213-252-2953; Website: www.idepsca.org; Contact 1: Raul Anorve, Executive Director; Contact 2: Nelson Motto; Email 1: infoidepsca@ idepsca.org; Email 2: ranorve@idepsca.org

Instituto Laboral de la Raza, 2947 16th Street, San Francisco, CA 94117; Phone: 415-431-7522; Fax: 415-431-4846; Website: www.ilaboral.org; Contact: Sarah M. Shaker; Email: info@ ilaboral.org

Korean Immigrant Workers Advocates (KIWA), 3465 West 8th Street, 2nd Floor, Los Angeles, CA 90005; Phone: 213-738-9050; Fax: 213-738-9919; Website: www.kiwa.org; Contact 1: Danny Park, Executive Director; Contact 2: Vy Nyugun, Organizer; Email 1: kiwa@kiwa.org; Email 2: dannypark@kiwa.org

La Raza Centro Legal/San Francisco Day Laborer Program, 474 Valencia Street, Suite 295, San Francisco, CA 94103; Phone: 415-575-3500; Fax: 415-255-7593; Website: www.lrcl.org; Contact 1: Renee Saucedo; Contact 2: Hillary Ronen: Email 1: daylabor@lrcl.org; Email 2: renee@lrcl.org

Maintenance Industry Cooperation Trust Fund, 704 Hartford Avenue, Los Angeles, CA 90017; Phone: 213-833-1972; Contact 1: Lilia Garcia; Contact 2: Javier Amaro

Malibu Community Labor Exchange (MCLE), P.O. Box 2273, Malibu, CA 90265; Phone: 310-457-1614; Fax: 310-457-8684; Website: www.malibulaborexchange.org; Contact: Mona Beth Loo, Executive Director; Email 1: info@malibulaborexchange.org; Email 2: malibumona@earthlink.net

Mujeres Unidas y Activas, 3543 18th Street, San Francisco, CA 94110; Phone: 415-621-8140; Fax: 415-861-8969; Contact: Juana Flores, Co-Director of Programs; Email: mua@mujeresunidas.net

National Day Laborer Organizing Network (NDLON), 2533 West Third Street, Suite 101, Los Angeles, CA 90057; Phone: 213-353-1333; Fax: 213-353-1344; Contact 1: Pablo Alvarado; Contact 2: John Arvisu; Email: palvarado@chirla.org

Organización de Trabajadores Agrícolas de California, P.O. Box 30424, Stockton, CA 95213; Phone: 209-933-6086; Contact: Luis Magaña

People Organized to Win Employment Rights (POWER), 32 7th Street, San Francisco, CA 94103; Phone: 415-864-8372; Fax: 415-864-8373; Website: www.fairwork.org; Contact: Steve Williams, Executive Director; Email: power@unite-to-fight.org

Pilipino Workers' Center, 153 Glendale Boulevard, 2nd Floor, Los Angeles, CA 90026; Phone: 213-250-4353; Fax: 213-250-4337; Website: www.pwcsc.org; Contact: Aquilina Soriano-Versoza, Executive Director; Email: pilworker@pwcsc.org

Pomona Day Laborer Center, 1682 West Mission Boulevard, Pomona, CA 91766; Phone: 909-397-4215; Fax: 909-622-9880; Contact: Mike Nava; Email: firme09@yahoo.com

Support Committee for Maquiladora Workers, Craftsman Hall, 3909 Centre Street #210, San Diego, CA 92103; Phone: 619-542-0826; Fax: 617-295-5879; Website: http://enchantedweb sites.com/maquiladora/; Contact: Mary Tong; Email: scmw@juno.com

The Temporary Workers Employment Project/Working Partnerships USA, 2102 Almaden Road, Ste. 107, San Jose, CA 95125; Phone: 408-269-7872; Fax: 408-269-0183; Website: www.wpusa.org

Union Sin Fronteras, P.O. Box 66, 722 Vine Street, Coachella, CA 92236; Phone: 760-398-5183; Fax: 760-398-5183; Contact: Ventura Gutierrez; Email: unionsinfronteras@hotmail.com

Watsonville Law Center—Agricultural Workers Access to Health Project, 521 Main Street, Suite H, Watsonville, CA 95076; Phone: 831-722-2845; Fax: 831-761-3295

COLORADO

El Centro Humanitario para Los Trabajadores, 2260 California Street, Denver, CO 80205; Phone: 303-292-4115; Fax: 303-291-2109; Website: www.centrohumanitario.net; Contact: Minsun Ji, Executive Director; Email 1: info@centrohumanitario.net; Email 2: mji@centro humanitario.net

DISTRICT OF COLUMBIA

DC Employment Justice Center, 1350 Connecticut Avenue, NW, Suite 600, Washington, DC 20036-1712; Phone: 202-828-9675; Fax: 202-828-9190; Website: www.dcejc.org; Contact 1: Judith M. Conti, Director; Contact 2: Kerry O'Brien; Email: jconti@dcejc.org

FLORIDA

Coalition of Immokalee Workers (CIW), P.O. Box 603, Immokalee, FL 34143; Phone: 239-657-8311; Fax: 239-657-8311; Website: www.ciw-online.org; Email: workers@ciw-online.org

Farmworker Association of Florida, (FWAF), 815 South Park Avenue, Apopka, FL 32703; Phone: 407-886-5151; Fax: 407-884-6644; Website: www.farmworkers.org/fwafpage.html; Contact: Tirso Moreno; Email: apopkafwaf@aol.com

Farmworker Network for Economic and Environmental Justice, 815 South Park Avenue, Apopka, FL 32703; Phone: 407-886-5151; Fax: 407-877-0031; Website: www.farmworkers.org/fwspage.html; Contact: Carols Marentes, Cochairperson; Email: marentes@farmworkers.org

Miami Worker Center, 6127 NW 7th Avenue, Miami, FL 33127; Phone: 305-759-8717; Fax: 305-759-8718; Website: http://sficwj.org; Contact 1: Gihan Perera; Contact 2: Tony Romano; Email 1: info@theworkerscenter.org; Email 2: gihan@theworkerscenter.org

South Florida Interfaith Committee for Worker Justice—Miami Workers' Rights Initiative, 260 NE 17th Terrace, Suite 200, Miami, FL 33132; Phone: 305-576-5001, x28; Fax: 305-576-1718; Website: http://miamiworkerscenter.org; Contact 1: Bruce Jay, Coordinator; Contact 2: Ronald Martinez; Email: interfaith@nscdade.org

UNITE for Dignity, 1405 NW 167 Street, Suite 200, Miami, FL 33169; Phone: 305-623-3000; Fax: 305-623-3071; Contact: Anna Fink; Email: annalfink@hotmail.com

ILLINOIS

Albany Park Workers' Center, 4174 North Elston Avenue, Chicago, IL 60618; Phone: 773-588-2641; Contact: Miguel Rios; Email: guzman7628@sbcglobal.net

Centro de Derechos Humanos Simon Bolivar, 11 South Porter, 1B, Elgin, IL 60120; Contact: Sergio Cedillo

Chicago Area Workers' Center, 3047 West Cermak Road, Suite 7, Chicago, IL 60623; Phone: 773-230-0351; Fax: 773-542-5069; Contact 1: Tim Bell; Contact 2: Dolores Tapia, President; Email: erobers@hotmail.com

Chicago Coalition for the Homeless, 1325 South Wabash, Suite 205, Chicago, IL 60605-2521; Phone: 312-435-4548; Fax: 312-435-0198; Website: www.chicagohomeless.org; Contact 1: Ed Shurna, Executive Director; Contact 2: Cindy Boland; Email 1: info@chicagohomeless.org; Email 2: eshurna@chicagohomeless.org; Email 3: cindy@chicagohomeless.org

Chicago Home Care Organizing Project (CHOP), c/o SEIU Local 880, 650 South Clark Street, 2nd Floor, Chicago, IL 60605; Phone: 312-939-7490, x134; Fax: 312-939-8256; Website: www.seiu880.org; Contact: Keith Kelleher, Head Organizer; Email: seiu880@acorn.org

Chicago Interfaith Worker Rights Center, 1020 West Bryn Mawr, 4th Floor, Chicago, IL 60660; Phone: 773-728-8400; Fax: 773-728-8409; Website: www.chicagointerfaith.org; Contact 1: Jose Oliva; Contact 2: Kim Bobo; Email 1: joliva@nicwj.org; Email 2: joliva@nicwj.org

Latino Union of Chicago, 1619 West 19th Street, Chicago, IL 60608; Phone: 312-491-9044; Fax: 312-491-9046; Contact: Jessica Aranda, Executive Director; Email 1: latinounionofchicago@ yahoo.com; Email 2: jessicaaranda@sbcglobal.net

San Lucas Worker Center, 2914 West North Avenue, Chicago, IL 60647; Phone: 773-227-6633; Website: www.sanlucasworkers.com; Contact: Ari Glazer; Email 1: info@sanlucasworkers .com; Email 2: ari@sanlucasworkers.com

INDIANA

St. Joseph Valley Project—Indiana Interfaith Workers' Rights Center, 2015 W. Western Avenue, Suite 209, South Bend, IN 46629; Phone: 574-287-3838; Contact 1: Juan Hernandez, Steering Committee Chair; Contact 2: Greg Jones; Email: Hernandez_jmh1961@yahoo.com

Workers' Project, Inc., 1520 Profit Drive, Fort Wayne, IN 46808; Phone: 260-373-0373; Website: www.workersproject.org; Contact: Gregor Koso; Email: gakoso@workersproject.org

MAINE

Maine Rural Workers Coalition, 145 Lisbon Street., 2nd Floor, Lewiston, ME 04240; Phone: 207-753-1922; Fax: 207-753-1226; Website: www.gwi.net/~mrwc; Contact: José Soto, Executive Director; Email 1: mrwc@gwi.net; Email 2: josemrwc@gwi.net

MARYLAND

Casa de Maryland (main office), 310 Tulip Avenue, Takoma Park, MD 20912; Phone: 301-431-0110; Fax: 301-431-4179; Website: www.casademaryland.org; Contact 1: Francisco Cartagena; Contact 2: Silvia Navan; Email 1: fcartagena@casamd.org; Email 2: snavas@casamd.org

Casa Obrera, 113 South Broadway, Baltimore, MD 21231; Phone: 410-732-7777

Centro de Empleo Trabajadores Hacia el Progreso (worker center), 337 New Hampshire Avenue, Takoma Park, MD 20913; Phone: 240-432-5958

Centro de Empleo y Liderazgo, 734 East University Boulevard, East Silver Spring, MD 20903; Phone: 301-431-0110; Website: www.casademaryland.org; Contact: Gustavo Torres, Executive Director; Email 1: yotagri@casamd.org; Email 2: info@casamd.org

MASSACHUSETTS

Brazilian Immigrant Center, 139 Brighton Avenue, Suite #7, Allston, MA 02134; Phone: 617-783-8001; Fax: 617-562-1404; Website: www.braziliancenter.org/; Contact 1: Fausto de Rocha, Director; Contact 2: Marcony Almeida, Outreach Coordinator; Email: bic@brazilian center.org

Chinese Progressive Association/Workers Center, 33 Harrison Avenue, 3rd Floor, Boston, MA 02111; Phone: 617-357-4499; Fax: 617-357-9611; Website: www.cpaboston.org; Contact: Lydia Lowe, Executive Director; Email: justice@cpaboston.org

Merrimack Valley Project Worker Center, 35 Jackson, Lawrence, MA 01840; Phone: 978-686-0650; Contact: Loren MacArthur

Pioneer Valley Workers Center, c/o Anti-Displacement Project, 57 School Street, Springfield, MA 01105; Phone: 413-739-7233; Contact: Caroline Murray; Email: caroline@a-dp.org

SEIU Local #615, Voice and Future Worker Center, 60 Canal Street, 6th Floor, Boston, MA 02114; Phone: 617-523-6150; x422; Fax: 617-742-4896; Contact: Weezy Waldstein

MICHIGAN

Michigan Organizing Project (MOP), 350 South Burdick Street, Suite 310, Kalamazoo, MI 49007; Phone: 269-344-1967; Website: www.michiganorganizing.org; Contact 1: John Musick; Contact 2: Erin Ashmore; Email 1: musick@michiganorganizing.org; Email 2: erin@michiganorganizing.org

MINNESOTA

Centro Campesino, 104 1/2 West Broadway Street, Suite 206, Owatonna, MN 55060; Phone: 507-446-9599; Fax: 507-446-1101; Website: www.centrocampesino.net; Contact Pedro-Jesus Romero-Menendez; Email 1: pedro@centrocampesino.net; Email 2: justicefreedom8@hotmail.com

Resource Center of the Americas, 3019 Minnehaha Avenue, Minneapolis, MN 55406-1931; Phone: 612-276-0788; Fax: 612-276-0898; Website: www.americas.org; Contact: Teresa Ortiz; Email 1: info@americas.org; Email 2: tortiz@americas.org

Twin Cities Religion and Labor Network (TCRLN), c/o Bethany Lutheran, 2511 East Franklin Avenue, Minneapolis, MN 55406; Phone: 612-332-2055; Website: www.tcrln.org; Contact 1: Bob Hulteen; Contact 2: Julia Dreier; Email 1: bob@tcrln.org; Email 2: juliadreier629@yahoo.com

MISSISSIPPI

Mississippi Poultry Workers' Center, 383 South 4th Street, Morton, MS 39117; Phone: 601-918-4615; Contact 1: Kathy Sykes, Community Organizer; Contact 2: Angela Stuesse, Community Outreach & Education Associate

Mississippi Workers Center for Human Rights, 213 Main Street, Greenville, MS 38701; Phone: 662-334-1122; Fax: 662-334-1274; Website: www.msworkerscenter.org; Contact 1: Jaribu Hill, Executive Director; Contact 2: Marsha Watson, Treasurer; Email: rightsms@bellsouth.net

MONTANA

Working for Equality and Economic Liberation (WEEL), P.O. Box 345, Helena, MT 59624; Phone: 406-495-0497; Website: www.weelempowers.org; Contact: Jodi Medlar, Executive Director; Email: jmedlar@weelempowers.org

NEBRASKA

Omaha Together One Community (OTOC), 7262 Mercy Road, Suite 102, Omaha, NE 68124; Phone: 402-344-4401; Fax: 402-344-4272; Website: www.otoc.org; Contact 1: Tom Holler, Executive Director; Contact 2: Sergio Sosa, Organizer; Email 1: omahatogether@qwest.net; Email 2: tomholler@cox.net

NEW JERSEY

Casa Freehold, 3 Vougth Avenue, Freehold, NJ 07728; Phone: 732-685-3846; Contact 1: Juan Carlos; Contact 2: Fidela San Miguel; Email 1: irwinsanchez12@hotmail.com; Email 2: tjb3011@aol.com

Comité de Apoyo a los Trabajadores Agrícolas, P.O. Box 510, Glassboro, NJ 08028; Phone: 609-881-2507; Fax: 609-881-2027; Website: www.cata-farmworkers.org; Contact: Nelson Carrasquillo, Executive Director; Email 1: cata@cata-farmworkers.org; Email 2: catanc@aol.com

New Labor, 103 Bayard Street, 2nd Floor, New Brunswick, NJ 08901; Phone: 732-246-2900; Website: www.newlabor.net; Contact: Rich Cunningham, Executive Director; Email 1: info@newlabor.net; Email 2: richcunningham@newlabor.net

United Labor Agency/Bergen County Day Laborer Project, 205 Robin Road, Suite 220, Paramus, NJ 07652; Phone: 201-967-1546; Fax: 201-967-1547; Contact: Amanda Garces, Organizer; Email: agcolombia@aol.com

Wind of the Spirit, P.O. Box 345, Morristown, NJ 07963; Phone: 973-538-2035; Fax: 973-538-1082; Website: www.windofthespirit.net; Contact 1: Diana Mejia; Contact 2: Miguel Patiño; Email 1: windofthespirit1@aol.com; Email 2: dmejia@terra.com

NEVADA

Alliance for Workers' Rights, 1101 Riverside Drive, Reno, NV 89503; Phone: 775-333-0201; Fax: 775-333-0203; Contact: Tom Stoneburner, Director; Email: nvawr@aol.com

NEW YORK

Andolan Organizing South Asian Workers (LIC), P.O. Box 2087, Long Island City, NY 11102; Phone: 718-390-7264; Fax: 718-728-1768; Contact: Gulnahar Alam, Director; Email: andolan _organizing@yahoo.com

Capital District Workers' Center, 33 Central Avenue, Albany, NY 12210; Phone: 518-482-5595; Contact 1: Fred Pfeiffer; Contact 2: Yacob Williams; Email: fredunit@nycap.rr.com

Centro de Hospitalidad, 100 Park Avenue, Staten Island, NY 10302; Phone: 718-488-1544 x134; Contact 1: Rev. Terry Troia; Contact 2: Ramon Carreon

Centro Independiente de Trabajadores Agricolas (CITA), P.O. Box 78, 32 North Main Street, Florida, NY 10921; Phone: 914-651-5570; Fax: 914-651-5572; Contact: Aspacio Alcantara, Director; Email: cita@warwick.net

Chinese Staff and Workers' Association (CSWA), P.O. Box 130401, New York, NY 10013; Phone: 212-334-2333; Fax: 212-334-1974; Website: www.cswa.org; Contact: Wing Lam, Executive Director; Email: cswa@cswa.org

Coalicion Hispana de Ossining, Ossining, NY 10562; Phone: 914-941-7822; Contact: Cecilia Gutierrez; Email: nocaima@msn.com

Committee Against Anti Asian Violence—Women Workers Project, 2473 Valentine Avenue, Bronx, NY 10458; Phone: 718-220-7391; Fax: 718-220-7398; Website: www.caaav.org; Contact: Sung E. Bai; Email: justice@caaav.org

Community Voices Heard, 170 East 116th Street, Suite 1E, New York, NY 10029; Phone: 212-860-6001; Fax: 212-996-9481; Website: www.cvhaction.org; Contact 1: Paul Getsos, Executive Director; Contact 2: Gail Aska; Email 1: paul@cvhaction.org; Email 2: gail@cvhaction.org

Cortland Workers' Rights Board, 26 Court Street, Cortland, NY 13045-2604; Phone: 607-756-5582; Fax: 607-756-5582; Contact: Linda Smith; Email: cwrb@odyssey.net

Damayan Migrant Workers Association, 410 West 40th Street, New York, NY 10018; Phone: 212-564-6057; Contact 1: Ana Liza Caballes; Contact 2: Linda Abad

Domestic Workers United, 2473 Valentine Avenue, Bronx, NY 10458-5305; Phone: 718-220-7391, x23; Contact: Ai Jen Poo; Email: apoo@caav.org

Filipino Workers Center, 122 West 27th Street, 10th Floor, New York, NY 10001; Phone: 212-741-6806; Email: filipinoworker@aol.com

Hispanic Resource Center of Larchmont and Mamaroneck, P.O. Box 312, Mamaroneck, NY 10543; Phone: 914-835-1512; Fax: 914-835-1551; Contact: Harold Lasso, Executive Director; Email: Hrc10543@aol.com

Hispanic Westchester Coalition, 46 Waller Avenue, White Plains, NY 10605; Phone: 914-948-8466 ex. 16; Contact: Graciela Hayman; Email: WHC1060@aol.com

Latino Workers Center (LWC), 191 East 3rd Street, New York, NY 10009; Phone: 212-473-3936; Fax: 212-473-6103; Contact: Monica Santana; Email: centrolatino@hotmail.com

Make the Road by Walking, 301 Grove Street, Brooklyn, NY 11237; Phone: 718-415-7690; Fax: 718-418-9635; Website: www.maketheroad.org; Contact 1: Oona Chatterjee; Contact 2: Andrew Friedman; Email: oona@maketheroad.org

Mexican American Workers Association, 39 West 14th Street, #204, New York, NY 10011; Phone: 646-259-5474; Contact: Rosario Cera; Email: amat@yahoo.com

Neighbors' Link, 27 Columbus Avenue, Mount Kisco, NY 10549; Phone: 914-666-3410; Contact: Sheelah Highland; Email: sheehyland@aol.com

New York Taxi Workers' Alliance, 37 East 28th Street, Room 302, New York, NY 10016; Phone: 212-627-5248; Fax: 212-741-4563; Contact: Bhairavi Desai, Staff Coordinator; Email: bhairavi desai@aol.com

Proyecto de los Trabajadores Latinoamericanos, 1080 Willoughby Avenue, 2nd Floor, Brooklyn, NY 11221; Phone: 718-628-6222; Fax: 718-628-4111; Website: www.latinamericanworkers project.org; Contact 1: Oscar Paredes, Director; Contact 2: Javier Gallardo; Email 1: trabajadores@msn.com; Email 2: javigallardo@msn.com

Restaurant Opportunities Center of New York (ROCNY), 99 Hudson Street, 3rd Floor, New York, NY 10013; Phone: 212-343-1771; Fax: 212-343-7217; Website: www.rocny.org; Contact 1: Saru Jayaraman, Executive Director; Contact 2: Fekkak Mamadouh, Assistant Director; Email 1: saru@rocny.org; Email 2: mamadouh@rocny.org

Work Experience Program (WEP)/Workers Together! (WWT!), c/o Fifth Avenue Committee, 141 Fifth Avenue, Brooklyn, NY 11217; Phone: 718-857-2990; Fax: 718-857-4322; Contact 1: Benjamin Dulchin, Organizer; Contact 2: John Kest, Coordinator

Workers' Awaaz, P.O. Box 471, Jackson Heights, NY 11372-0471; Phone: 718-565-0801; Fax: 718-565-0836; Website: www.workersawaaz.org; Contact: Shahbano Aliani; Email 1: workers awaaz@yahoo.com; Email 2: wa@workersawaaz.org

Workplace Project, 91 North Franklin Street, Suite 207, Hempstead, NY 11550; Phone: 516-565-5377; Fax: 516-565-5470; Contact 1: Nadia Marin-Molina; Contact 2: Carlos Canales; Email 1: workplace@igc.org; Email 2: nadiamarin@yahoo.com

NORTH CAROLINA

Black Workers for Justice, P.O. Box 1863, Rocky Mount, NC 27802; Phone: 252-977-8162; Contact 1: Saladin Muhammad, National Chairperson; Contact 2: Ajamu Dillahunt; Email 1: bwfj@igc.org; Email 2: naeema@gateway.net

Central North Carolina Workers'—Beloved Community Center, P.O. Box 875, Greensboro, NC 27406; Phone: 336-230-0001; Contact 1: Maryln Baird; Contact 2: Ana Maria Jones

Eastern North Carolina Interfaith Workers Rights Center, 303A East 4th Avenue, Red Springs, NC 28377; Phone: 910-843-9012; Contact: Sallie McLean

North Carolina Occupational Safety and Health Project (NCOSH), P.O. Box 2514, Durham, NC 27715; Phone: 919-479-0514; Fax: 919-289-4857; Website: http://ncosh.igc.org; Contact: Amy Kuffman; Email: ncosh@igc.org

Poultry Workers Project/Center for Women's Economic Alternatives (CWEA), P.O. Box 722, Murfreesboro, NC 27910; Phone: 252-332-4179; Fax: 252-332-6091; Contact: Bernice Sessoms

Southerners for Economic Justice, 331 West Main Street, Box 38, Durham, NC 27701; Phone: 919-401-5907; Fax: 919-401-9708; Contact: Cynthia Brown

Western North Carolina Interfaith Workers Rights Center, P.O. Box 667, Morganton, NC 28680; Phone: 828-432-5080; Contact 1: Francisco Risso; Contact 2: Juan Ignacro Montes

OHIO

Cincinnati Interfaith Workers' Justice Center, 215 East 14th Street, Cincinnati, OH 45202; Phone: 513-621-4336; Website: www.esop-cleveland.org/issues/daylaborers; Contact 1: Don Sherman; Contact 2: Monica McGloin; Email: shermandonr@earthlink.net

Day Laborer's Organizing Committee, 12002 Miles Avenue, 3rd Floor, Cleveland, OH 44105; Phone: 216-429-0757; Fax: 216-641-0286; Contact: Oren Casdi; Email: oren_esop@ameritech.net

Farm Labor Organizing Committee (FLOC), AFL-CIO, 1221 Broadway Street, Toledo, OH 43609; Phone: 419-243-3456; Fax: 419-243-5655; Website: www.floc.com; Contact: Beatriz Maya; Email 1: info@floc.com; Email 2: bmayal@floc.com

OREGON

Centro Cultural, P.O. Box 708, Cornelius, OR 97113; Phone: 503-359-0446; Fax: 503-357-0183; Website: www.centrocultural.org; Contact 1: Sabino Sardineta, Executive Director; Contact 2: Romula Xol; Email 1: arturo@centrocultural.org; Email 2: sabino@centrocultural.org

ENLACE, 320 SW Stark, Suite 410, Portland, OR 97204; Phone: 503-295-6466; Fax: 503-295-6402; Contact: Peter Cervantes Gautschi; enlaceintl@aol.com

Pineros y Campesinos Unidos del Noreste, 300 Young Street, Woodburn, OR 97071; Phone: 503-982-0243; Fax: 503-982-1031; Website: www.pcun.org; Contact 1: Ramon Ramirez; Contact 2: Larry Kleinman; Email: formworkerunion@pcun.org

VOZ, 330 SE 11th Avenue, Portland, OR 97214; Phone: 503-233-6787; Fax: 503-232-6449; Website: www.portlandvoz.org; Contact: Romeo Sosa; Email: romeo@portlandvoz.org

PENNSYLVANIA

Heartland Labor Capital Network c/o Steel Valley Authority, One Library Place, Suite 201, Duquesne, PA 15110; Phone: 412-460-0488; Fax: 412-460-0487; Website: www.heartlandnet work.org; Contact: Tom Croft, Project Director; Email 1: heartland.sva@att.net; Email 2: t.w.croft@att.net

Immigration Resource Center, AFL-CIO, 22 South 22nd Street, 2nd Floor, Philadelphia, PA 19103; Phone: 215-564-6910; Fax: 215-665-1973

Philadelphia Unemployment Project, 1201 Chestnut Street, Suite 702, Philadelphia, PA 19107; Phone: 215-557-0822; Fax: 215-557-6981; Website: www.philaup.org; Contact: John Dodds; Email: PHILAUP@aol.com

RHODE ISLAND

Dare to Win—Direct Action for Rights & Equality, 340 Lockwood Street, Providence, RI 02907; Phone: 401-351-6960; Fax: 401-351-6977; Website: www.daretowin.org; Contact: Sara Mersha, Lead Organizer; Email 1: dare@daretowin.org; Email 2: dare_sara@hotmail.com

United Workers Committee, 626 Broad Street, Center Falls, RI 02863; Phone: 401-728-5920; Fax: 401-724-5550; Contact: Mario Bueno; Email: progresolatino@aol.com

SOUTH CAROLINA

Carolina Alliance for Fair Employment (CAFÉ), 1 Chick Springs Road, Suite 110-B, Greenville, SC 29609; Phone: 864-235-2926; Fax: 864-235-9691; Website: www.cafesc.org; Contact: Carol Bishop, Executive Director; Email 1: cafe@igc.org; Email 2: msckbishop @aol.com

TEXAS

Border Agricultural Workers Project/Union de Trabajadores Agricolas Fronterizos (UTAF), 201 East Ninth Avenue, El Paso, TX 79901; Phone: 915-532-0921; Fax: 915-532-4822; Website: www.farmworkers.org/bawppage.html; Contact: Carlos Marentes, Director

Central Texas Immigrant Workers' Rights Center (CTIWoRC), 510 South Congress Avenue, Suite 206, Austin, TX 78704; Phone: 512-474-0007 x102; Fax: 512-474-0008; Website: www.equaljusticecenter.org; Contact 1: Julien Ross, Coordinator; Contact 2: Amanda Garces; Email: julien@equaljusticecenter.org

Fuerza Unida, 710 New Laredo Highway, San Antonio, TX 78211; Phone: 210-927-2294; Fax: 210-927-2295; Website: http://fuerzaunida.freeservers.com; Contact 1: Petra Mata, Co-Coordinator; Contact 2: Viola Casares, Co-Coordinator; Email: fuerzaunid@aol.com

Gulfton Area Neighborhood Organization (GANO), 6006 Bellaire, Suite 104, Houston, TX 77081; Phone: 713-665-1284; Fax: 713-665-7967; Contact: Nelson Reyes; Email 1: nereyes@msn.com; Email 2: carecen@evi.net

Harris County AFL-CIO, Justice & Equality in the Workplace Program (JEWP), 2506 Southerland Street, Houston, TX 77023; Phone: 713-923-9473; Contact: Richard Shaw

La Mujer Obrera, 2000 Texas Avenue, El Paso, TX 79901; Phone: 915-533-9710; Fax: 915-544-3730; Website: www.mujerobrera.com; Contact: Maria Flores

Southwest Public Workers' Union (SPWU), 1416 East Commerce Street, San Antonio, TX 78205; Phone: 210-299-2666; Fax: 210-299-4009; Contact: Chavel Lopez

UTAH

Justice, Economic Dignity and Independence for Women (JEDI), 150 South 600 East, Suite 5B, Salt Lake City, UT 84102; Phone: 801-364-8562; Fax: 810-323-9452; Website: www.jedi4women.org; Contact: Bonnie Macri; Email: jedi@networld.com

VERMONT

Vermont Workers' Center, P.O. Box 883, Montpelier, VT 05601; Phone: 802-229-0009; Website: www.workerscenter.org; Email: info@workerscenter.org

VIRGINIA

Coal Employment Project, P.O. Box 682, Tazwell, VA 24651; Phone: 504-988-5877; Fax: 504-988-5877; Website: www.thekeep.org/cep/; Contact: Cosby Ann Totten

Tenants' and Workers' Support Committee (TWSC), P.O. Box 2327, Alexandria, VA 22301; Phone: 703-684-5697; Fax: 703-684-5714; Website: www.twsc.org; Contact: Jon Liss, Organizing Director; Email: jliss@twsc.org

Virginia Justice Center for Farm and Immigrant Workers, 6066 Leesburg Pike, Suite 620, Falls Church, VA 22041; Phone: 703-778-3450; Fax: 703-778-3454; Website: www.justice4all.org

Virginia Justice Center for Farm and Immigrant Workers, 1000 Preston Avenue, Suite A, Charlottesville, VA 22903; Phone: 434-977-0553; Fax: 434-997-0558; Website: www.justice4all.org

WASHINGTON

Casa Latina, 220 Blanchard Street, Seattle, WA 98121; Phone: 206-956-0779; Fax: 206-956-0780; Website: www.casa-latina.org; Contact: Hilary Stern, Executive Director; Email 1: info@casa-latina.org; Email 2: hilary@casa-latina.org

Filipino Workers Action Center, 2809 Beacon Avenue, Suite 18, Seattle, WA 98144; Phone: 206-763-9611; Contact: Ace Saturay, Executive Director; Email: fwac9@yahoo.com

Washington Alliance of Technology Workers (WASHTECH/CWA), 2900 Eastlake Ave. E Suite 200, Seattle, WA 98103; Phone: 206-726-8580; Fax: 206-323-6966; Website: www.washtech

.org; Contact: Marcus R. Courtney, Organizer; Email 1: contact@washtech.org; Email 2: courtney@washtech.org

Washington Farmworkers Union, P.O. Box 337, Granger, WA 98932; Phone: 509-854-2442; Fax: 509-854-2442; Contact 1: Daniel Ezequiel Morfin; Contact 2: Bill Nicasio

WISCONSIN

9 to 5, National Association of Working Women, 152 West Wisconsin Avenue, Suite 408, Milwaukee, WI 53203; Phone: 414-274-0925; Fax: 414-272-2870; Website: www.9to5.org; Contact: Linda Garcia Barnard; Email 1: 9to5@9to5.org; Email 2: lindagb@9to5.org

Faith Community for Worker Justice—Milwaukee Interfaith Workers' Rights Center, 633 South Hawley Road, Milwaukee, WI 53214; Phone: 414-475-3539, x13; Website: www.worker justice.org; Contact: Bill Morris; mclcfaith@ameritech.net

Interfaith Coalition for Worker Justice of South Central Wisconsin, 2300 South Park Street, Suite 6, Madison, WI 53713; Phone: 608-255-0376; Contact 1: Patrick Hickey; Contact 2: Deborah Herman; Email 1: worker@workerjustice.org; Email 2: Deborah_herman@earthlink.net

Voces de la Frontera, 1027 South 5th Street, Milwaukee, WI 53204; Phone: 414-297-8264; Contact 1: Christine Neumann-Ortiz, Director; Contact 2: Alexis Cazco; Email 1: cineumann@aol.com; Email 2: vocesdelafrontera@sbcglobal.net

NOTES

INTRODUCTION

1. As of 2003, the Economic Policy Institute found that 30.4 precent of black workers and 39.8 percent of Latino workers earned poverty-level wages. Lawrence Mishel, Jared Bernstein, and Sylvia Allegretto, *The State of Working America 2004/2005* (Ithaca: Cornell University Press, 2005), Tables 2.11 and 2.12, pp. 132–33.
2. Even after seventy-one Thai garment workers made international headlines after having been found in a locked apartment complex in Almonte, California, having been held there under slave labor conditions for as long as seven years, deportation proceedings were initiated as soon as the workers were freed. They were eventually able to get special visas based on their status in the case.
3. In my earlier work, I describe a phenomenon called community unionism. Community unions are defined as modest-sized community-based low wage workers that focus on issues of work and wages in their communities. They are characterized by three signature strategies. First, they develop ongoing relationships with workers not just at their workplaces but also in their communities and not just on the basis of occupational identity but other aspects of identity as well—like ethnicity and race. Second, given the decentralized nature of many low wage industries, they do their organizing across a range of firms. Third, in the communities in which they operate, they focus on shifting the terms of the debate and building support for stronger wage enforcement and public policy initiatives. Worker centers, my focus in this book, are a very important subset of the world of community unions. See Janice Fine, "Community Unions and the Revival of the American Labor Movement" in *Politics and Society* 33, no. 1 (March 2005), 153–99.
4. Lawrence Goodwyn, *The Populist Moment: A Short History of the Agrarian Revolt in America* (Oxford: Oxford University Press, 1976) Preface and Introduction.
5. The second stage of the research was to complete forty survey interviews, which were conducted during the summer and fall of 2003. Thirty-four of the forty organizations surveyed are working primarily with immigrants. The final stage of research was to carry out nine case studies (these were in addition to the forty groups included in the survey). All of the nine focus on working with immigrants, although two of them, CAFÉ and the Tenants' and Workers' Support Committee, work extensively with African American workers as well as immigrants. In fact, CAFÉ was founded out of the African American freedom struggle.

CHAPTER 1. ORIGINS AND CHARACTERISTICS OF WORKER CENTERS

1. During the 1930s and 1940s, there was widespread agreement in the labor movement that organizing the south was critical to their long-run success. After World War II, the CIO launched Operation Dixie, a massive campaign to organize southern workers, which did not succeed. For some analysis of the reasons for this failure see Michael Golfield, *The Decline of Organized Labor in the United States* (Chicago and London: University of Chicago Press, 1987) 238–42 and Philip S. Foner, *Organized Labor and The Black Worker 1619–1981* (New York: International Publishers, 1976), 269–93.
2. Telephone interview with Katie Quan, January 2005
3. Many centers referred to the Chinese Staff and Workers Association in New York City's Chinatown and the Workplace Project on Long Island as organizations they had drawn their inspiration and organizational models from.
4. "A *labour market* concerns the activities of hiring and supplying certain labour to perform certain jobs, and the process of determining how much shall be paid to whom in performing what tasks. In addition, the way in which wages move and the mobility of workers between different jobs and employers falls within this definition. . . . In practice, the definition of a *local labour market* is established on the assumption that its key characteristic is that the bulk of the area's population habitually seek employment there and that local employers recruit most of their labour from that area." David W. Pearce, ed., *MIT Dictionary of Modern Economics*, 4th ed. (Cambridge, MA: MIT Press, 1995), 237, 251.
5. Steven C. Pitts, *Organize . . . to Improve the Quality of Jobs in the Black Community: A Report on Jobs and Activism in the African-American Community*, University of California at Berkeley Center for Labor Research and Education, May 2004.
6. Roger Waldinger, ed., *Strangers at the Gates: New Immigrants in Urban America* (Berkeley: University of California Press, 2001), 37–38.
7. Ibid., 37.
8. Ibid., 6.
9. "What We Have," internal IDEPSCA document, November 12, 2003.

CHAPTER 2. PUTTING WORKER CENTERS IN CONTEXT

1. Diane Schmidley, "U.S. Census Bureau, Current Population Reports," *Profile of the Foreign-Born Population in the United States: 2000*, Special Studies No. P23–206, U.S. Census Bureau, December 2001; and *Immigrant Families and Workers: Facts and Perspectives* "The Dispersal of Immigrants in the 1990s," Brief No. 2, November 26, 2002. Also see Jeffrey S. Passel, Randy Capps and Michael Fix "Undocumented Immigrants: Facts and Figures" Urban Institute Immigration Studies Program (Washington DC: January, 2004).
2. Michael Fix, *Tabulations of Current Population Survey* (Washington, DC: Urban Institute: November 2001).
3. According to the Northeastern University Center for Labor Market Studies, half of the new workforce of the 1990s were immigrants in comparison to 10 percent in the 1970s. Andrew Sum, Ishwar Khatiwada, Paul Harrington with Shela Palma, *New Immigrants in the Labor Force and the Number of Employed New Immigrants in the U.S. from 2000 through 2003: Continued Growth Amidst Declining Employment Among the Native-Born Population* (Boston: Center for Labor Market Studies, Northeastern University, December 2003), 1–3.
4. In 2000, 26 percent of immigrant workers had employer-provided health insurance. Shannon Blaney and Leighton Ku, *Health Coverage for Legal Immigrant Children: New Census Data Highlight Importance of Restoring Medicaid and SCHIP Coverage* (Washington, DC: Center on Budget and Policy Priorities, October 2000).
5. William A. V. Clark, "The Geography of Immigrant Poverty: Selective Evidence of an Immigrant Underclass," in *Strangers at the Gates: New Immigrants in Urban America*, Roger Waldinger, ed. (Berkeley: University of California Press, 2001), 173.
6. Migration Policy Institute, *Migration Information Source, Data Tools, Immigration: A Historical Perspective*, "Immigration to the United States by Decade: Fiscal Years 1821 to 2000 (in millions)," and

"Foreign-born Population by Region of Birth as Percentage of the Total Population of the United States: 1850–2000," from U.S. Census Bureau, *Historical Census Statistics on the Foreign-Born Population of the United States: 1850 to 1990*, Working Paper No. 29, U.S. Government Printing Office, Washington, DC, 1999, http://www.migrationinformation.org/GlobalData/charts/final.fb.shtml.

7. David T. Beito, *From Mutual Aid to the Welfare State: Fraternal Societies and Social Services, 1890–1967* (Chapel Hill: The University of North Carolina Press, 2000), 17.

8. Ibid., 17.

9. Schmidley, "U.S. Census Bureau, Current Population Reports," 2001.

10. See Princeton University Office of Population Research as cited in the draft report by Anne Farris, *The House We All Live In: A Report on Immigrant Civic Participation* (New York: Carnegie Corporation of America, 2003), 3; and Jeffrey Passel, "New Estimates of the Undocumented Population in the United States," *Migration Information Source* (Washington, DC: Migration Policy Institute, May 22, 2002).

11. These numbers are from Waldinger and Jennifer Lee, "New Immigrants in Urban America" in *Strangers at the Gates*, Waldinger, ed., 30–79.

12. Rhoda Amon, "Long Island: Our Story/Shifting Sands and Fortunes," *Newsday*, March 30, 1998.

13. The 18.1 million net jobs created between 1979 and 1989 involved a loss of manufacturing (1.6 million) and mining (266,000) jobs and an increase in the service sector (19.3 million) jobs. The largest amount of job growth (14.2 million) was in the two lowest paying service sector industries—retail trade and services (business, personnel, and health). Taken together, these two industries accounted for 79 percent of all new net jobs over the 1979–1989 period and 72.9 percent of all new jobs in 1989–2000. Lawrence Mishel, Jared Bernstein, and Heather Boushey, *The State of Working America 2002–03* (Ithaca: Cornell University Press, 2003), 121–34. In 2003, 24.3 percent of the workforce earned poverty-level wages. Mishel, Bernstein, and Allegretto, *The State of Working America 2004–2005* (Ithaca: Cornell University Press, 2005).

14. Whereas in the fifties, sixties and seventies, most U.S. workers, but especially blue collar workers, were shielded from competitive unstructured labor markets, today a growing number of workers are not. Doeringer and Piore estimated that, in the 1960s, fewer than one in five members of the U.S. workforce could be found in these markets which were characterized by temporary work, transient labor, low formal skill levels, and unstable, unstructured capital-labor relationships at the point of production. Peter B. Doeringer and Michael J. Piore, *Internal Labor Markets and Manpower Analysis* (Lexington: D.C. Heath and Company, 1971).

15. The 18.1 million net jobs created between 1979 and 1989 involved a loss of manufacturing (1.6 million) and mining (266,000) jobs, and an increase in the service sector (19.3 million) jobs. The largest amount of job growth (14.2 million) was in the two lowest-paying service sector industries—retail trade and services (business, personnel, and health). Taken together, these two industries accounted for 79 percent of all new net jobs over the 1979–1989 period and 72.9 percent of all new jobs in 1989–2000. Lawrence Mishel, Jared Bernstein, and Heather Boushey, *The State of Working America 2002–03* (Ithaca: Cornell University Press, 2003), 121–34. In 2003, 24.3 percent of the workforce earned poverty-level wages. Mishel, Bernstein, and Sylvia Allegretto, *The State of Working America 2004/2005* (Ithaca: Cornell University Press, 2004).

16. Howard Wial, "Minimum Wage Enforcement and the Low-wage Labor Market," MIT Task Force on Reconstructing America's Labor Market Institutions, Working Paper #WP11, August 1, 1999, 18. Available at http://mitsloan.mit.edu/iwer/tfwial.pdf.

17. "Whether measured by inflation-adjusted budgets, the number of investigators, or the number of Fair Labor Standards Act Compliance actions taken, the enforcement resources of the Wage and Hour Division are smaller today than they were twenty years ago. The WHD's inflation-adjusted budget for fiscal year 1998 was 7 percent below its level in fiscal year 1979. The number of investigators dropped by 11 percent between 1979 and 1998, and the number of compliance actions were 34 percent lower." Wial, "Minimum Wage Enforcement," 21.

As an illustration of the problem, in the garment industry today, David Weil estimates that "given the probability of inspection and the expected civil penalty, the predicted cost of noncompliance is about $780 compared to the cost of compliance of $6700." Weil goes on, "Facing this trade-off, a rational contractor should choose noncompliance on a period by period basis—even given a moderate level of aversion to being caught. This simple calculus, played out in the context of extremely competitive product markets for sewing contractors, explains the economics underlying the intransigence of the sweatshop problem, even with more aggressive enforcement activity." David Weil, "Regulating Noncompliance to Labor Standards: New Tools for an Old Problem," *Challenge* (January–February 2002): 5.

18. Kate L. Bronfenbrenner, "Employer Behavior in Certification Elections and First-Contract Campaigns: Implications for Labor Law Reform," in *Restoring the Promise of American Labor Law,* Sheldon Friedman, Richard W. Hurd, Rudolph A. Oswald, and Ronald L. Seeber, eds. (Ithaca: Cornell University Press, 1994), 75–89. Bronfenbrenner also found that in 32 percent of elections in which workers had voted in favor of the union, workers were still without a contract two years after the election.

19. A national survey conducted by Rogers and Freeman estimated that 40 million nonunion workers say they would join a union if one were available to them. They estimate that although 13.5 percent of U.S. workers belonged to unions in 2002, if workers were able to freely join a union without employer interference, that number would be 47 percent. Richard Freeman and Joel Rogers, *What Workers Want* (New York: Cornell University Press, 1999).

20. I would like to thank Howard Wial for providing me these statistics.

21. Beito notes that while it is well known that fraternal organizations and mutual-aid societies flourished among eastern and southern European immigrants, they "also existed among groups not usually identified with the new immigration," including Mexicans, Japanese-Americans, Chinese immigrants, and especially African-Americans." Beito, *From Mutual Aid to the Welfare State,* 17.

22. See, for example, Hadassa Kosak, *Cultures of Opposition: Jewish Immigrant Workers, New York City, 1881–1905* (Albany: State University of New York Press, 2000), and Michael R. Weisser, *A Brotherhood of Memory: Jewish Landsmanshaftn in the New World* (New York: Basic Books, 1985).

23. While the Workmen's Circle is still in existence, its smaller membership is largely comprised of older retired workers and younger progressives interested in a secular Jewish identity. Its base is no longer among present-day craft and industrial workers, and it no longer provides extensive social services.

24. Historian Lawrence Glickman is quoted in Robert Pollin and Stephanie Luce, *The Living Wage: Building a Fair Economy* (New York: The New Press, 1998), 27.

25. Kim Voss, *The Making of American Exceptionalism: The Knights of Labor and Class Formation in the Nineteenth Century* (Ithaca: Cornell University Press, 1993), 81.

26. Kathryn Kish Sklar, *Florence Kelley and the Nation's Work: The Rise of Women's Political Culture, 1830–1900* (New Haven and London: Yale University Press, 1995), 174–75.

27. Nelson Lichtenstein, Susan Strasser, and Roy Rosenzweig, *Who Built America? Working People and the Nation's Economy, Politics, Culture, and Society* (New York: Worth, 2000), 221–23.

28. Ann Withorn, "To Serve the People" (Ph.D. diss., Brandeis University, 1977), 130.

29. Karen Pastorello, "A Power among Them: Bessie Abromowitz Hillman and the Making of the Amalgamated Clothing Workers of America" (Ph.D. diss., State University of New York at Binghamton, 2001), 60–64, 76–77.

30. Beito, *From Mutual Aid to the Welfare State,* makes several interesting arguments about why these organizations stopped providing insurance over time, including the rise of the New Deal and the replacement of fraternal forms of insurance by government programs as well as the passage of laws that held the organizations to fiduciary standards they could not meet. On the decline of civic organizations, including fraternal and mutual aid societies, see Theda Skocpol, *Diminished Democracy: From Membership to Management in American Civic Life* (Norman: University of Oklahoma Press, 2003), especially chapters 4 and 5.

31. From the official website of the Legal Services Corporation, http://www.lsc.gov/.

32. Nelson Lichtenstein, *State of the Union: A Century of American Labor* (Princeton, NJ: Princeton University Press, 2002), 10.

CHAPTER 3. ORGANIZING AT THE INTERSECTION OF ETHNICITY, RACE, GENDER, AND CLASS

1. January 2004 telephone interview.

2. Nancy Abelman and John Lie, *Blue Dreams: Korean Americans and the Los Angeles Riots* (Cambridge: Harvard University Press, 1995), 49–84 and 85–118.

3. Interviews with Danny Park and Paul Lee, December 2003, all subsequent quotations are drawn from this interview.

4. From KIWA's Semiannual Report (Winter 2003).

5. Manuel Orozco, "Remittances to Latin America and the Caribbean: Issues and Perspectives on Development" Report Commissioned by the Office for the Summit Process, Organization of American States (Washington, DC: September, 2004) 2.

6. Peggy Levitt, *The Transnational Villagers* (Berkeley: University of California Press, 2001), 18–19.

7. Ibid., 3.

8. Ibid., 19.

9. Interview with Marcella Cervantes, October 2003, all subsequent quotes are from this interview.

10. However, even for immigrant workers involved in a union drive, NLRA protections are not guaranteed. In the Hoffman Plastics decision in 2002, the Supreme Court held that undocumented workers were not entitled to the remedy of back pay under the NLRA. Since that time, employers have tried to use Hoffman to weaken the rights of undocumented immigrant workers involved in organizing drives.

11. A May 2004 study of immigrant union members by the Migration Policy Institute found that between 1996 and 2003, the number of foreign-born union members increased from 1.4 million to 1.8 million, or by 24 percent. See Migration Policy Institute, *Immigration Facts,* no. 7, May 2004.

12. Interview with Lupe Hernandez, December 2003.

13. Interview with Kim Bobo, April 2003, all subsequent quotations are from this interview.

14. Interview with Kimi Lee, December 2003, all subsequent quotations are from this interview.

15. Interview with Jose Oliva, April, 2003, all subsequent quotations are from this interview.

16. Interview with Father Damien Zuerlain, October 2003, all subsequent quotations are from this interview.

17. Interview with Marcello Lopez, May 2004, all subsequent quotations are from this interview.

18. Interview with Sergio Sosa, October 2003, all subsequent quotations are from this interview.

19. Interview with Raul Anorve, February 2004, all subsequent quotations are from this interview.

20. Interview with Jon Liss, May 2003.

21. David Fitzgerald, "Beyond 'transnationalism': Mexican hometown politics at an American labour union," *Ethnic and Racial Studies* 27, no. 2 (March 2000), 237–40.

22. See Carol Zabin and Luis Escala Rabadan, "Mexican Hometown Associations and Mexican Immigrant Political Empowerment in Los Angeles," *Nonprofit Sector Research Fund Working Paper Series,* The Aspen Institute (Winter 1998).

23. Ruth Milkman and Kent Wong, "The 1992 Southern California Drywall Strike" in *Organizing Immigrants: The Challenge for Unions in Contemporary California,* ed. Ruth Milkman (Ithaca: Cornell University Press, 2000), 181.

24. Leon Fink, *The Maya of Morganton: Work and Community in the Nuevo New South* (Chapel Hill: University of North Carolina Press, 2003), 34–78.

25. Ibid., 54.

26. Interview with Muhammed Tasleem Khan, October 2003, all subsequent quotations are from this interview.

27. Interview with Irma Solis, June 2004, all subsequent quotations are from this interview.

28. Interview with Mulgeta Yimer, May 2003.

29. When confronted by KIWA about the workers' unpaid wages, the owner threatened to call the INS, which is what catalyzed the organization to move to a boycott so quickly.

30. Interestingly, Lee says the Asian workers have mixed reactions when they walk in the door of the GWC. "In the Asian community it's totally different because yeah we're Asian, but then because we're young and we're American-born the workers themselves kind of have this 'who are you?' reaction. The Asian immigrants . . . have the kind of stereotype that someone who's going to help them is a white person in a suit, and it's going to be an older guy. They're going to be a lawyer or something like that. When they see us, we're young and we're American-born and we don't know things. . . . When we talk to them more, and they see that we have been able to win things and help things, they trust us more."

31. Interview with Helen Chien, December 2003, all subsequent quotations are from this interview.
32. Interview with Joann Lo, December 2003, all subsequent quotations are from this interview.
33. Interview with Jaime Vargas, June 2004, all subsequent quotations are from this interview.
34. Interview with Carol Bishop, May 2004, all subsequent quotations are drawn from this interview.
35. Sheila Allen, "CAFÉ Working to Bridge the Gap between the Latino Community," *Darlington News and Press,* June 27, 2002, 5b.
36. See Nelson Lim, "On the Backs of Blacks? Immigrants and the Fortunes of African-Americans," in *Strangers at the Gates,* ed. Waldinger, 186–227; and Roger Waldinger, *Still the Promised City: African-Americans and the New Immigrants in Postindustrial New York* (Cambridge: Harvard University Press, 1996).
37. Miriam Ching Yoon Louie, *Sweatshop Warriors* (Boston: South End Press, 2001), 124.
38. Pierette Hondagneu-Sotelo, *Domestica: Immigrant Workers Cleaning and Caring in the Shadows of Affluence* (Berkeley: University of California Press, 2001), 9.

CHAPTER 4. DELIVERING SERVICES ON THE FRONTLINES

1. In her doctoral dissertation on social movements and social services, Ann Withorn hypothesized that "the broader the social change goals and more 'alternative' the ideology, the more sympathetic the movement will be to service delivery." Ann Withorn, "To Serve the People," Brandeis University doctoral dissertation, Waltham, Massachusetts, July 1977, 130.
2. Derek Park, Steven Lee, Rose Sohn, and Bona Hong, "Ten Years at a Worker Empowerment Clinic," KIWA report (Los Angeles: February 2003).
3. Janice Fine, "Community Unions in Baltimore and Long Island: Beyond the Politics of Particularism" (Ph.D. diss., Massachusetts Institute of Technology, 2003), table 4.2, p. 109.
4. Oliva interview, May 2003.
5. Alvarado interview, December 2004.
6. During the period between the project's founding in 1992 and the end of 1995, 40 percent of the total labor complaints (accounting for about 360 workers) brought to the clinic had to do with non- or underpayment of wages.
7. According to Gordon, immigrant workers went to the state Department of Labor as opposed to the federal for two reasons. First, many of them were exempt from the federal wage laws because their employers had less than $500,000 in gross revenues a year and did not put goods into the stream of interstate commerce. Of course, this included the vast majority of restaurants, contractors, and landscaping companies for whom they worked. Second, because of the link between the federal Department of Labor and the Immigration and Naturalization Service, even those workers who were covered by the federal minimum wage laws preferred to deal with the state Department of Labor.
8. This whole section is drawn from a paper Jennifer Gordon prepared for the Carnegie Foundation ("The Campaign for the Unpaid Wages Prohibition Act") as well as various documents, statements, and affidavits provided to me by the Workplace Project staff as part of its files on the Department of Labor.
9. Park, Lee, Sohn, and Hong, "Ten Years at a Worker Empowerment Clinic."
10. Fine, "Community Unions in Baltimore and Long Island," 111.
11. Alvarado interview, December 2004.
12. Knutti interview, April 2003.
13. In addition to my own interviews, I am very grateful to Meredith DeSpain, of the Lyndon B. Johnson School of Public Affairs at the University of Texas at Austin, for sharing her case study on CAWRI.
14. Readers interested in a broader analysis about the Workplace Project's Legal Clinic should see chapter 5 of Jennifer Gordon, *Suburban Sweatshops* (Cambridge: Harvard University Press, 2005).
15. Domenzain interview, December 2004.
16. Lee interview, November 2004.
17. Austin Police Department letter of October 29, 2003: "According to Texas Penal Code (Chapter 31.04, Theft of Service), a person commits an offense if, with intent to avoid payment of service that

he knows is provided only for compensation: (4) He intentionally or knowingly secures the performance of the service by agreeing to provide compensation and, after the service is rendered, fails to
make payment after receiving notice demanding payment. For purposes of this section, intent to
avoid payment is presumed if: (1) the actor absconded without paying for the service or expressly refused to pay for the service in circumstances where payment is ordinarily made immediately upon
rendering of the service, as in hotels, campgrounds, recreational parks, restaurants, and comparable
establishments."

18. Ross's quotes are taken from Julien Ross, "A Fair Day's Pay: The Problem of Unpaid Workers in
Central Texas," *Texas Hispanic Journal of Law and Social Policy* 10, no. 1 (Fall 2004): 144–46, 155.

19. Arvizu interview, December 2004.

20. Alvarado interview, May 2004.

21. This is excerpted from the text entitled "Order, Decision or Award of the Labor Commissioner, October 24, 2002," Labor Commissioner State of California, Department of Industrial Relations, Division of Labor Standards Enforcement.

22. Domenzain interview.

23. Lee interview, December 2004.

24. "Hull House, in spite of itself, does a good deal of legal work. We have secured support for deserted
women, insurance for bewildered widows, damages for injured operators, furniture from the
clutches of the installment store." Jean Bethke Elshtain, *The Jane Addams Reader* (New York: Basic
Books, 2002) 44.

25. Ibid., xxi.

26. See Withorn, "To Serve the People," 361.

27. Ibid., 127–28.

28. As of 1996, all legal service agencies operating under funds provided by the Legal Services Corporation are prohibited from representing undocumented immigrants, as well as from filing class actions, challenges to welfare reform, rulemaking, lobbying, litigation on behalf of prisoners, and representation in drug-related public housing evictions.

CHAPTER 5. ECONOMIC ACTION ORGANIZING

1. Ultimately I understand power to mean the ability to compel an individual or an institution to do
something they really don't want to do or the ability to grant to/or withhold from an individual or
institution something they really want. The most important source of economic and political power
for grassroots community organizations is the "power of organized people" as voters, consumers,
and producers.

2. "I use 'political incorporation' rather than 'inclusion' or 'assimilation'—two terms often applied to
the political experience of new immigrants. Both terms suggest less conflict and disagreement than
is common in political entry—to be assimilated or included in a polity seems almost to be absorbed
into it. 'Incorporation' is a better term because it indicates both inclusion and the formation of the
group that is being incorporated. To say that a group has been incorporated into a polity signals the
formation of that group as a new and distinctive part of the polity. This implies change in the polity,
and the possibility of conflict between the new group and other political agents." David Plotke, "Immigration and Political Incorporation in the Contemporary United States," in Charles Hirschman,
Philip Kasinitz, and Josh DeWind, editors, *The Handbook of International Migration: The American
Experience* (New York: Russell Sage Foundation, 1999), 298.

3. "We have little data on the prevalence of such outsourcing, except within the manufacturing sector. . . . One manufacturing survey has found that from 1986 to 1987, 23.9 percent of firms contracted out at least some of their janitorial services" (Abraham and Taylor 1996). Another analysis of
this survey, using a follow-up questionnaire, finds that 57.4 percent of metalworking and machinery
plants "usually" outsource some part of their machining operations (Harrison and Kelley 1993). A
more recent clue for all industries can be had from the 1999 Staffing and Structure Survey conducted
by the American Management Association, which finds that 49.6 percent of firms reported job cuts

in 1999, virtually unchanged from the 50 percent in 1995. Of the companies cutting jobs during this five-year period, fully 44.6 percent reported that "the work was transferred to other entities" (for example outsourcing and subcontracting) (American Management Association 1999) 189. Annette Bernhardt, Martina Morris, Mark S. Handcock, and Marc A. Scott, *Divergent Paths: Economic Mobility in the New American Labor Market* (New York: Russell Sage Foundation, 2001), 188.

4. For blacks it is 32 percent and Latinos 42.5 percent. The poverty-level wage is the hourly wage that a full-time, year-round worker must earn to sustain a family of four at the poverty threshold, which was $8.70 in 2001. From Lawrence Mishel, Jared Bernstein, and Sylvia Allegretto, *The State of Working America 2004/2005* (Ithaca: Cornell University Press, 2004).

5. In a random survey of 153 of their members in Boston, SEIU 615, the heavily Latino janitor's local and worker center with a large number of part-time, non-English speaking workers, a large percentage of which are undocumented, found that 42 percent of its members had been in the country for ten years or more and 71 percent for six years or more.

6. The common definition of a hiring hall is "a union operated placement center where jobs from various employers are allotted to registered applicants according to a set order based usually on rotation or seniority." *The American Heritage® Dictionary of the English Language,* 4th ed. (New York: Houghton Mifflin Company, 2000).

7. The billboard says: "Need workers? LA City Day Laborers 4 blocks away. Don't pick up day laborers at the Home Depot. Thanks for helping the community of North Hollywood."

8. Bernard Cordon, "Damned if You Do: Home Depot's Labor Problem," *Forbes Magazine* 16 (August 11, 2003), 19.

9. Interview with Mrs. Lee, December 2003, all subsequent quotations are drawn from this interview.

10. Mark Erlich, *With Our Hands: The Story of Carpenters in Massachusetts* (Philadelphia: Temple University Press, 1986), 18.

11. Workplace Project, *Annual Narrative Report to the Public Welfare Foundation* (Hempstead, New York: January 1–December 31, 1999).

CHAPTER 6. RELATIONSHIPS WITH UNIONS

1. They also sought to relocate major packing operations from traditional centers in areas like Iowa and Illinois and move further into rural Nebraska, western Kansas, as well as Colorado and the Texas Panhandle.

2. This background material is drawn from Karen Olsson, "The Shame of Meatpacking," *The Nation,* September 16, 2002; David Bacon, "The Kill Floor Rebellion," *The American Prospect* 13, no. 12 (July 2002); and Charles Craypo, "Meatpacking: Industry Restructuring and Union Decline," in *Contemporary Collective Bargaining in the Private Sector,* Paula B. Voos, ed. (Madison: University of Wisconsin/Industrial Relations Research Association, 1994), 63–96.

3. Tom Holler interview, October 2003, all subsequent quotes are from this same interview.

4. Sergio Sosa interview, October 2003, all subsequent quotes are from this same interview.

5. Marcella Cervantes interview, October 2003, all subsequent quotes are from this same interview.

6. Donna MacDonald interview, October 2003.

7. Also, every month the center sponsors a legal clinic, a workers rights workshop, and a union organizing workshop. All three are led or co-led by workers who have become active leaders in the center.

8. Jose Oliva interview, April 2003, all subsequent quotes, except when noted, are from this interview.

9. Dan McMann interview, April 2003, all subsequent quotes are from this interview.

10. Tim Leahy interview, April 2003, all subsequent quotes are from this interview.

11. Cintas is the major target of a national organizing campaign that UNITE-HERE has launched in the apparel industry. According to the company website, "Cintas is the largest uniform supplier in North America. . . . We operate 351 facilities in the U.S. and Canada, including 15 manufacturing plants and seven distribution centers that employ more than 28,000 people."

12. Jose Oliva interview, November 2004.

13. Yanira Merino interview, February 3, 2004.

14. Sara Flocks interview, November 2004, all subsequent quotes are from this interview.

15. Kevin Fitzpatrick interview, October 2003, all subsequent quotes are from this interview.

16. Michael Luo, "New York Cabs to Charge More, But You Can Put It on Plastic," *New York Times*, March 31, 2004, A1, A21.

17. New York Taxi Workers Alliance, "Petition to Initiate Rulemaking Pursuant to 35RCNY 11–01 (2002)," 1–7. Much of the research is contained in the "Chart Book on Wages, Operating Costs, and Cost of Living for Taxicab Drivers in New York City," prepared for the Taxi Workers Alliance by the Brennan Center for Justice at NYU School of Law, 2002.

18. Rizwan Raha interview, October 2003.

19. Gilbert Gorman, *The Taxicab: an Urban Transportation Survivor* (Chapel Hill: University of North Carolina Press, 1982), and "Taxi!" *Atlantic Monthly* (May 1994), 16–23; *Taxi Dreams* (2001), Thirteen/WNET and the Public Broadcasting System, at http://www.pbs.org/wnet/taxidreams/index .html.

20. CAAAV's goal is to build a movement among what it calls the "new working class" in Asian communities who are "often left out of formal organizing because they are considered 'noncitizens' not only in terms of their immigration or citizenship status, but their extra-legal status as non-traditional workers." Excerpted from a CAAAV proposal, July 16, 2004. CAAAV was also the incubator of the Domestic Workers Union.

21. Interview with Bhairavi Desai, October 2003, and articles by Anuradha G. Advani, "Against the Tide: Reflections on Organizing New York City's South Asian Taxicab Drivers," in *Making More Waves: New Writing by Asian American Women*, Elaine H. Kim, Lilia V. Villanueva, and Asian Women United of California, eds. (Boston: Beacon Press, 1997); and Mohammed Kazem, Rizwan Raja, Biju Mathew et al. "Reorganizing Organizing: Immigrant Labor in North America," in "Satyagraha America," *Amerasia Journal* 25, no. 3 (1999–2000): 171–81.

22. According to Bhairvi Desai, as of spring 2005, approximately fifty-six hundred drivers have signed forms saying that they wish to be members of the NYTWA, about one thousand are dues-paying members.

23. Interview with Paul Lee, December 2003, all subsequent quotations are drawn from this interview.

24. Interview with Mr. Park, December 2003, all subsequent quotations are drawn from this interview.

25. From Voice and Future Fund, "Common Stream Grant Report Form," July 15, 2004.

26. From grant proposal by Weezy Waldstein, "Building Services Career Paths Planning Project: Building the Future for Immigrant Workers and Boston," grant proposal, Voice and Future Fund, Boston, Mass., 2004.

27. Richard B. Freeman and James L. Medoff, *What Do Unions Do?* (New York: Basic Books 1984).

28. Telephone interview with Pablo Alvarado, January 18, 2005, all subsequent quotations are drawn from this interview.

29. Of course, some of these difficulties are a function of day labor itself and may be impossible to address. Is day labor a long-term livelihood or a short-term bridge to more permanent employment? UCLA Professor of Urban Studies Abel Valenzuela found that while 30 percent of day laborers in Los Angeles had been in the United States for less than a year, and 23 percent for between one and five years, close to 25 percent had been here for five to ten years and 23 percent for ten years or more. We can see from these numbers that many day laborers are not newcomers and are remaining or at least going back and forth between day labor and other types of employment. But many day laborer organizers report that their leadership base requires constant reorganizing as people move on to permanent employment or return to their home countries. Whether day laborer work could support more traditional union hiring halls remains an open question. Abel Valenzuela, Jr., "Day Laborers in Southern California: Preliminary Findings from the Day Labor Survey," Center for the Study of Urban Poverty, Institute for Social Science Research, UCLA, May 30, 1999.

30. In this context, by "recognizing" a worker center, I mean acknowledging they exist by returning a phone call or agreeing to a meeting, not recognizing them in the traditional employment relations sense of a firm granting formal recognition of the union's right to bargain on behalf of employees.

31. Freeman and Medoff, *What Do Unions Do?* 7–8.

32. Richard B. Freeman, "Spurts in Union Growth: Defining Moments and Social Processes," National Bureau of Economic Research Working Paper No. w6012*, April 1997.

33. Telephone interview, December, 2003.

CHAPTER 7. PUBLIC POLICY ENFORCEMENT AND REFORM

1. When first enacted, the FLSA covered perhaps 20 percent of American workers. By 1996, it covered an estimated 65 percent of all American workers. In 1961 coverage was expanded to workers in the construction, retail, and service industries. In 1966, coverage was extended to 9 million more workers when hospitals, nursing homes, and educational institutions were added. Minimum wage coverage expanded again in 1974, when private household workers and additional employees of state and local government were added. But in 1976, state and local government workers were removed from FLSA coverage, and they were not restored to coverage until 1985. In 1977, Congress, by lowering the threshold minimum level volume of annual sales that determined whether a firm had to pay minimum wage, extended coverage to many small businesses. See Willis Nordlund, *The Quest for a Living Wage* (Westport, CT: Greenland Press, 1997), and the U.S. Department of Labor, Wage and Hour Division, *Minimum Wage and Overtime Hours Under the Fair Labor Standards Act* (Washington DC: U.S. Department of Labor, 2003).

2. "The minimum wage used to bring a family of three with one full-time worker above the official poverty line. Now it doesn't bring a full-time worker with one child above the line. A full-time, year-round worker earning $5.15 an hour makes $10,712 a year, a family with two minimum wage earners $21,424. Only households with two adults working full-time, no children, and employment health benefits can meet their minimum needs budget at this wage." Holly Sklar, Laryssa Mykta, and Susan Wefald, *Raise the Floor: Wages and Policies that Work for All of Us* (New York: Ms. Foundation for Women, 2001), 49.

3. All of the data in this paragraph are from Howard Wial, "Minimum Wage Enforcement and the Low-wage Labor Market," MIT Task Force on Reconstructing America's Labor Market Institutions, Working Paper #WP11, August 1, 1999, 10–12. Available at http://mitsloan.mit.edu/iwer/tfwial.pdf.

4. See U.S. Bureau of Census (1997), 544, Table 845, as cited by Wial, "Minimum Wage Enforcement." "Whether measured by inflation-adjusted budgets, the number of investigators, or the number of Fair Labor Standards Act Compliance actions taken, the enforcement resources of the Wage and Hour Division are smaller today than they were 20 years ago. The WHD's inflation adjusted budget for fiscal year 1998 was 7 percent below its level in fiscal year 1979. The number of investigators dropped by 11 percent between 1979 and 1998, and the number of compliance actions were 34 percent lower." Wial, ibid., 15. As an illustration of the problem, in the garment industry today, David Weil estimates that "given the probability of inspection and the expected civil penalty, the predicted cost of noncompliance is about $780 compared to the cost of compliance of $6,700." Weil goes on, "Facing this trade-off, a rational contractor should choose noncompliance on a period by period basis—even given a moderate level of aversion to being caught. This simple calculus, played out in the context of extremely competitive product markets for sewing contractors, explains the economics underlying the intransigence of the sweatshop problem, even with more aggressive enforcement activity." David Weil, "Regulating Noncompliance to Labor Standards: New Tools for an Old Problem," *Challenge* 45, no. 1 (January–February 2002): 47–74.

5. Wial, "Minimum Wage Enforcement," 6–7.

6. "The majority of the state's workers' compensation laws include 'aliens' in the definition of covered employees. Entitlement to lost wages under state workers' compensation laws turns on state statutes and their definition of 'worker' or 'employee.' State courts in California, Colorado, Connecticut, Florida, Georgia, Iowa, Louisiana, Nevada, New Jersey, New York, Pennsylvania, and Texas have specifically held that undocumented workers are covered under their state workers' compensation laws." National Employment Law Project, "Low Pay, High Risk State Models for Advancing Immigrant Workers Rights," New York, NY (November 2003), 59.

7. Ibid., 44–57.

8. However, federal courts have held that Hoffman is not relevant to back pay under the FLSA and have made rulings favorable to plaintiffs. See *Flores v. Albertson's Inc,* 2002WL 11623 (CD Cal 2002); *Liu v. Donna Karan International Inc.,* 2002 WL 1300260 (SD NY 2002). See U.S. Department of Labor Fact Sheet #48, "Application of U.S. Labor Laws to Immigrant Workers: Effect of Hoffman Plastics Decision on Laws Enforced by the Wage and Hour Division" (Washington DC: U.S. Department of Labor, 2002).

9. Wial, "Minimum Wage Enforcement," 33.

10. Mike Sherry, Cindy Gonzalez, and Leslie Reed, "Meatpacking Probe Applauded," *Omaha World Herald*, September 25, 1999, 1A and 56.

11. Ibid.

12. Don Walton, "Johanns Vows to Support Hispanic Workers," *Lincoln Journal Star*, February 2, 2000, 1a and 12a.

13. The Garment Worker Center, the Maintenance Trust Fund, KIWA, and CHIRLA.

14. Interview with Lillia Garcia, February 10, 2004, all other quotations are taken from this interview.

15. Interview with Henry Huerta, January 27, 2004, all other quotations are taken from this interview.

16. Tom Gallagher, "Tough on Crime? The Decline of Labor Law Enforcement in California," *California Works*, June 27, 2001.

17. They first wanted to call it the Office of Immigrant Affairs, but this name was deemed to be too controversial.

18. In addition to the four worker centers, the advisory board regularly included the labor commissioner, the chief of enforcement in the L.A. office, and the director of the LWI office.

19. Garcia e-mail to author, November, 2004.

20. Richard Shaw interview, February 23, 2004, all subsequent quotations are from this interview. Additional information was gleaned from the "Justice and Equality in the Workplace Program" brochure and the Workers Center Project proposal in possession of author.

21. "Although perhaps counter-intuitive at first glance—how could a person who is not allowed to work be entitled to a minimum wage?—Congress has recognized that the only way to remove the incentive for an unscrupulous employer to hire undocumented workers and pay them sub-minimum wages is to punish those who do so." Jennifer Gordon, "The Campaign for the Unpaid Wages Prohibition Act: Latino Immigrants Change New York Wage Law: The Impact of Non-Voters on Politics and the Impact of Political Participation on Non-Voters," *Report to the Carnegie Foundation*, 1998, 8.

22. According to Gordon, immigrant workers went to the state Department of Labor as opposed to the federal for two reasons. First, many of them were exempt from the federal wage laws because their employers had less than $500,000 in gross revenues a year and did not put goods into the stream of interstate commerce. Of course, this included the vast majority of restaurants, contractors, and landscaping companies for whom they worked. Second, because of the link between the federal Department of Labor and the Immigration and Naturalization Service, even those workers who were covered by the federal minimum wage laws preferred to deal with the state Department of Labor. Ibid., 7.

23. Gordon wrote: "This decision took three months to make. Over a series of three Workplace Project monthly membership meetings, members discussed the problems they had been facing at the DOL and developed a list of additional information they would need to figure out the causes of those problems (for example, knowledge about how the DOL was supposed to function, and about the New York State political system). We presented workshops with this information. Our members used it and their own experience to analyze the immediate and deeper causes of the problems that they saw, and to brainstorm short and long-term solutions. Looking at the solutions in light of the organization's resources at that time, they decided to focus their energy on a legislative campaign." Ibid., 10.

24. The bill was also opposed behind the scenes by the state DOL until it began to look like a fait accompli.

25. Jordan Rau, "A Fight for Fair Pay: State Labor Agency's Reinforcement of Rules Requiring Proper Wage for Workers Has Waned during Pataki's Tenure" *Newsday*, April 11, 2004, 3.

26. Telephone interview with author, June 2004.

27. Ai Jen Poo telephone interview with author, June 2004, all other quotations are drawn from this interview.

28. Brian Kavanaugh telephone interview with author, June 2004, all other quotations are drawn from this interview.

29. When it was first enacted in 1938, the Fair Labor Standards Act excluded private household workers, but was amended in 1974 and now guarantees private domestic workers the right to receive minimum wages and overtime pay. The amendment covers a range of domestic occupations, including

housekeepers, maids, cooks, and butlers. Any domestic employee who works more than eight hours in a single workweek is entitled to receive the minimum wage. Pierette Hondagneiu-Sotelo writes, "Most people involved in domestic work, employers as well as employees, still do not know that wage and hour regulations cover paid domestic work. The reason for their ignorance is obvious: virtually no attempt has been made by the government or media to educate domestic workers and employers about these laws. If we examine newspaper editorials and reports on regulations concerning paid domestic work, especially those published after the Zoe Baird debacle, we find an overwhelming focus on employment taxes, not wages and hours. Often, through no fault of their own, employers remain unaware of the various laws protecting domestic workers employment rights." This problem is what the New York City Council hoped to address in requiring employers to sign the statement. See Pierrette Hondagneu-Sotelo, *Domestica: Immigrant Workers Cleaning and Caring in the Shadows of Affluence* (Berkeley: University of California Press, 2001), 211–16.

30. Statistics are from the ACORN Living Wage Resource Center, referenced by Chris Tilly in "Living Wage Laws in the United States: The Dynamics of a Growing Movement," in Charles Tilly and Maria Kousis, eds. *Economic and Political Contention in Comparative Perspective* (Boulder, CO: Paradigm Press, 2005).

31. Excerpted from the Chinese Progressive Association, *Workers Organizing Center Update,* San Francisco, CA, February 2004.

CHAPTER 8. IMMIGRANT RIGHTS AND SOCIAL JUSTICE

1. "We passed the law. It passed because I was the presiding officer. I dole out committees. I dole out every single thing. I made it in everyone's vested interest to do the right thing and vote for this. There were Republicans that voted for it. I had budget deals all over the place going." Interview with Paul Tona, June 2004.

2. Some police departments across the country have been asked to conduct immigration raids, and this has been a source of controversy and point of organizing for community organizations.

3. Each drivers' license applicant must demonstrate proof that he or she is either a U.S. citizen; has been lawfully admitted for permanent or temporary residence; is a conditional permanent resident or has a pending or approved application for asylum; or is a refugee, a nonimmigrant with a valid unexpired visa, has a pending or approved application for temporary protected status, has approved deferred action status, or has a pending application for permanent residence or conditional permanent residence. Applicants who present a nonimmigrant visa, a pending application for asylum, a pending or approved application for temporary protected status, proof of approved deferred action status, or a pending application for permanent residence or conditional permanent residence may receive only a "temporary" drivers' license. These temporary licenses are valid only for the period of the applicant's authorized stay in the United States. In any case in which the state issues a drivers' license that does not satisfy REAL ID's requirements, the license must clearly state on its face that it may not be accepted by any federal agency for any official purpose. This summary relies on the National Immigration Law Center May 12, 2005, website posting: "Summary of the Driver's License Provisions in the REAL ID Act of 2005 as Made Part of the Emergency Supplemental Appropriations Act for Defense, the Global War on Terror, and Tsunami Relief (Public Law No: 109-13)," http://www.nilc.org/.

4. U.S. Department of Labor, *Employment and Earnings,* January 1999.

CHAPTER 9. THE INTERNAL LIFE OF WORKER CENTERS

1. Robert D. Putnam, *Bowling Alone: The Collapse and Revival of American Community* (New York: Simon and Schuster, 2000).

2. Sidney Verba, Kay Lehman Schlozman, and Henry E. Brady, *Voice and Equality: Civic Voluntarism in American Politics* (Cambridge: Harvard University Press, 1995).

3. "Let's go back to literacy. . . . When people who can read and write Spanish come to our centers to learn English, we help them learn the capacity to teach others how to read and write Spanish. . . . so

they are teaching literacy while also learning how to acquire English. In that way, people feel they are not just getting but also giving. That is *capacitación*—developing peoples' capacities."

4. The Supreme Court ruled in April 2002 in *Hoffman Plastic Compounds vs. NLRB* that undocumented workers fired for their union support are not entitled to back pay, which has imperiled their right to organize.

5. Bhairavi Desai e-mail, January 17, 2005.

6. Maria Mottolla telephone interview, October 2004

7. Jennifer Gordon, telephone interview, December 2004.

8. Angelica Salas, telephone conversation, January 2005.

9. Gihan Pereira telephone interview, April 2004.

CHAPTER 10. NETWORKING, STRUCTURES, AND PRACTICES

1. The Mexican American Legal Defense and Education Fund (MALDEF) and the Puerto Rican Legal Defense and Education Fund provide and finance the legal representation.

2. National Day Laborer Organizing Network, "From Hopes to Realities: Our 2003–2004 Accomplishments," Los Angeles, California, August 2004, 5.

3. Ibid., 4.

4. For an excellent history of ACORN's worker organizing efforts see Vanessa Tait, *Poor Workers' Unions: Rebuilding Labor from Below* (Boston: South End Press, 2005) 131–65.

5. Cesar Chavez, *On Money and Organizing* (La Paz, CA: United Farm Workers, 1971).

6. Ibid.

7. Interview with Rich Cunningham, January 28, 2005, and e-mail message, January 29, 2005, all subsequent quotations are drawn from these.

8. This section on Casa Maryland draws upon research conducted in February 2005 by Ed Gramlisch at the Center for Community Change as well as an April 2005 conversation with Gustavo Torres by the author.

9. Myra Glassman telephone interview, October 2004, all subsequent quotations are drawn from this interview.

10. Madeline Talbott telephone interview, October 2004, all subsequent quotations are drawn from this interview.

11. Ginny Goldman telephone interview, October 2004, all subsequent quotations are drawn from this interview.

CHAPTER 11. A HOLISTIC ASSESSMENT OF THE WORKER CENTER PHENOMENON

1. For a detailed theoretical discussion of social movement organizations see Doug MacAdam, John D. McCarthy, and Mayer N. Zald, eds., *Comparative Perspectives on Social Movements* (New York: Cambridge University Press, 1996).

2. Aldon Morris, *The Origins of the Civil Rights Movement: Black Communities Organizing for Change* (New York: The Free Press, 1984), 40–76. Morris is taking on the "resource mobilization" school of social movement theorists who argued that external resources were key to the success of the civil rights movement.

3. See Janice Fine, "Community Unions in Baltimore and Long Island: Beyond the Politics of Particularism," (PhD. dissertation, Massachusetts Institute of Technology, 2003), chapters four and five.

4. See Steven Lukes, *Power: A Radical View* (London: MacMillan Education, 1974), and John Gaventa, *Power and Powerlessness: Quiescence and Rebellion in an Appalachian Valley* (Urbana: University of Illinois Press, 1980), 1–32.

5. From Elshtain, *The Jane Addams Reader*, 26.

6. By scale we mean the size of the organization or the relative magnitude of the membership base.

7. For very trenchant analysis related to this point, see Steve Jenkins, "Organizing, Advocacy and Mem-

ber Power," *Working USA: The Journal of Labor and Society* 6, no. 2 (2002): 56–89. Jenkins is a former organizer and attorney at Make the Road by Walking, a worker center in Bushwick, Brooklyn.

8. See Morris, *The Origins of the Civil Rights Movement.* Morris offers many examples in chapters 3, 4, and 5. See, for example, pp. 65–66 about the Tallahassee bus boycott. "The financial base of this movement was also rooted in the black church. In Reverend Speed's words: 'The bulk of the money came from the black people in the community, from church to church.' In p. 281 Morris makes plain his claim that "my research demonstrates that the overwhelming majority of local movements were indigenously organized and financed."

9. *Relational power* is a term that is used by the Industrial Areas Foundation (IAF) and other faith-based organizations to describe the type of power their organizations seek to build. "Unilateral power represents 'power over' others . . . 'relational power' . . . is the 'power to' act collectively together." Mark R. Warren, *Dry Bones Rattling: Community Building to Revitalize American Democracy* (Princeton, NJ: Princeton University Press, 2001), 68. The term was initially coined by Bernard Loomer in "Two Conceptions of Power," *Criterion* 15, no. 1 (Winter 1976): 12–29.

10. For a very insightful discussion of low-wage worker organizing and relational power, see Margaret Gray's excellent paper for the 2004 American Political Science Association annual convention entitled "Low-wage Worker Advocacy: Leveraging Allies and Compensating for Constraints."

11. Many thanks to Rebecca Smith at the National Employment Law Project for sharpening this point.

12. Gary Marks, *Unions in Politics: Britain, Germany, and the United States in the Nineteenth and Early Twentieth Centuries* (Princeton, NJ: Princeton University Press, 1989), 46–49.

13. Ann Shola Orloff, "Origins of America's Welfare State," in *The Politics of Social Policy in the United States,* Margaret Weir, Orloff, and Skocpol, eds. (Princeton: Princeton University Press, 1988).

14. Susan C. Eaton, "Beyond 'Unloving Care': Linking Human Resource Management and Patient Care Quality in Nursing Homes," *International Journal of Human Resource Management* 2 (2003).

15. Lawrence Mishel, Jared Bernstein, and Sylvia Allegretto, *State of Working America 2004/2005* (Ithaca: Cornell University Press, 2005). In 2001, researchers at the Ms. Foundation for women found that eight dollars an hour is the amount needed for a single full-time worker to meet their minimum needs budget, excluding the cost of health benefits which many do not have.

16. Wial, "Minimum Wage Enforcement," 18.

17. The Industrial Standards Act allows Ontario's minister of labor after convening an industry-wide labor management conference at the request of workers or employers, to adopt regulations governing any minimum labor standards (minimum wages, maximum hours, overtime pay) to which a sufficient number of worker and employer representatives agreed at the conference. Each covered industry has an advisory committee that consists of three employer representatives and two union representatives.

18. Frances Fox Piven and Richard A. Cloward, "Rulemaking, Rulebreaking and Power," draft paper in possession of author.

BIBLIOGRAPHY

Abelman, Nancy, and John Lie. *Blue Dreams: Korean Americans and the Los Angeles Riots.* Cambridge: Harvard University Press, 1995.

Advani, Anuradha G. "Against the Tide: Reflections on Organizing New York City's South Asian Taxicab Drivers." In *Making More Waves: New Writing by Asian American Women,* ed. Elaine H. Kim, Lilia V. Villanueva, and Asian Women United of California. Boston: Beacon Press, 1997.

Bacon, David. "The Kill Floor Rebellion." *The American Prospect* 13, no. 12 (July 2002).

Beito, David T. *From Mutual Aid to the Welfare State: Fraternal Societies and Social Services, 1890–1967.* Chapel Hill: University of North Carolina Press, 2000.

Bernhardt, Annette, Martina Morris, Mark S. Handcock, and Marc A. Scott. *Divergent Paths: Economic Mobility in the New American Labor Market.* New York: Russell Sage Foundation, 2001.

Blaney, Shannon, and Leighton Ku. *Health Coverage for Legal Immigrant Children: New Census Data Highlight Importance of Restoring Medicaid and SCHIP Coverage.* Washington, DC: Center on Budget and Policy Priorities, October 2000.

Brennan Center for Justice, NYU School of Law. "Chart Book on Wages, Operating Costs, and Cost of Living for Taxicab Drivers in New York City." Prepared for the Taxi Workers Alliance, 2002.

Bronfenbrenner, Kate L. "Employer Behavior in Certification Elections and First-Contract Campaigns: Implications for Labor Law Reform." In *Restoring the Promise of American Labor Law,* ed. Sheldon Friedman, Richard W. Hurd, Rudolph A. Oswald, and Ronald L. Seeber. Ithaca: Cornell University Press, 1994.

Chavez, Cesar. *On Money and Organizing.* La Paz, CA: United Farm Workers, 1971.

Chinese Progressive Association. *Workers Organizing Center Update.* San Francisco, CA, February 2004.

Clark, William A. V. "The Geography of Immigrant Poverty: Selective Evidence of an Immigrant Underclass." In *Strangers at the Gate: New Immigrants in Urban America,* ed. Roger Waldinger. Berkeley: University of California Press, 2001.

Cordon, Bernard. "Damned if you do: Home Depot's Labor Problem," *Forbes Magazine* 16 (August 11, 2003), 19.

Craypo, Charles. "Meatpacking: Industry Restructuring and Union Decline." In *Contemporary Collective Bargaining in the Private Sector,* ed. Paula B. Voos. Madison: University of Wisconsin/Industrial Relations Research Association, 1994.

DeSpain, Meredith Lynn, "Cross-Sector Collaborations in Immigrant Worker Protection: Exploring Their Emergence and Considering Their Strategic Value for Worker Centers," (paper prepared for the Central Texas Immigrant Worker Rights Center, August 2004).

Eaton, Susan E. "Beyond 'Unloving Care': Linking Human Resource Management and Patient Care Quality in Nursing Homes." *International Journal of Human Resource Management* 11, no. 3 (2003): 591–616.

Elshtain, Jean Bethke. *The Jane Addams Reader.* New York: Basic Books, 2002.

Erlich, Mark. *With Our Hands: The Story of Carpenters in Massachusetts.* Philadelphia: Temple University Press, 1986.

Farris, Anne. *The House We All Live In: A Report on Immigrant Civic Participation.* New York, NY: Carnegie Corporation of America, 2003.

Fine, Janice. "Community Unions in Baltimore and Long Island: Beyond the Politics of Particularism." Ph.D. diss., Massachusetts Institute of Technology, 2003.

Fink, Leon. *The Maya of Morganton: Work and Community in the Nuevo New South.* Chapel Hill: University of North Carolina Press, 2003.

Fitzgerald, David, "Beyond 'Transnationalism': Mexican Hometown Politics at an American Labour Union," *Ethnic and Racial Studies* 27, no. 2 (March 2000), 237–40.

Foner, Philip S., *Organized Labor and The Black Worker 1619–1981.* New York: International Publishers, 1976.

Freeman, Richard B. "Spurts in Union Growth: Defining Moments and Social Processes." National Bureau of Economic Research, Working Paper No. w6012*, April 1997.

Freeman, Richard B., and James L. Medoff. *What Do Unions Do?* New York: Basic Books, 1984.

Freeman, Richard, and Joel Rogers. *What Workers Want.* Ithaca: Cornell University Press, 1999.

Gallagher, Tom. "Tough on Crime? The Decline of Labor Law Enforcement in California." *California Works* (June 27, 2001).

Gaventa, John. *Power and Powerlessness: Quiescence and Rebellion in an Appalachian Valley.* Urbana: University of Illinois Press, 1980.

Golfield, Michael, *The Decline of Organized Labor in the United States.* Chicago: University of Chicago Press, 1987.

Goodwyn, Lawrence. *The Populist Moment: A Short History of the Agrarian Revolt in America.* Oxford: Oxford University Press, 1976.

Gordon, Jennifer. "The Campaign for the Unpaid Wages Prohibition Act: Latino Immigrants Change New York Wage Law: The Impact of Non-Voters on Politics and the Impact of Political Participation on Non-Voters." *Report to the Carnegie Foundation,* 1998.

——. *Suburban Sweatshops: The Fight for Immigrant Rights.* Cambridge: Harvard University Press, 2005.

Gorman, Gilbert. *The Taxicab: an Urban Transportation Survivor.* Chapel Hill: University of North Carolina Press, 1982.

——. "Taxi!" *The Atlantic Monthly* (May 1994).

Gray, Margaret. "Low-wage Worker Advocacy: Leveraging Allies and Compensating for Constraints." Paper prepared for the American Political Science Association, 2004.

Hondagneu-Sotelo, Pierrette. *Domestica: Immigrant Workers Cleaning and Caring in the Shadows of Affluence.* Berkeley: University of California Press, 2001.

Jenkins, Steve. "Organizing, Advocacy, and Member Power." *Working USA: The Journal of Labor and Society* 6, no. 2 (2002): 56–89.

Kazem, Mohammed, Rizwan Raja, Biju Mathew, et al. "Reorganizing Organizing: Immigrant Labor in North America." In "Satyagraha America," *Amerasia Journal* 25, no. 3 (1999–2000): 171–81.

Korean Immigrant Worker Advocates. "Semiannual Report." Los Angeles, CA: Winter 2003.

Kosak, Hadassah. *Cultures of Opposition: Jewish Immigrant Workers, New York City, 1881–1905.* Albany: State University of New York Press, 2000.

Levitt, Peggy. *The Transnational Villagers.* Berkeley: University of California Press, 2001.

Lichtenstein, Nelson. *State of the Union: A Century of American Labor.* Princeton, NJ: Princeton University Press, 2002.

Lichtenstein, Nelson, Susan Strasser, and Roy Rosenzweig. *Who Built America? Working People and the Nation's Economy, Politics, Culture, and Society.* New York: Worth, 2000.

Lim, Nelson. "On the Backs of Blacks? Immigrants and the Fortunes of African-Americans." In *Strangers at the Gates: New Immigrants in Urban America,* ed. Roger Waldinger. Berkeley: University of California Press, 2001.

Loomer, Bernard. "Two Conceptions of Power." *Process Studies* 6, no. 1 (Spring 1976), 5–32.

Louie, Miriam Ching Yoon. *Sweatshop Warriors.* Boston: South End Press, 2001.

Lukes, Steven. *Power: A Radical View.* London: MacMillan Education, 1974.

Luo, Michael. "New York Cabs to Charge More, But You Can Put It on Plastic." *New York Times,* March 31, 2004, A1 and A21.

MacAdam, Doug, John D. McCarthy, and Mayer N. Zald, eds. *Comparative Perspectives on Social Movements.* New York: Cambridge University Press, 1996.

Marks, Gary. *Unions in Politics: Britain, Germany, and the United States in the Nineteenth and Early Twentieth Centuries.* Princeton, NJ: Princeton University Press, 1989.

Migration Policy Institute. *Migration Information Source, Data Tools, Immigration: A Historical Perspective,* "Immigration to the United States by Decade: Fiscal Years 1821 to 2000 (in millions)," and "Foreign-born Population by Region of Birth as Percentage of the Total Population of the United States: 1850–2000." U.S. Census Bureau, Working Paper No. 29, *Historical Census Statistics on the Foreign-Born Population of the United States: 1850 to 1990.* Washington, DC: U.S. Government Printing Office, 1999.

——. *Immigration Facts,* no. 7, May 2004.

Milkman, Ruth and Kent Wong. "The 1992 Southern California Drywall Strike" in *Organizing Immigrants: The Challenge for Unions in Contemporary California,* ed. Ruth Milkman. Ithaca: Cornell University Press, 2000.

Mishel, Lawrence, Jared Bernstein, and Sylvia Alegretto. *The State of Working America, 2004/2005.* Ithaca: Cornell University Press, 2004.

Mishel, Lawrence, Jared Bernstein, and Heather Boushey. *The State of Working America, 2002–2003.* Ithaca: Cornell University Press, 2003.

Morris, Aldon. *The Origins of the Civil Rights Movement: Black Communities Organizing for Change.* New York: The Free Press, 1984.

National Day Laborer Organizing Network. "From Hopes to Realities: Our 2003–2004 Accomplishments." Los Angeles, CA: August 2004.

National Employment Law Project. "Low Pay, High Risk: State Models for Advancing Immigrant Workers Rights." New York, NY: November, 2003.

New York Taxi Workers Alliance. "Petition to Initiate Rulemaking Pursuant to 35RCNY 11–01." New York, 2002.

Nordlund, Willis. *The Quest for a Living Wage.* Westport, CT: Greenland Press, 1997.

Olsson, Karen. "The Shame of Meatpacking." *The Nation* 16 (September 2002).

Orloff, Ann Shola. "Origins of America's Welfare State." In *The Politics of Social Policy in the United States,* ed. Margaret Weir, Ann Shola Orloff, and Theda Skocpol. Princeton, NJ: Princeton University Press, 1988.

Orozco, Manuel. "Remittances to Latin America and the Caribbean: Issues and Perspectives on Development" Report Commissioned by the Office for the Summit Process, Organization of American States, Washington, DC: September, 2004.

Park, Derek, Steven Lee, Rose Sohn, and Bona Hong. "Ten Years: The Worker Empowerment Clinic." Korean Immigrant Worker Advocates report. Los Angeles, CA: February 2003.

Passel, Jeffrey. "New Estimates of the Undocumented Population in the United States." *Migration Information Source.* Washington DC: Migration Policy Institute, May 22, 2002.

Pastorello, Karen. "A Power among Them: Bessie Abromowitz Hillman and the Making of the Amalgamated Clothing Workers of America." Ph.D. diss., State University of New York at Binghamton, 2001.

Pearce, David W., ed. *MIT Dictionary of Modern Economics.* 4th ed. Cambridge: MIT Press, 1995.

Pitts, Steven C. *Organize . . . to Improve the Quality of Jobs in the Black Community: A Report on Jobs and Activism in the African-American Community.* Berkeley: University of California Labor Center, May 2004.

Piven, Francis Fox, and Richard A. Cloward. "Rulemaking, Rulebreaking, and Power." Draft paper in possession of author.

Plotke, David. "Immigration and Political Incorporation in the Contemporary United States." In *The Handbook of International Migration: The American Experience,* ed. Charles Hirschman, Philip Kasinitz, and Josh DeWind. New York: Russell Sage Foundation, 1999.

Pollin, Robert, and Stephanie Luce. *The Living Wage: Building a Fair Economy.* New York: The New Press, 1998.

Putnam, Robert D. *Bowling Alone: The Collapse and Revival of American Community.* New York: Simon and Schuster, 2000.

Rau, Jordan. "A Fight for Fair Pay: State Labor Agency's Reinforcement of Rules Requiring Proper Wage for Workers Has Waned during Pataki's Tenure." *Newsday,* April 11, 2004, 3.

Ross, Julien. "A Fair Day's Pay: The Problem of Unpaid Workers in Central Texas." *Journal of Law and Social Policy* 10, no. 1XX (Fall 2004): 144–46, 155.

Sherry, Mike, Cindy Gonzalez, and Leslie Reed. "Meatpacking Probe Applauded." *Omaha World Herald,* September 25, 1999, 1A, 56.

Sklar, Kathryn Kish, *Florence Kelley and the Nation's Work: The Rise of Women's Political Culture, 1830–1900.* New Haven: Yale University Press, 1995.

Sklar, Holly, Laryssa Mykta, and Susan Wefald. *Raise the Floor: Wages and Policies that Work for All of Us.* New York: Ms. Foundation for Women, 2001.

Skocpol, Theda. *Diminished Democracy: From Membership to Management in American Civic Life.* Norman: University of Oklahoma Press, 2003.

Sum, Andrew, Ishwar Khatiwada, Paul Harrington with Shela Palma. *New Immigrants in the Labor Force and the Number of Employed New Immigrants in the U.S. from 2000 through 2003: Continued Growth Amidst Declining Employment Among the Native Born Population.* Boston: Northeastern University Center for Labor Market Studies, December 2003.

Tilly, Chris. "Living Wage Laws in the United States: The Dynamics of a Growing Movement." In *Economic and Political Contention in Comparative Perspective,* ed. Charles Tilly and Maria Kousis. Boulder, CO: Paradigm Press, 2005.

U.S. Department of Labor. "Application of U.S. Labor Laws to Immigrant Workers: Effect of Hoffman Plastics Decision on Laws Enforced by the Wage and Hour Division." U.S. Department of Labor Fact Sheet #48. Washington DC: Government Printing Office, 2002.

U.S. Department of Labor, Wage and Hour Division. *Minimum Wage and Overtime Hours Under the Fair Labor Standards Act.* Washington DC: Government Printing Office, 2003.

Valenzuela, Jr., Abel. "Day Laborers in Southern California: Preliminary Findings from the Day Labor Survey." Los Angeles: Center for the Study of Urban Poverty, Institute for Social Science Research, University of California at Los Angeles, May 30, 1999.

Verba, Sidney, Kay Lehman Schlozman, and Henry E. Brady. *Voice and Equality: Civic Voluntarism in American Politics.* Cambridge: Harvard University Press, 1995.

Voss, Kim. *The Making of American Exceptionalism: The Knights of Labor and Class Formation in the Nineteenth Century.* Ithaca: Cornell University Press, 1993.

Waldinger, Roger. *Still the Promised City: African-Americans and the New Immigrants in Postindustrial New York.* Cambridge: Harvard University Press, 1996.

——. "Introduction." *Strangers at the Gates: New Immigrants in Urban America,* ed. Waldinger. Berkeley: University of California Press, 2001.

Waldinger, Roger, and Jennifer Lee. "New Immigrants in Urban America." In *Strangers at the Gates: New Immigrants in Urban America,* ed. Waldinger. Berkeley: University of California Press, 2001.

Waldstein, Weezy. "Building Services Career Paths Planning Project: Building the Future for Immigrant Workers and Boston." Boston, MA: Voice and Future Fund, 2004.

Walton, Don. "Johanns Vows to Support Hispanic Workers." *Lincoln Journal Star,* February 2, 2000, 1a and 12a.

Warren, Mark R. *Dry Bones Rattling: Community Building to Revitalize American Democracy.* Princeton, NJ: Princeton University Press, 2001.

Weil, David. "Regulating Noncompliance to Labor Standards: New Tools for an Old Problem." *Challenge,* 45, no. 1 (January/February 2002), 47–74.

Weisser, Michael R. *A Brotherhood of Memory: Jewish Landsmanshaftn in the New World.* New York: Basic Books, 1985.

Wial, Howard. "Minimum Wage Enforcement and the Low-wage Labor Market." MIT Task Force on Reconstructing America's Labor Market Institutions, Working Paper #WP11, August 1, 1999. Available at http://mitsloan.mit.edu/iwer/tfwial.pdf.

Withorn, Ann. "To Serve the People." Ph.D. diss., 1977.

Workplace Project. *Annual Narrative Report to the Public Welfare Foundation.* January 1–December 31, 1999.

Zabin, Carol and Luis Escala Rabadan. "Mexican Hometown Associations and Mexican Immigrant Political Empowerment in Los Angeles." *Nonprofit Sector Research Fund Working Paper Series,* The Aspen Institute, Winter 1998.

INDEX

Addams, Jane, 34, 36, 95, 239, 252
advocacy, 2, 4–5, 12, 79–80
Ae Hwa Kim, 44–45
African Americans, 1, 18, 181; Latinos and, 17, 66–69
African American worker centers, 9, 16–18
Age Discrimination in Employment Act of 1967, 159, 160
Agoura Hills, 88–91
Alabama Christian Movement for Human Rights (ACMHR), 246
Alexandria, Virginia: childcare workers, 176–77; living wage ordinance, 177–78, 196; racial and economic justice issues, 191–92; taxi industry, 19, 50, 179. See also Tenants' and Workers' Support Committee
alliance-building, 14, 239–43; cross-class, 35–36, 39
Alliance for Justice, 85. See also Workplace Project
Alvarado, Pablo, 56, 78, 81, 89, 107–9, 112–14, 146, 202
Amalgamated Clothing and Textile Workers Union (ACTWU), 24–25, 36, 239
American Federation of Labor (AFL), 35
American Federation of Labor-Congress of Industrial Organizations (AFL-CIO), 39–40
American Federation of State, County, and Municipal Employees (AFSCME), 177
American Friends Service Committee (AFSC), 153, 229
Americans with Disabilities Act of 1990, 159
Andolan, 174
Anorve, Raul, 57, 68–69, 113, 115, 153, 202, 207–8, 294n.3

Ansco, 126–28
anti-immigrant bias: attacks, 181–88; campaigns, 57–60; organizations, 54–55, 183–84; in unions, 153, 170–71
antiunion campaigns, 32–33, 125–26, 129, 141–43
apprenticeship programs, 116, 127, 170
Araujo, Lillian, 118
Arlandria neighborhood (Alexandria), 191–92
Arvizu, John, 88–89
asbestos workers, 130–33
Asia–Latin America Solidarity Project, 44–45
Asian-American workers, 178
Asian immigrants, 11, 19, 26, 137, 174, 287n.30; Latino immigrants and, 62–65. See also taxi industry
Asian Immigrant Women's Advocates (AIWA), 70, 104
Asian Law Caucus, 91
Asian Pacific American Legal Center of Southern California, 91, 227
Assembly Bill 633, 89–91
Assi Market campaign, 139–43
Associated Communities Organized for Reform Now (ACORN), 155, 230, 233, 235–38
attorneys, volunteer, 78
Austin Police Department (APD), 87–88, 288n.17
AUTO, 179, 203

Baltimore, 177, 250
Baltimoreans United In Leadership Development (BUILD), 250
bank drafts, 235–38

Baptists, 53
barbajanes (crooks), 116
Baumgarten, Deborah, 174
Beito, David T., 28
Benjamin, Roberta, 68
Berg Manufacturing, 129–30
Bernhardt, Annette, 102
Bishop, Carol, 67
Black Workers for Justice (BWJ), 9, 16–17
Bobo, Kim, 49–50, 52, 53, 132–33
Boston Workforce Development Initiative, 144
Bowling Alone (Putnam), 201
boycotts, 40, 62, 104–6, 110, 147, 251, 296n.8
Brady, Henry E., 201
Brazilian immigrants, 45
Brennan Center, 136, 138
Brewer, Gale, 175
Briggs, Franklin, 68
Brookhaven Citizens for Peaceful Solutions
    (BCPS), 183
budgets and fund-raising, 217–23
Building Services Career Paths Planning Project,
    144
Bureau of Field Enforcement (southern Califor-
    nia), 164, 166
Bureau of Labor Statistics, 194
Bush, George W., 189

CAFÉ. *See* Carolina Alliance for Fair Employ-
    ment
California Apparel News, 105
California Department of Labor Standards En-
    forcement Division (DLSE), 91
California labor codes, 80
California Labor Commissioner, 80, 110
California Works Foundation, 165
campaigns, 251–52. *See also individual cam-
    paigns*
campus action campaigns, 106
Canada, 265, 296n.17
Canales, Carlos, 50, 185–86
card-check recognition, 129–30, 141, 143, 262
CARECEN, 16
Caribbean immigrants, 19, 174
Caring Hands Workers Association, 119
Carolina Alliance for Fair Employment (CAFÉ),
    45, 70; African Americans and Latinos in,
    67–68; job rights workshops, 49, 178–79; ori-
    gins, 9, 24–25; racial and economic justice is-
    sues, 192–93; service delivery, 93; soccer league
    and, 55–56, 75; Youth Center, 68
Carpenters Union, 125–27
Carroll, William, 68
Casa Maryland, 16, 92, 94, 97, 130–33, 235

Case Farms, 17, 132
Catholic Campaign for Human Development, 53
Catholic Charities, 115, 185–86, 229
Catholic Church, 52–54
Center for Community Change, 228, 229, 241,
    260
Center for Creative Nonviolence, 191
Central American immigrants, 11, 14, 16, 19, 47,
    52
central labor councils (CLCs), 155. *See also* Har-
    ris County Central Labor Council; Omaha
    Central Labor Council
Central Texas Immigrant Workers Rights Center
    (CTIWoRC), 87–88
Centro De Derechos Laborales, 190
Cervantes, Marcella, 47, 54, 70, 71, 123
Chavez, Cesar, 233, 234
check cashing privileges, 96–97, 112
check-wiring service, 94, 97
Cheesecake Factory, 134
Chicago Area Workers Rights Initiative
    (CAWRI), 82–84, 130
Chicago Federation of Labor (CFL), 129
Chicago Homecare Organizing Project (CHOP),
    235–36
Chicago Interfaith Committee on Workers Is-
    sues, 22, 125
Chicago Interfaith Workers Rights Center
    (CIWRC), 21–24, 49, 51–52; legal clinic, 82–84,
    96; networks and, 226, 239; service delivery,
    75–77; unions and, 125–30
Chicago Trade and Labor Assembly, 36
Chien, Helen, 63–64, 65, 75, 213
childcare workers, 32, 50, 176–77, 196
Child Health Insurance Program (CHIP),
    196–97
child labor laws, 35
Chinese immigrants, 16, 17, 19, 63–65, 218
Chinese Progressive Association (CPA), 16, 178,
    217
Chinese Staff and Workers Association, 9
Chinese Worker Organizing Center, 218
Cho, Cindy, 213
Cho Sung Galbi (restaurant), 110
churches, 51–55, 121, 255, 296n.8
Church of the Resurrection, 182, 183–84
Cicero Flexible Products, 128
Cintas, 129, 148, 290n.11
citizenship, dual, 45
Civil Rights Act of 1964, 159–60
civil rights movement, 72, 246, 295n.2, 296n.8
civil society, 2, 201
Clark Construction, 131
Cloward, Richard A., 267

Coalition for Humane Immigrant Rights of Los
    Angeles (CHIRLA), 56, 78, 89, 107; budget,
    217; hiring halls, 24, 113–14; networks and, 224,
    226, 227
Coalition of Immigrant Worker Advocates
    (CIWA), 163–69, 226
Coalition of Immokalee Workers (CIW), 94,
    106, 178, 196
code of conduct, 134, 147, 179
collection process, 81
collective action skills, 30
Collective Agreement (Quebec), 265
collective voice/institutional response face of
    worker centers, 148–50, 197–99, 249–52
Colombian immigrants, 45
Committee Against Anti-Asian Violence
    (CAAAV), 26, 137–38, 174, 291n.20
Communidad Salud/the Healthy Community
    Project, 192
communities, 133; home country connections
    and, 42–48. See also churches
community-based organizing projects, 3, 7
community-based unions, 139–40, 283n.3
community election, 143
community institutions, 55–60
ConAgra Beef, 71, 123
Congress of Industrial Organizations (CIO), 121
consciousness-raising, 118
construction industry, 152–53, 169–71; tax issues,
    187–88. See also day laborers
construction unions, 152–53, 170–71
contingent employment, 178–79, 263
conventions, national, 225–26
cooperatives, 70–71, 118–19
craft unions, 114, 146
critical thinking skills, 207–8
cross-agency cooperation, 264
cross-class and cross-ethnic alliances, 4, 35–36,
    39
cross-country alliances, 43
CSI Staffing, 68
culture clashes, 124–25
Cunningham, Rich, 234–35
Cuomo, Mario, 173
Cypress Park site, 107–9

data collection, 79–80, 138, 198
Davis, Andrea, 204–5
Davis, Gray, 58, 89, 164, 169, 189, 227
Day Laborer Band, 202
day laborers, 16, 24, 50; anti-day laborer ordi-
    nances, 88–89; asbestos workers, 130–33; Farm-
    ingville, 54–55, 58–60, 182–85; Freeport, 115,
    182, 185–88; harassment of, 54–55, 112–13; hiring

halls, 24, 113–15, 152, 217, 290n.6; leadership de-
    velopment, 50, 202; national networks, 224–26;
    shape-up sites, 182–85; unions and, 108–9,
    115–16, 152. See also construction industry
day laborer worker centers, 39, 40, 145–46; al-
    liance-building, 239–40; economic action or-
    ganizing, 112–16; Home Depot and, 107–9;
    IDEPSCA and, 194; systems for job assign-
    ments, 113–14
Day Labor Fairness and Protection Act, 225
D.C. Employment Justice Center, 78
decentralization, 102
decision-making, 214–16, 225, 231
DeCoster Egg Farms, 160–61
Department of Consumer Affairs, 175
Department of Homeland Security, 181, 190
Department of Industrial Relations (California),
    164
Department of Labor (DOL), 24, 79–80, 285n.15,
    288n.7. See also Wage and Hour Division
Department of Labor Standards and Enforce-
    ment, 169
Desai, Bhairavi, 51, 137, 215–17, 220, 223
Divergent Paths: Economic Mobility in the New
    American Labor Market (Bernhardt et al.), 102
Division of Labor Standards Enforcement, 87,
    166
documentation, 48, 127, 131
Domenzain, Alejandra, 86, 91, 166
Domestic Violence Is Real workshops, 192–93
domestic workers: Fair Labor Standards Act and,
    175, 293–94n.29; homecare industry, 230, 235–36;
    housekeepers, 50–51. See also childcare workers
Domestic Workers Bill of Rights, 174–76, 197
Domestic Workers Union (DWU), 70, 149,
    174–76, 197
Dominican immigrants, 19, 45–46
Dominican Republic, 45
Downtown Labor Center (UCLA), 227
driver's licenses, 93, 180, 189–90, 227, 294n.3
drywall trade, 58
DT Sewing, 90
dual citizenship, 45
DuBois, W. E. B., 102
dues, 219–23, 232–33; bank drafts, 237–38

economic action organizing: cooperatives,
    118–19; day laborer worker centers, 112–16;
    economic development and, 116–18; KIWA
    and, 109–12; strengths and weaknesses, 144–56;
    targeting corporate employers, 103–7; unions
    and, 114–16, 143–45
economic justice, 53, 191–94
economic opportunity centers, 117

Economic Policy Institute, 263
economic power, 256–58
economic studies, 69
economy, 4, 31–33, 285n.13; ethnic, 140. *See also* globalization
education, 190; ESL classes, 24–25, 49, 73, 91–92, 96, 235; literacy skills development, 193–94, 294–95n.3; political, 5, 43; popular, 13, 24, 206–8, 231; racial and economic justice issues, 191–93
Elephant Snack (restaurant), 111
El Maguey, 58
El Monte Slave Labor case, 227
El Paso, Texas, 116–18
El Puente Community Development Corporation, 117
Employee Free Choice Act, 156, 262
employee leaders, 134
employers: arrests of, 87–88; bankruptcy, 80, 81, 126–27; campaigns against unions, 32–33, 125–26, 129; *empresarios* (entrepreneurs), 116–17; evasion of responsibility, 80–82, 87, 105, 126–27; firing of workers for union activity, 32–33, 126, 129, 163; liability for sweatshop abuses, 89–91; responsibility for subcontractors, 104–6; scare tactics, 47–48; targeting, 103–7; violations in California, 166–67
employment agencies, licensing requirements, 175–76
Employment Report (IL), 83
empresarios (entrepreneurs), 116–17
enforcement. *See* public policy enforcement
ENLACE, 12, 227–28, 242
entrepreneurial training centers, 117
Equal Employment Opportunity Commission (EEOC), 159, 160–61
Equal Justice Center, 229
Erlich, Mark, 114
ESL classes, 24–25, 49, 73, 91–92, 96, 235
ethnic economy, 140
ethnic identity, 13, 40; home country connections and, 42–48
ethnicity: cross-class and cross-ethnic alliances, 4, 35–36, 39; networks and, 33–34

faces of power, 250, 267
faces of worker centers: collective voice/institutional response, 148–50, 197–99, 249–52; monopoly face, 145–48, 194–97, 251–52
Fair Immigration Reform Movement (FIRM), 188–89, 260–62
Fair Labor Standards Act of 1938 (FLSA), 32, 91, 157–58, 175, 259, 292n.1, 293–94n.29; suggested reforms, 263–65

faith-based organizing groups, 11, 14, 120
family reunification, 44
Farah Clothing Factory, 9
Farmingville, Long Island, 54–55, 58–60, 182. *See also* day laborers
Farmingville (movie), 182
Farm Labor Organizing Committee, 17
Farmworker Association of Florida, 77, 94, 97
federal labor laws, 157–59, 176
Federal Unpaid Wages Bill, 263
Filipino immigrants, 11, 16, 19, 43–44, 174
Filipino Worker Center of Los Angeles, 16, 43, 226
financial services, 94, 96–97
Fink, Leon, 58
First Amendment, 89
Fitzgerald, David, 57
Fitzpatrick, Kevin, 136, 138
Flocks, Sara, 133, 134–35
Florida, minimum wage requirements, 178
Ford Foundation, 115
Forever 21 campaign, 104–6, 147, 251
foundations, 218–19, 233, 254–55
Fourteenth Amendment, 89
Fourth Circuit Court of Appeals, 160
fraternal organizations, 33–34, 95, 97
Freeman, Richard B., 145, 149, 151, 266
Freeport, Long Island, 115, 182, 185–88
Freeport Community Development Agency, 186
free speech areas, 89
free trade zones, 44
Freire, Paulo, 13, 206, 208
Fuerza Laboral Feminina, 70–71
funding, 112, 217–23, 254–55

Garcia, Alejandro, 205–6
Garcia, Lilia, 164, 165, 168
Garment Fund, 87
garment industry, 9, 16–17, 62, 283n.2, 285n.15, 290n.11; economic action organizing, 116–18; job losses, 144–45, 208; lawsuits, 89–91; networks, 230–31; subcontracting, 104–6
Garment Worker Center (GWC), 17, 20, 49–50, 62–65, 70, 150, 168; budget, 218; data collection and advocacy, 79; funding, 219–20; internal structure, 204; legal clinic, 86–87; networks and, 226; service delivery, 75, 93, 96; staffing and decision-making, 211, 213; workforce development and, 144–45
Gaventa, John, 250, 267
gender issues, 69–71
George Meany Center, 132
Giuliani, Rudolph, 26, 138
Glacken, William F., 185–88

Glassman, Myra, 236, 238
globalization, 13, 42–48, 208
global justice and democracy movement, 9, 117, 245
Glover, Danny, 138
Golden Era of immigration, 28–29; institutional infrastructure, 36–38; support systems during, 33–36; worker centers, parallels with, 38–40
Golden Gate Restaurant Association, 134
Goldman, Ginny, 237–38
Goodwyn, Lawrence, 3
Gordon, Jennifer, 79, 206, 219, 288nn.7–8, 293nn.21–23
Great Migration, 28
grocery workers campaign, 139–43
Guadalupanos, 57
Guatemalan immigrants, 17, 132
Gutierrez, Luis, 225

H-2A guest worker program, 160
Harris County Central Labor Council, AFL-CIO, 169–71
health insurance, 115, 196–97, 266
health issues, 73, 192
health services, 92–93
Healthy Fair Koreatown, 143
Henry, Kathleen, 50
Hernandez, Lupe, 49, 63–64, 104, 211–12
Hernandez, Mike, 107
Hidalgo, immigrants from, 58–60, 182
High Fashion Institute, 116–17
hiring halls, 24, 113–15, 152, 217, 290n.6
Hoffman Plastics decision, 160, 230, 258, 260–61, 289n.10, 292n.8, 295n.4
Holler, Tom, 46–47, 121–23, 203
homecare industry, 230, 235–36
home country connections, 42–48, 56–60
Home Depot, 107–9, 225
Home Rule party, 186
hometown associations (HTAs), 36, 56–60
Hondagneu-Sotelo, Pierette, 70, 293–94n.29
Hong, Ray, 44
Hong Kong, domestic workers, 174
Hornick, Connie, 182–85
Hotel Employees and Restaurant Employees Union (HERE), 9, 17, 43, 133–35, 147–48, 188
hotel industry, union/worker center cooperation, 133–35, 148
hot goods, 91, 263
hot shop workplaces, 129, 148, 151
housekeepers, 50–51
housing, 125, 191
Houston, 169–71
Houston's Dirty Little Secret, 169

Huerta, Henry, 164–65, 168–69
Hull House, 34–36, 239, 252, 289n.24
hunger strikes, 110, 178
hybrid organization, 12

identification, 12, 93–94, 235; REAL ID Act, 189–90, 294n.3
Immigrant Funders' Collaborative, 227
Immigrant Law Project (NYU), 175
immigrants: current situation, 101–3; employment status, 1, 27–29; patterns, 4; population increase, 190; poverty rates, 27–28; reasons for working in United States, 29–30; rights, 5; scare tactics used against, 47–48; second great migration, 28–31. *See also* undocumented workers; *individual ethnic groups*
Immigrant Workers Freedom Ride, 188–89
Immigrant Workers' Union, 25, 139–43
Immigration and Naturalization Service (INS), 181, 288n.7. *See also* Department of Homeland Security
immigration laws and policies, 24, 27–28, 44, 180–82, 187–88; 1990s, 28–29. *See also individual laws and policies*
immigration reform, 5, 188–90, 260–62
impact litigation, 88–91, 113
independent contractors, 135–39, 153–54. *See also* subcontracting
independent unions, 135–43; KIWA grocery workers campaign, 139–43; New York Taxi Workers Alliance as, 135–39
individual taxpayer identification number (ITIN), 94, 112, 189
Industrial Areas Foundation (IAF), 46–47, 120, 210, 229–30, 233, 296n.9
industrial unions, 258
industry-specific organizing, 20–21
industry teams, 85–86
informal sector, 102
injuries, 25, 32, 68, 73, 111, 122, 139
inspection sweeps, 167–68
institutional infrastructure, Golden Era, 36–38
Instituto de Educación Popular del Sur de California (IDEPSCA), 24, 57, 68–69, 107, 224; hiring halls, 113–14; racial and economic justice issues, 193–94; services provided, 76; staffing and decision-making, 211; unions and, 153–54
insurance programs, fraternal organizations, 97
intake clinics, 166–67, 169
Inter Civic Council (ICC), 246
Interfaith Worker Justice (IWJ), 12, 49–50, 153, 229, 240–42; Harris County AFL-CIO and, 169–71

internal life of worker centers, 5, 13, 201; budgets and fund-raising, 217–23; leadership development, 202–6; membership, 208–11; staffing and decision-making, 211–17
International Brotherhood of Electrical Workers (IBEW), 153
international publicity campaigns, 106
International Workers Day, 226–27
International Workers of the World (IWW), 35
internet campaigns, 106
Iowa Beef Products (IBP), 121–22
Iraq War, 138

janitorial industry, 17–18, 92, 144, 148, 165, 215
Jessica McClintock campaign, 104–5
job losses, 144–45, 208, 289–90n.3
job rights workshops, 25, 49, 65–66, 178–79
Jobs with Justice (JwJ), 22, 155, 204, 228–29
Johanns, Mike, 162, 163, 205–6
jornaleros, 202
JP Stevens, 24–25
justice, economic and racial, 53, 137–38, 191–94
Justice and Equality in the Workplace Program (JEWP), 170
Justice Department, 158
Justice for Janitors, 144, 148, 215

Kavanaugh, Brian, 175–76
Kelley, Florence, 34–36
Kelly, Ellen, 186, 187, 188
Khan, Muhammed Tasleem, 58
K-Mart, 16
Knights of Labor, 34
Knutti, Connie, 83, 84
Korean immigrants, 11, 19, 25–26; Latinos, relations with, 44–45, 110–11, 142; women, 69–70
Korean Immigrant Worker Advocates (KIWA), 25–26, 44, 48, 75, 247; collective voice and, 149–50; economic action organizing, 109–12; market workers justice campaign, 139–43, 156; multicultural organizing, 61–63; networks and, 226; restaurant campaign, 146–47; service delivery, 76, 79–80, 93; staffing, 71, 212
Korean-Latino employment relations, 44–45, 110–11, 142
Korean Restaurant Owners Association, 110
Koreatown (Los Angeles), 45; market workers justice campaign, 139–43, 156; multicultural organizing, 61–63

Laborers International Union (LIU), 58, 130–33
Laborers' Union, 17
Labor Immigrant Organizing Network (LION), 226

Labor in the Pulpits, 23
labor laws, 157–61, 176, 244, 262; applicable to undocumented workers, 74, 172, 293n.21. See also law enforcement
labor market, 284n.4
labor market institutions, worker centers as, 245–48
labor movement, immigrant views of, 51–52
Labor Notes, 226
La Mujer Obrera (LMO), 9, 116–18
language differences, 19–20, 62–63
Latino, as term, 19
Latino immigrants, 11, 19; African Americans and, 17, 66–69; Asian immigrants and, 62–65; Catholic Church and, 52–54; janitors, 17–18; Koreans, relations with, 44–45, 110–11, 142
Latino Neighborhood Association, 193
law enforcement, 88–89, 185, 261, 294n.2; employer violations and, 87–88, 115
lawful presence requirement, 189
lawsuits: filed by corporations, 105; group, 81, 264; impact litigation, 88–91, 113; restaurant workers, 110
leadership development, 5, 13, 22, 55, 202–6, 231–32; cooperatives and, 118–19; day laborers, 50, 202; public school parents, 193; as strength, 248–49; women and, 70, 118–19
Leased Drivers Coalition (LDC), 137
Lee, Kimi, 50, 62, 147, 230–31; on Forever 21 campaign, 104–5; on internal life of worker centers, 204, 208, 214–16; on service delivery, 86, 91, 93
Lee, Mrs., 75, 212
Lee, Paul, 62, 63, 64, 65, 66, 110, 111, 139–41
legal advocacy model, 78
legal clinics, 74–82, 96, 197–98; Central Texas Immigrant Workers Rights Center, 87–88; Chicago Interfaith Workers Rights Center, 82–84; federally funded, 74, 289n.28; Garment Worker Center, 86–87; Workplace Project, 85–86
Legal Services Corporation, 37
Levitt, Peggy, 45–46
licensing process for employment agencies, 175–76
Liechtenstein, Nelson, 41
Lim, Nelson, 69
Liss, Jon, 57, 191, 215, 220
literacy, 193–94, 294–95n.3
Little Village, 236
living wage campaigns, 177–78, 195–96, 259, 296n.15
Lo, Joann, 63–65, 105–6, 215
local industry committees, 265

Long Island: anti-immigrant attacks, 182–85; Unpaid Wages Prohibition Act, 172–74. *See also* Farmingville; Freeport
Long Island Association, 184
Lopez, Marcello, 55–56, 75
Los Angeles, local network, 226–27
Los Angeles Alliance for a New Economy (LAANE), 196
Los Angeles Garment Worker Center. *See* Garment Worker Center
Los Angeles riots, 44
Los Angeles Times, 111
Los Derechos de Trabajadores (CIWA), 165
Louie, Miriam Chang Yoon, 69–70
low-income families, percentage of immigrants, 27
low-wage worker advisory board, 164, 169
low-wage workers: current situation, 101–3; skilled and unskilled categories, 259–60. *See also* immigrants; undocumented workers
Lukes, Steven, 250, 267
Lutherans, 53

McClintock, Jessica, 104–5
MacDonald, Donna, 124, 163
McMann, Dan, 125–27
Maintenance Cooperation Trust Fund, 164, 165
Manpower, 179
manufacturing industries, 31
maquiladoras, 118, 228
marches and demonstrations, 226–27
Marin-Molina, Nadia, 85–86, 116, 185–86, 212
Mariscal, Max, 212
Marks, Gary, 258
Martini, John, 152–53
matrícula consulars, 112
Maurstad, David, 162–63
Mayan immigrants, 58
meatpacking industry, 32, 45–47, 120–25, 195; church involvement, 53–54; enforcement and, 162–63; new Big Four, 122; soccer leagues and, 56; "Workers Bill of Rights," 162–63, 195
media, 55, 81, 106–7, 111, 123, 170, 256; framing of economic development, 249–50
media, ethnic, 111
Medoff, James L., 145, 149, 266
membership of worker centers, 14, 208–11; cooperative requirements, 119; dues, 219–23, 232–33, 237–38; institutional, 210; requirements, 85, 99, 111–12, 210, 232–33; size of, 252–53; size of as weakness, 232–33
Merino, Yanira, 131–33

Methodists, 53
Mexican-American Legal Defense and Education Fund (MALDEF), 89, 225
Mexican consulate, 45, 59, 68, 112, 170
Mexican immigrants, 9, 11, 19, 45, 49, 51–52
Mexico: Home Depot and, 109; *maquiladoras,* 118, 228; networks with, 227–28
Miami Workers Center (MWC), 22, 223
micro-enterprise incubator programs, 117
Migrant and Seasonal Agricultural Worker Protection Act (AWPA), 160
Milkman, Ruth, 58
minimum wage, 25, 31, 73, 158, 263; applies to undocumented workers, 172, 293n.21; campaigns, 177–78, 196; restaurant industry, 110–11, 134. *See also* wages
Mississippi Workers Center for Human Rights, 22, 160
Monclova II, 228
monitoring, 90–91, 197–98, 265–66; of Department of Labor, 79–80
monopoly face of worker centers, 145–48, 194–97, 251–52
monopoly power, 266
Montgomery Improvement Association (MIA), 246
moral legitimacy, 151, 198–99, 256
Morris, Aldon, 246, 295n.2, 296n.8
Mottolla, Maria, 216
movement-building process, 3, 100; alliance-building, 14, 35–36, 39, 239–43
Mujeres Unidas y Activas, 119
Muller v. Oregon, 35
multicultural organizing, 61–66
multiemployer bargaining, 161, 262
multiemployer consultative committees, 265
Multiethnic Immigrant Worker Organizing Network (MIWON), 189, 226–27
multiethnic worker center exchange, 227
Multi-Fiber Agreement (MFA), 144–45, 208
multinational corporations, boycotts of, 147
mutual aid organizations, 33–34

NAFTA, 9, 117
Narro, Victor, 202
National Alliance For Fair Employment (NAFFE), 228, 243
national boycott campaigns, 104–6
National Campaign on Jobs and Income Support, 229
National Day Laborer Organizing Network (NDLON), 12, 56, 78, 81, 89, 146, 188, 224–26, 228, 240, 241–42; asbestos workers and, 131–32; Home Depot and, 107–9

National Employment Law Project (NELP), 155, 225, 230, 242–43

National Immigration Law Center (NILC), 230, 243

National Interfaith Committee on Worker Justice, 11, 17, 52, 132

National Labor Relations Act (NLRA) of 1937, 32, 48, 160–61, 262; exclusion of domestic workers, 175, 176; independent contractors not covered, 136–37, 153–54

National Labor Relations Board (NLRB) election process, 129, 139, 140, 141, 262

National Low-wage Worker Task Force, 155

national networks, 12, 22, 43–44, 216, 224–26

National Organizers Alliance (NOA), 228–29

Nebraska Beef, 47, 163

Neighborhood Funders Group (NFG), 218–19

networks, 5, 224–27; ethnic, 33–34; inclusion of worker centers, 227–31; informal, 58; local, 226, 240–41; national, 12, 22, 43–44, 216, 224–26. *See also* National Day Laborer Organizing Network

New American Opportunity Campaign, 189

New Deal, 97, 158, 161

New Homes for Chicago, 125

New Labor, 234–35

Newsday, 80, 173

New York Department of Labor, 172

New Yorker, 106

New York Farm Bureau, 173

New York Foundation (NYF), 216–17

New York Taxi Workers Alliance (NYTWA), 19, 26, 51, 58, 61, 149, 153–54, 195; budget and fund-raising, 217; dues, 220, 223; fare increase campaign, 179; as independent union, 135–39, 149, 153–54; membership, 210, 211; racial justice focus, 137–38; services provided, 77, 92–93; staffing, 215–17

New York Times, 80, 106

New York University Law School, 26

no match letters, 180

nongovernmental organizations (NGOs), 14

nonstandard work arrangements, 31–32; contingent employment, 178–79, 263; independent contractors, 135–39, 153–54; subcontracting, 31, 101–2, 104–6, 258, 289–90n.3; temporary employment, 25, 68, 178–79

Occupational Health and Safety Act of 1970 (OSHA), 160

Office of Low Wage Industries (OLWI), 166–69

offices of low-wage industries, 264

Oliva, Jose, 51–52, 76–77, 83–84, 126, 128–30, 213

Omaha, 46–47

Omaha Central Labor Council, 123

Omaha Together One Community (OTOC), 21, 47, 51, 53–54, 149; health services, 92; immigration issues and, 190; internal structure, 203; living wage campaign, 178; networks and, 229; popular education, 207; soccer leagues and, 56; UFCW and, 120–25; "Workers Bill of Rights" and, 162–63, 195

Ontario Industrial Standards Act, 265, 296n.17

Operating Engineers, 153

organizational structures and practices: issues of strategic alliance-building and networking, 239–43; strengths an weaknesses, 231–39. *See also* networks

organizing, 2–4, 12; community-based, 3, 7; employer retaliation against, 47–48; faith-based, 11, 14, 120; general areas, 100–101; geographic focus, 21–22; industry-specific, 20–21; multicultural, 61–66; reactive, 98, 129, 148, 151. *See also* economic action organizing; social justice agenda

orientation sessions, 85

Oscar Romero Health Center, 93

O'Sullivan, Terrence, 132

Our Lady of Guadalupe, 53–54

outreach and recruitment, 4, 48–51, 55–60, 73; church and, 51–55

outsourcing, 31, 289–90n.3

Oxfam America, 106

painters, 115–16

Park, Danny, 44, 61–62

Park, Mr., 141–42

Pasadena, California, 193–94

Pasadena Day Laborer Center, 68–69, 114

passports, 49, 112

Pataki, George, 173, 199

Peace and Justice Committee, 55

peer counselors, 86–87

Peirera, Gihan, 223

Pequa Jong (restaurant), 110

Philippines, overseas workers and, 43

picketing, 81–82, 84, 110, 126

Pitts, Steven, 18

Piven, Frances Fox, 267

place-based focus, 13

political education, 5, 43

political incorporation, 101, 289n.2

political parties, 36

political power, 255–56, 258–60

Pomona Economic Opportunities Center, 16

Poo, Ai Jen, 175, 176

popular education, 13, 24, 206–8

Populist Moment, The (Goodwyn), 3

portable health insurance and pension benefits, 266
poultry industry, 17, 132
poverty-level wages, 102, 290n.4
poverty rate of immigrants, 27–28
power, 100, 255–60, 267, 289n.1; economic, 256–58; political, 255–56, 258–60; relational, 255–56, 296n.9
prehire agreements, 262
presentations, 48–49
Presumed Guilty (video), 68
prevailing wage violations, 169–71
privatization, 196
production chain, 101–2
Progressive Era, 35, 259
Prop L, 178
Proposition 187, 57–58, 173
public policy enforcement, 100, 157, 198, 250; certification training program, 168; Harris County AFL-CIO and Interfaith Worker Justice, 169–71; inadequacy of, 31, 158–59, 165–66, 285n.15, 292n.4; inspection sweeps, 167–68; new paradigms, 264–66; organizing to pass new laws, 177–79; partnering with government to insure, 162–71; policy changes to strengthen compliance and improve, 171–77; TWSC and childcare workers, 176–77
public policy reforms, 260–66
public regulatory agencies, taxi industry, 135, 136
Putnam, Robert, 201

Rabadan, Luis Escala, 57
race issues, 181
racial and ethnic discrimination, 68, 73, 101, 160, 245
racial justice, 137–38, 191–94
raffling of jobs, 113–14
Raja, Rizwan, 137
Ramos, Rhina, 81
rancheros, 106
Rau, Jordan, 173
REAL ID Act, 189–90, 294n.3
relational power, 255–56, 296n.9
restaurant industry: economic action organizing, 109–10; KIWA campaign, 146–47; minimum wage, 110–11, 134; union/worker center cooperation, 133–35
Restaurant Opportunities Center of New York (ROC-NY), 17, 93, 119, 247
Restaurant Workers Association of Koreatown (RWAK), 25, 75, 111–12; collective voice and, 149, 150
Restaurant Workers Justice Campaign, 25, 109

retraining funds, 117
Right to Organize campaigns, 260
Roofers United, 152

Sachem Quality of Life Committee, 183–84
Salas, Angelica, 219
San Francisco, living wage campaign, 178
Sara Lee Corporation, 228
Schlozman, Kay Lehman, 201
Schwarzenegger, Arnold, 58, 169, 189, 227
Second Great Migration, 28–31
security guards, 154
self-help programs, 36, 86–87
September 11th 2001 terrorist attacks, 17, 47, 75, 181, 189, 227
service delivery, 2, 4, 12, 72–73, 112, 288n.1; ESL and other classes, 24–25, 49, 73, 91–92, 96, 235; financial services, 94, 96–97; funding and, 219; health services, 92–93; ideology of movement and, 96, 98–99; impact litigation, 88–91; industry-based approach, 98; range of services, 73, 76; strategic needs of movement and, 95–96, 97–98; strengths and weaknesses of model, 94–99; of utilized service, 95–96. *See also* legal clinics
Service Employees International Union (SEIU), 48, 92, 137, 147–48, 154, 195; Local 615, 17–18, 92; Local 880, 230, 235
service industries, 31, 80. *See also individual industries*
settlement houses, 34–37, 39, 94–95
sexual harassment, 73, 160–61
Shaw, Richard, 169–71
Sheen, Martin, 191
shop stewards, 149, 154
Sicily, Illinois, 128
Sklar, Kathryn Kish, 34
small claims court, 174
Snyder, Mitch, 191
soccer leagues, 55–56, 75, 235
social insurance laws, 266
Socialist party, 37
social justice agenda, 5, 72; countering anti-immigrant attacks, 182–88; fighting for racial and economic justice, 191–94; impact of policies on immigrants, 180–82; strengths and weaknesses of public policy activities, 194–200. *See also* justice, economic and racial
social movement organizations (SMOs): 1960s, 95–96; worker centers as, 245–48
social movements, 72, 231
social purpose businesses, 117–18
Social Security numbers, 47, 180, 189–90
social wage, 41

Solidarity Sponsoring Committee (Baltimore), 229, 249–50
Solis, Irma, 59–60, 213
Soriano, Aquilina, 43
Sosa, Sergio, 56, 122, 123
South, 9, 178–79, 284n.1
South Asian immigrants, 11, 174
Southeast Asian immigrants, 11, 174
Southerners for Economic Justice (SEJ), 24–25
South Korea, democracy movement, 44
special master, 134
Spitzer, Eliot, 174
staffing, 71, 78, 211–14, 248–49
State Federation of Labor (Nebraska), 123
State Labor Commissioner (California), 165
state laws, 159
strikes, 122, 126, 138
subcontracting, 31, 101–2, 104–6, 258, 289–90n.3. See also independent contractors
successor employer liability, 90
support systems, during Golden Era, 33–36
Supreme Court, 35, 132, 160
suspended workers, 142–43
sweatshops, 17, 89–91
Sweatshop Warriors (Louie), 69–70
Sweatshop Watch, 91, 225, 227, 230–31

Taco Bell campaign, 106, 147, 251
Taft Hartley provisions, 262
Talbott, Madeline, 236–38
Tallahassee bus boycott, 296n.8
task forces, 167–68
Taxi and Limousine Commission (TLC), 136, 137
taxi industry, 19, 26, 50, 75, 179; creation of independent union, 135–39. See also New York Taxi Workers Alliance
tax issues, construction industry, 187–88
technical assistance, 216–17, 225
temporary employment, 25, 68, 178–79
Temporary Protected Status (TPS), 47
Tenango, Mexico, 60
tenant evictions, 22, 67, 191
Tenants' and Workers' Support Committee (TWSC), 20, 50, 57, 147–48, 247; budget and fund-raising, 217; childcare workers and, 176–77; driver's licenses and, 189; dues, 220–21; internal structure, 203–4; living wage campaign, 178, 196; membership, 210, 211; racial and economic justice issues, 191–92; service delivery, 93; staffing and decision-making, 211; tenant evictions and, 22, 67, 191; UNITY, 203, 205; women and, 70, 192
Texas Penal Code, 87–88
textile industry. See garment industry

theft of services provision, 87–88, 288–89n.17
tipped employees, 134
Title VII (Civil Rights Act of 1964), 159–60
tomato pickers, 106
Tona, Paul, 55, 183–84, 294n.1
Torres, Crispin, 129
Torres, Gustavo, 235
town hall hearings, 111
training centers, 117, 132
transnational villagers, 46

underground economy, 165
undocumented workers: antiunion campaigns and, 142–43; benefits of independent contractor status to, 138–39; firing of, 32–33, 126, 129, 163, 295n.4; labor laws applicable to, 74, 172, 293n.21; length of time in country, 102–3, 290n.5, 291n.29; not covered by labor laws, 159–60; reasons for, 29–30; reluctance to file complaints, 167–68; remedies available to, 160–61; residential construction and, 152–53. See also immigrants
unfair labor practices, 128
Union of Needletrades, Textiles and Industrial Employees (UNITE), 17, 128, 147–48
unions, 48, 57, 84, 92, 194–95, 285–86n.17; anti-immigrant sentiment, 153, 170–71; collective voice/institutional response face and, 148–50; community-based, 139–40, 283n.3; construction industry, 152–53, 170–71; craft, 114, 146; day laborers and, 108–9, 115–16, 152; decline of, 1–2, 16–17, 36, 244–45; density, 151; economic action organizing and, 114–16, 143–45; employer campaigns against, 32–33, 125–26, 129, 141–43; ethnic culture and, 154; Home Depot and, 108–9; independent, 135–43; industrial, 258; Laborers International Union (LIU), 130–33; limitations on, 123–25; as models for worker centers, 39–40; monopoly face and worker centers, 145–48; South, strategies and, 133; views of worker centers, 128–29; workforce development and, 143–45. See also Omaha Together One Community; union/worker center relationships
union/worker center relationships, 4, 128–29; clashes, 124–25; grocery workers, 139–43; hotel industry, 133–35; improving, 150–56; project suggestions, 155–56
United Day Laborers of Long Island, 149, 186
United Electrical Workers Union (UE), 129
United Farm Workers (UFW), 233
United Food and Commercial Workers (UFCW), 21, 51, 111, 120–25, 163; local 211, 149; Local #770, 139, 140; OTOC and, 120–25

United Labor Unions (ULU), 230
United Students Against Sweatshops, 147
UNITY cooperative (Workplace Project), 50–51, 70–71, 118–19, 203
UNITY (TWSC), 203, 205
unpaid wages, 73, 78–79, 172–74, 198
Unpaid Wages Prohibition Act, 172–74, 198
U.S. Students Against Sweatshops, 106
USA Today, 123
utilized services, 95–96

Valenzuela, Abel, Jr., 291n.29
Van Arsdale, Henry, 137
Vargas, Jaime, 66
Vargas, Roman, 112
Verba, Sidney, 201
violence, 54–55, 137, 192–93
visas, 261
voice, 149
Voice and Future Fund, 144
voluntarism, 35–36, 40
Voz Laboral, 48–49

Wage and Hour Division (DOL), 82–84, 229, 240, 242, 264–65; inadequacy of, 158–59, 292n.4
Wage Claim Adjudication Office (Los Angeles), 164
wage disputes, 73, 79, 288n.6; intake clinics, 166–67, 169
wage guarantee, 90
wages: poverty-level, 102, 290n.4; prevailing wage violations, 169–71; union *vs.* nonunion, 194; unpaid, 73, 78–79, 172–74, 198. *See also* minimum wage
Waldinger, Roger, 69
Weil, David, 285n.15, 292n.4
welfare-to-work program, 50
Wet Seal, 90–91
What Do Unions Do? (Freeman and Medoff), 145, 149
Withorn, Ann, 95–98, 288n.1
women, 9, 69–71; leadership development, 70, 118–19
Women's Employment Rights Center, 91
Women's Leadership Group (TWSC), 192
women's movement, 72
Women Workers Project (CAAAV), 174
Wong, Kent, 58
worker centers: broad agenda, 13–14; budgets and funding, 254–55; collective voice/institutional response face, 148–50, 197–99, 249–52; comparison with progressive era movements, 94–95; contact list of, 271–82; distinguishing

features of, 11–14; founded in response to decline of unionization, 16–17; greatest strengths of, 248–52; as labor market institutions, 245–48; major weaknesses of, 252–55; mapping, 2–3; monopoly face aspect, 145–48, 194–97, 251–52; networks of, 224–27, 240; origins of, 4, 14–18; outreach and recruitment, 4, 48–51, 55–60; parallels with Golden Era, 38–40; participants, 19–22; regions, 7, 19; rise of, 244–45; as social movement organizations, 245–48; strategy as weakness, 253–55; sustainability of, 254–55; three waves of formation, 5–11. *See also* day laborer worker centers; internal life of worker centers; leadership development; membership of worker centers; social justice agenda; union/worker center relationships; *individual worker centers*
workers, profile of, 19–22
Worker Sanctuary Program, 128
"Workers Bill of Rights" (meatpacking industry), 162–63, 195
workers compensation laws, 159, 179, 292n.6
Workers Hardship Fund, 110
Workers Organizing Center (CPA), 178
workers rights courses, 49, 85, 92, 207
workers rights handbooks, 24, 49, 50, 75–77
Workers' Rights Manual (CIWRC), 75–77
Worker's Rights Project (WRP), 24–25
workfare recipients, 204
workforce development, unions and, 143–45
working hours, 35
Workmen's Circle, 33–34, 38–39, 286n.21
Workplace Project, 16, 48–49, 59–60, 66, 149, 239; budget, 217–18; countering anti-immigrant attacks, 182–88; data collection and advocacy, 79–80; hiring hall trailer, 115; internal structure, 203; leadership development, 206; legal clinic, 85–86; membership, 210; popular education, 207; power of, 256; service delivery, 98; staffing, 212; UNITY (house-cleaners cooperative), 50–51, 70–71, 118–19, 203; Unpaid Wages Prohibition Act and, 172–74, 198
World Social Forum, 41
World War I, 28

Yellow Cab drivers. *See* taxi industry
Yimer, Mulgeta, 61, 75
Young Workers United (YWU), 133, 178, 247
Yum Brands, 106

Zabin, Carol, 57
Zacatecas Club, 57
zoning process, 107–9
Zuerlain, Damien, 53–54

ABOUT EPI

The Economic Policy Institute was founded in 1986 to widen the debate about policies to achieve healthy economic growth, prosperity, and opportunity.

Today, despite rapid growth in the U.S. economy in the latter part of the 1990s, inequality in wealth, wages, and income remains historically high. Expanding global competition, changes in the nature of work, and rapid technological advances are altering economic reality. Yet many of our policies, attitudes, and institutions are based on assumptions that no longer reflect real world conditions.

With the support of leaders from labor, business, and the foundation world, the institute has sponsored research and public discussion of a wide variety of topics: globalization; fiscal policy; trends in wages, incomes, and prices; education; the causes of the productivity slowdown; labor market problems; rural and urban policies; inflation; state-level economic development strategies; comparative international economic performance; and studies of the overall health of the U.S. manufacturing sector and of specific key industries.

The institute works with a growing network of innovative economists and other social science researchers in universities and research centers all over the country who are willing to go beyond the conventional wisdom in considering strategies for public policy.

Founding scholars of the institute include Jeff Faux, former EPI president; Lester Thurow, Sloan School of Management, Massachusetts Institute of Technology; Ray Marshall, former U.S. secretary of labor, professor at the LBJ School of Public Affairs, University of Texas; Barry Bluestone, Northeastern University; Robert Reich, former U.S. secretary of labor; and Robert Kuttner, author, editor of *The American Prospect*, and columnist for *Business Week* and the Washington Post Writers Group.

For additional information about the institute, contact EPI at 1660 L Street NW, suite 1200, Washington, DC 20036; (202) 775-8810; or visit www.epinet .org.

ABOUT THE AUTHOR

Janice Fine is a member of the faculty of the School of Management and Labor Relations at Rutgers University, a senior fellow at the Center for Community Change and a research associate at the Economic Policy Institute. For many years, she has written about the labor movement and community organizing as well as the influence of money in American politics, and has been the recipient of fellowships from the Open Society Institute as well as the Industrial Performance Center at the Massachusetts Institute of Technology. In addition to her academic work, Fine has worked as a community, labor, and electoral organizer for more than twenty years. From 1981 to 1983 she was the president of the United States Student Association. During the 1980s, she worked for the AFL-CIO in Broward County, Florida; Massachusetts Fair Share in Boston; the Jackson '88 presidential campaign; and numerous other electoral campaigns. During the 1990s, she founded the New England Money and Politics Project at Northeast Action and played a leading role in passing the nation's first "Clean Election" law in Maine. Until 2003, she was the organizing director at Northeast Action, the hub of a regional network of statewide progressive coalitions and citizen action groups.